CW01430881

FIRST (CITY)
BRIGADE THE
MANCHESTER
REGIMENT
A RECORD
1914-1918

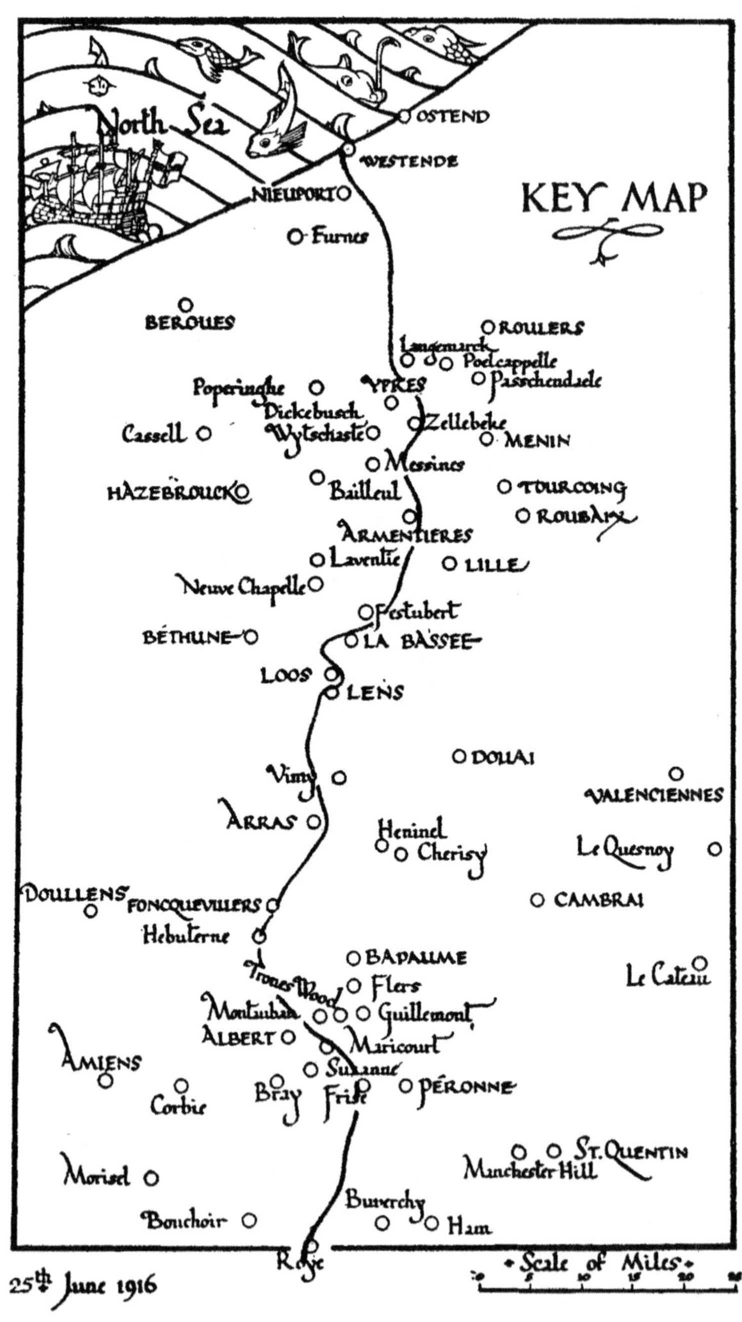
North Sea
OSTEND
WESTENDE
KEY MAP
NIEUPORT
Furnes
BERGUES
ROULERS
Langemarck
Poelcappelle
Passchendaele
Poperinghe
YPRES
Dickebusch
Zellebeke
Cassell
Wytschaete
MENIN
Messines
HAZEBROUCK
Bailleul
TOURCOING
ROUBAIX
ARMENTIERES
Laventie
LILLE
Neuve Chapelle
Festubert
BÉTHUNE
LA BASSEE
LOOS
LENS
DOUAI
Vimy
VALENCIENNES
ARRAS
Heninel
Cherisy
Le Quesnoy
DOULLENS
FONCQUEVILLERS
CAMBRAI
Hebuterne
BAPAUME
Trones Wood
Flers
Le Cateau
Montauban
Guillemont
ALBERT
Maricourt
AMIENS
Suzanne
Corbie
Bray
Frise
PÉRONNE
St. QUENTIN
Morisel
Manchester Hill
Buverchy
Bouchoir
Ham
Roye
25th June 1916
Scale of Miles
0
5
10
15
20

SIXTEENTH : SEVENTEENTH EIGHTEENTH : NINETEENTH BATTALIONS : : : : THE MANCHESTER REGIMENT

(FIRST CITY BRIGADE)

A Record 1914-1918

MANCHESTER
SHERRATT & HUGHES
34 CROSS STREET
MCMXXIII

Printed and bound by Antony Rowe Ltd, Eastbourne

BY GRACIOUS PERMISSION

This History

IS DEDICATED TO

HIS MAJESTY THE KING

GEORGE FALKNER
& SONS PRINTERS
MANCHESTER &
LONDON

FOREWORD

IN 1919 *it was decided to have the History of the Regular Battalions rewritten from their creation to date, and also the hope was expressed that the History of* ALL *Battalions of "The Manchester Regiment" would be written, and the whole combined into a work worthy of the Regiment and the City it has so nobly represented. In accordance with this most desirable object a Sub-Committee was formed in Manchester—in addition to the Regular Battalions' Committee—with Lieut.-Colonel H. L. James, C.B., as Chairman, and the following Chapters from the War Diaries and different sources of information, as well as those of other Battalions, have been produced under their able direction.*

To their first Chairman, and to Colonel H. C. Darlington, C.B., C.M.G., T.D., Lieut.-Colonel F. Bentley, T.D., Lieut-Colonel G. Ramsbottom, D.S.O., Major A. G. Foord, D.S.O., Captain J. H. Worthington, Captain R. Hobkirk (Hon. Accountant), Captain H. C. Bardsley (Hon. Secretary), Major C. C. Stapledon (1922) *Commanding Depot; to Mr. H. Tinsley Pratt (Portico Library, Manchester), Lieut.-Colonel D. A. Hailes (late Royal Marine Light Infantry)—and to all who have generously contributed to the fund—including the Artistes of the Manchester Theatres—are due the thanks of all interested in our Regiment.*

At the request of the Manchester History Sub-Committee, as the first Commander of this most gallant Brigade, and as Chairman of the Regular History Committee, I write to introduce this Volume to the Regiment and to the Public. I need hardly say, too, how much I have been honoured by their request, or that the task is merely a labour of love.

No one who had to do with the Raising or Training of the City Battalions can ever forget the extraordinary enthusiasm and the ready response, from the first appeal, when the First City—16th Battalion—was raised, under Lieut.-Colonel J. C. Crawford, to the completion of the Second City—91st Infantry Brigade.

The splendid work, under the auspices of the Earl of Derby, K.G., carried out by the Lord Mayor, the Manchester Organising Committee—the late Sir E. Tootal Broadhurst, Bart., Mr. E. M. Phillips, Captain Arthur Taylor, Mr. Kenneth Lee and Mr. Vernon Bellhouse—under the Chairmanship of the late, and much lamented, Sir Herbert Dixon, Bart., assisted by Colonel F. R. McConnel, Major L. Sington, and many others, including the Employers, and members of the Medical profession, will be long remembered in Manchester. All combined patriotically to raise Brigades to add to the old Regiment, which were destined so nobly to uphold, and increase its honour, and that of the City from which they literally "SPRANG INTO BEING." *The spirit displayed by the men from the warehouses and offices was a source of perpetual joy and admiration to all who had to do with them, and a certain augury of what was to be expected from Battalions so well supplied with old-fashioned Lancashire "grit."*

Personally, when I look back to those early days of the War, it is a great pleasure to recall the cordial assistance I received from the late Sir Herbert Dixon, Bart., the late Lieut.-Colonel C. L. Petrie, D.S.O., Staff-Captain Arthur Taylor, and the late Brigade-Major H. F. Montgomery, D.S.O. (afterwards so foully done to death in Dublin), and all the first Commanding Officers.

At that time, too, the services of Retired Regular and Volunteer Officers, Warrant Officers and Non-Commissioned Officers were invaluable.

What Sir Ian Hamilton had said on unveiling the South African War Memorial had come to pass, thus—

> *"Manchester has also cause for deep pride and thankfulness at the thought she could, if it were needed, call up Battalion after Battalion to fight in a just cause. Battalions who would be inspired by the memory and example of those heroic comrades who had gone on before."*

To-day when we look back and read this story of persistent gallantry, endurance and self-sacrifice, we can realise how nobly men of all ranks from Manchester helped in the just cause and how regimental esprit de corps was maintained.

On reading the long Casualty Rolls, surely, no one can fail to realise the immensity of the Regimental sacrifice, and of the irreparable losses of the people of Manchester. Yes, losses of high and low, of rich and poor—an equality of sacrifice—so now, and always, let there be rendered to them an " Equality of Remembrance and of Homage."

As will be well remembered Major General T. H. Shoubridge, C.B., C.M.G., D.S.O., on 1st July 1920—the anniversary of the Somme—paid a glowing tribute to the deeds of the Regiment in the Great War, and he said he saw a great deal of the 16th, 17th, 18th and 19th Battalions in France, and could only recall with emotion the way they went into action on the glorious 1st July. Their taking of Montauban was probably the turning point of the battle. He also spoke of " The Salient," " Trones Wood," " Beaumont Hamel," " Passchendaele," and of the glorious stand at " Manchester Hill." " It was an epic and there was never a greater stand during the War than the stand of the 16th Manchester's on the immortal little hill in front of St. Quentin."

In the following chapters will be found an account of the above and many other splendid services of all four Battalions. When we read them with just pride, let us also remember the patient ENDURANCE *of all and the losses incurred during month after month of trench warfare in what were called comparatively quiet times at the Front.*

In the past sometimes it has been said that Manchester provided the smallest men for the army. If that be true it should also be recorded that nature supplied them with hearts abnormally large, strong and charged with valour.

> * *" Of this Regiment it may be said once for all that none more devoted, and none more valiant has passed in this War through the Valley of the Shadow of Death."*

* *Lieut.-General Sir James Willcocks*

Many pages can be written filled with messages of thanks and of praise, or taken from orders, or books about different Battalions, or the Regiment in general, and when the History of all the Battalions has been completed Manchester will possess a record of patriotic service difficult to surpass.

May the same spirit, the same courage, endurance and grit displayed in the past by Lancashire Officers and Men of all Ranks live on and on, from generation to generation, and always be at the service of the Sovereign, old England, and the Empire in War and in Peace.

H. C. E. WESTROPP
Brigadier-General

Armistice Day
11*th November* 1922

CONTENTS

Explanation of Abbreviations

"*b*"—born "*e*"—enlisted "d"—died "d. of w."—died of wounds
"k. in a."—killed in action "F. & F."—France & Flanders (including Italy)

N.B.—When the place of enlistment is followed by the name of another place in brackets, the latter place represents the deceased soldier's place of residence

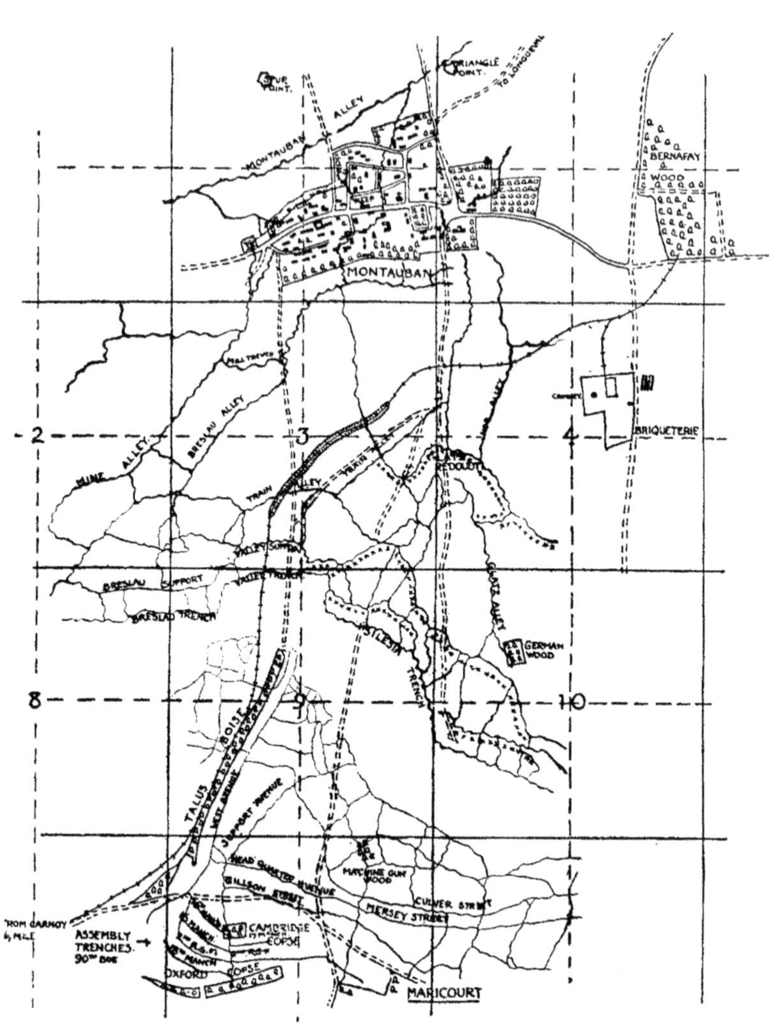

ATTACK ON MONTAUBAN
1ST JULY 1916

16TH

CONTENTS

APPENDIX

CHAPTER I

FORMATION AND EARLY TRAINING

THE 1st City Battalion consisted of the first batch of recruits that clamoured for enlistment after the public announcement of the project to form a " Pals " Battalion was made on August 27th, 1914. On September 1st the Lord Mayor swore in some 800 in a body, and on September 4th the men were posted to Companies, employees from large firms being put in the same platoon wherever possible. A supply of ex-regular N.C.O's was found to lick the raw material into shape. Young officers were selected from candidates for commissions, and senior officers with previous experience were put in charge of companies for training. Events followed in rapid succession.

On September 5th the mufti-clad, straw-hatted battalion marched to the Town Hall and was inspected by the Lord Mayor. On the 9th " A " Company marched to Heaton Park to prepare the Camp. On the 10th Lieut.-Colonel J. C. Crawford arrived and assumed Command; and on the 12th the rest of the Battalion paraded at the Artillery H.Q. and marched to Heaton Park in the rain, which developed to a downpour at night.

Much humour and quaint irony attended the transformation of a thousand thorough-going civilians into soldiers. The first complaint occurred as the men were told off to their tents, the likeliest looking man, often a boy scout with some notion of drill and camp-life, being put in charge. One O.C. Company on going round to inspect the tents found a deputation drawn up and the following respectful protest was made by an ancient " private " (afterwards known as " father "). " If you please, sir, you've placed us in a bit of a predicament. It's this way, you see, we all come from the same warehouse, and him as has been made the head of the tent is the office boy, sir, and I'm the head of the department ! "

Soon recruit training was in full swing. Company Commanders and N.C.O's taking the men, the R.S.M. taking the young officers.

Captain E. G. Sotham, of the 2nd Manchesters', took over the duties of Adjutant on October 4th, and lectured nightly to the young officers.

The Code of Discipline can only be applied to a body of high-spirited civilians by degrees, but gradually by progressive drill, marching, and barrack-routine, the instinct of obedience was learned. Drill has been, and always must be, the foundation of discipline, for by drill obedience becomes instinctive and cohesion a necessity of nature, and the will of the individual is subordinated to that of his leaders. To the civilian soldier, and perhaps particularly to the independent Lancashire " lad " this lesson does not come easily. The importance of the individual and the preservation of existence are everything in times of peace, but discipline in war means the effacement of the individual and readiness for unquestioning sacrifice. It involves a revolution in mental outlook, and the higher the intelligence and education of the men, the harder, perhaps the lesson. In the " Pals " all classes were mingled in the ranks. The packer from the basement and the commissionaire from the door were, as often as not, put in command of their seniors in the warehouse. One sergeant humorously complained to his officer that he was in an inferior social position to every man in his platoon. Everyone, however, was united for a common purpose. The irresistible wave of volunteer patriotism, the faith in the righteousness of their cause, overcame all individual interest and personal consideration. The quick intelligence of the city clerk proved to be splendid material. Training and fresh air soon gave him the physical stamina he required, and his naturally quick wit gave him a dash and initiative that, when once it was subordinated, made him a soldier of the finest type.

Heaton Park formed an admirable training-ground, its great undulations affording opportunity for instructions in extended order drill, use of ground, visual training and judging distance, with close-order drill as the foundation. But for route-marches, the sets and tram-lines of the Manchester area were not so attractive, and the greatest insistence was always made on " march discipline." The Battalion, too, always prided itself on its " guards," and under the critical eye of the Adjutant and R.S.M. these maintained a high standard of smartness, and competition for " the stick " was keen.

The C.O's hut inspection, when, after six or seven weeks, huts took the place of tents, became an important event of the week, involving as it did the drudgery of floor and table scrubbing and attention to minute details that count for so much in the sub-structure of discipline in a regiment, for steadiness in battle is built up by discipline in quarters as well as on the march and on the barrack square.

Orderly Room reinforced what drill and training began, and gradually instilled into the troops the great gulf that is fixed between civil and military law. The daily ritual went on, with the resultant C.B. and detentions and reprimands, and increasing " crime sheets " and a vast fund of humorous incident.

The first prisoner for C.O.'s orderly room was marched in before an admiring crowd, clad in bowler hat, a tail coat and brown boots. It was with delight that the uninitiated saw the Sergeant-Major remove his hat, without any ceremony, for the Sergeant-Major was what a Sergeant-Major should be. The awkward squad, under his inimitable tuition, provided a new novelty for Manchester sightseers to watch. The nearness to home and comfort lured men to overstay their week-end leave, and provided the C.O. with much occupation.

" How dare you come back on Tuesday? Explain yourself, Private ———."

" Well, sir, it's like this yer—I met some friends from Newcastle on Saturday night, and I thought it far better to get over the effects of 'ome, rather than in the guard room."

So the weeks flew by—those first happy weeks, full of novelty and enthusiasm. The pale-faced clerk developed into a bronzed and burly soldier. The longing to get at the Boche gave zest to all, from the highest to the lowest.

Soon blue uniforms were provided, and dummy rifles, and the "Tramguards" paraded through the city, exceedingly proud of their substitute for khaki. They were inspected by Generals, and the Lord Mayor and their Colonel in Chief, Lord Derby. They became cinema actors, and delivered a dashing attack, which later figured on the screen as " A Night Attack in Flanders." They were vaccinated, innoculated, lectured on sanitation and other important subjects, given " M " and " D." They were paid in postal orders and realised new money values.

The feeding arrangements were a vital question. These were originally in the hands of the Refreshment Department of the Corporation Parks' Committee, the men messing in the Tearoom near the Hall. Dinner of cold meat one day, hash the next, with cheese, lettuce, pickles or jam on alternate days for tea, led to a press campaign for the improvement of rations. Accordingly, on October 26th, the Regiment took over its own feeding and cooking arrangements under the Quartermaster, Lieut. F. Walker, D.C.M. Conditions then improved. Rations were more than plentiful, so much so that it was said that the orderly officer discovered eleven whole loaves and a ham in the swill tubs. Rabbit-pie and turkeys were consumed in large numbers, and the cooks, it afterwards transpired, rolled two barrels of beer from the canteen into the evergreens and buried them—like the dog and bone—providing rubber tubes for the sucking up of the cheering liquor.

Meanwhile the drums and bugles played their eternal tunes, and the old familiar songs made route marches tolerable. "Tipperary," "Farewell, Little Girl, Little Girl," "Here's to the good old beer," "Keep the home fires burning," resounded through the lanes of Droughts and Jericho. Night operations varied the monotony, and trench digging, and the young officers read up "outposts" at high pressure and retailed it to the men immediately afterwards. Section drill was followed by company drill, and the greatest day of all was the occasion of the first battalion drill, with the Adjutant on his famous Rhinosaurus.

All the many specialists that form an integral part of an infantry battalion were in course of time taught their particular duties and brought up to a state of efficiency. The stretcher bearers and sanitary men under the M.O., the storesmen and cooks, butchers and shoemakers, tailors and pioneers under the Q.M. The Lewis gunners, the signallers, the scouts, the bombers and the band were taught their jobs and, when horses and mules arrived, the transport were selected from men whose civil occupation gave them special aptitude.

On January 8th, 1915, the battalion marched with the rest of the Brigade from Heaton Park through the streets of the city to the Free Trade Hall, where Brigadier-General Westropp, on taking over command of the Brigade, delivered a stirring address on the traditions of the Manchester Regiment.

"It is the history of regiments," he said, "it is their pride, and it is their traditions, which make a regiment illustrious, which make it formidable in the field, and when weapons and numbers alone will not avail, they give the regiment its glory and its confidence." The soldierly appearance of the men in their march through the streets of Manchester made a profound impression, and they received a great ovation from vast crowds. Gigantic police-horses, lent for the occasion for the use of senior officers, added to the martial impression! But Heaton Park was still a kind of "nursery," with parents and lovers hovering around its walls. This could not, of course, go on for ever, and events now pointed towards the move to Grantham.

On March 21st, 1915—destined to prove a historic day for the Battalion that held Manchester Hill in 1918—the Sixteenth marched past Lord Kitchener at the Town Hall with the rest of the City Battalions, 12,000 men in all, the Second City Brigade coming over from Morecambe for the day. This parade provided an unbroken hour of marching men. The following is an extract from Western Command Order, 1434, dated 22-3-15.

"The General Officer Commanding in Chief Western Command is desired by Field-Marshal Earl Kitchener, K.P., G.C.B., &c., Secretary of State for War, to express his complete satisfaction with the appearance and marching of the detachments R.A., R.E., and the Infantry Battalions which passed him in Liverpool and Manchester yesterday. He warmly appreciates the spirit which has prompted both officers and men to offer their services, in many cases under difficult circumstances, and he is convinced that when they get to the Front, they will in every way be a very valuable addition to the Army in the Field."

The Manchester Guardian in a leading article on March 22nd voiced the significance of this parade and the particular character of the battalions.

"Only now and then in these months of war has it been forced fully home to us that we are living history, but the dullest could not see the march of the twelve thousand yesterday without knowing that of this his children's children will be told. Nor could he see it without a deep and quickening sense of his personal relation to the facts behind it. For Manchester's army is Manchester, and the new army is Britain, in a way no soldiers ever have been before or, it is to be hoped, will ever need be again. The people who cheered and the people who marched were not spectators and a spectacle. They were kin in the truest sense, and every eligible man who watched the City Battalions swing by must have felt it an incongruous thing that he was not on the other side of the barrier."

On April 11th there was a memorable Church Parade to Manchester Cathedral, every inch of floor space being occupied by men of the Brigade.

Brigade Sports held at Heaton Park on April 21st formed a fitting occasion for a final leave-taking. Huge crowds, numbering 20,000 people, watched the events which were keenly contested, the Sixteenth winning the cup.

On April 24th, 1915, the Sixteenth left Manchester, entraining for Grantham. The whole of the newly-formed 30th Division, commanded by Major-General W. Fry, C.V.O., C.B., were encamped in huts in Belton Park, Lord Brownlow's seat. The 1st City Brigade, now known as the 90th Infantry Brigade, was commanded by Brigadier-General H. C. E. Westropp, with Major Petrie, D.S.O., Brigade Major, and Captain Arthur Taylor, who had done good work as an original member of the committee which formed the City Battalions, Staff-Captain.

From the huts the great stretch of level turf of the deer park formed an admirable parade-ground. Discipline was tightened, training became more advanced. Field-days in Harlaxton Park, trench digging and routine in Willoughby Park, route marches of anything from 20 to 28 miles with full pack, and shooting with real rifles on a real range in real khaki were the order of the day. The troops were getting restless—" What did you do in the Great War, Grandpa ? "—" Oh, Willy, dear, I attacked Syston Hall near Grantham." So they joked.

The troops were inspected by the G.O.C. Division, and Lieut.-General Sir Archibald Murray. Lieut.-Col. Crawford left the Battalion early in June to command the 1st Battalion in France, and Lieut.-Col. C. L. R. Petrie, D.S.O., assumed command. On September 2nd Brigadier-General C. J. Steavenson took over the command of the 90th Brigade from Brigadier-General H. C. E. Westropp.

The Pull Through, a bright and breezy publication was suppressed after two successful editions. The concert troop provided an outlet for the latent talent in the Battalion. The cricket eleven won many victories.

At length the final move was made to Lark Hill Camp, Salisbury Plain, for the last lap of training on September 7th. Field-days, Brigade and Divisional training, the firing of Part III new Army Musketry course, in which the Battalion held first place in the Brigade, and the field-firing course rounded off the tiresome and arduous training. General Paget, G.O.C.-in-Chief, Salisbury Plain District, inspected the Division and on November 4th Lord Derby made the final inspection for the King, who was prevented from coming in person owing to his accident whilst in France. His Majesty sent the following message :—

" Officers, non-commissioned officers and men of the 30th Division, on the eve of your departure for Active Service I send you my heartfelt good wishes. It is a bitter disappointment to me that owing to an unfortunate accident I am unable to see the Division on parade before it leaves England, but I can assure you that my thoughts are with you all. Your period of training has been long and arduous, but the time has now come for you to prove on the field of battle the results of your instruction.

From the good account that I have received of the Division I am confident that the high traditions of the British Army are safe in your hands, and that with your comrades now in the Field you will maintain the unceasing efforts necessary to bring this War to a victorious ending.

Goodbye and God Speed

GEORGE R.I."

LIST OF THE OFFICERS WHO PROCEEDED OVERSEAS WITH THE BATTALION

C.O. : Lieut.-Col. C. L. R. Petrie, D.S.O. *Second-in-Command :* Major A. C. Kempster. *Adjutant :* Capt. E. G. Sotham.

"A" Company: Capt. J. H. Worthington, *O.C.*; Capt. W. Elstob, Lieut. P. J. Mead, Sec.-Lieut. G. L. Q. Henriques (*Scout Officer*), Sec.-Lieut. C. W. K. Hook, Sec.-Lieut. E. S. Slack.

"B" Company: Capt. F. Walker, D.C.M., *O.C.*; Capt. J. J. Payne, Lieut. F. E. Behrens (*Bombing Officer*), Lieut. J. M. Oliver, Sec.-Lieut. E. L. Rhodes, Sec.-Lieut. J. E. G. Percy.

"C" Company: Capt. R. E. Roberts, *O.C.*; Lieut. W. J. S. Davidson, Sec.-Lieut. R. K. Knowles, Sec.-Lieut. R. Gibbon, Sec.-Lieut. G. A. Barber.

"D" Company: Capt. H. S. Greg, *O.C.*; Capt. W. M. Johnson, Lieut. A. B. Dalgliesh, Lieut. R. H. Megson (*Signal Officer*), Sec.-Lieut. T. A. H. Nash, Sec.-Lieut. S. R. Allen.

Lewis Gun Officer: Lieut. G. P. Morris. *Transport Officer:* Lieut. L. F. Wilson. *M.O.:* Capt. F. S. Fletcher. *Q.M.:* Lieut. and Q.M. J. T. Ball. *Chaplain:* Rev. R. W. Balleine, C.F.

The following officers were with the Battalion during training:—

First C.O.: Lieut.-Col. J. C. Crawford (left to command 1st Battalion Manchester Regiment). *Second-in-Command:* Major D. Comyn. Lieut.-Col. H. Ledward, Capt. H. H. Cunliffe, Capt. H. S. Wheatley-Crowe, Capt. M. H. R. Patey (transferred to Division's Cyclists), Capt. Sir W. N. M. Geary, Bart., Lieut. A. J. C. Sington, Lieut. R. O. Philips (rejoined within a few weeks of embarkation), Sec.-Lieut. H. de D. Dyer, Sec.-Lieut. W. J. Clarke (transferred to Division's Cyclists), Capt. Arthur Taylor (appointed Staff-Captain to the 90th Brigade, Sept. 4th, 1915).

Reserve officers at Heaton Park:—

Sec.-Lieuts. J. Hayward Browne, E. Prestwich, G. M. Bles, E. G. Clayton, C. E. Day, O. C. de C. McDonnel, S. G. Turner, E. M. Tuke, H. R. Cook, D. H. Roberts, T. C. V. Matthews, A. F. D. Knight, N. A. Smith, G. C. Harriman.

Early on the dark cold morning of November 6th, 1915, the Sixteenth marched from Lark Hill Camp to entrain at Amesbury for Folkestone. The crossing to Boulogne was calm and uneventful, and feeling very proud of themselves, the "Pals" fell in on the quay and marched with band playing up the hill to the rest camp for the night. Then the rain came down in torrents, the mud deepened, and the next day, wet and miserable, they entrained in cattle-trucks and jolted the long slow journey to Pont Remy. The Battalion set out in pitch darkness, in a deluge of rain, accompanied by peals of thunder, up a long winding hill, with overweighted packs. At last St. Ricquier was reached, but it was a drenched, ruffled and weary regiment that sank down in billets as the grey dawn broke. The long training, however, stood the test, and, next day the weather cleared, sleep and food did their work, and a pleasant week of training in frost and snow was spent in the peaceful little town with its fine fifteenth-century church. In the " place " before the great Western Tower the band played to friendly inhabitants, who had not hitherto had English troops billeted on them, and much pleasant fraternising beguiled the spare time.

On the 17th the trek began through many miles of France, a new country to the majority of the men. Oh, those dismal reveilles in the dark, the bustle of preparation, the hurried breakfast, the blanket rolling and packing on the waggon, the billet-cleaning and inspection—for a clean billet meant a good battalion! Then the fall in, and inspection in the grey dawn, and the Colonel's command to move off at the starting point, and the long swinging routine of march discipline over the long straight roads of France. The hourly halts, the songs, the familiar band-tunes, and the mid-day meals as the men crowded eagerly round the steaming cookers (or " galloping Lockhart's "). Then followed the arrival in the new billets—the comforting tea, the search for the estaminet, and the certain sleep. The first night was spent at Brucamps, and the next day, marching by St. Ouen and Flesselles, a stay was made at Villers Bocage until November 27th. Thence the Battalion moved to Bonneville for further training. From this dilapidated village, stretched along two streets, in the shape of an elongated X, the Sixteenth set off at length for their baptism of fire on December 7th. The night was spent in a muddy camp of tents at Couin, within view of Verey lights and the sound of guns, and next day, marching by platoons at intervals, the Battalion entered the village of Hebuterne.

Here it received a warm reception. Suddenly, as the leading Company was entering the " place " heavy shelling was concentrated down the road, and among the casualties Lieut. Behrens was severely wounded. The behaviour of the troops under these trying circumstances was admirable. Eventually Companies were paired off for instruction with seasoned troops of the Gloucester and Worcester Regiments, and were initiated into the routine of trench life. A less promising beginning could hardly be imagined. It rained continuously until the last day—and then it froze. The mud-caked Battalion marched away from Hebuterne, on the 14th, to Louvencourt. Next day it returned, via Beauquesne, to the old billets at Bonneville. Here Christmas was spent, memorable for the fire which broke out in a farm-building. Collaborating with the local fire-brigade, consisting of an archaic hand-cart manned by ancient and excitable greybeards, the troops spent the whole night fighting the fire, which raged till 6 a.m. " Naked lights" afterwards became a sore subject.

THE SOMME

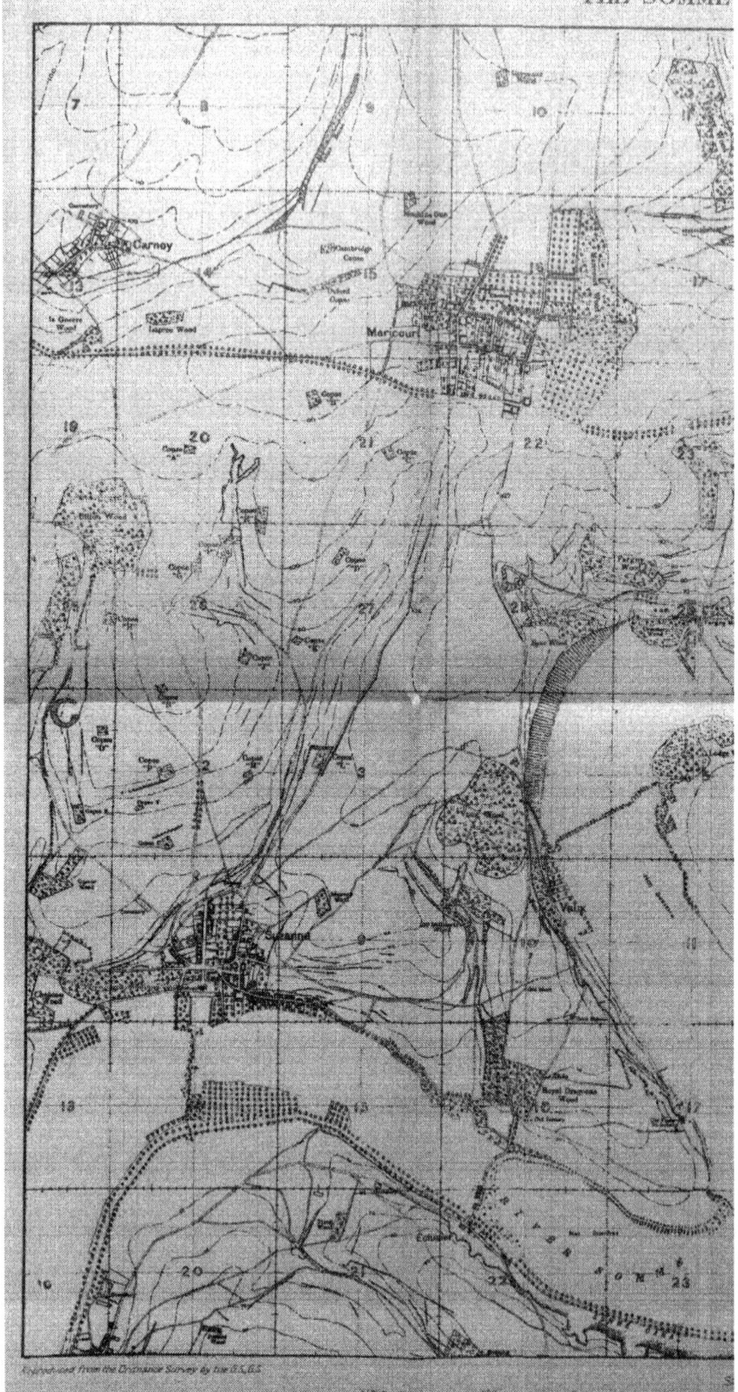

AREA • MAP B.

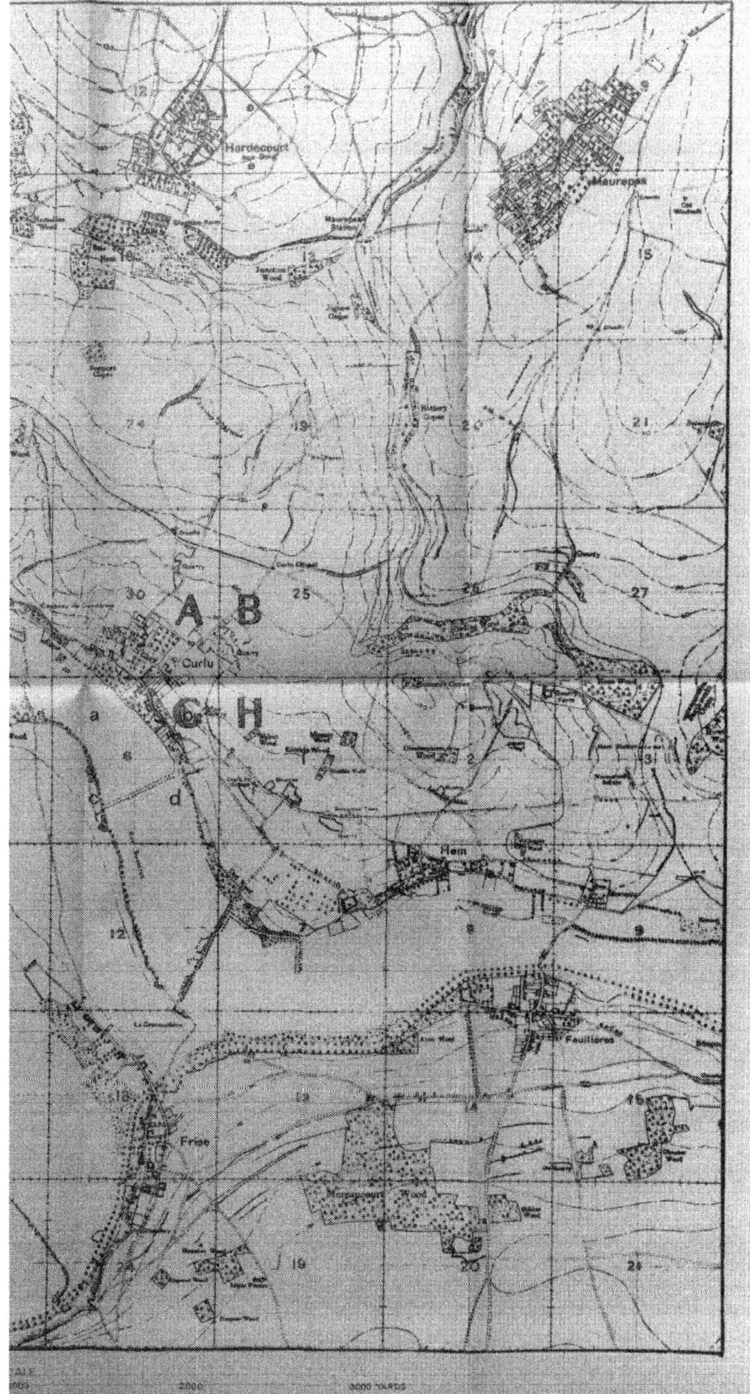

Hardecourt
Maurepas
A
B
Curlu
C
H
a
d
Hem
Feuillères
Frise
Maurepas Wood

CHAPTER II

IN THE MARICOURT AREA *

"THE Great War," says Doyle in his "British Campaign: 1916," "had now come into its second winter, a winter which was marked by an absolute cessation of all serious fighting upon the Western front. Enormous armies were facing each other, but, until the German attack upon the French lines of Verdun at the end of February, the Infantry of neither side was seriously engaged." This passage serves to explain the succeeding phase through which the Sixteenth passed.

On January 1st, 1916, the 30th Division was ordered to take over the line of the Somme, near Eclusier, from the 5th Division; the 5th Division of the French Army being on the right, and the 15th British Brigade on the left. At 2 p.m. on January 2nd the Sixteenth set out from Bonneville for the Somme. The first night was spent at Talmas, the second at La Hoossoye, the third at Chipilly, after a march of seventeen miles. On the 5th they marched, via Bray and Suzanne, to Maricourt, taking over the Maricourt defences from the 1st Devons. Next day they relieved the 15th Royal Warwicks in the front line trenches. Three days were spent in the line, two in Maricourt, followed by three more in the line, and on the 12th the Battalion was relieved by the 17th Manchesters, and moved for the first time into billets in Suzanne.

When the Sixteenth came to Suzanne, as the billeting area for the front line by Maricourt, it was a comparatively quiet and *healthy* spot. Civilian inhabitants still lingered there although it was only two miles behind the front line. The *Marquis* shared his *Château* with Brigade Headquarters. It was said that Suzanne was a "rest cure"—well, it may have been! The great Château of brick and stone, largely rebuilt on the old plan during the nineteenth century, was the nucleus of the place. It stood among trees at the foot of a hill up which the village ran, with great gates and spacious forecourt, and a formal water-garden linked up with the Somme. The gardens were fallen into sad neglect from the days of their glory, in the period of the "grande noblesse." Tapestries and furniture,

* See Map B

and state-coaches in the eighteenth century stable block recalled its former splendour. Now the place rang with the busy life of Brigade Headquarters; staff officers and horses, cars and orderlies were in possession, and deep in the stable cellar was the dressing station. On the axial line of the forecourt, planned in the *grand manner* of the period, Centre Street, with the church to its left, ran up the hill towards Maricourt, with West Street and East Street looping to left and right, whilst Cannon Street lay under the brow of the hill, leading to Eclusier. Along these roads lay the barns and cottages that housed the troops during their periods of "rest"; flimsily constructed of half timber and mud, with solidly-built cellars. North Street crowned the valley, in the chalk side of which Manchester fatigues burrowed tunnelled dug-outs under the direction of the 11th South Lancs. (Pioneers), and below the crucifix lay the cemetery that proved the last resting-place for many a Manchester man.

It may have been the knowledge that a new Division had come in, or the fact that our artillery paid more attention to Maurepas and Guillemont, but, be that as it may, the village of Suzanne became a scene of liveliness.

On the 13th January the guard having mounted with due ceremony outside the Battalion orderly room, an unusual number of officers and "accused" were gathered in the precincts, and just as the C.O. was "telling off" a prisoner a high explosive shell burst with a crash a few yards away. The blood was seen trickling down the pale face of the "accused," who remained standing to attention—the room was filled with dust and broken glass and debris; but a trap door leading to a deep cellar was discovered, and soon C.O. and prisoner, Adjutant and Sergt.-Major and the rest were mixed up under the protecting vault.

The same morning twelve men of "B" Company were wounded, and the 2nd R.S.F.'s had many casualties. Houses fell like packs of cards—brick-dust filled the air, as the enemy artillery registered systematically down the streets. It was soon found that the civilian inhabitants must be evacuated, and the mournful procession of old men and women, girls and children began. The French cling to their homesteads, and the pathos of their exodus, carrying such of their worldly goods as they could from their crumbling homes, emphasized the devastating effect of the war

It has been said that in war, for every three days' fighting there are three months drudgery and routine, and from January until July, except for short spells of training behind the line, the Sixteenth went the round of Suzanne—Maricourt, Maricourt—Suzanne, with the 17th Manchesters as their opposite number, and a routine varying from four to two days' reliefs. The two mile march from billets in Suzanne to Maricourt and the front line trenches was along the road that skirted Maricourt valley, dotted with its battery positions. Across the near horizon stretched the great Peronne road, with its dwindling avenue of trees. The straggling village of Maricourt, with its château, its brewery, its battered cottages, and orchards and farm courtyards was sheltered by Maricourt Wood, and had a defence system of its own, making it a "point d'appui" in case the front line should go. It was the centre of an important salient that formed the extreme right of the British front. On the right the 18th Manchesters held posts on the Somme Marshes and at Fargny Mill, facing the Chapeau de Gendarme. Thence the trenches rose steeply in front of Fargny Wood, and on past the enigmatical sunk "Y" Wood, the crest of which was held by the Germans across the Peronne Road. From this point it followed a line about 100 yards in front of the perimeter of Maricourt Wood, at a northern extremity of which it bent at right angles to Machine Gun Wood. This portion was held by battalions of the King's Liverpool Regt. (89th Brigade). They were miserable trenches—with a wretched and inadequate system of communication that caused irritating blocks during relief, the wire was thin, dug-outs there were none—only a few splinter-proof shelters. Some of the platoons in the front line—and a number of posts—were completely isolated.

During the winter all that could be done was to struggle with the mud and maintain what defence existed, but it was a very different line that was handed over to the French before the Somme offensive, and the 30th and 18th Divisions must share the credit for the fine trench system that was laboriously built up during the spring of 1916. In front stretched the bare rolling landscape of Picardy. On the right were the great bend of the wide Somme basin and the villages of Curlu and Frise. In the centre came the hamlet of Hardecourt, and, beyond, Maurepas. Bois d'en Haut, Nameless Wood, and Faviere Wood fronted Hardecourt. On the right came Maltzhorn Farm, and further round rose the great green masses of Trones and Bernafay Woods, the Briqueterie and Montauban. Later all these landmarks on the daily horizon were destined to become historic in the great Somme struggle.

On the 24th January there was a violent bombardment of Maricourt, shells coming over in incredible numbers. The wood resounded with the crash of trees and the incessant shriek and whistle overhead. The 17th Kings were brought up to man the Maricourt defences and were reinforced by one and a half companies of the 17th Manchesters. The Sixteenth Headquarters took up battle positions in the Wood.

The 28th was the Kaiser's birthday and an attack on a grand scale appeared imminent. As a matter of fact the bombardment was made to cover the flank of the attack which the Germans launched on the French on the other side of the Somme. The men did not realise the full significance of this operation at the time. Frise was taken from the French, the enemy advanced to within almost a mile of Brigade Headquarters, and had this important turning movement penetrated a few hundred yards more into the French lines, it is said that the whole Maricourt salient would have been lost. But the French rushed up reinforcements and drove the enemy back within safety limits. The French 75's firing incessantly day and night were a revelation of artillery power, and our guns gave effective aid by enfilade fire across the river. It was one of the first uses the enemy had made of lachrymatory or tear shells, which caused the eyes to stream and rendered our gunners almost impotent.

On the 31st the Sixteenth were relieved after eight hard days in the line. Billets two miles or less from the front line trench do not necessarily constitute a *rest*, especially when the time is spent burrowing chalk dug-outs. But everything, it is said, has its compensations. If Suzanne attracted shells it had the most refreshing hot douche baths on the Cappy Road, where the lousy, muddy, rat-ridden Tommy could regain his self-respect. Here, too, the parcels from home provided a never failing delight and supplemented the dull, if ample, monotony of rations.

Note.—A complaint having been sent in by the Battalion that there was no pork in the " Pork and Beans " the reply, having passed through Brigade, Division, Corps and Army, came back.

" With reference to the complaint made by the Manchesters that there is no pork in the ' Pork and Beans ' it should be understood that the pork has been absorbed by the bean."

Episode of Black Watch Relief in Maricourt Trenches

Whilst holding the line in front of Maricourt the Sixteenth went through a form of relief with a Battalion of the Black Watch. The Highlanders had come in full strength from training and rest behind and were in splendid condition. The crowded trenches contained a strange medley of Scotch and Lancashire, and at length the last platoon of the relieved company was heard passing the O.C. Company's dug-out, the " relief complete " form was just filled in, when the telephone rang and the Adjutant's voice was heard—" Relief cancelled." There was a fine display of language that night, no reasons were given—and shortly before dawn the " Jocks " withdrew. Two days later a battalion of the Gordons relieved the Manchesters.

It is said that important strategical reasons dictated this strange proceeding—but months after—on the dead body of a German Colonel was discovered an entry in his diary to this effect:

"The Manchesters holding the Maricourt trenches opposite us were relieved by the Black Watch. Just as the relief was complete it was cancelled and the Manchesters were recalled. The interesting conversation between the Adjutant of the Manchesters and the Company-Commander in the front line was heard by our telephone tapping machine."

Shortly afterwards many precautions were wisely introduced in the use of telephone conversations to the forward Company Headquarters.

The Battalion remained in the Maricourt-Suzanne area until the 17th March, taking the usual spells in the trenches. During the earlier part of this period there had been several falls of snow and much rain. The trenches were in a wretched condition, and the weather was bitterly cold. Damp gum-boots, mud-caked ground sheets and capes, anti-frost-bite grease, and gas alarms were the order of the day. The ration parties carried their heavy "dixies" through knee-deep mud, cold night watches alternated with mud-shifting and water-pumping. Yet these hardships were borne with that cheerfulness, determination and grit which is as essential to the success of modern war as prowess in battle. There was one redeeming feature in the twenty-four hour round—the rum issue! "Rum up!" was most joyous of all sounds. The most rabid *pussyfoot* would fall under these conditions. Always issued by the Company officer to his men, it constituted an almost sacred rite, a bond of sympathy and comradeship. Now at least the circulation would flow as the comforting liquor coursed through the frozen veins, and life seemed possible once more.

On March 17th the Battalion was relieved in Suzanne by the 7th Buffs and marched to Bray, where it dug long straight cable trenches seven feet deep in chalk. On the 28th it marched to Corbie and on the following day "A" Company marched to Ribemont, leaving one platoon at Bonnay, while "B" Company went to Longpre.

The period March 29th to April 12th was spent on Corps' fatigues, and on the 13th the Battalion marched to Coisy, and on the following day to Breilly, eight miles west of Amiens, for training.

Winter in the trenches is apt to make men forget that they are soldiers. The round of clearing mud, consorting with rats and doing "sentry go" in frost and snow makes for a loss of self-respect, and a loosening of discipline, and does not form an ideal preparation for spring offensives. Accordingly these periods of training behind were essential for the efficiency of the fighting troops. Discipline was strictly enforced. The daily routine was marching, drill, musketry and tactics. It was at this time that the following incident occurred, which is a commentary on the " temper " of the troops on manœuvres, after the realities of the line.

The customary hours of marching, enlivened with exercises in advanced and flank guards under heavy loads brought the tired Brigade to a position from which a lofty hill was dimly visible on the other side of a wide valley. The Brigadier (mounted) in a few stirring words having issued his orders for attacking an imaginary enemy represented by red flags, the following observations by a small and perspiring Manchester " Pal " were overheard :—

" After an imaginary *tot* of rum we goes over an imaginary top and attacks an imaginary enemy. What I wants to know is—why the 'ell can't we imagine the whole bloody thing's over and jimmy off 'ome."

A Brigade Horse Show was held in a vast natural amphitheatre near Picquigny. Competition was keen, the day propitious, the effect on the Transport miraculous. Perhaps the Company cook-cart was the greatest revelation. Brass gleamed, paint shone, knives and axes were like polished bayonets and the cooks themselves were clean. The Sixteenth won the event and many others. The tiny ammunition mule's tail and coat were like silk ; horses heavy and horses light, mules of every size and variety proudly displayed themselves to an amazed and delighted crowd. Limbered waggons threaded their speedy way through biscuit tins, for all the world like the Military Tournament at Olympia. There was also a horse race.

On the 29th March the Battalion set out for Corbie, a distance of seventeen miles, and the splendid appearance of the men was much commented on.

The hardships of the winter were now over and milder weather set in. On the morning of the 1st May the troops bathed in the Somme, and afterwards marched to Suzanne. Next day they were once more in the Maricourt sector, in trenches south of the Peronne Road, and next to their old sub-sector, " A " and " B " Companies being in the line. The Germans suspecting that a new Division had come in instituted a series of " hurricane hates," or intense bombardments, as a preparation for a raid. Suddenly in the night these terrifying concentrations of gunfire would obliterate a post, enveloping it in sheets of flame. On the 3rd a sap was destroyed, trenches were blown in, four men were killed, and an officer and seven other ranks wounded. At 11 p.m. on the 5th a similar " hate " killed four more and wounded six, making terrible havoc of a post of " A " Company. The 6th and 7th passed quietly, and on the following day the Battalion was relieved by the 18th Manchesters and returned to Suzanne.

On the night, 13th/14th May, the enemy opened heavy fire on the trenches and batteries in the Maricourt-Suzanne area. Successive raids and attacks made on the 2nd Royal Scots Fusiliers and the 18th Manchesters were driven off by machine gun and rifle fire, but an advanced sap-head held by the latter, which lay only some fifteen yards from the nearest enemy post, after a terrific bombardment, provided them with identification. Two prisoners of the 63rd German Regiment were brought in. The casualties on the British side were between fifty and sixty, chiefly from shell fire. On the night of the 14th the Battalion relieved the 18th Manchesters, remaining in the line until the 19th.

For the rest of the month all was quiet. The weather was good, trenches were revetted, wire was strengthened, and the routine of trench warfare reached a high standard of efficiency. Petrie Avenue, an important new communication trench leading from " S Works " strong point on the Suzanne-Maricourt Road, was constructed.

By way of diversion a front line Company instituted " five o'clock hate teas."

The F.O.O., the Stokes and Heavy "football" mortar officers, the West Spring gun and the Company rifle grenades collected all available rounds, and gave the enemy trench on the edge of " Y " Wood a little return of their own intensive concentration. At a given hour the calm of " peace time in the trenches " was broken by a few short lively minutes, and the eager infantry watched with delight the soaring missiles and the spurts of earth and flame as the mortars rent the trenches and broke the wire, while the field guns " sprinkled them with shrapnel." Then before the whizz-bang retaliation came, all sought safety.

About this time a raid on a grand scale was contemplated on mysterious " Y " Wood, but after five days of expectation it never came off. Rehearsals behind the line in the Maricourt valley and reconnaissance from the line strung the troops up to a pitch of eager expectancy, and had an excellent effect on the *morale*. A Company Commander having explained the plan of operation to his men asked if anyone had any questions to ask. A large and burly Pioneer rose to the invitation.

" Now, sir, you've told us what t'bombers 'ave to do. What I wants to know is, if any o' them bleeding Boches tries to molest us, while us is diggin', would it be legitimate to kill 'em with a spade ? "

The continued German pressure at Verdun had reached a high point in June, and it was recognised that only an early allied attack on the western end of the line could ease the situation. Sir Douglas Haig had placed himself and his armies at the disposal of General Joffre, and an attack over a broad front was in preparation.

On June 1st the 90th Brigade was relieved by the famous French XXth Corps—which included "The Iron Division"—the picked *Gladiator* Corps of our Allies. They took over the section of the British line north of the Somme in order to ensure a closer co-operation at the junction of the English and French Armies. For some days before the relief the line was full of eager French officers of all arms, making their reconnaissances, and a warm *entente* was instituted. The XXth Corps had done great things in the Verdun battle, and came from a period of recuperation at full strength. Immediately the whole area began to hum like a beehive. Battery positions were constructed for the great concentration of guns, swarms of French labour corps set systematically to work. Our men envied the admirable distinction made by our Allies between the fighting and working troops. The Lewis Gun and Mitrailleuse were eagerly compared, the condition of the trenches, particularly the sandbag revetments and the sanitary arrangements were warmly admired. "C'est epatant!" exclaimed the eager *poilu*, "you Eenglish make yourselves so veery confortable."

Commandant Chevallier, 79th French Infantry, relieved the Sixteenth. The relief itself passed off uneventfully. Every precaution was taken. Our Verey lights continued in use for a few nights so that the French parachute rocket should not tell the enemy what had taken place. The Infantry "stood to" all through the first night, and to the liaison officers of the Battalion who stayed with them for a time it was curious to behold in the old familiar trenches the bearded *poilu* with his strange *tin* hat, his sky-blue great coat, and his long thin bayonet. They expressed great surprise at the youthful appearance of the Sixteenth boys.

"Ils sont tous enfants! Mais, I should like to go over ze tops with dem, dey are magnifiques!"

It was considered an honour to be placed next to the picked troops of France, and the smoothness with which the relief was conducted augured well for the confidence and friendship which was to be proved in the weeks to come.

From the old Maricourt sector the Sixteenth moved into camp at Etinehem on the night of the 1st/2nd June, where they rested and received drafts, and on the 10th relieved the 18th King's (Liverpools) in 2.1. subsector, on the other side of Maricourt, in order to study the ground over which they were shortly to attack.

The following episode took place during the course of this relief.

In a muddy communication-trench leading up to Maricourt a weary Company was telescoped in an interminable block—the guide had lost his way—rain was falling, an occasional bullet whistled overhead and packs weighed like lead. Through the darkness emerged the still more miserable figures of the "Liverpool Pals" returning from the line. The Company humorist recollecting, no doubt, the final inspection of the Division by Lord Derby on Salisbury Plain, a dazzling scene of "spit and polish," was heard to exclaim: "Eh! Eh! If that there Durby could see 'is *pets* now it w'd turn 'is bloody 'air grey."

Hard days of enemy bombardment followed while the Battalion occupied the line facing Montauban, Bernafay Wood, Trones Wood, and Briqueterie. The whole trench system was a bustle of preparation for the coming battle, working parties were everywhere, both French and English, and 200 men of the 16th and 18th were detailed on the night of the 13th to dig a new "jumping off" trench in front of the old line, near the salient where the French army joined the British. The covering party was placed, the men had been allotted their tasks, the sods were removed and digging only just begun when, with a crash, the German artillery and machine guns blazed into fury. The combined English and French guns promptly and effectually retaliated. Along the whole line the working-parties dashed to the front trench and with about two men to the yard rapid rifle-fire was opened. But many casualties were inflicted in the crowded English line. Lieut. Fowler, in charge of the covering party, and Lieut. R. O. Philips were severely wounded, the latter whilst helping the return of the working party with great gallantry, and two men were killed and fourteen wounded. The cause of this outburst was a German raid which was made in order to discover the join between the French and British armies. It is said that they succeeded in obtaining identification of the French XXth Corps at the extreme left-hand sap of the French line.

On the 16th the Battalion was relieved by the 2nd Bedfords, and moved to the Bois de Taille for breakfast. Next day they marched to Heilly where they entrained for Ailly-sur-Somme and thence marched to Le Mesge, via Picquigny. Singing, and with a swing, they reached billets at 11-30 p.m. after having marched twenty-four miles. This was a severe test and was a great credit to the regiment when it is remembered that they came straight from the line with their feet soft from the trenches.

On the 19th the Division began an admirable and systematic training for its first great battle under its new Commander, Major-General Shea, who had succeeded Major-General Fry.

The whole trench system had been reproduced in facsimile at Briquemesnil. Silesia trench, the Glatz redoubt and the topography of Montauban itself, with all its streets marked out, with dummy hedges, and Montauban Alley, the final objective were there. Here, day after day, the attack was practised, there being no respite until every man was familiar with the part he had to take. On one occasion the Division carried out the operation entirely without officers, and it was effected without a hitch.

On the 21st the Sixteenth had moved to billets at Oissy, where, on the 24th, a last memorable concert was held in the Château grounds. In a peaceful setting of trees the men lay at their ease on the grass, with the little group of officers on the terrace, and listened to the old familiar songs of Grantham and Lark Hill.

On the 26th June there was a march to Ailly, train thence to Mericourt, and a further march brought the Battalion to Etinehem at 10 p.m. The British attack had been planned for the 28th, but the weather proved so tempestuous that it was necessarily delayed. Meanwhile, the week-long bombardment of the enemy roared incessantly.

At 7 p.m. on 30th June the Sixteenth marched from Etinehem, reaching its assembly trenches that lay by Cambridge Copse in the Maricourt area at 12-45 midnight, being inspected on the way by the Divisional Commander and the Brigadier.

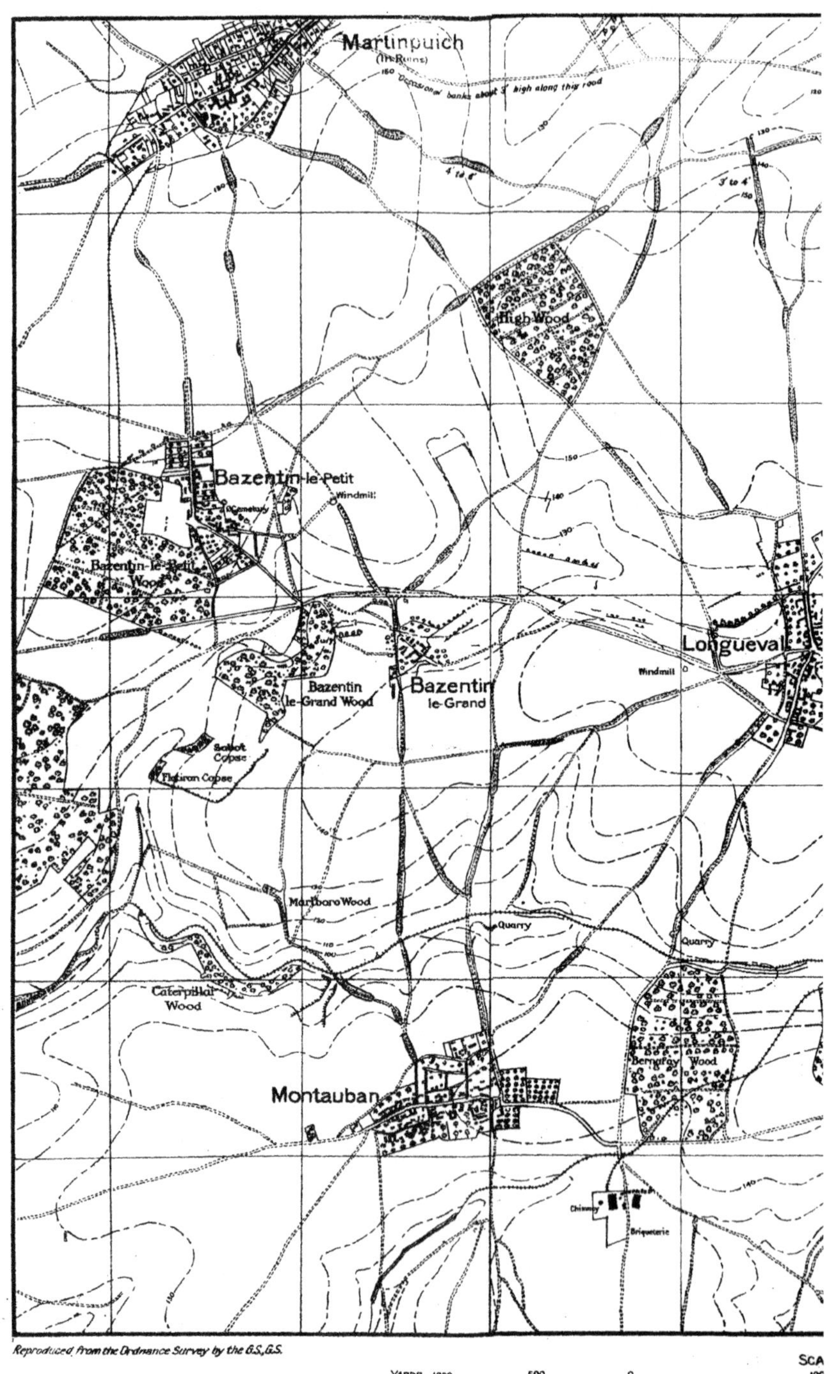
Martinpuich
(In Ruins)
Occasional banks about 3' high along this road
4' to 6'
3' to 4'
High Wood
Bazentin-le-Petit
Windmill
Cemetery
Bazentin-le-Petit Wood
Longueval
Windmill
Bazentin le-Grand Wood
Bazentin le-Grand
Sabot Copse
Flatiron Copse
Marlboro Wood
Quarry
Quarry
Caterpillar Wood
Montauban
Bernafay Wood
Chimney
Briqueterie
Reproduced from the Ordnance Survey by the G.S.,G.S.
SCA
YARDS 1000 500 0 100

AREA · MAP A.

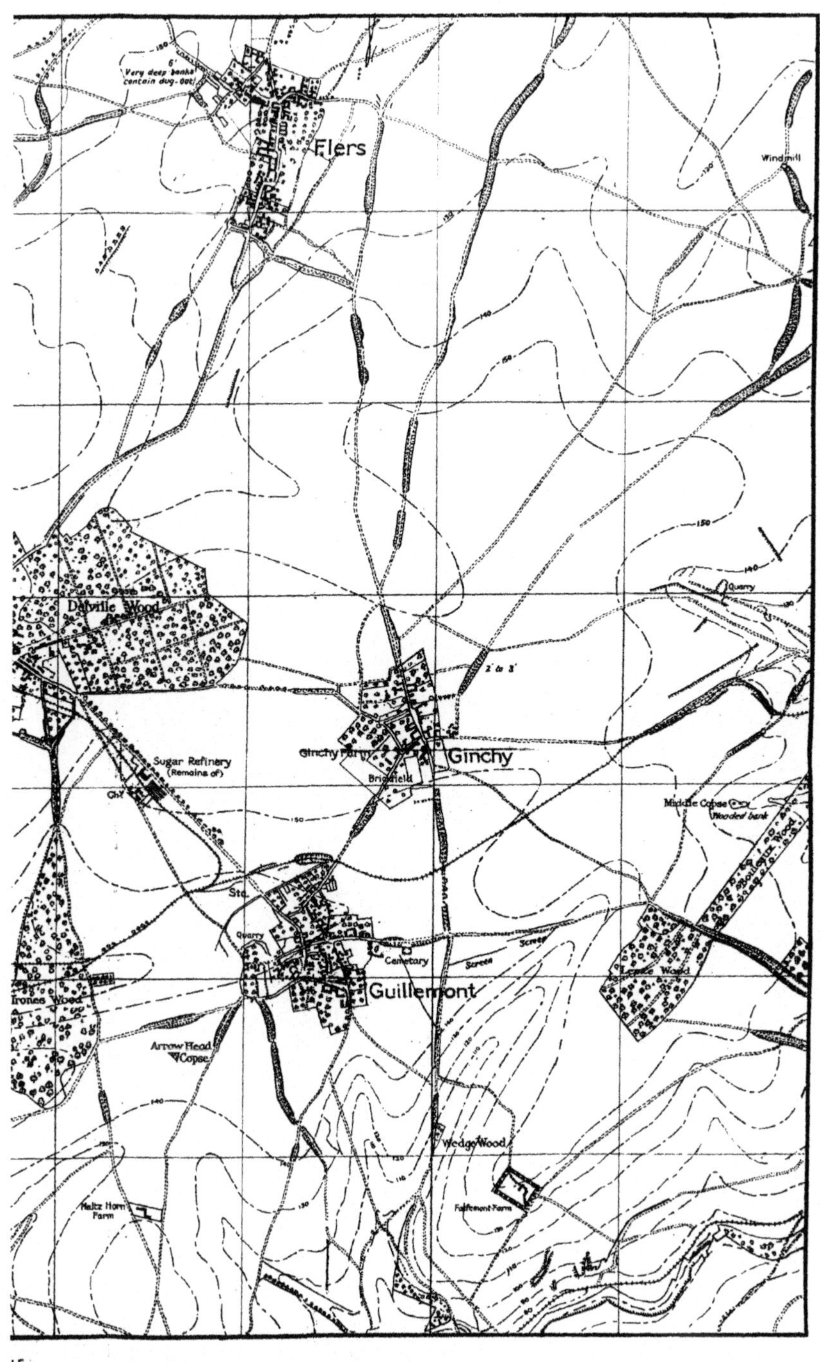

LE
0 2000 3000 YARDS

CHAPTER III

THE BATTLE OF THE SOMME*

MONTAUBAN : TRONES WOOD : GUILLEMONT

THE " Big Push " had come at last.

The Battle of the Somme stretched from where Snow's VIIth Corps faced the Gommecourt Salient, at its northern end, to Congreve's XIIIth Corps facing Montauban, on the south side of the British line, where it touched the French XXth Corps on the river Somme itself, with a battle front of 20 miles. Hundreds of thousands were to leap from their trenches into the open and carry all before them. The New Armies were to prove the fruits of their long training.

The XIIIth Corps was to attack with the 30th Division on the right, and having the 18th Division on the left, and the 9th Division in Reserve. The furthest objective of the 30th Division was the important village of Montauban, a pivotal position in the German Reserve Line. The first wave of the attack was upon the enemy front-line system, with the 89th Brigade on the right and the 21st Brigade on the left. These troops were to seize Briqueterie and Glatz Redoubt. The 90th Brigade was then to " leap-frog " through and seize the village.

The dispositions of the 90th Brigade were as follows :

Its left lay on the Talus Boisé—a long thin wood that separated it from the 18th Division—and then along the track leading north to Montauban. Its right was on the track west of Machine Gun Wood, running through the west end of Glatz Redoubt to Montauban.

The objective of the Sixteenth was Montauban Alley, an important German trench some two hundred yards in advance of the further perimeter of the village, with its left in line with the western end of Montauban, its right by Triangle Point where it touched the 17th Manchesters. The 2nd Royal Scots Fusiliers and the 18th Manchesters were in support and reserve. " B " Company had the left of the firing line, " A " Company the right, " C " Company being in support, and " D " Company in Reserve.

* See Map A

This great attack of July 1st, 1916, was the first important action in which the Sixteenth had been engaged. It would be impossible to exaggerate the feeling of optimism and expectation that filled all ranks. Here was the great test. The thoroughness of the training, the short respite behind after the hardships of trench routine, the stupendous bombardment to which the enemy had been subjected for one week, the evidences on all sides of preparation and strength had served their purpose.

After a cramped cold night in the crowded Assembly Trenches the day broke in mist and haze, that lifted, as if according to plan, shortly before zero. The sun shone in a cloudless sky ; our captive balloons and aeroplanes, to the accompaniment of shrieking shells, dominated the air. At 7-30 a.m., after a final bombardment of the utmost intensity, the first lines of Divisions went over the top. The great attack had begun. The tension was tremendous. As far as the eye could see to right and left the great waves of little khaki-clad figures were rolling back the enemy. The first trench was taken. Then the news spread from man to man—" The French have taken Hardecourt and Favière Wood ! The Germans are surrendering all along the line ! " The heartening rum-ration gave the finishing touch ; bayonets flashed in the sun ; and at 8-30 the Battalion leaped to its advance.

It was the last time the old original Sixteenth, that had hung together from its civilian beginning, through the long wearisome training and the drudgery and hardship of trench routine could be said to exist intact. It is true that three hundred were to remain for the bloody tangles of Trones Wood, one hundred for the unfortunate attempt on Guillemont, but for the assault of Montauban, it was a unit complete in personnel, officered by its original leaders. These were the Clerks and Warehousemen of the 1st City Battalion who came of their own free will in the early days of the War. Their spirit lived on in the gallant few who survived, but that July 1st paid heavily for its splendid achievement.

There were three thousand yards to traverse across the battered maze of intricate entrenchments, across a churned up earth strewn with grey corpses, amidst a deafening crash of sound and the shrill zip-zip-zip of the stinging machine-gun bullets. White puffs of shrapnel burst against the clear blue sky with the songs of larks challenging the shrieking shells. In little columns of artillery formation the attacking waves passed through the 21st Brigade that had already taken the first enemy line, on, into the unknown. They came under a heavy machine gun fire. The little columns extended but the 18th Division was held up at Pommiers Ridge and enfilade fire mowed down the advancing waves. Bands of " Kamarades " with shaking hands held high were passed for succeeding waves to deal with; the shattered wreck of trenches gave place to green fields and a crest before a dip, beyond which our barrage formed an almost solid wall of spouting earth, convulsing the ground in sickening upheaval. Steady as on parade at Heaton Park, or Grantham, the lines pressed on until our barrage caused an enforced and irritating check. Then the guns lengthened range, the attackers swept up the final slope and poured into Montauban, led by the C.O. Hardly one brick had been left upon another, but little nests of machine gunners and strong points had to be tackled. They fought their way through, driving those who resisted into cellars before a hail of bombs. Several hundreds of prisoners were taken, and by 10-30 a.m. the village was in our hands and the final objective, Montauban Alley, had been reached.

Battalion Headquarters was established, communications were effected with Brigade Headquarters. "A" "B," and "C" Companies were consolidating Montauban Alley, having "D" Company in support in the village. All the officers of "A" and "B" Companies were out of action, and Lieut. Nash was sent up at 11-30 a.m. to help Captain Johnson in the front line, the latter taking the right half, the former the left half of the firing line. Touch was obtained with the 17th Manchesters on the right, but on the left where there was an exposed flank, a bombing block was made until late in the afternoon, when the 18th Division came up.

An eager handful rushed the gun-pits beyond the Alley, firing at the fleeing gunners as they rushed down the hill, and chalked the name of their unit on the three first guns to be taken in the Battle of the Somme. The men were exhausted, and suffering from the reaction which follows hard fighting, but they had to work feverishly in order to consolidate the position they had won. Eventually sentry groups were told off, Lewis guns posted and normal routine instituted. Finally, the weary troops were able to snatch some sleep. There were no means of communicating with the Artillery, there were no Verey pistols (owing to casualties) and there remained little more than a dozen bombs in the firing line. Lieut. Harvey, of "D" Company, was sent up, making a total of three officers in the line.

At mid-day the Germans began to shell the village. The ground between Montauban Alley and the village appeared at times one sheet of flame. The ground in front fell away into Caterpillar Wood Valley, and the firing line could only command a field of fire of some hundred yards. It had been impossible to occupy, according to plan, Spur Point, an important position in advance of Montauban Alley, which commanded the valley, as our guns were shelling the spot. Consequently the Germans were able to mass their first real counter attack, which was launched at 9-30 p.m. It was beaten off by 10-15 p.m. and but for heavy shelling all was quiet. But the position was so precarious for the small exhausted garrison that all through the night they "stood to" at their firing position—the remains of their ammunition laid out on the parapet at their side. They were shelled throughout the night, and, as there had been no opportunity of filling their water bottles since the evening of the 30th, they were in great distress through thirst.

At 3 a.m., just as dawn was breaking, and the order to "stand down" was about to be issued, long lines of grey figures in great-coats and helmets were seen advancing over the ridge, shoulder to shoulder—on they came, wave after wave.

The second counter attack had begun!

There was no need to issue fire orders. As the Germans topped the ridge our men opened rapid fire with deadly precision, many climbing out on to the parapet to get a better *field of fire*. The Lewis guns served splendidly. It had been said: "You can, no doubt, take the village, but can you hold it?" "We can do it," said the men, and they did. The lonely wounded, lying among their dead comrades on the ground behind the village under the starry sky, heard the hellish crash of the enemy artillery preparation, and the rattle of the Lewis gun and rifle fire; saw great jets of flame among the trees of the village and the clustering rockets. "Can they hold on—will the stampede overwhelm us?" They were barely 150 strong, with 1,000 yards of trench to hold. There were no means of communicating to the guns direct—but the attack was broken up solely by rifle fire. Four waves had been dispersed when our artillery came into action and put up a barrage that rendered further attack impossible. But all was not over. The enemy had broken into Montauban Alley between our extreme right post and the junction with the 17th Manchesters. "Bombers forward" was the order. But there were no bombs. The enemy were driven back, however, and another block established on the right of the Battalion line.

At 2-30 p.m. the firing line was relieved by the 2nd Wilts and, taking with them one Mills bomb and 300 rounds of S.A.A.—all that they had—they filed along the trench, which was still being shelled, and so across the dreary tangle of the battle-field back to the Assembly Trenches. They had done their job but they were tired—overwhelmingly tired. They had had no sleep, to speak of, for sixty hours, battling for a day and a night and another day against overwhelming odds, without water, without bombs, with ammunition low, yet they had maintained their winnings. And as the battered remnant sank down exhausted the Padre said: "Boys—I know you are fagged out, but there are still many wounded lying out. I want some of you to help me to get them in." And they stood up to a man. No praise can be too high for those Junior N.C.O.'s and Senior Privates who took the lead when officers and sergeants fell. Of " A " Company alone all the officers and three of the four platoon-sergeants were killed or wounded before the village was reached. Forty men died and sixty were wounded in the one action. All the officers of " B " Company were likewise out of action and there were 88 casualties.

It is impossible to single out special acts of gallantry from an almost general devotion to duty.

Of the Company-Commanders, Captain Worthington, O.C. " A " Company, was severely wounded in lung, hand and thigh ; Captain F. Walker, D.C.M., O.C. " B " Company, lost both his eyes ; Captain Johnson, O.C. " C " Company, was killed when gallantly commanding the firing line in the final counter-attack ; and Captain Elstob alone remained, eventually to command the Battalion, win the V.C., and a hero's grave at Manchester Hill in 1918.

Lieut. Allen was killed whilst trying to rescue Lieut. Kerry, the Lewis Gun officer, who subsequently died of wounds then received.

List of Officers who took part in the Attack on July 1st 1916

Lieut.-Col. C. L. Petrie, D.S.O.; Capt. and Adjutant E. G. Sotham; Capt. J. H. Worthington, O.C. " A " Company (wounded); Capt. F. Walker, D.C.M., O.C. " B " Company (wounded) ; Capt. W. M. Johnson, O.C. " C " Company (killed) ; Capt. Elstob, O.C. " D " Company (wounded slightly and remained) ; Lieut. G. P. Morris (wounded) ; Lieut. Megson (wounded slightly and remained) ; Lieut. Hook (wounded) ; Lieut. Allen (killed) ; Lieut. Slack (wounded) ; Lieut. Nash (wounded) ; Lieut. Barr (wounded) ; Lieut. Kerry (died of wounds 1918) ; Lieut. W. Swain (wounded) ; Lieut. E. Prestwich (wounded) ; Lieut. E. L. R. Horley (wounded) ; Lieut. Faux (wounded) ; Lieut. Hanscombe (wounded) ; Lieut. Harvey (wounded) ; Capt. Heathcote, R.A.M.C. ; Rev. R. W. Balleine.

What was left of the Battalion was withdrawn to Happy Valley, off the Bray-Albert Road, where it remained in bivouac until the 8th, when it returned to its old Assembly Trenches, Cambridge Copse. and spent the next day carrying for the Brigade.

TRONES WOOD

Of all forms of fighting in the Great War, wood fighting proved to be the most terrible. Trones Wood, High Wood, Delville Wood are associated with the most disastrous and costly actions of the great Somme Battle. Trones Wood was the first of these, and the 30th Division was the first to attack it. The first attempt to dislodge the enemy was made on July 8th by the 21st Brigade. There was no suspicion of the strength of the German position, and the attack was repulsed within two hours. At 1 p.m. on the same day the 21st Brigade renewed their attempt, attacking with the 2nd Wilts from the side of Bernafay Wood. About 3 p.m. the 18th and 19th Manchesters came up in support, and there was some very severe fighting. Towards evening a detachment of the 17th King's Liverpools came up to strengthen this attack, and it was then determined to withdraw the shattered 21st, and replace it by the 90th Brigade. Maltzhorn Trench was at once taken over by a party of 2nd Royal Scots Fusiliers of this latter Brigade, who threw themselves with zest into the attack and captured about one hundred and sixty prisoners.

At 6-40 a.m. on July 9th the third attack was launched against Trones Wood, in which the 17th and 18th Manchesters took part. By 8 a.m. they had extended the position already held, and had almost cleared the wood of enemy troops. A terrific German bombardment, however, followed which resulted in such heavy losses to the two Manchester Battalions that they were compelled to fall back, in consequence of which the Royal Scots Fusiliers had to sacrifice the northern portion of Maltzhorn Trench. At 2-30 p.m. intelligence was received that the 17th and 18th Manchesters had evacuated Trones Wood, and the Sixteenth were ordered to move, via Glatz Redoubt, to Sunken Road, Briqueterie, from which point the Battalion was to attack and occupy the south and south-western part of Trones Wood. Accordingly the C.O., Lieut.-Col. Petrie, D.S.O., with two and a half Companies, started at once via Glatz Redoubt and worked up Sunken Road; the other one and a half Companies followed from Glatz Redoubt and Chimney Trench. This movement was carried out under very heavy artillery fire.

At 6-40 p.m. the Battalion formed up on Sunken Road to attack Trones Wood. The advance was carried out under heavy shrapnel, high explosive and machine-gun fire. The rapidity of advance, however, enabled the Battalion to avoid the barrage without serious loss. When the Battalion reached the line—Trones Alley and south-western edge of Trones Wood—a single Company of the 18th Manchesters was found still in occupation of the southern corner of the Wood, supporting the right flank of the newly arrived Battalion. The attackers bombed up Trones Alley to a desired point, which they blocked, and then retired, leaving a standing patrol in the Alley, just inside the western edge of the Wood. The southern portion of the Wood was found to be thickly entangled with fallen trees and thorny undergrowth. At 8 p.m. the situation was as follows :—

Headquarters and Reserve Company in Sunken Road; three Companies occupying Trones Alley and south-western edge of Wood. 11-45 p.m. brought urgent orders from Brigade Headquarters that the northern portion of Trones Wood must be cleared of the enemy before dawn, as the success of the present operations depended upon it. Accordingly three Companies of the Sixteenth, reinforced by one Company of South African Infantry were detailed to carry out this operation, which was to be done by means of vigorous patrolling of the Wood. The timber growth, however, proved so dense that it was found impossible to do much before daylight. To fill the gaps in the line caused by the withdrawal of the Manchesters for this purpose a further Company of South African Infantry was put under orders of the O.C. Sixteenth, and, leaving Sunken Road, went into the line in Maltzhorn Trench between the Sixteenth's right and the 2nd Royal Scots Fusiliers' left. At 4 a.m. on the 10th the Brigade artillery barrage was placed on the northern edge of the Wood. By 5 a.m. the South African Company reported wood clear of Germans. Four machine guns were then sent up to assist in defence of the Wood. Half an hour later a reverse occurred. The enemy throwing a strong attacking party against the Wood again occupied its southern end, cutting off some of the Manchester's patrols. The Reserve Company of Manchesters was then sent up from Sunken Road to drive the Germans back from the southern edge of the Wood. This they succeeded in doing, and re-occupied the trenches just outside the Wood. The activity of the enemy snipers and bombers prevented a further advance. Meanwhile it was reported that the Germans were massing strong forces in the centre of the Wood. At 8 a.m. a party of 18th Manchesters arrived, and were sent up to reinforce the trenches. Under urgent orders from Brigade Headquarters further patrols were sent out during the day, and at 6-45 p.m. the Wood was reported clear of the enemy, except the southern and south-western edge. Lieut.-Col. Petrie, in command of these operations, received intimation that at 9-30 p.m. one Company of the 17th K.L.R. would attack Trones Alley and south-western corner of the Wood, and that the 16th and 18th Manchesters and South African Infantry would conform. It was further intimated that the artillery barrage would be put on the Wood at 10-30 p.m., and that the attacking troops were to be clear of the Wood by that time. But after the most strenuous and gallant efforts to dislodge them the enemy still held the Wood.

In the morning the position had seemed more hopeful, but the Germans had quickly seized upon the gap in the line between the

Sixteenth and the 2nd Royal Scots Fusiliers, and through this they had made their way. Consequently after much confused fighting and very heavy shelling the night of July 10th found the Wood once more in the occupation of the enemy.

At 2 a.m. on the 11th, the troops were withdrawn from the trenches fringing the Wood and retired upon Sunken Road. The Sixteenth were relieved by the K.L.R. and by 4 a.m. were back in Maricourt Trenches.

Officers who took part in Trones Wood Operations (July 8th—11th)

Lieut.-Col. C. L. Petrie, D.S.O.; Capt. and Adjutant E. G. Sotham; Lieut. J. M. Oliver, O.C. "A" Company (missing, believed killed); Capt. J. J. Payne, O.C. "B" Company (wounded); Lieut. W. S. Davidson, O.C. "C" Company (wounded); Capt. W. Elstob, O.C. "D" Company (wounded); Lieut. R. H. Megson, *Signal Officer*; Lieut. Stafford Badger; Lieut. E. H. K. Smithers (killed in action); Sec.-Lieut. T. A. H. Nash (wounded); Sec.-Lieut. G. M. Harvey; Sec.-Lieut. S. E. Jackson; Sec.-Lieut. B. M. E. Baker; Sec.-Lieut. E. W. Venner (missing, believed killed); Sec.-Lieut. H. G. Scudamore; Sec.-Lieut. A. O. Hoskins.

Other Ranks: 15 killed in action, 85 missing, 81 wounded—181.

At 3 p.m. on the 11th July the Manchesters evacuated Maricourt and marched to Bois Celestins, arriving there at 7 p.m. The following day they rested. On the 13th they marched to Daours, remaining there until the 19th. Here training was continued. The Battalion marched to Bois Celestins on the 19th, and to Happy Valley on the 20th. Here reorganisation and training was carried out. Lieut.-Col. Petrie, D.S.O., returned to England, and Major H. Knox took over the command.

Guillemont

Trones Wood was eventually taken by the 54th Brigade on July 14th. Mametz Wood had also been captured. Thus, having broken the German line, it was resolved to carry the attack forward with the least possible delay. Bazentin was taken by the British on July 14th, thus making a gap in the second line. To develop this gain it became necessary to push forward to the left in the direction of Pozières, and on the right towards Guinchy and Guillemont.

The Manchesters were detailed to take part in the attack upon Guillemont. On the afternoon of July 22nd the Battalion received orders to leave Happy Valley and move to Mansel Copse area. This destination was reached at 6 p.m. and the Battalion bivouacked for the night. On the 23rd they moved to the Assembly Trenches, Cambridge Copse, and on the 24th the Battalion took up a position north of the old German front line. Here patrols went out at night to reconnoitre the ground between Trones Wood and Guillemont.

The Sixteenth had done splendidly at Montauban and Trones Wood, but two important actions in ten days are enough for any troops, and the survivors of the Sixteenth were reinforced by drafts from twenty-eight different Battalions. Lieut.-Col. Knox, who had succeeded Lieut.-Col. Petrie, had indeed a hard task to perform. He had only a handful of officers left and very few N.C.O.'s, to say nothing of the men. The drafts arrived two weeks before the attack on Guillemont, and one of these weeks had been spent in Assembly Trenches expecting every night to receive orders to attack the following morning. The men did not know their leaders.

The attack on Guillemont had been arranged for the morning of July 30th. At 8-30 p.m. on the 29th they moved off for the " jumping off " position. Lieut.-Col. Knox decided to move the Battalion in single file and this proved very successful, in spite of a heavy gas shell bombardment which came down as they were approaching Bernafay Wood, and caused a break in the line and some delay and many casualties. The position was reached at 3-0 a.m. Zero hour was 4-45. The weather was very thick, the fog being so dense that it was difficult to see more than a few yards ahead. The 89th Brigade advanced from the right and the 90th upon the left, the latter being directed straight for the village. The Sixteenth (90th Brigade) went forward in three waves, and on reaching the railway running through the sector, formed up steadily. Using the railway as a guide they pushed on towards Guillemont. On passing through the German wire, which had been battered by the British artillery, heavy machine-gun and rifle fire was met with on both flanks—on the left owing to Guillemont station being still in the hands of the enemy, and on the right owing to touch with the 18th Manchesters not being obtained, the heavy mist making it impossible to distinguish immediate surroundings. Casualties were very heavy, nests of enemy machine guns being quarried in solid rock. These played havoc with the attack, and after several gallant attempts to overcome them the Battalion was driven back and the remnant withdrawn to a line slightly in advance of the original point of attack.

The 2nd Royal Scots Fusiliers and 18th Manchesters managed to reach the village and hold on, but the German barrage fell so thickly behind them that they were cut off, and neither help nor munitions could reach them. Two Companies of the 17th Manchesters made their way through the barrage, but failed to alleviate the situation.

"Of the 18th Manchesters few returned, and two Companies of the 16th Manchesters were not more fortunate. They got into the village on the extreme north, and found themselves in touch with the 17th Royal Fusiliers of the Second Division; but neither Battalion could make good its position. It was one of the tragic episodes of the great Somme Battle." (Doyle: "1916 Campaign.")

The following were the casualties of the Sixteenth in the Guillemont Attack:—

Capt. J. H. Hawkins (missing, believed killed); Sec.-Lieut. F. G. Breet (killed); Sec.-Lieut. C. M. Williams (died of wounds); Sec.-Lieut. H. G. Plested (missing, believed killed); Sec.-Lieut. T. C. Haynes (wounded); Sec.-Lieut. G. C. Harryman (died of wounds seven days later); Sec.-Lieut. R. E. S. Tucker (died of wounds); Sec.-Lieut. S. C. Jackson (died of wounds).

Of Other Ranks: 17 killed, 97 wounded, 97 missing.

During the early hours of July 31st the Battalion was relieved and was ordered to reassemble at Mansel Copse, near Mametz.

CHAPTER IV

FESTUBERT, FLERS AND BELLACOURT

A QUIETER period now awaited the Sixteenth. On August 1st it was resting in Mansel Copse, and the next day it marched to Mericourt, entraining for Longpré, near Amiens, where the 3rd was spent cleaning up. On the 4th it entrained for Berguette, and was billeted at Busnettes on the 5th for training. It was now attached to the XI Corps, First Army, and was on the 10th inspected by Lieut.-General Sir R. C. B. Haking, First Army Commander, who congratulated the men on their smart turn-out. On the 11th it marched to billets at Essats, near Bethune, where it remained until September 2nd—training and supplying working parties.

September 3rd brought the Battalion again into the fighting area, when it took over the southern sector of Festubert Trenches from the 15th West Yorks—one Company of 17th Manchesters being lent to make up the strength. This tour, which lasted five days, was very quiet, and there were no casualties. Patrols and wiring parties went out nightly. On the 8th the Sixteenth was relieved by the 17th Manchesters and on the same day took over the village line from 2nd Royal Scots Fusiliers, a spell which lasted for six days. From the 14th to 16th the Battalion was again in the Festubert Trenches, three men being killed. On the latter date the 11th East Lancashires relieved, and the Sixteenth marched to Bethune. The Festubert sector was the first taste the Sixteenth had experienced of Flanders, water being so near the surface that trenches were only dug some two feet deep, sandbag walls being built upon either side for cover. On the 17th the Battalion left Bethune and marched to billets in Busnettes, which it left on the 18th for Chocques. Here it entrained for Candas; marching thence to billets at Beauval, for two days' training. The 21st September to the 4th October were spent at Flesselles.

On October 4th the Battalion left Flesselles and moved by motor-bus to Buire, and from the 6th to the 10th it was at Fricourt Camp. On the morning of the 10th the Battalion marched via Montauban—now wonderfully changed, with roads cleared, huts in course of erection everywhere, and the outskirts one mass of transport lines—with the intention of occupying Flers Trench and Support.* On reaching Longueval, however, word was received that there was no room in the trenches, so a halt was made on ground west of Delville Wood, and the troops bivouacked for the night. Next morning they marched to Flers Support and Grove Alley, with Headquarters in Flers Support, where they remained in Reserve for the attack on Bayonet Trench and Le Transloy on the 12th, which was unsuccessful, and in the evening they were ordered to move up and reinforce the 17th Manchesters in the front line and Gird Support. It was an exciting relief for the enemy was nervous after the attack which had been made in the afternoon and consequently his artillery and flares were very active. The trenches being shallow, particular care was necessary in advancing. The Battalion accomplished the relief in good time considering the difficulties, and was in positions by 10 p.m. with Headquarters in Gird Trench. Next day the area was heavily shelled and that part of the system occupied by Battalion Headquarters in Gird Trench, where the shelter was very inadequate, was so severely hammered that Lieut.-Col. Knox decided to find fresh accommodation for the Headquarter's Sections. He had only gone some fifty yards when a shell burst on the parapet at his side and wounded him so severely that he died in about ten minutes. His death was a serious loss to the Battalion.

Lieut.-Col. Knox (2nd Battalion Manchester Regiment) was a gallant soldier who, in the short time during which he had been in command of the Battalion, had done wonders with the men. He took command in July, after Trones Wood, when the Battalion had suffered heavy casualties, and he had to infuse the Sixteenth's spirit into a Battalion then largely composed of troops who had joined from other units. Lieut.-Col. Knox, however, handled the men with consummate tact, and there can be no doubt that the Battalion was at the highest pitch of efficiency when he took it into action on October 12th.

In the evening Major W. Elstob took over the command, and the following days were fully occupied in worrying the enemy by every possible means. On the 14th orders were received to move Headquarters from Gird Trench to a position off Gird Support, nearer the enemy, and on the following morning this was heavily shelled. On the morning of the 16th the Battalion was ordered to evacuate the front line to enable our artillery to bombard the enemy lines and in the evening of the same day the 2nd Yorks took over this section of the trenches, the Sixteenth moving back to Switch Trench, some 2,000 yards in the rear.

On the 17th the Battalion was in reserve, and "A" and "D" Companies were ordered to hold the front line in support of the

* See Map A.

attack to be made by the 21st Brigade on the following morning, and to occupy Flers Trench on the 18th. In the early morning of the 20th October they marched back to Montauban Camp, where they remained until the 22nd. It was a much needed rest for the previous ten days had been a most trying experience owing to the thick mud and continuous heavy fire.

On the 22nd the Battalion marched to Ribemont, and on the 26th moved by motor-bus to Sus St. Leger for training until the 28th, when it left for billets at Bailleulval. On the 29th it relieved the 8th Sherwood Foresters in the left section of Bellecourt Trenches, about five miles south of Arras and opposite Blairville, which was in German hands.

During this month of October, besides losing its C.O., the Battalion had the following casualties :—

Two officers wounded.

Other Ranks: killed, 20; died of wounds, 8; missing, 1; wounded, 64.

From November 1st, 1916, until January 7th, 1917, a quiet spell of trench warfare ensued. The routine was regular, five days in the line and five days in support or reserve billets at Bailleulval, villages almost in the front line still being occupied by civilians.

The last tour of the front line of this sector commenced on December 30th. Rain had been falling steadily for a few days and the communication-trenches were in many parts impassable. Relief in the sector took place by daylight, and it was remarkable that although bunches of our men must have been constantly seen by the Germans, whose observation from Blairville was excellent, no enemy artillery or machine gun activity took place. It was one of those curious unarranged armistices which were occasionally met with up and down the line. Probably the Germans were having equal difficulty with their trenches, and had no wish to stir up unpleasantness. The Battalion only lost two men killed during the two months.

On January 8th a move was made to billets at Warlutz, and on the 24th to Dainville near Arras. Two months were spent in this area supplying working parties to help the 1st Canadian Pioneer Battalion in railway construction (Doullens—Pommern). This was in connection with an extensive railway scheme in preparation for a big offensive.

CHAPTER V

IN THE ARRAS SECTOR

HENINEL : CHERISY

FROM March the 1st to the 12th the Sixteenth were at Halloy working on railway construction between Doullens and Arras. They were in billets at Grenas from the 12th to the 19th, when they moved to Monchiet, and on the 21st they marched through Agny to Mercatel, where the outpost line was taken over from the 19th K.L.R.

Whilst in the Doullens area, in addition to railway work, odd moments had been seized for training in preparation for an early spring offensive and a " picture ground " of full scale was marked out near Halloy, representing the territory around the village of Mercatel, which had been alloted to the Sixteenth for an attack. This had only just been completed and one day devoted to a careful walk over the ground when the news came that the Germans had commenced to retire and the Battalion was ordered to move forward and follow them up.

A few days later the Sixteenth were advancing over the very ground of the " picture " near Halloy, and the sight of the strong defence that the Germans had built was enough to make all feel it was just as well that it had not been necessary to drive him out at the point of the bayonet.

The enemy in his retirement had systematically laid the country waste. Every village was demolished, every cross road and bridge blown up, every tree laid low. It was a country utterly desolate. This ruthless and thorough destruction made the question of supplies exceedingly difficult, and great credit is due to the R.E. and transport services in the way they overcame the obstacles that had been prepared to disorganise pursuit.

An interesting period of semi-open warfare followed, outpost skirmishes being frequent, and our line advanced some hundred yards nearly every night. There was slow, steady shelling by the enemy during the first two days and on the 24th the Germans attacked the Battalion's right at 5-50 a.m. and were repulsed by Lewis gun and rifle fire. The Sixteenth remained in the line until the 29th.

Sec.-Lieut. W. Clark and three other ranks were killed and many were wounded during this tour of duty in the outpost line around Mercatel and Henin.

On the 29th the Manchesters were relieved by the 2nd Battalion Yorks Regiment, and marched to billets at Bellacourt, for rest and working parties, until the 2nd April, when they again took over the line from the 2nd Yorks, continuing to hold this position until the 7th, when they handed over to the 2nd Bedfords and moved to Ficheux.

When in the Mercatel-Henin area an amusing affair occurred one night. Certain enemy posts had been causing considerable annoyance, so it was decided to scupper their garrisons and hold the posts. A raiding party advanced under cover of darkness to the most important post of all at some cross roads and found it empty. They at once began to put it into a state of defence, keeping a careful watch in case it should prove to be an enemy " trap." Soon a small party of Germans were seen approaching in a careless manner, evidently with no idea that there were strangers near, so they were allowed to come on unchallenged and were promptly taken prisoners. It turned out that the group that had been holding the post had moved off before their relief arrived, so both the post and the relief were captured. The German counter-attack was successfully repulsed. For this smart piece of work Sergeant Leech, the N.C.O. in charge, received the D.C.M. He showed great initiative and gallantry in commanding his Platoon, which was without an officer.

On the 9th April the Sixteenth were still in reserve at Ficheux, and the same day the battle of Arras began in atrocious weather, the Third Army attacking the Hindenburg Line. The Battalion was ordered to move up in close support, south of Mercatel, in the afternoon of the 9th. The following day information was received that the Hindenburg Line was cleared of the enemy opposite Heninel, and the Battalion was ordered to move across and assemble at a position on the north-western side of the village. Marching at 2 p.m. they were met with heavy machine-gun and rifle fire at the cross roads west of St. Martin and the following dispositions were taken up :—

" D " Company along the Neuville-Vitasse and St. Martin Road.

" A," " B " and " C " Companies along Nagpur Trench.

A reconnaissance showed that the Germans had again occupied a portion of the Hindenburg Line from the Nepal Trench to the south-east, and were right across the line of advance. It is almost superfluous to go deeply into details as to what that meant. The strength of the Hindenburg Line, the wonderful construction of the trenches, the numerous dug-outs—deep enough to withstand the heaviest shelling—the belt upon belt of thick, closely-staked barb-wire, formed a picture permanently engraved on the memory of all who were there.

It was decided to establish a temporary line between Neuville-Vitasse and St. Martin Road, with Battalion Headquarters in the old Mill. At 10 o'clock on the same night orders came to attack the flank of the opposing troops in the Hindenburg Line by bombing down from the north-west of Natal Trench, and thus secure the system known as " The Cot," on the south-east side of Natal Trench, in co-operation with the 1/9th London Regiment and the 7th Middlesex Regiment. " A " Company was detailed for this operation which began at 4-30 a.m., the objective being successfully carried by 2 p.m. Some two or three hours later the Company was relieved by the 18th Manchesters and rejoined the Battalion in its old position.

On the 12th the positions were handed over to the 1st Middlesex and 4th Suffolk Regiments and the Battalion marched to billets at Bailleulval, and on the following day to Souastre, where it remained until the 18th. The Division had been actively engaged in the sector for over a month, and the few days' rest and training at Souastre, near Gommecourt, were in preparation for a new attack on a larger scale all along the British line.

The Sixteenth marched on the afternoon of the 18th to a section of trenches in the Neuville-Vitasse area, arriving there in the early hours of the following morning, and later in the day moved forward to " The Cot " in readiness to attack Cherisy.

At 4-45 a.m. on the 23rd the 90th Brigade commenced its attack on the German position at Cherisy, east of Heninel. The disposition of the troops was :—

17th Manchesters on the right ; 2nd Royal Scots Fusiliers on the left ; with the Sixteenth in immediate support.

The attack was conceived on the " leap frog " plan, the leading waves having objectives some half the distance towards Cherisy, whilst the second and third waves were to push forward to points in and around the village itself. The Sixteenth supplied special bombing parties for the advance in addition to acting in close support. The advance was met by extremely heavy machine-gun fire, and by a destructive artillery barrage. The machine guns being placed in strong concrete shelters had withstood the hammering of our artillery.

Our troops fought hard and doggedly throughout the day and many parties succeeded in penetrating to their objectives, but by night-fall very little ground had been gained whilst the loss had been appalling. The German resistance was very strong from the first, and, as indicated, the advance was at a heavy cost and there was but small consolation to be found in the fact that the enemy in their counter-attacks suffered even more severely.

The Sixteenth remained in occupation of their position, " The Cot," until April 27th.

In the operations April 23rd/27th the Battalion suffered the following casualties :—

Killed in action : Capt. R. H. Megson, Capt. L. F. Wilson, Lieut. C. W. K. Hook, Sec.-Lieut. J. A. Ingram.

Wounded : Capt. W. T. D. Wickam, Second-Lieutenants J. L. L. Smith, W. Laughland, R. A. M. J. McDonnell, J. A. Smith, H. R. W. Smith, G. M. Harvey, F. W. Caiger.

The casualties amongst other ranks were : 31 killed in action, 56 missing, besides a great many wounded. At the close of the action, which was one of the toughest encounters in the history of the Battalion, it numbered less than 100 in all ranks.

On the 27th the Sixteenth marched to Arras, entrained for St. Pol, and marched thence to billets in Croisettes, remaining in this neighbourhood until 21st May, when it moved by way of Hestrus, Westrehem and Guarbecque to La Kreule, two miles north of Hazebrouck, arriving there on the 25th.

The C.O. wrote at the time :—

" We have been marching a great deal lately, and I am glad to say that the Battalion has marched very well. For two days never a man fell out. It has been a triumph in this hot weather, and I am proud of the men."

The Battalion remained at La Kreule training until the 31st, when it entrained at Caestre for St. Omer, moving thence by bus to billets at Acquin.

The Sixteenth was now bound for the Ypres area, and left Acquin on June 6th, by bus, for billets near Hielehoeux, to the west of Poperinghe, where it was held in reserve for General Plumer's successful attack on the Messines Ridge.

It was here until the 9th, when it marched to Toronto Camp, providing working parties there until it relieved the 2nd Yorks in the trenches in the Hooge Sector (14th–20th June.) This was one of the worst trench-sectors the Battalion had experienced, and there were over fifty casualties.

Amongst acts of special gallantry during this tour mention may be made of Corporal G. Simpson. At great personal risk he picked up a smoking bomb from a fire-bay and disposed of it, thereby saving the lives of several men. He was awarded the Military Medal.

On the 21st the Sixteenth marched to Ottawa Camp, and after several further moves—Reninghelst, Zutkerque, Wippenhoek and Château Segard—reached the fighting area at Zillebeke Bund on the night of July 28th.

CHAPTER VI

THE THIRD BATTLE OF YPRES

ZILLEBEKE BUND : MESSINES : WYTSCHAETE

THE general attack against the Flanders Ridge, in the Ypres area, was now in preparation, and this was launched at dawn on July 31st. For the three successive days before the attack some excellent reconnaissance was made by the Battalion to ascertain the forward assembly positions for the attack, and remove obstacles and wire. Colonel Elstob on the night of July 27th/28th personally took out a large party, consisting of all the Company Commanders and a representative of each section in the Battalion, and they actually penetrated to the German support trenches, thus gaining invaluable information about the ground over which the advance was to be made. The party all arrived back safely, and were resting in Stanley Trench, some three hundred yards in rear of our front line, when our artillery opened a practice hurricane barrage. The Germans thinking that this was the prelude to our attack replied vigorously, and obliterated every bay of Stanley Trench except the few occupied by the C.O. and his party. By the greatest good fortune they came off scathless. The knowledge thus obtained of the S.O.S. targets of the enemy guns saved considerable loss on the morning of the attack, as the troops assembled in advance of them in "No Man's Land," with their "jumping off" point little over fifty yards from the German front line. There were five Divisions detailed for the attack in this area, three of which were in the line and two in support. Those in the line, counting from the north, were the Eighth, with its left on the Ypres-Roulers railway and its right on Sanctuary Wood, the Thirtieth Division in the centre, and the Twenty-fourth opposite Shrewsbury Forest, with its right resting upon the Zillebeke-Zandvoorde Road. In support was the Twenty-fifth Division upon the left and the Eighteenth Division upon the right.

On the night of July 30th/31st the whole Battalion was east of Stanley Street by 1-15 a.m. and organised into its approximate assembly positions in Sanctuary Wood by 3-15 a.m. as follows :—

"A" Company, first wave. "B" Company, second wave. "D" and "C" Companies, third wave. "A" Company was only forty yards from Jackdaw Trench, the remaining Companies being thirty to fifty yards behind in their respective waves. During the assembly touch was gained with the 18th Manchesters on the right, and touch with the 1st Worcesters on the left, was obtained immediately after the attack commenced. The assembly was carried out quietly and without knowledge of the enemy—a fine performance, since it was carried out in darkness.

At zero hour, which was 3-50 a.m., in the dim grey light of dawn, the 30th Division in company with the Eighth swept forward to their objectives behind a perfect wall of flame, formed by the incredibly rapid bursting of innumerable shells. The barrage was one of the most concentrated in the history of the War. It seemed impossible that anything could live in it, but small groups of the enemy popped up here and there to be dealt with by our troops as they advanced. Within five minutes of zero the whole Battalion was across the enemy line and well on its way to the final objectives, between Clapham Junction and Surbiton Villas.

The 90th and 21st Brigades formed the first line. The resistance was strong, the fire heavy, and the losses considerable, so that the attackers could do no more than carry the front line trenches and repulse repeated counter-attacks during the day. Though the attack, as a whole, was not entirely successful, the Sixteenth gained all their objectives well within the hour, and Battalion Headquarters was established in Jackdaw Trench by 4-10 a.m.

At 5 a.m. Colonel Elstob went forward to clear up the situation, as no reports were coming through. Passing through part of Sanctuary Wood and reaching the left edge of the Wood near the bend of the Ypres-Menin Road, there was found to be considerable confusion owing to units being very mixed up. The group of dug-outs and trenches just north of the bend in the road, and machine gun and sniping fire from the direction of Surbiton Villas and Stirling Castle, were causing trouble and casualties. The C.O. got the men together and, moving in small parties, they dashed across the road and began to "mop up" the dug-outs and tunnel. It appeared that the troops on the immediate left were held up on the eastern edge of Château Wood. Having gained a knowledge of the local situation on the left, and attempting to clear up the situation Colonel Elstob returned to his Battalion Headquarters at 10-30 a.m. This episode and the previous reconnaissance were typical examples of the C.O.'s bold, fearless and thorough leadership. The attack was carried out under the worst possible weather conditions. The day had opened with a slight mist and low hanging clouds, which by mid-day had turned into heavy rain. By nightfall these conditions, combined with the Flanders mud, made everything sticky, and progress was a matter of the greatest difficulty. The downpour lasted for nearly a week and was largely responsible for preventing the initial success of July 31st being exploited to the fullest advantage. As it was, Tanks became mud-logged, and heavy guns almost immovable.

The Sixteenth took between thirty and forty prisoners, and lost Captain E. Brodrick killed in action, Sec.-Lieut. J. C. Jackson missing, and ten officers wounded. Of other ranks twenty-two were killed, forty-two missing, and one hundred and eighty-eight wounded.

On August 1st the Battalion was relieved by the 2nd Bedfords and marched to Château Segard. The autumn rains lasted for many weeks and the dreary downpour added immensely to the difficulties of a country which at the best of times is soft and water-laden. For the space of two months operations on a grand scale were impossible. Impassable mud and water covered the whole German front.

On August 2nd the Sixteenth marched to a camp near Dickebusch, and on the 3rd to Wippenhoek. On the 4th the Battalion reached Steenvoorde, in the Eecke area, and rested and cleaned up until the 7th, when it moved to billets at Courte-Croix, near Caestre. The 10th to the 21st were spent in training near Berthen, and the 22nd to the 27th in camp near Kemmel. On the 28th a portion of the Messines trenches were taken over and from then until the second week in November various periods were spent in and out of trenches in this and the Wytschaete area, with Kemmel Hill Camp as the Battalion's resting-place. During the month of September seven men were killed and thirty-three wounded, four of whom died of their wounds. October was a flat time and there was no activity but training and the building of hutments. From the 11th to the 25th November Strazeele, Steenvorde and Alberta Camps were occupied, and on the 25th the Battalion relieved the 1/6th Cheshires in the front line (Ypres-Menin Road) left sector, remaining there until relieved by the 17th Manchesters on the 30th. December was spent in a similar manner, in Alberta Camp, Gheluvelt and Polderhoek trenches, Stirling Castle and Chippena Camps, and Christmas was celebrated in an important part of the line near Zonnebeke, this being the first time the Sixteenth had actually been in the front line for Christmas Day—1915 Christmas having been spent in rest billets at Bonneville, near Doullens, and 1916 Christmas in reserve at Bailleulval, south of Arras.

Lieut.-Col. Elstob temporarily commanded the Brigade at this period, and the Acting-C.O. of the Sixteenth was wounded, Battalion Headquarters being blown in.

On the 30th December the Battalion moved out of the line to a camp on the outskirts of Reninghelst, near Poperinghe, having had one man killed and twenty-one wounded during the month.

CHAPTER VII

THE SECOND BATTLE OF THE SOMME

THE ST. QUENTIN FRONT

THE New Year of 1918—the fourth and last of the Great War—opened with chequered prospects for the Allies. In distant subsidiary fields of action the developments and prospects were good, but a terrible menace was banking up on the Western Front. The Russian Alliance had broken down and as a result of this huge defection the entire forces of Germany and Austria, together with much captured Russian Artillery were available for the war in France and Flanders. From November to March an endless succession of troop trains were conveying men and material for use on the Western Front. But some little time was yet to pass before the storm broke.

During the month of January the Sixteenth were employed in training and reorganising.

January 1st–4th were spent in cleaning up at Chippena Camp. On the 5th the Battalion proceeded by train from Dickebusch to Ebbinghem, and marched thence to Lynde. On the 7th it entrained at Steenbecque for Longueau, and marched thence to La Neuville. During the remainder of the month it moved to Vauvillers, Neste, Esmery Hallon, Salency, Sincency and Pierremande—which was the Brigade Reserve on the extreme right of the British Army in France. The Battalion remained in Brigade Reserve during the early days of February. On the 6th a draft of thirteen officers and two hundred and eighty other ranks joined the Battalion from the 19th Manchesters. This was due to a redistribution of units which took place just then. The 18th Battalion was taken out of the Brigade and eventually became the 17th entrenching Battalion. At the same time the 17th Battalion of the Manchesters was transferred from the 90th to the 21st Brigade.

The Acting-C.O., Major R. Gibbon, M.C., of the Sixteenth, welcomed the draft from the 19th Manchesters in the Y.M.C.A. Hut at Sincency in the following terms :—

" I arranged for you all to come here this morning as it is a special occasion. You officers, N.C.O.'s and men of the 19th Battalion Manchester Regiment must feel pretty sore at finding your Battalion split up, and believe me that very natural feeling is appreciated by us all. Higher authorities, however, have decided on a reorganisation of the formation of the Army and, as all alterations and innovations do, it is bound to hit somebody or other pretty hard for a time, though it is done with great hopes of improvement in fighting efficiency. Fighting is what we are all here for, and the only way of fighting well is to have good organisation. It is, therefore, up to us all to enter heart and soul into the new organisation, make it a big success, and by so doing lick the Boche.

Your Battalion is part and parcel of us. You were formed at the same time that we were. You trained in England in the same areas that we did. When the 90th Brigade was formed it consisted of the 16th, 17th 18th and 19th Battalions Manchester Regiment, and we came out to France in November 1915 in that formation.

Shortly after arrival the 19th Battalion was transferred to the 21st Brigade, in accordance with principles laid down by G.H.Q. At that time, to say the least of it, we were keenly disappointed. We were parting from old and tried friends, and I do not mind confessing that efforts have been made on several occasions to get you back to this Brigade.

Thus, though in different Brigades, we have fought together on the Somme, near Arras and at Ypres. Where the 19th have been there the Sixteenth were also to be found. Your commanding officer, Colonel Macdonald was, as you know, originally Adjutant of the 17th Battalion, and is known and admired by us all. It is, therefore, a very real pleasure to greet troops who have been under his command. I have no desire to bore you with a long speech, but from the foregoing remarks I trust I have made it clear that we do not regard you as strangers amongst us. Indeed, very much to the contrary. We welcome you as old friends who have rejoined us again. The number of your Battalion may be different to ours but remember that you belong to the same Regiment—a Regiment with great traditions and honours. And to those battle honours both the 19th and 16th Battalions have added no small measure since their arrival in France.

I will, therefore, conclude by giving you on behalf of Lieut.-Col. Elstob, who is at present on leave, and on behalf of all ranks a most hearty welcome to our Battalion, together with the expression of a sincere hope that you will not find it difficult to settle down and regard the Sixteenth as your own Battalion."

On February 8th this composite Battalion was relieved by the 2/7th Battalion London Regiment (58th Division), and marched to Manicamp. Two days later it was at Quesny. On the 11th it moved to Ognolles, and here, on the 13th, the Division was inspected by the Commander-in-Chief (Field-Marshal Sir Douglas Haig). There was a general salute and march past in column of platoons. The next few days were spent on railway work, and Col. Elstob took the opportunity of captaining the 30th Division Rugby football team against a French team in Paris. On the 20th the Battalion marched from Ognolles to Ham. The 22nd found the Battalion in Brigade reserve at Etreillers, working on defensive positions.

During the better part of the first three weeks of March the Battalion remained in the Etreillers area, on the St. Quentin front, preparing for the German grand attack which was known to be impending, and on the 18th took over Manchester Hill Redoubt.

The British battle line, stretching roughly a matter of fifty miles from the Scarpe to the Oise, was defended by twenty-four Divisions, or about 200,000 infantry, while it was reckoned that the Germans had some sixty Divisions in their front line with about thirty Divisions in immediate reserve. It was also believed that the German concentration of gun power was more than double that of the British.

The storm broke along the entire line on the morning of March 21st. A preliminary bombardment commenced about 5 a.m. and contained a large proportion of gas-shells which searched the rear lines and battery positions as well as the front defence.

General Maxse's XVIIIth Corps held the ground from the Oinignon Valley to a point just west of St. Quentin, and had three Divisions in the line. These were the 61st on the left, the 30th in the centre, and the 36th reaching towards the south. General Williams' 30th Division, with which we are here concerned, had two Brigades in the line, the 21st and 90th, with General Stanley's Brigade (King's Liverpools) in reserve. The front line held by this Division was about 4,000 yards in extent, stretching from the immediate west of St. Quentin to the Somme, and included two strong points, Manchester Hill and the Epine de Dallon.

CHAPTER VIII

THE SECOND BATTLE OF THE SOMME—*continued*

MANCHESTER HILL *

AND

LIEUT.-COL. WILFRITH ELSTOB, V.C., D.S.O., M.C.

THE fighting along the entire front of the 30th Division was of the most desperate character. The forward Battalions were the Sixteenth and the 2nd Wilts. Rushing through the gaps in the defenders' line by sheer weight of numbers the Germans flung themselves upon the forward zone, where after long fighting which lasted well into the afternoon, they gained possession of the two posts already mentioned, and finally broke into a small piece of the battle line near Savy.

Both the 90th and 21st Brigades lost very heavily during these attacks, but the subsequent calling up of the 18th and 19th King's Liverpools (Stanley's 89th Brigade) from Beauvois helped to stem the tide. Consequently, notwithstanding the weight and fury of the attack, the 30th Division still held the enemy at bay as late as 4 o'clock in the afternoon of March 22nd, but it was subsequently found advisable to withdraw and fall back upon Ham.

The part played by the Sixteenth in their defence of Manchester Hill is a record that will hold its own with any defensive battle of the war.

Manchester Hill formed an important *point d'appui* in the British "Outpost System," which acted as a buffer zone to absorb the first shock of attack and break it up. It covered the main "Battle Position" held by the Brigade round Savy, and controlled the important St. Quentin–Savy Road, with another strong point, L'Epine de Dallon, a mile to its right, the hamlet of Francilly-Selency a mile to the left, and the Bois de Savy half a mile behind.

* See Map C.

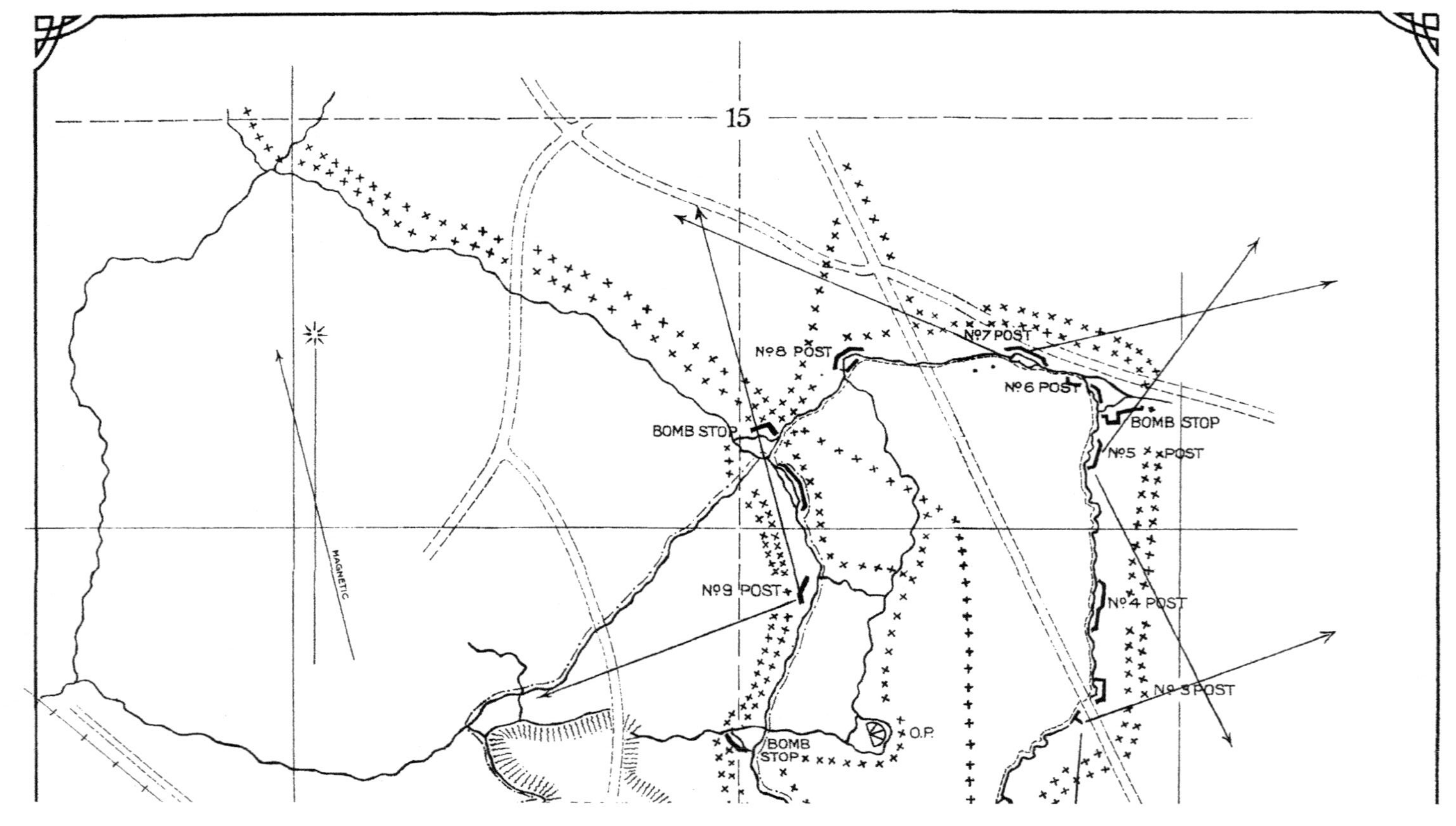
15
№ 8 POST
№ 7 POST
№ 6 POST
BOMB STOP
BOMB STOP
№ 5 POST
№ 9 POST
№ 4 POST
№ 3 POST
O.P.
BOMB STOP
MAGNETIC

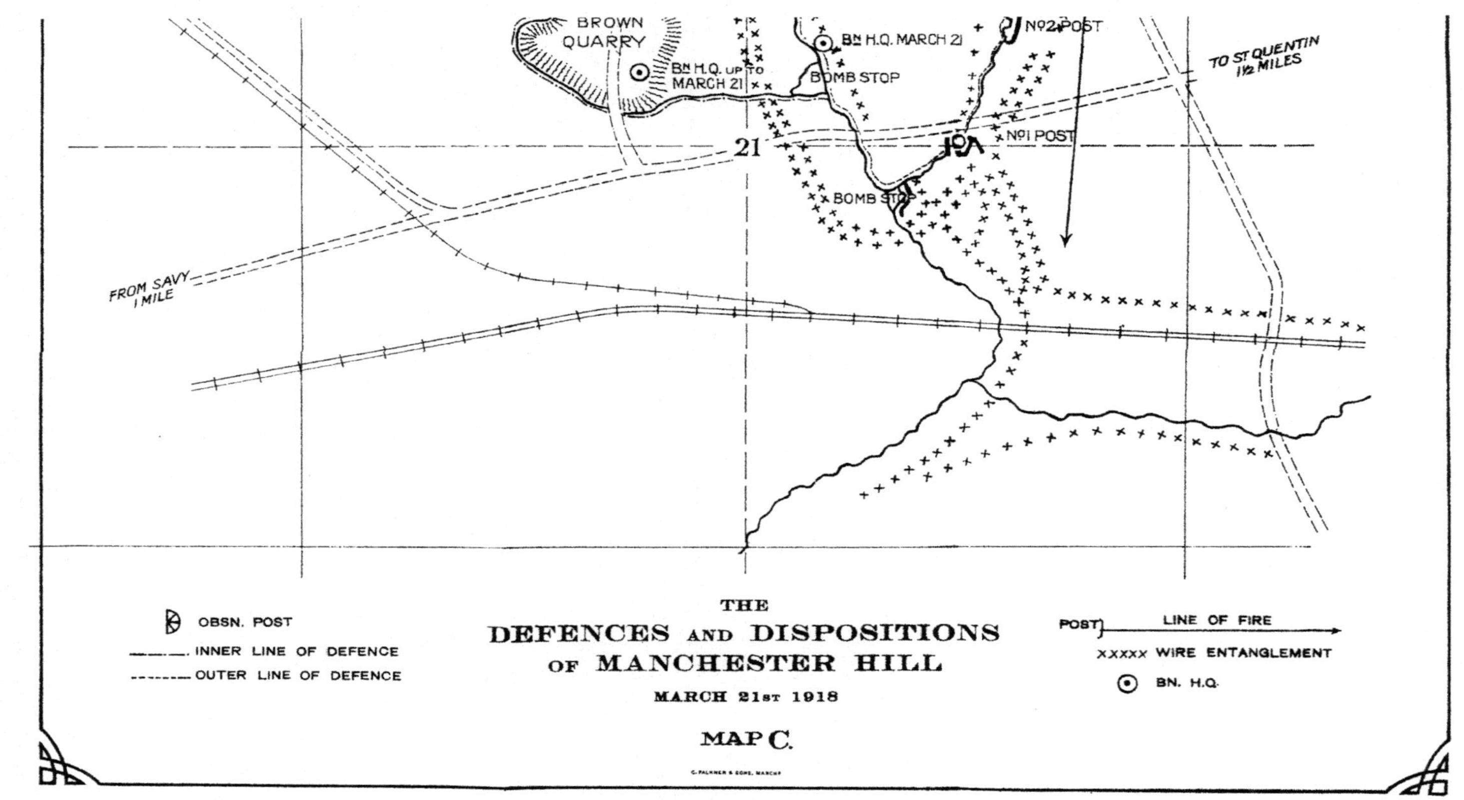

THE
DEFENCES AND DISPOSITIONS
OF MANCHESTER HILL
MARCH 21ST 1918

MAP C.

A mile and a half due east the road dipped suddenly into St. Quentin and here, close to their front line, which ran near the crest, the Germans had made a tremendous concentration of guns to support the coming grand attack. Safe in the hollow the vast army of storm troops waited, for our artillery had been instructed not to shell this large and important French town heavily.

Manchester Hill was a tactical feature of great strength. It was not a high eminence, but rather a bare swelling undulation, commanding an admirable field of fire in every direction. It was backed by the "Brown Quarry" on its reverse slope which afforded excellent cover and location for dug-outs. On either side clearly defined valleys were commanded by machine guns. It was a position naturally strong, and the trace of its trenches, the location of its posts, the organisation of its cross fire and the strength of its wire rendered it, for a clear day, almost impregnable. Mere penetration on a narrow front is of little value to the enemy if the garrison of important tactical localities hold their ground. The principle of defence and depth combined with the system of Redoubts on the back area of the Battalion led to very extended areas being given to Battalions to hold, and the sector held by the Sixteenth had a frontage of some 2,000 yards and a depth of nearly two miles.

The distribution of the Battalion was as follows :—

Right front—"A" Company. *O.C.*, Captain E. N. Ashe, M.C.
Left front—"B" Company. *O.C.*, Captain J. Guest.

Supporting : Right front—"C" Company. Two Platoons independently under Captain P. Heywood. Left front—"C" Company. Less two Platoons. *O.C.*, Captain Pritchard.

Manchester Hill Redoubt : Battalion Headquarters, with "D" Company (*O.C.*, Lieut. D. J. Clark), under the immediate command of Col. Elstob.

Strong Machine Gun Corps posts commanded the valleys, Stokes Mortar emplacements were on the crest of the Quarry, and our artillery fire was controlled from the ferro-concrete observation post that stood on the summit of the Hill.

Before taking over the sector on the night of the 18th March Col. Elstob fully explained to his men the system of defence. They went into the line prepared. It was known that the great attack was imminent and that they had been selected to bear the brunt of the first onslaught.

Again and again he warned them to be ready for a bombardment lasting possibly several days, and said that they must stem the enemy advance and not cause other troops to be sacrificed in regaining a lost position. Pointing to the blackboard showing the dispositions he said, " This is Battalion Headquarters. Here we fight and here we die."

As they marched up to the line, the Platoon singing competition was judged by the Divisional Commander, and when the band turned back (for they were not to go into action) the C.O. said :

" Those are the only fellows that will come out alive."

" *It must be impressed upon all troops actually allotted to the defence of any position, whether in the outpost system or the main battle position, that so far as they are concerned there is only one degree of resistance, and that is to the last round and to the last man.*"

The Colonel had not failed to impress the Regulation on his troops.

It was hoped that the Battalion would have time to get accustomed to the ground before the attack began. The first night passed quietly, and next day all was still. The great upland and its surrounding valleys were freshly green, untouched by shells and peculiarly soothing to eyes accustomed to the churned-up soil of Ypres and the Somme battlefield.

Another quiet night followed, except that in anticipation of an attack next dawn a British Projector-gas attack was mainly directed at St. Quentin, causing as was afterwards found, many casualties. Another uneventful day of anxious expectation passed. The attack was timed to begin on the morning of the 21st.

The night 20th/21st March was calm and still. The sky was clear, the moon almost at full. A careful system of patrols covered the front throughout the night, but no signs of enemy activity were reported. The Colonel visited all the posts of the right half Battalion the left half being also visited from Battalion Headquarters. At 5-30 a.m. the final patrol went out. Time wore on. No news was sent in, the silence was complete. At 6-30 a.m. the roar of innumerable guns broke the uncanny calm. High explosives, shrapnel, and worst of all, gas shells shrieked through the air. The sky was lit up with great flashes. The much talked-of bombardment had begun. But still no enemy movement could be perceived, and that for good reason—a fog had succeeded the clear and placid night—a fog made increasingly dense by the smoke of the bursting shells. Nothing could have been more disastrous. The wide front, the defence in depth, the valleys now no longer death traps, gave the enemy everything that he could desire.

At 7-30 a.m. the front line Companies reported that everything appeared normal on their fronts, and that the enemy shells were falling behind their sectors. The C.O. gave orders to move Battalion Headquarters from the Brown Quarry to Battle Headquarters on Manchester Hill. Battle Headquarters dug-out and observation post and signal station lay some 300 yards east of the Quarry and mid-way between the Artillery observation post and the Savy-St. Quentin Road, near an important junction of trenches that formed a pivotal point on the inner ring of the Redoubt. The C.O. visited all the posts in the Redoubt, encouraging the men and telling them what to do. Shortly after 8 a.m. the bombardment became more intense, and the telephone wires to the Companies failed, though a buried cable ensured communication with Brigade.

About 8-30 a.m. the first news of the commencement of the attack reached the Battalion Headquarters, a runner bringing information that " A " Company Headquarters was almost surrounded. Within a few minutes similar news came from " B " Company.

The thick fog made observation impossible and neutralised the elaborate scheme of machine gun defence which should have proved an impenetrable barrier up the valleys. A scream was heard as one of our sentries was bayoneted. Three years later an English tin hat was found bashed in by a rifle butt near a machine gun post—*with nine German rifles lying round it.*

About 9 a.m. a forward post on the left front of the Redoubt sent back word that they were engaged at close quarters with the enemy, and simultaneously the attack developed on the right posts, and from then on the desperate struggle raged until late in the afternoon, with the Colonel the heart and soul of the defence. Gradually the fog lifted, and by 11-30 there was a glint of sunshine breaking through, and on all sides masses of the enemy could be seen advancing by half-companies in file. The break through was complete on either side. Special troops were left to settle with Manchester Hill.

The stand made round the Colonel by the garrison of this small Redoubt is an epic in our military history. Completely surrounded they fought against overwhelming odds. Many of them were not used to fighting. Cooks, signallers, batmen and police—all the " odd-job " collection that make up an Infantry Battalion Headquarters—rose to the occasion, inspired by the supreme example of their Commander.

Our artillery had been rendered impotent, the Stokes mortars had expended all their ammunition. The British Infantry with rifle and bayonet and Lewis gun, bomb and revolver had to bear the brunt alone. At the end the German field guns were brought up within sixty yards.

In a battle where all ranks behaved so splendidly it is hard to single out names for special mention. No honours were bestowed, except the posthumous V.C. for the Commanding Officer, but the following were specially noticeable :—

Major R. GIBBON, M.C., who went to France with the Battalion in 1915 and remained with it throughout, gallantly helped to stay many of the rushes during the morning until severely wounded in the right arm and shoulder by a " pine-apple " bomb.

Captain SHARPLES, the Adjutant of the Battalion, was prominent for his cheery encouragement of the men, both by word and deed, always on the firestep where the enemy pressed over-closely, firing with a quiet confidence, until he was killed.

The M.O., Captain WALKER, R.A.M.C., behaved fearlessly throughout, frequently leaving his crowded aid-post to dress dangerous cases in the battle line. Later in the day, when the enemy rushed the Quarry, it was entirely owing to Captain Walker's determined stand that they did not blow up the aid-post. Whilst they were throwing bombs down the entrance he dashed up the dug-out steps, at great personal risk of meeting a grenade half way, or a bayonet at the top, and succeeded in convincing them that it was a Red Cross Station.

Corporal STENSON, the medical corporal, showed great courage in dressing the wounded, though badly wounded himself in the early stages of the attack.

R.S.M. POTTER, D.C.M., and C.S.M. F. J. BROWN, M.C., of " D " Company, were also very prominent in maintaining the ammunition supply, leading quickly-organised bombing parties to counter-attack whenever the enemy gained a lodgment, and encouraging others to fight every inch of ground.

Sergeant HOY, the Lewis gun sergeant, accounted for hundreds of the enemy. With two young soldiers he fought a post on the western edge of the Quarry, firing towards Savy. He continued firing until the enemy were upon him, and whilst changing the pan two sprang at him and he was killed with a revolver shot.

The stand made at Manchester Hill by the Sixteenth must ever be particularly associated with the name of the commanding officer, Lieut.-Col. WILFRITH ELSTOB.

Finding that the enemy had entered the Redoubt by the trench leading from the Savy—St. Quentin Road, he erected a bombing block between the attackers and Headquarters dug-out. Although sniped at and bombed by the enemy, he replied by emptying his revolver on an enemy bombing party a few yards down the trench, accounting for them all, and when his revolver ammunition was exhausted he continued to hold single-handed with bombs the bombing post he had erected against some half-dozen successive bombing attacks. The enemy subsequently abandoned these tactics and after a sharp bombardment made an attack over the top with large numbers. Colonel Elstob took up a rifle and played a great part in holding back these assailants, and only a few reached the parapet of the trench, into which they threw bombs. The C.O. was wounded for the first time, but after being dressed he returned to the defence, walking about regardless of the fire from every side, and cheering the men wherever he went.

"You are doing magnificently, boys! Carry on—keep up a steady fire and they'll think there's a Battalion here."

When ammunition ran low he crossed and recrossed the bullet-swept Quarry with fresh supplies from the dump. A shell blew him five yards, but laughing he picked himself up and exclaimed: "They can't damned well kill me!"

In spite of three wounds he continued to fight with rifle, bayonet, revolver and bomb. Throughout the fight he kept in communication with the Brigade.

"The Manchester Regiment will hold Manchester Hill to the last man." The romance of that amazing conversation on the buried cable between the Colonel and the Brigadier will not die. A staff-officer at Brigade Headquarters reported the episode as follows:

"At about 11 o'clock Col. Elstob informed me that the Germans had broken through and were swarming round the Redoubt. At about 2 p.m. he said that most of his men were killed or wounded, including himself; that they were all getting dead beat, that the Germans had got into the Redoubt and hand-to-hand fighting was going on. He was still quite cheery. At 3-30 he was spoken to on the telephone and said very few were left and that the end was nearly come. After that no answer could be got."

In these messages the gallant Commander, cut off by countless thousands, voiced as if from another world the vivid story of the battle against hopeless odds, with that cheery determination which cannot but thrill the imagination. One survivor tells that the last words the C.O. used to him were "Tell the men not to lose heart. Fight on!" The enemy in a last desperate assault called upon him to surrender. He still held his ground, firing from the firestep some twenty-five to thirty yards up the trench. Colonel Elstob replied: "NEVER!" and fell back dead with a bullet through his brain. That was the end. It was now shortly after four o'clock, and the battered remnant of the garrison, wounded and exhausted, surrendered.

Wilfrith Elstob embodied all that was noblest in the Regiment he loved so well. "If I die," he wrote to a friend on the eve of the battle, "do not grieve for me, for it is with the Sixteenth that I would gladly lay down my life."

A boyhood spent in the quiet seclusion of a Cheshire vicarage taught him to love the big simple things of life. Educated at Christ's Hospital, he came to Manchester University, where he took his degree and the Diploma in Education, for from early years it had been his ambition to be a schoolmaster. After a year's teaching at the Lycée, at Beauvais, and another studying at the Sorbonne in Paris, he became a Master of Merchiston Castle School, Edinburgh. On the outbreak of war this student and athlete, with no previous military training enlisted as a private. He was gazetted Second-Lieutenant in the 16th Battalion Manchester Regiment, shortly after its formation, and rose not only to command it in many a fight, but temporarily commanded his Brigade. He was a man of splendid physique and commanding bearing. A modest and retiring idealist in times of peace, the war brought forth all the latent power of the man. His was one of those fine natures which combined in a remarkable degree tenderness and strength, innate dignity and humility, generosity and restraint. Men instinctively trusted him. The announcement conferring the posthumous honour of the VICTORIA CROSS reads as follows:—

"For most gallant and heroic conduct displayed during the fight at Manchester Redoubt near St. Quentin on the 21st March, 1918. Through many hours Lieut.-Col. Elstob set the highest example of cool heroism, determination, endurance and fine soldierly bearing. During the preliminary bombardment this officer constantly visited the posts in the Redoubt, encouraging the men. As repeated attacks developed Lieut.-Col. Elstob always personally controlled the defence at the threatened point. Sometimes fighting with his revolver, at other times with rifle and bayonet, and again with bombs. In one assault the enemy made a lodgment in the work and commenced bombing the trench. Lieut.-Col. Elstob with great dash attacked the party himself, driving them back and inflicting seven casualties. He then superintended the construction of a block under heavy fire. At another time, when ammunition was required, this officer made several hazardous journeys under severe fire, first accompanied by another man, and subsequently alone, and succeeded in replenishing the supply. Throughout the day Lieut.-Col. Elstob showed the most fearless disregard of his own safety. Though thrice wounded, and when he must have been suffering the most acute pain, his cheerfulness, encouragement and noble example inspired the very fine defence made."

Though Manchester Redoubt was surrounded in the first waves of the attack (and Lieut.-Col. Elstob was thus prevented from exercising command over the rest of the Battalion) it held out until late in the afternoon. . . . .

Sometime after this (3-20 p.m.) the post fell, overcome by vastly superior forces, supported by guns, brought close up. Of the original garrison of eight officers and one hundred and sixty other ranks, only two officers and fifteen other ranks survived. Lieut.-Col. Elstob was killed in the final assault, having carried out to the end what he had impressed on his men before the battle—

"Here we fight, here we die!"

CHAPTER IX

THE RETREAT FROM HAM AND SPOIL BANK

WHEN Manchester Hill fell Captain W. G. Brittlebank took over temporary command of the shattered remnants of the Sixteenth, but owing to the almost entire loss of officers and N.C.O.'s, and the nature of the fighting, the survivors were widely scattered. The first real effort to reorganise was made by Major Roberts, an original officer of the Sixteenth, whose force comprised the Brigade School, of which he was Commandant, and such stragglers of the old Battalion as he could collect—in all two subalterns and seventy men—for the bitter and unequal rear-guard action. On reaching the Nesle-Noyen Canal he took up a position with the object of holding the bridges at Buverchy and Ramiecourt, setting out a line of posts along the western bank east of Moyencourt. No hostile movement was evident until 4-30 p.m. on the 24th, when small bodies of troops were seen converging on both the bridges. Simultaneously a heavy shrapnel barrage, which continued for an hour, was opened along the whole Battalion front. All was then quiet until 5 p.m. on the 25th, when the village of Buverchy was occupied in force and machine gun fire was concentrated on the bridge. At the same time an advance was made, under the cover of trees at Château Robecourt, on the bridge of Ramiecourt, which synchronised with a yet wider flanking movement on the enemy left. The rifle was the only defensive weapon available, but though it was used with deadly effect, the odds were too great. The enemy flanking movement continued and at 6 p.m. the troops holding Ramiecourt Bridge, which had not been destroyed, were compelled to fall back to avoid being completely cut off.

A defensive flank was then thrown out along the Moyencourt-Buverchy Road, and an attempt to relieve the situation by a counter-attack had to be abandoned owing to heavy losses. A serious loss was sustained by the fatal wounding of Major Roberts, whose hastily organised defences and gallant leadership had served a purpose and had like many other local engagements a far reaching effect on the battle as a whole. The position was now desperate. It was found that the left flank was entirely open with the exception of a Company of French troops. In fact, it had been open since 12 noon. With both flanks in the air, with no definite knowledge of the general position, and an entire lack of higher authority, a further retirement was inevitable, and eventually a new line was taken up, in conjunction with the French east of Cressy, which was held until a general retirement was made on Roye.

At 5 p.m. on the 27th the Battalion took part in the general evacuation of Roye and marched along the main Amiens Road to Bouchoir, where it arrived at mid-day, and was ordered to man reserve positions approximately 700 yards west of the village. It was here strongly reinforced by the Divisional Signalling School and Traffic Control men, making in all a strength of 450.

The 2nd Royal Scots Fusiliers were in the front line, the 2nd Bedfords in support.

At 9 a.m. on the 29th Bouchoir was heavily shelled. The troops in the front and support lines retired, the enemy occupied the village and owing to heavy casualties the Sixteenth took up an alternative position. They counter-attacked and established a line 200 yards from the outskirts of Bouchoir, and then made a further attempt to retake the village, but were unsuccessful owing to the heavy losses sustained from the enemy machine guns, trench mortars and light artillery.

The position 200 yards from the village was, however, held until a general retirement was ordered on the morning of the 31st, when the Sixteenth moved to Moreuil and Morisel through a new line which had been established by the French, no formal relief taking place.

Throughout the retreat the men behaved splendidly, in spite of hardships, privation and fatigue. Camaraderie and humour did not fail even in the darkest hours, and a mere boy was heard to remark that they ought to go down to posterity as "The New Contemptibles." Equipment was discarded, some of the men having five or six bandoliers slung over their shoulders. It was described as " more like rabbit shooting than rearguard fighting "—but they became so tired that they could hardly drag one foot after another, and when they lay down to fire they frequently fell asleep and were with difficulty aroused to continue the next retirement. Weary and dazed with fighting they were continually faced with fresh German troops in overwhelming numbers. When they were not fighting they were marching or digging under the most demoralising conditions. But they kept their faces to the enemy and held him at bay.

A few words here with reference to the two officers who served the longest with the Battalion may not be out of place.

Captain R. K. KNOWLES and Captain and Q.-M. J. T. BALL, M.C., for some two years in France were in happy accord as Transport Officer and Q.-M. respectively. These two were in no small part responsible for the maintaining of a high spirit of *morale* in all ranks, both in and out of the line. "An army marches on its stomach" it is said. An army fights on its stomach and an army hangs on to the battered trenches and water-logged shell holes on its stomach—and not once during the whole of the time did rations fail to materialise. In the midst of an attack, with but the scantiest of detail as to where the Battalion was to be found, the T.O. or the Q.-M., or both appeared at the appointed time full of smiles and good-cheer—and in the middle of the battle of Trones Wood the Q.-M. arrived on his black "prehistoric" circus horse with bottles of rum slung around him. It was thought by many that the lot of the Transport and Q.-M. Stores was "a little bit of heaven" as compared with the front line, but pitch dark nights, imperfect tracks, continuously swept by long range machine gun fire, and here and there a special "hate" from all the enemy guns within range, did not conduce to too great a feeling of ease and comfort. And for the back area, who of the Sixteenth does not remember how many prizes were carried off for "turn-out" by the Transport?

Up to March 21st, 1918, Captain and Q.-M. Ball continued his splendid work, but on that day he was severely wounded whilst attending to the clearing of the stores from the village of Etreillers, and even then it was only under compulsion that he was despatched in an ambulance for hospital, his one wish being to get *at* the Boche—not away from them. Hospital claimed him till some months after the Armistice, so that he was unable to rejoin and help to finish the war in which he had seen so much service and done so much to uphold the efficiency of the Sixteenth.

After the disastrous attack of the Germans in March, 1918, Captain (then Lieut.) Knowles took command of "B" Company and showed even greater qualities as a Company Commander than he had exhibited as T.O. Fearless, considerate, yet firm, he quickly had a Company second to none, which he had the proud privilege of piloting through the final great day of November 11th, 1918, at the same time achieving the record for continuous service with the Sixteenth, having joined them at the birth of the Battalion in August, 1914.

The Battalion was not allowed much respite for recuperation after the rigours of the terrible retreat, and it was soon destined to take part in another important and bloody operation.

On the 5th April it moved to a new area, entraining at Fouquieres for Rousbrugge and proceeding thence by bus to a camp near International Corner. On the 7th it marched to Kempton Park, becoming Brigade reserve, and Major W. H. Colley, 2nd Yorks, took over the command.

April 12th found the Sixteenth again manning battle positions, with Headquarters at Gournier Farm, and four days later all troops forward were withdrawn west of the Steenbeek, leaving the Battalion in the front line, reinforced by a Company of the 17th Manchesters. Two Companies of the 18th Belgian Infantry Regiment relieved them on the 17th of April and they marched to Moulon Camp, near Elverdinghe, and on the 18th to St. Lawrence Camp.

On the 19th the Sixteenth was formed into two Companies, and with the remainder of the 17th Manchesters (less Headquarters) a Composite Battalion was formed, under the command of the Sixteenth's Headquarters, which marched to camp at Busseboom and thence took over the front line at Spoil Bank, on the south side of the Ypres-Comines Canal, from two Companies of the 6th Cameron Highlanders. On the 24th April they were relieved by No. 2 Batt. 39th Composite Brigade, and moved into close support at Spoil Bank and Lock 8

In the morning of the 25th the enemy attacked south of the Ypres-Comines Canal, and one Company of the Manchesters counter-attacked to restore the situation, the rest of the Battalion forming a defensive flank from Shelley Farm—Voormezeele. As at Manchester Hill thick mist came to the aid of the attacking enemy, who overran the forward posts on the 26th and drove the remnants of the Battalion from the Spoil Bank line to Lock 8. Casualties were heavy and five officers were killed. They fell back on Scottish Camp and the survivors, with the exception of Headquarters, were absorbed in the 2nd Yorks, and proceeded on the 29th to man trenches near Ouderdom. Simultaneously, Headquarters and Details rejoined transport lines near Poperinghe and on May 2nd moved by road to bivouacs outside Steenvoorde, and on the following day to Buyscheere, where they were joined on the 10th by the Company which had been attached to the 2nd Yorks.

The Sixteenth was now reduced to a Cadre of ten officers and forty-nine other ranks, and together with the band, which had been selected as the Divisional band, moved on May 16th by way of Audricq and Woincourt to Monthieres, and became affiliated to the 1st Batt. 140th Regiment, U.S. Army, to assist in its training. From the 17th May to the 11th June they were at Moncheaux and were then transferred to the 3rd Batt. 138th Regiment, U.S. Army, and remained with the latter from the 12th to the 15th at Bazinval.

What was left of the Battalion was now bound homewards to replenish its attenuated ranks. Gamaches was reached on the 15th, and Boulogne on the following day, the night being spent at Ostrohove Rest Camp. Folkestone was reached on the 17th and they moved thence by rail to Brookwood Station and Cowshot Camp, where they remained until the early days of July, resting and receiving larger drafts of officers and men.

The Sixteenth had, meanwhile, been transferred to the 14th Division (42nd Infantry Brigade).

CHAPTER X

BACK TO YPRES AREA AND THE END OF THE GREAT WAR

THE short spell in England, during the fortnight or so of June and July, must have been a welcome change to the few war-worn survivors of the original Sixteenth.

But the end of the struggle—though so near—was not yet. The Battalion was filled up with drafts and re-equipped, and on July 4th, 1918, left Brookwood for Folkestone, reaching Boulogne the same day and spending the night at Ostrohove Rest Camp. On the following day it moved to Baincthun, thence by way of Mesnil and Sanghen to Tournehem. General Sir Henry Plumer, commanding the Second Army, inspected the Battalion on the 17th ; a draft of three hundred and ninety-four men joined from the Base Depot ; and from that time on to the 22nd August the Manchesters were engaged in general training. On the 17th August Sports were held in the cricket field at Guemy. On the 23rd August the Battalion marched from Tournehem to Nortkerque and entrained for Proven, marching thence to Tunnellius Camp. On the 29th it relieved the 1/5th the K.O.S.B.'s in the left Divisional sector of the 2nd Corps front—the 42nd Infantry Brigade being at that time in reserve.

On September 3rd the band rejoined from " H " Depot, and on September 5th the Sixteenth relieved the 33rd London R.B. in the line of the left brigade sub-sector, Ypres sector. On the 13th the Manchesters were relieved by the 29th D.L.I. and marched to Brake Camp. On the 15th they proceeded by light railway to Winnizeele, where they were billeted in the Steenvorde area. The 19th was spent at Dominion Camp, the 20th on the march to the Dickebusch Bund area, and on the 21st they relieved the 14th Argyle and Sutherland Highlanders in the Voornezeele Brigade sector. On the 26th the Battalion was relieved in the line by the 6th Wilts, and on the 14th by A. and S.H. and marched to Ouderdom, except " C " Company which moved to Dickebusch Bund. On the 27th the Battalion, less " C " Company marched, to the Eizenwalle area to act in support in an attack that was pending.

At 5-30 a.m. on September 28th the 42nd Infantry Brigade attacked the enemy lines and carried all its objectives. The Germans had evidently lost heart in the business, consequently the supporting Battalion of Manchesters was not called upon to take any active part. " C " Company carried S.A.A. and stores from Hemil Dump to the front line after the objectives had been gained. The Battalion marched to Micmac Camp after the position had been consolidated and on October 1st to the Wytschaete area. On the 2nd it moved to Neuve Eglise, via Wulverghem, and thence by light railway to Hell Fire Junction, Ypres. The 3rd was spent resting in shelters and dug-outs in the old front line at Hell Fire Corner. On the 4th the Battalion entrained at Hell Fire Junction for Zonnebeke, where it was billeted in old dug-outs, shelters and tents. From the 5th to the 12th it acted as labour party in road construction, earning high praise from the Corps Commander for the work accomplished. The 13th and 14th were spent in the Drauoute-Kemmel area, the 15th at Wulverghem, and from there it moved to a position in front of Comines, remaining there until the 17th when it moved to La Barbe. On the 20th it was at Luigne, in the Quevacamps area, and on the 28th took over the front line at Espierres. Two days later it was relieved by the 6th Wilts and went into billets at Doltinges, the town being shelled at intervals. On the night of the 27th the Manchesters were again in the front line at Espierres. On the night 29th/30th October two Platoons of " A " Company and two Platoons of " B " Company successfully carried out a minor operation—crossing the river Scheldt in two places and establishing posts on the east bank. Five prisoners and two machine guns were taken. For this piece of work the Battalion was warmly congratulated by the Divisional Commander.

On the 31st the Manchesters were relieved and marched to transport lines, moving thence to billets at Les Balons, near Wattrelos, Belgium, remaining until 8th November when they marched to Petit Audenarde and billeted there awaiting orders.

November 11th was Armistice Day.

On the 14th the Battalion was back at Les Balons, and throughout December and January, February and March, 1919, was smartening up, carrying out ceremonial parades, helping in agricultural work and indulging in sports. Meanwhile the demobilisation of officers and men began.

On January 25th, 1919, a colour party consisting of Captain T. Hawkins, M.C., D.C.M., M.M., and Sec.-Lieut. G. S. Kay, two warrant officers, six sergeants and thirty-two rank and file proceeded to The Square, Roubaix, for the presentation of the Battalion Colours by Lieut.-General Sir Beauvoir de Lisle, K.C.B., D.S.O., Commanding Fifth Army.

On the 31st March two officers and one hundred other ranks were sent as a draft to the 1/5th Border Regiment, and on the 27th six officers had left to join the 51st Manchester Regiment, Second Army, as volunteers for the Army of Occupation.

On April 30th the Battalion, being down to cadre strength, awaited orders for embarkation, but it was not until the 6th June that it was finally dispersed, when the cadre party proceeded to Lille Demobilisation Camp, taking the Colours with them.

On July 1st, 1920, the Colours of the Sixteenth and other Manchester Battalions were consecrated at the Regimental Depôt, Ashton-under-Lyne, and handed over by Major-General T. H. Shoubridge, C.B., C.M.G., D.S.O., commanding the East Lancashire Division and district. At noon the Colours were paraded in Albert Square, Manchester, afterwards being carried to the Manchester Cathedral, followed by a large representative contingent of old members of the Battalion, where they were delivered into the keeping of the Dean and Chapter, to be preserved with those of the other City Battalions.

Appendix I
HONOURS

Photo *Caswall Smith*

LIEUTENANT-COLONEL WILFRITH ELSTOB, V.C., D.S.O., M.C.
16TH BATTALION MANCHESTER REGIMENT

Victoria Cross

ELSTOB, WILFRITH *T/Lt.-Col., 16th Batt.* *Gazetted 9th June* 1919

For most conspicuous bravery, devotion to duty and self-sacrifice at Manchester Redoubt, near St. Quentin, on the 21st March 1918.

During the preliminary bombardment he encouraged his men in the posts in the Redoubt by frequent visits and when repeated attacks developed controlled the defence at the points threatened, giving personal support with revolver, rifle and bombs. Single handed he repulsed one bombing assault, driving back the enemy and inflicting severe casualties.

Later when ammunition was required he made several journeys under severe fire in order to replenish supply.

Throughout the day Lt.-Col. Elstob, although twice wounded, showed the most fearless disregard of his own safety, and by his encouragement and noble example inspired his command to the fullest degree. The Manchester Redoubt was surrounded in the first wave of the enemy attack, but by means of buried cable Lt.-Col. Elstob was able to assure his Brigade Commander "That the Manchester Regiment will defend Manchester Hill to the last."

Some time after the post was overcome by vastly superior forces, and this very gallant officer was killed in the final assault, having maintained to the end the duty which he impressed on his men, namely "Here we fight and here we die."

He set the highest example of valour, determination, endurance and fine soldierly bearing.

Also received Military Cross, 1*st Jan.* 1917, *and D.S.O.* 1*st Jan.* 1918
k. in a., 21*st March* 1918

DISTINGUISHED SERVICE ORDER

Name	Rank	Place and date of deed	Gazetted
ELSTOB, Wilfrith .. V.C., M.C.	T/Lt.-Col.	k. in a. 21-3-18	1-1-18

MILITARY CROSS

Rank	Name	Gazetted	Remarks
Q. & Hn. Lt.	BALL, John Thomas ..	1-1-18	
6723, C.S.M.	BROWN, Fredk. James Mann	18-6-17	
T/Capt.	ELSTOB, Wilfrith .. .. V.C., D.S.O.	1-1-17	K. in a., 21-3-18
T/Sec.-Lt.	HALL, William Ernest James	26-9-17 9-1-18	
T/Capt.	HAWKINS, Thomas .. D.C.M. (3-6-16), M.M. (1-9-16) in S. Staffs. 1916 ..	26-7-18	
T/Capt.	GIBBON, Robert	1-1-18	
T/Sec.-Lt.	McQUINN, Wallace	18-2-18	D., 6-8-18 (P. of W.)
T/Sec.-Lt.	SOUTHWORTH, Francis ..	2-4-19 10-12-19 18-7-18	l'Escault River, 29/30-10-18
T/Sec.-Lt.	WHITTLE, Reginald Alfred..	26-9-17 9-1-18	
Sec.-Lieut.	COMPTON, Robert .. .. (4th S. Lancs.) *attached* 16th	15-2-19 30-7-19	St. Eloi, 24/25-9-18

DISTINGUISHED CONDUCT MEDAL

No.	Name	Rank	Place and date of deed	Gazetted
17/8361.	ALTON, A.	Pte.		28-3-18
64421.	BROOKES, L. ..	Pte.	Espierres. 29/30-10-18	3-6-19 11-3-20
40903.	DODDEMEAD, C. ..	Pte.	St. Quentin	3-6-18 21-10-18
47213.	ETCHELLS, W. ..	L/Cpl.		1-1-18 17-4-18
26519.	GILBERT, J. ..	C.S.M.	St. Quentin	3-9-18
7111.	GOWAN, H.	Sgt.	Montauban	1-1-17 13-2-17
43008.	LEECH, R.	Sgt.	Henin. 27-4-17 ..	18-6-17
7191.	PENNINGTON, T. E.	Sgt.	Montauban and Trones Wood	1-1-17 13-2-17
277049.	POTTER, H. W. ..	Sgt.		1-1-18 17-4-18
43046.	POTTER, W. J. ..	R.S.M.		1-1-18 17-4-18
12453.	SALTER, F.	L/Cpl.	St. Quentin ..	3-9-18

MILITARY MEDAL

No.	Name	Rank	Place and date of deed	Gazetted
6712.	ALLEN, H.	C.S.M.	Trones Wood.. ..	19-2-17
6207.	ARNFIELD, T. ..	L/Sgt.	Gheluvelt	3-3-18
7194.	ARRANDALE, S. R.	Sgt.	IX Corps.	19-3-18
6828.	BAINS, G.	Pte.	Montauban	23-8-16
1048.	BARBER, W. H. ..	L/Sgt.	Zillebeke Bund ..	18-10-17
40899.	BARTLES, J. ..	Pte.	St. Quentin	16-7-18
41846.	BATCHELOR, A. ..	Pte.	St. Quentin	16-7-18
7599.	BOWIE, D.	Pte.	Montauban	16-11-16
33284.	BROOKS, C. H. ..	Pte.		28-1-18
2789.	BROWN, F.	Cpl.	Héninel-Cherisy ..	9-7-17
7091.	COLEMAN, A. ..	L/Cpl.	Zillibeke Bund ..	28-9-17
	" " (*Bar*)	Sgt.	St. Quentin ..	18-7-18
26580.	COLLINS, G. ..	Pte.	St. Quentin	29-8-18
6855.	CROMPTON, S. ..	Sgt.	Zillibeke Bund ..	28-9-18
6368.	DAWSON, S. P. ..	Pte.	Montauban	16-11-16
35448.	DEAN, J.	Pte.	St. Quentin	16-7-18
6235.	DEAVILLE, A. ..	Pte.	Guillemont	19-2-17
6735.	DICKENSON, S. ..	L/Cpl.	Héninel-Cherisy ..	9-7-17
6980.	DRABBLE, A. ..	Cpl.	Bellecourt	19-2-17
57326.	EBLING, J. B. ..	Sgt.	Esquierres	23-7-19
7345.	ELSWORTH, A. ..	A/Cpl.	Zillebeke Bund ..	28-9-18
43073.	FLANAGAN, M. ..	Pte.	Héninel-Cherisy ..	9-7-17
6988.	FOSTER, J.	Cpl.	Zillebeke Bund ..	28-9-17
6246.	FROUD, C. T. ..	Pte.	Montauban	16-11-16
7374.	GLEAVE, W. ..	Sgt.	Héninel-Cherisy ..	9-7-17
7113.	GREAVES, W. ..	Pte.	Montauban	11-11-16
29226.	GREENALL, F. ..	Pte.	Zillebeke Bund ..	28-9-17
139443.	GRIMSHAW, H. ..	Sgt.	St. Quentin	26-8-18
3201.	HOBSON, E... ..	Pte.	IX Corps	19-3-18
41865.	HODGSON, P. ..	L/Cpl.		13-3-18
46817.	HOPKINSON, A. H.	Pte.	IX Corps	19-3-18
6386.	HORFORD, T. ..	Sgt.	Héninel-Cherisy ..	9-7-17
7343.	HOWELLS, J. ..	Cpl.		29-8-18
12944.	HULBERT, S. ..	L/Cpl.	Zillebeke Bund ..	28-9-17
6762.	IRLAM, S. D. ..	L/Cpl.	Zillebeke Bund ..	28-9-17
6636.	JOWLE, R.	L/Cpl.	Montauban	21-9-16
7128.	KIRKPATRICK, R.	Pte.	Maricourt	11-11-16
48668.	LUTMAN, H. J. ..	Pte.	St. Quentin	16-7-18
43109.	MANGER, J. ..	Pte.	St. Quentin	16-7-18
11604.	MARSH, O. G. ..	Sgt.		9-7-19
6527.	MEIN, W. .. .. (*Posthumous*)	Pte.	Montauban	19-2-17
38002.	MULLIN, H. ..	Cpl.	Zillebeke Bund ..	28-9-17
7038.	PALMER, H. ..	L/Cpl.	Montauban	23-8-16
29626.	PETTECREW, E. ..	Pte.	Héninel-Cherisy ..	9-7-17
11910.	PILKINGTON, A. E.	Cpl. (L/Sgt.)	St. Quentin	16-7-18
51516.	POOLTON, H. ..	Pte.	Esquieres	14-5-19
40890.	PRESSLEY, F. ..	Sgt.	Zillebeke Bund ..	28-9-17
6545.	PROFFITT, A. ..	Cpl.	Héninel-Cherisy ..	9-7-17
6424.	RIDDICK, W. ..	L/Cpl.	Maricourt	3-6-16
6676.	SHEARD, G. ..	Pte.	Montauban	16-11-16
48495.	SHEARD, T. S. ..	Sgt.	St. Quentin	16-7-18
7055.	SIMPSON, G. ..	Cpl.	Zillebeke Bund ..	21-8-17

MILITARY MEDAL—*continued*

No.	*Name*	*Rank*	*Place and date of deed*	*Gazetted*
6683.	SMITH, R.	Pte.	Maricourt	11-11-16
29617.	THOMPSON, W. ..	Pte.	Zillebeke Bund ..	28-9-17
48527.	TOPPING, T. ..	Pte.	St. Quentin	16-7-18
6442.	WALKER, A. ..	L/Sgt. (Sgt.)	Gheluvelt	13-3-18
102461.	WARLOW, W. ..	Pte.	Zillebeke Bund ..	28-9-17
277745.	WATERHOUSE, W.	L/Cpl.	St. Quentin	29-8-18
6445.	WAYNE, F.	Pte.	Montauban	16-11-16
4694.	WILLIAMSON, J. ..			
23036.	WOOLLEY, T. ..	Pte.	Zillebeke Bund ..	28-9-17
6822.	WORDSWORTH, G.	Pte.	Montauban	16-11-16
40885.	WRIGHT, C. E. ..	Pte.	Gheluvelt	13-3-18

MERITORIOUS SERVICE MEDAL

No.	*Rank*	*Name*	*Gazetted*
7090.	R.Q.M.S. ..	CARR, S.	29-8-18
37316.	Pte. ..	MAHY, E. E.	17-6-18
6534.	R.Q.M.S. ..	MORRIS, W.	3-6-19
6694.	Cpl. ..	TYLDESLEY, A. J.	18-1-18
6570.	Cpl. ..	WATSON, A.	17-6-19
6702.	C.Q.M.S. ..	WINNING, T. A...	3-6-19
6823.	Sgt. ..	WORRALL, F.	3-6-19
6944.	Sgt. ..	WORRALL, W.	18-1-19

FOREIGN DECORATIONS

BELGIUM—CROIX DE GUERRE

No.	*Rank*	*Name*	*Gazetted*
7055.	Sgt. ..	SIMPSON, George	12-7-18
7820.	Pte. ..	STRINGER, James	4-9-19

FRANCE—CROIX DE GUERRE

No.	*Rank*	*Name*	*Gazetted*
20842.	Sgt. ..	CALDERBANK, S.	19-7-19

FRANCE—MEDAILLE MILITAIRE

No.	*Rank*	*Name*	*Gazetted*
17324.	L/Cpl. ..	COXON, Harry	14-7-17
6241.	L/Cpl. ..	EDGE, H.	7-5-17

RUSSIA—MEDAL OF ST. GEORGE

No.	*Rank*	*Name*	*Gazetted*	*Remarks*
6636.	Pte.	JOWLE, Robert, M.M. ..	15-2-17	4th Class

APPENDIX II

OFFICERS KILLED

(IN ORDER OF DATE)

OFFICERS KILLED (in order of date)

Rank	*Name*	*Date*	*Place*
T/Capt.	JOHNSON, Morton William ..	2-7-16	Montauban
T/Lieut.	OLIVER, John Milner	9-7-16	Trones Wood
T/Lieut.	SMITHERS, Edward Henry Keith (11th B. Man. R.) *attached*	9-7-16	Trones Wood
Sec.-Lieut.	VENNER, E. W.	9-7-16	Trones Wood
T/Sec.-Lt.	ALLEN, Sydney Raymond ..	12-7-16	Montauban
T/Sec.-Lt.	MONTAGUE, Williams Charles .. (25th B. Man. R.) *attached*, d. of w.	29-7-16	Guillemont
T/Sec.-Lt.	BRETT, Francis Joseph .. .. (25th B. Man. R.) *attached*	30-7-16	Guillemont
Capt.	HAWKINS, John Noel .. .. (27th B. Man. R.) *attached*, d. of w.	30-7-16	Guillemont
Sec.-Lieut.	PLESTED, Horace George .. (4th B. Man. R.) *attached*	30-7-16	Guillemont
Lt.-Col.	KNOX, Hubert .. .. .. (2nd B. Man. R.) *attached*	13-10-16	Flers
T/Sec.-Lt.	CLARK, William	27-3-17	Mercatel
T/Lieut.	HOOK, Cyril Walter Keenan ..	23-4-17	Héninel
T/Capt.	MEGSON, Robert Hargraves ..	23-4-17	Héninel
T/Capt.	WILSON, Laurence Farrer.. ..	23-4-17	Héninel
Sec.-Lieut.	INGRAM, John Aldred .. .. (6th B. Man. R.) *attached*	23-4-17	Héninel
Sec.-Lieut.	RYLANDS, Frank .. (d. of w.)	25-4-17	
T/Lieut.	BRODRICK, Edward .. .. (13th B. Man. R.) *attached*	31-7-17	Zillebeke Bund
Sec.-Lieut.	JACKSON, John Cooper .. .. (3rd B. Man. R.) *attached*	31-7-17	Zillebeke Bund
Lieut.-Col.	ELSTOB, Wilfrith .. .. .. V.C., D.S.O., M.C.	21-3-18	St. Quentin
Capt.	ASHE, Edward Neville, M.C. .. (8th B. Man. R.) *attached*	21-3-18	St. Quentin
Sec.-Lieut.	LEWIS, Charles .. .. .. (6th B. Man. R.) *attached*	21-3-18	St. Quentin
Cpt.-Adjt.	SHARPLES, Norman (*attached*)	21-3-18	St. Quentin
T/Major	ROBERTS, Rupert Edward (d. of w.)	26-3-18	St. Quentin
Sec.-Lieut.	DINNIS, George Hugh	28-4-18	Ypres-Comines Canal
Sec.-Lieut.	HILTON, Robert .. .. (d.)	29-4-18	
T/Sec.-Lt.	McQUINN, Wallace (d. P. of W.)	6-8-18	
Lieut.	KERRY, Arnold John St. Ledgier (d.)	14-2-18	
Capt.	PRITCHARD, O. T.	21-3-18	St. Quentin
A/Capt.	GUEST, J.	21-3-18	St. Quentin
A/Capt.	HEYWOOD, P. H.	21-3-18	St. Quentin
Lieut.	CLARKE, J.	21-3-18	St. Quentin
Sec.-Lieut.	BENTLEY, J. A.	21-3-18	St. Quentin
Sec.-Lieut.	BIRCHENOUGH, J. A.	21-3-18	St. Quentin
Sec.-Lieut.	DEAN, W.	21-3-18	St. Quentin
Sec.-Lieut.	DURRANT, F. J.	21-3-18	St. Quentin
Sec.-Lieut.	HAYES, F.	21-3-18	St. Quentin
Sec.-Lieut.	KEELING, F. W.	21-3-18	St. Quentin
Sec.-Lieut.	PLEASANCE, M. D.	21-3-18	St. Quentin
Sec.-Lieut.	BRADWELL, E.	28-4-18	Ypres-Comines Canal

OFFICERS KILLED (in order of date)—*continued*

Rank	*Name*	*Date*	*Place*
Sec.-Lieut.	JONES, ...	28-4-18	Ypres-Comines Canal
Sec.-Lieut.	RINGHAM, H. T.	28-4-18	Ypres-Comines Canal
Sec.-Lieut.	SHAW, F. S.	28-4-18	Ypres-Comines Canal
Sec.-Lieut.	WOODACRE, A.	28-4-18	Ypres-Comines Canal
T/Sec.-Lt.	FINDLAY, Scott, ... (19th B. Man. R.) *attached*	8-5-18	Berryscheere

APPENDIX II
continued
W.O.'s, N.C.O.'s
AND MEN
KILLED

ABBOTT	Joseph, *b* Manchester, *e* Manchester (Salford, Lancs.), 7536, Pte., k. in a., F. & F., 9-7-16.
ACHESON	Stanley, *b* St. John's, Manchester, *e* Manchester (Liverpool), 6826, Sgt., k. in a., F. & F., 9-7-16.
ADAMSON	Harold William, *b* Manchester, *e* Manchester (Moss Side, Manchester), 252015, Pte., d. of w., F. & F., 6-8-17.
ADAMSON	James Hamilton, *b* Whitehaven, Cumb., *e* Manchester (Chorlton-cum-Hardy, Manchester), 6201, A/C.S.M., k. in a., F. & F., 9-7-16.
ADSHEAD	John Edward, *b* Newton Heath, Manchester, *e* Manchester, (Miles Platting, Manchester), 7487, Pte., d. of w., F. & F., 2-7-16.
AINSWORTH	Robert Willie, *b* Chelfield, Radcliffe, Lancs., *e* Heaton Park, Manchester (Radcliffe), 7447, Pte., d. of w., F. & F., 2-7-16.
ALBAN	Louis, *b* St. Michael's, Manchester, *e* Manchester (Ancoats, Manchester), 6202, Pte., k. in a., F. & F., 1-7-16.
ALDRED	Joseph, *b* Leigh, Lancs., *e* Manchester (Miles Platting, Manchester), 27076, Pte., k. in a., F. & F., 27-11-16.
ALLEN	Thomas William, *b* Dunham Massey, Cheshire, *e* Manchester (Stretford, Manchester), 33679, Pte., d. of w., F. & F., 10-7-16.
ALLISON	William, *b* Harpurhey, Manchester, *e* Manchester (Salford, Lancs.), 27099, Pte., k. in a., F. & F., 9-7-16.
ALLOTT	Arthur, *b* Deepcar, Sheffield, *e* Manchester (Dewsbury, Yorks.), 13548, L/Sgt., d., F. & F., 26-3-18.
ALLPORT	Francis James, *b* Hallow, Worcester, *e* Upton-on-Severn (Earl's Croome, Worcester), 42290, Pte., k. in a., F. & F., 28-7-17.
ARMITAGE	Ernest, *e* Oldham, Lancs., 39652, Pte., k. in a., F. & F. 21-3-18.
ASHLEY	William Thomas, *b* Kinsey Heath, Audlem, Cheshire, *e* Manchester (Crewe), 27370, L/Cpl., k. in a., F. & F., 30-7-16.
ASHTON	Charles Edward, *b* Hightown, Manchester, *e* Manchester (Rhodes, Manchester), 7074, Sgt., k. in a., F. & F., 23-4-17.
ASHTON	James, *b* Heywood, Lancs., *e* Bury, Lancs. (Heywood), 54659, Pte., d., F. & F., 25-10-18.
ASHTON	James Ewart, *b* Northwich, Cheshire, *e* Manchester (Winnington, Northwich), 12506, Cpl., k. in a., F. & F., 8-5-18.
ASHTON	Rowland Otto, *b* Chorlton-on-Medlock, Manchester, *e* Manchester (Chorlton-on-Medlock), 6713, Pte., k. in a., F. & F., 1-7-16.
ASPLEY	Charles Joseph, *b* Presteign, Radnor, *e* Shrewsbury (Walton Kington, Radnor), 54657, Pte., k. in a., F. & F., 21-3-18.
ASTON	Leonard, *b* Harpurhey, Manchester, *e* Manchester (Blackley, Manchester), 6208, Pte., k. in a., F. & F., 1-7-16.
ATHERTON	Henry, *b* Over Winsford, Cheshire, *e* Manchester (Moss Side, Manchester), 6335, L/Cpl., k. in a., F. & F., 9-7-16.
ATKINS	Randolph Thomas, *b* Miles Platting, Manchester, *e* Manchester (Harpurhey, Manchester), 27151, Pte., d. of w., Home, 28-10-16.
BAGLEY	Brian Capendale, *b* Wing, Rutland, *e* Oakham, Rutland (Wing.), 40894, Pte., k. in a., F. & F., 18-10-16, formerly 24819 Leicester R.

BAILEY Percy James, *b* South Normanton, Derby, *e* Manchester (South Normanton), 7424, Sgt., k. in a., F. & F., 23-4-17.

BAKER Frederick George, *b* Summerstown, London, *e* St. Pancras, Middlesex (Highbury), 47541, L/Cpl., k. in a., F. & F., 21-3-18, formerly 309221 R.E.

BALFE Francis, *b* Kirkdale, Liverpool, *e* Manchester (Levenshulme, Manchester), 6458, Pte., d. of w., F. & F., 6-7-16.

BALL Harry, *b* Leigh, Lancs, *e* Leigh, 7698, Pte., k. in a., F. & F., 1-7-16, formerly 28310 10th Hussars.

BALLARD Herbert, *b* St. George's, Manchester, *e* Manchester (Moss Side, Manchester), 7075, Cpl., k. in a., F. & F., 9-7-16.

BAMBER Henry Charles, *b* Manchester, *e* Manchester (Chorlton-on-Medlock, Manchester), 203252, Pte., d., F. & F., 23-7-18.

BANCROFT John, *b* Broughton, Manchester, *e* Manchester (Lower Broughton, Manchester), 6714, Pte., k. in a., F. & F., 14-10-16.

BARLOW Henry, *e* Manchester (Eccles, Lancs.), 251625, Pte., d. of w., Home, 25-10-18.

BARRETT Harold, *b* Broughton, Manchester, *e* Manchester (Lower Broughton, Manchester), 7197, Pte., k. in a., F. & F., 18-1-16.

BARROW Joseph, *b* Knutsford, Cheshire, *e* Manchester (Mobberley, Cheshire), 19321, L/Cpl., k. in a., F. & F., 23-4-17.

BARSBY John Edward, *b* Daybrook, Notts., *e* Nottingham, 43102, L/Cpl., k. in a., F. & F., 28-11-17, formerly 1/10996 Notts and Derby R.

BATLEY Harold, *b* Harpurhey, Manchester, *e* Manchester, 6954, L/Cpl., k. in a., F. & F., 9-7-16.

BEAN Frederick, *b* Helpston, Northants., *e* Peterborough, Northants (Helpston), 50994, Pte., k. in a., F. & F., 21-3-18, formerly G/19292 Middlesex R.

BEBINGTON Neil Campbell, *e* Bootle, Liverpool, 252628, Pte., d. of w., F. & F., 27-4-18, formerly 5059 King's Liverpool R.

BEEVER George, *b* Stoke-on-Trent, Staffs., *e* Manchester (Rydal Mount, Glossop, Derby.), 6462, Pte., k. in a., F. & F., 1-7-16.

BELFIELD Harry, *b* Ashton-u-Lyne, Lancs., *e* Failsworth, Lancs. (Ashton-u-Lyne, Lancs.), 33164, Pte., k. in a., F. & F., 27-7-17.

BELL Andrew, *b* Salford, Lancs., *e* Manchester (Salford), 6716, L/Cpl., k. in a., F. & F., 31-7-17.

BELL Ernest Victor, *b* Sydenham, Kent, *e* Chelsea, Middlesex (Oxted, Surrey), 59178, Pte., k. in a., F. & F., 21-3-18, formerly T4/160287 R.A.S.C.

BELL Frederick William, *b* Manchester, *e* Manchester (Harpurhey, Manchester), 33270, Pte., k. in a., F. & F., 23-4-17.

BELL Robert Edward, *b* Manchester, *e* Manchester (Harpurhey, Manchester), 33488, Pte., d. of w., F. & F., 11-5-17.

BELL William, *b* York, *e* Manchester (Walmgate, York), 7355, Sgt., k. in a., F. & F., 23-4-17.

BENN Thomas, *b* Gorton, Manchester, *e* Manchester (Bradford, Manchester), 11472, Pte., k. in a., F. & F., 21-3-18.

BENNETT Frank, *b* Barton, Eccles, Lancs., *e* Manchester (Barton), 6463, Cpl., k. in a., F. & F., 9-7-16.

BENNETT Robert, *b* Pendlebury, Lancs., *e* Manchester (Pendlebury), 7360, L/Cpl., k. in a., F. & F., 21-3-18.

BENTLEY Charles, *b* Hulme, Manchester, *e* Manchester (Gorton. Manchester), 6582, Pte, k. in a., F. & F., 13-2-16.

BENTLEY Edward, *b* Helmshore, Bury, Lancs, *e* Manchester (Bury), 7392, Pte., k. in a., F. & F., 9-7-16.

BERRY William Henry, b Marylebone, Middlesex, *e* Marylebone, 27158, L/Cpl., k. in a., F. & F., 30-7-16, formerly 2729 R.W. Kent R.

BESWICK Harry Bowden, *b* Stockport, Cheshire, *e* Manchester (Chorlton-cum-Hardy, Manchester), 6465, Cpl., k. in a., F. & F., 30-7-16.

BIBB Richard, *b* Birmingham, *e* Lichfield, (Birmingham) 43115, Pte., d. of w., F. & F., 26-4-17, formerly 10598 Border R.

BILLINGTON Harry, *b* Manchester, *e* Manchester (Moston, Manchester), 19704, Cpl., k. in a., F. & F., 23-4-17.

BISHOP Sidney Melvil, *b* London, *e* Heaton Park, Manchester (Chorlton-cum-Hardy, Manchester), 7411, L/Cpl., k. in a., F. & F., 9-7-16.

BLEARS Frank Eric, *b* Eccles, Lancs., *e* Manchester (Eccles), 6585, Pte., k. in a., F. & F., 30-7-16.

BLOMLEY Albert, *b* Chadderton, Oldham, Lancs., *e* Oldham, 49790, Pte., k. in a., F. & F., 31-7-17.

BLOOD John, *b* Manchester, *e* Manchester, 35459, Pte., d., F. & F., 3-9-17.

BOARDMAN Ellis, *b* Ancoats, Manchester, *e* Heaton Park, Manchester (Clayton, Manchester), 7436, Pte., k. in a., F. & F., 23-4-17.

BOOTH Charles Henry, *b* Burslem, Staffs., *e* Manchester (Colchester, Essex), 26153, Pte., d., F. & F., 25-10-18.

BOOTH William, *b* Hyde, Cheshire, *e* Denton, Lancs., 49443, L/Cpl., k. in a., F. & F., 27-4-18.

BOTTRILL Christopher Thomas, *b* Shelley, Huddersfield, *e* Manchester (Chorlton-cum-Hardy, Manchester), 6837, Sgt., k. in a. F. & F., 1-7-16.

BOULD Thomas, *b* Dinting, Derby, *e* Manchester (Hyde, Cheshire), 20616, Pte., d. of w., F. & F., 2-5-18.

BOURKE Henry George, *b* Homerton, Middlesex, *e* London, 64405, Pte., k. in a., F. & F., 29-10-18, formerly 5646 R.A.P. Corps.

BOWDEN William, *b* Salford, Lancs., *e* Manchester (Pendleton, Lancs.), 1473, Cpl., k. in a., F. & F., 23-4-17.

BOWDEN William Howard, *e* Manchester (Chorlton-on-Medlock, Manchester), 275982, Sgt., k. in a., F. & F., 31-7-17.

BOYD Frank Cooper, *b* Manchester, *e* Manchester, 35463, Pte., k. in a., F. & F., 12-10-16.

BOYSON Fred, *e* Bugbrooke, Northants, (Rothersthorpe, Northants), 51004, Pte., d. of w., F. & F., 29-9-17, formerly G/86540 Middlesex R.

BRADBURY John, *b* Manchester, *e* Manchester (Newton Heath, Manchester), 18400, Cpl., d., F. & F., 31-7-17.

BRADDOCK Albert, *b* Brierley, Manchester, *e* Manchester (Fallowfield, Manchester), 53294, Pte., k. in a., F. & F., 27-4-18, formerly T/062807 R.A.S.C.

BRANNAGAN John William, *b* Manchester, *e* Manchester (Salford, Lancs.), 7584, Pte., k. in a., F. & F., 9-7-16.

BRENNAN Philip, *b* Hulme, Manchester, *e* Manchester (Hulme), 7081, Pte., k. in a., F. & F., 1-7-16.

BRIGGS Ambrose, *b* Ashton-u-Lyne, Lancs., *e* Manchester (Blackpool, Lancs.), 6470, Pte., k. in a., F. & F., 9-7-16.

BRIGGS John, *b* Harpurhey, Manchester, *e* Manchester (Heaton Chapel, Chester), 6347, Pte., d. of w., F. & F., 3-7-16.

BRIGGS Vincent Joseph, *b* Ashton-u-Lyne, Lancs., *e* Manchester (Blackpool, Lancs.), 6471, Pte., k. in a., F. & F., 30-7-16.

BRITTAIN Leonard Radcliffe, *b* Eccles, Lancs., *e* Manchester (Eccles), 7648, Pte., d. of w., F. & F., 3-7-16.

BROADBENT Thomas, *b* Altrincham, Cheshire, *e* Manchester (Altrincham), 6960, Sgt., k. in a., F. & F., 9-7-16.

BROADY James, *b* Ashton-on-Mersey, Cheshire, *e* Manchester (Urmston, Lancs.), 7202, Pte., d. of w., Home, 22-7-16.

BROCKLEHURST John, *b* Middlewich, Cheshire, *e* Manchester (Middlewich), 6345, Sgt., k. in a., F. & F., 1-7-16.

BROWN Frank, *b* Ardwick, Manchester, *e* Manchester (Chorlton-on-Medlock, Manchester), 6845, Pte., k. in a., F. & F., 1-7-16.

BROWN Horace, *b* Haughton, Denton, Lancs., *e* Manchester (Denton), 6844, L/Cpl., k. in a., F. & F., 1-7-16.

BROWN John William, *b* Chorlton-on-Medlock, Manchester, *e* Manchester (Chorlton-on-Medlock), 57347, Pte., d., F. & F., 26-10-18, formerly 39915 N. Lancashire R.

BROWN William Isherwood, *b* Turton, Bolton, Lancs., *e* Manchester (Altrincham, Cheshire), 6219, Cpl., d., F. & F., 3-3-16.

BROWNING Frederick Thomas, *b* Maidstone, Kent, *e* Maidstone (Canning Town, Essex), 51005, Pte., k. in a., F. & F., 31-7-17, formerly G/19298 Middlesex R.

BRUCE Harry, *b* Manchester, *e* Manchester (Lower Broughton, Manchester), 7633, Pte., k. in a., F. & F., 9-7-16.

BRUNT Arthur Ernest, *b* Bethnal Green, Middlesex, *e* Hackney Baths, Middlesex (Homerton, London), 41850, Pte., d. of w., F. & F., 26-4-17, formerly 4424 E. Surrey R.

BUCKLEY Henry, *b* St. Paul's, Hulme, Manchester, *e* Manchester (Chorlton-on-Medlock, Manchester), 8460, Pte., k. in a., F. & F., 23-4-17.

BUMBY Richard, *b* Manchester, *e* Manchester (Harpurhey, Manchester), 6742, Pte., k. in a., F. & F., 29-7-16.

BUNTING Lawrence, *b* Bonsall, Derby, *e* Mansfield, Notts., 43101, Pte., k. in a., F. & F., 21-3-18, formerly 19224 Notts and Derby R.

BURGESS John, *b* Hooley Hill, Lancs., *e* Ashton-u-Lyne, Lancs. (Hooley Hill), 49133, Pte., k. in a., F. & F., 27-4-18.

BURNS Daniel Patrick Henry, *b* Manchester, *e* Manchester (Wolverhampton), 7551, Pte., k. in a., F. & F., 3-5-16.

BURNS John Alfred, *b* Manchester, *e* Manchester (Openshaw, Manchester), 7346, L/Cpl., d., F. & F., 27-7-18.

BURNS Thomas Henry, *b* Collyhurst, Manchester, *e* Manchester, 7682, Pte., k. in a., F. & F., 30-7-16.

BURTON Frank, *b* Swinton, Lancs., *e* Manchester (Swinton), 6726, Pte., k. in a., F. & F., 1-7-16.

BUSH Ernest Herbert, *b* Brentford, Middlesex, *e* Brentford, 41821, Pte., k. in a., F. & F., 23-4-17, formerly 3886 E. Surrey R.

BUTLER James Edward, *b* Chesham, Bucks., *e* Chesham, 43071, L/Cpl., k. in a., F. & F., 30-7-17, formerly 22328 Oxf. & Bucks. L.I.

BUTLER John James, *b* Wheelock, Cheshire, *e* Crewe, Cheshire (Wheelock), 54671, Pte., k. in a., F. & F., 21-3-18.

CADMAN Harry, *b* Oldham, Lancs., *e* Hollinwood, Oldham (Failsworth, Manchester), 29111, Pte., d. of w., F. & F., 2-4-17.

CALEY Charles, *b* Douglas, I.O.M., *e* Manchester (Chorlton-on-Medlock, Manchester), 538, L/Cpl., k. in a., F. & F., 23-4-17.

CARMAN Phillip, *b* Shipley, Yorks., *e* Bradford, Yorks., (Lister Hills, Bradford), 61586, Pte., k. in a., F. & F., 29-10-18, formerly 205482, W. Rid. R.

CARRIGAN Myles, *b* Newton Heath, Manchester, *e* Manchester (Newton Heath), 203236, Pte., k. in a., F. & F., 21-3-18.

CARTWRIGHT Samuel, *b* Huntsley, *e* Stockport, Cheshire (Heaton Norris, Cheshire), 43208, Pte., k. in a., F. & F., 21-3-18, formerly 33169 Cheshire R.

CAUNT Arthur, *b* St. Pancras, Middlesex, *e* Bloomsbury, Middlesex (King's Cross, Middlesex), 41851, Pte., d. of w., F. & F., 3-5-17, formerly 4514 E. Surrey R.

CHADBOURNE William, *b* Blackwell, Alfreton, Derby, *e* Blackwell, 40902, Pte., d., F. & F., 13-1-17, formerly 2449 Notts & Derby R.

CHADWICK Albert, *b* Harpurhey, Manchester, *e* Manchester (Blackley, Manchester), 6476, L/Cpl., k. in a., F. & F., 16-9-16.

CHAPMAN Leonard, *b* Old Trafford, Manchester, *e* Manchester (Rusholme, Manchester), 7368, Cpl., k. in a., F. & F., 1-7-16.

CHASE George Frederick, *b* Middleton, Manchester, *e* Manchester, (Stockport, Cheshire), 7646, Pte., k. in a., F. & F., 27-1-16.

CHATERS John Charlton, *b* Hunslet, Yorks., *e* Manchester (Gorton, Manchester), 6968, Pte., k. in a., F. & F., 1-7-16.

CLARK Arthur Neil, *b* Manchester, *e* Manchester (Gorton, Manchester), 49648, Pte., d. of w., F. & F., 27-11-17.

CLARK James, *b* Manchester, *e* Manchester (Harpurhey, Manchester), 31192, Pte., k. in a., F. & F., 27-4-18.

CLARK James Albert, *b* Manchester, *e* Manchester (Harpurhey, Manchester), 48863, L/Cpl., k. in a., F. & F., 27-4-18.

CLARKE Albert, *b* Leicester, *e* Leicester, 41027, L/Cpl., d. of w. F. & F., 5-5-18, formerly 5301 Leic. R.

CLARKE Albert Robert, *b* St. Mary's, Battersea, Surrey, *e* Wimbledon, Surrey (Battersea), 41822, L/Cpl., k. in a., F. & F., 12-4-17, formerly 4523 E. Surrey R.

CLARKE George, *b* Altrincham, Cheshire, *e* Manchester (Altrincham), 6849, Cpl., d. of w., F. & F., 17-7-16.

CLAY Arthur, *b* Manchester, *e* Manchester (Pendleton, Manchester), 7632, Pte., k. in a., F. & F., 1-7-16.

CLEGG George Reginald, *b* Warrington, Lancs., *e* Manchester (Warrington), 6227, L/Cpl., k. in a., F. & F., 23-4-17.

CLEGG James, *b* Ardwick, Manchester, *e* Manchester (Ardwick), 6226, Pte., k. in a., F. & F., 9-7-16.

CLOUGH Henry, *b* Failsworth, Lancs., *e* Oldham, Lancs. (Glodwick, Oldham), 29462, Pte., k. in a., F. & F., 21-3-18.

COACKLEY Arthur Cory, *b* Manchester, *e* Manchester (Levenshulme, Manchester), 31313, Pte., k. in a., F. & F., 9-7-16.

COATES John William, *b* Leeds, *e* Chorlton-on-Medlock, Manchester (Denton, Manchester), 6970, Pte., k. in a., F. & F., 1-7-16.

COLE James, *b* Oldham, Lancs., *e* Hollinwood, Lancs. (Werneth, Oldham), 48972, Pte., k. in a., F. & F., 31-7-17.

COLLINGE Elijah, *b* Harpurhey, Manchester, *e* Manchester, 27100, Pte., k. in a., F. & F., 21-3-18.

COLLINS Harry George, *b* Willesden, Middlesex, *e* Croydon, Surrey (Willesden), 41783, Pte., k. in a., F. & F., 21-3-18, formerly 11477 E. Surrey R.

COLLINS John, *b* Oldham, Lancs., *e* Ashton-u-Lyne, Lancs. (Oldham), 29457, Pte., k. in a., F. & F., 23-4-17.

COLLINS William, *b* Pendleton, Manchester, *e* Salford, Lancs. (Pendleton), 25273, Pte, k. in a., F. & F., 23-4-17.

COLLIER Matthew, *b* Tyldesley, Lancs., *e* Atherton, Lancs. (Tyldesley), 302888, Pte., k. in a., F. & F., 15-6-17.

CONNOLLY Thomas, *b* Glasgow, *e* Manchester (Beswick, Manchester), 3895, Pte., d. of w., F. & F., 18-10-16.

COOKE Louis Fisher, *b* Norwich, *e* Norwich, 61515, Pte., d. of w., F. & F., 27-9-18, formerly 350868 Essex R.

COOKSON Charles, *b* Collyhurst, Manchester, *e* Manchester (Blackpool, Lancs.), 47246, Pte., k. in a., F. & F., 24-5-18, formerly 2445 Lancashire Fus.

CORKHILL John Robert, *b* Beswick, Manchester, *e* Manchester (Chorlton-on-Medlock, Manchester), 6596, Sgt., k. in a., F. & F., 12-10-16.

CORLEY Ezekiel, *b* Ramsbottom, Manchester, *e* Manchester (Lower Broughton, Manchester), 6853, Pte., d. of w., F. & F., 8-7-16.

CORY Charles Samuel, *b* Northampton, *e* Northampton, 51010, Pte., d. of w., F. & F., 1-8-17, formerly G/86531 Mid'sex R.

COVENTRY John, *b* Withington, Manchester, *e* Manchester (Ladybarn, Manchester), 6361, L/Cpl., k. in a., F. & F., 1-7-16.

COWELL John, *b* Cheetham, Manchester, *e* Manchester (Beswick, Manchester), 6977, Pte., d., F. & F., 3-3-16.

CRIMMINS William, *b* London, *e* Marylebone, Middlesex, 41857, Pte., k. in a., F. & F., 21-3-18, formerly 4443 E. Surrey R.

CROMPTON Frederick, *b* Salford, Lancs., *e* Manchester (Bradford, Lancs.), 302909, Pte., k. in a., F. & F., 16-6-17.

CROSBY Robert, *b* Chorlton-on-Medlock, Manchester, *e* Manchester (Chorlton-on-Medlock), 13698, Pte., d. of w., F. & F., 22-9-17.

CURRY Fred, *b* Oldham, Lancs., *e* Oldham, 27468, Pte., k. in a., F. & F., 15-10-16.

CURTAIN Timothy, *b* Earlstown, Lancs., *e* Ashton-u-Lyne, Lancs. (Hollinwood, Lancs.), 36276, Pte., k. in a., F. & F., 21-3-18.

CUSACK Henry, *b* Peel Green, Lancs., *e* Ashton-u-Lyne, Lancs. (Winton, Manchester), 302774, Pte., d. of w., F. & F., 28-12-17.

CUSICK John Herbert, *b* Oldham, Lancs., *e* Oldham, 50264, Pte., d. of w., F. & F., 9-4-18.

DAKIN Edward Fisher, *b* Reddish, Cheshire, *e* Manchester (Moss Side, Manchester), 6598, Pte., k. in a., F. & F., 1-7-16.

DANIELS Harry Hewitt, *b* Manchester, *e* Manchester (Moston, Manchester), 25977, Pte., k. in a., F. & F., 31-7-17.

DAVENPORT Harold, *b* Oldham, Lancs., *e* Ashton-u-Lyne, 33219, L/Cpl., d. of w., F. & F., 22-10-18.

DAVIDSON Thomas, *b* Dromore, Co. Down, *e* Belfast, 24882, Pte., k. in a., F. & F., 28-12-17.

DAVIES Alfred, *b* Crewe, Cheshire, *e* Manchester (Salford, Lancs.), 303010, Pte., k. in a., F. & F., 26-9-18.

DAVIES Harold, *b* Miles Platting, Manchester, *e* Manchester (Miles Platting), 6734, Sgt., k. in a., F. & F., 22-9-17.

DAVIES James Frederick, *b* Moss Side, Manchester, *e* Manchester (Moss Side), 6856, Pte., k. in a., F. & F., 1-7-16.

DAVIES John Henry, *b* Liverpool, Lancs., *e* Manchester, Lancs. (Durban, South Africa), 302012, L/Cpl., k. in a., F. & F., 31-7-17.

DAVIES John Norman, *b* Llansaintffryd, Monmouth, *e* Ashton-u-Lyne, Lancs. (Moss Side, Manchester), 29623, Pte., d. of w., F. & F., 31-7-17.

DAVIES William, *b* Manchester, *e* Manchester (Ancoats, Manchester), 22901, Pte., k. in a., F. & F., 31-7-17.

DAWSON Frank Taylor, *b* Bolton, Lancs., *e* Sale, Cheshire, 77439, L/Cpl., k. in a., F. & F., 29-10-18, formerly 292026 R.W. Fus.

DAWSON Herbert, *b* Bury, Lancs., *e* Manchester (Bury), 6232, L/Sgt., k. in a., F. & F., 23-4-17.

DAWSON James, *b* Bury, Lancs., *e* Hollinwood, 48790, Pte., d. of w., F. & F., 1-4-18.

DAWSON James Thomas, *b* Rusholme, Manchester, *e* Manchester (Gorton, Manchester), 6233, Pte., k. in a., F. & F., 21-3-18.

DEAKIN John, *b* Patricroft, Manchester, *e* Manchester (Eccles, Manchester), 7466, Pte., k. in a., F. & F., 1-7-16.

DEAN Henry, *b* Salford, Lancs., *e* Manchester (Salford), 6600, Pte., k. in a., F. & F., 9-7-16.

DEARNALEY William, *b* Preston, Lancs., *e* Oldham, 38104, Pte., d. of w., F. & F., 28-7-17.

DEAVILLE Arthur, *b* St. Philip's, Salford, Lancs., *e* Manchester (Salford), 6235, L/Cpl., d. of w., F. & F., 3-8-17, M.M.

DEWHURST Herbert, *b* Irlams-o'th'-Height, Lancs., *e* Manchester (Irlams-o'th'-Height), 6859, Cpl., k. in a., F. & F., 9-7-16.

DEVON Joseph, *b* Liverpool, *e* Liverpool (Edge Hill, Liverpool), 252611, Pte., k. in a., F. & F., 21-3-18, formerly 4220 Liverpool R.

DICKERSON Harold, *b* Salford, Lancs., *e* Manchester (Salford), 7677, Pte., k. in a., F. & F., 1-7-16.

DICKSON William, *b* Salford, Lancs., *e* Manchester (Salford), 7437, Pte., k. in a., F. & F., 1-7-16.

DILWORTH Albert Edward, *b* Kenilworth, Warwick, *e* Coventry, Warwick (Kenilworth), 64401, Pte., k. in a., F. & F., 25-9-18, formerly 45856 Essex R.

DOBSON Frank, *b* Oldham, Lancs., *e* Oldham, 32984, Pte., k. in a., F. & F., 23-4-17.

DOCHERTY John, *b* Glasgow, *e* Eccles, Manchester (Barton, Manchester), 37934, Pte., k. in a., F. & F., 27-7-17.

DOLAN Albert Martin, *b* St. Edmund's, Manchester, *e* Manchester, 6979, Pte., d. of w., F. & F., 16-9-16.

DOLEMAN Arthur, *b* Hulme, Manchester, *e* Manchester, 7079, Pte., k. in a., F. & F., 29-2-16.

DONNELLY Edward, *b* Manchester, *e* Manchester, 303305, Pte., k. in a., F. & F., 21-3-18.

DOOLEY Richard Abraham, *b* Manchester, *e* Manchester, 27117, Pte., k. in a., F. & F., 9-7-16.

DUFF Joseph Shackley, *b* Kendal, Westmorland, *e* Kendal, 43019, L/Cpl., k. in a., F. & F., 18-10-16, formerly 19570 Border R.

DUNKERLEY Edward, *b* Oldham, Lancs., *e* Oldham, 27421, Pte., k. in a., F. & F., 23-4-17.

DUNN — Arthur, *b* Lancaster, *e* Lancaster, 77115, Pte., k. in a., F. & F., 28-9-18.

DURR — John, *e* Manchester (Portwood, Stockport, Cheshire), 47239, Pte., d., F. & F., 6-6-18.

DYMOND — Charles Henry, *b* Forest Gate, Essex, *e* Bridgwater, Somerset, 252920, Pte., k. in a., F. & F., 29-10-18, formerly 291627 Devon R.

EACHUS — Douglas, *b* Northwich, Cheshire, *e* Manchester (Northwich), 6373, L/Cpl., k. in a., F. & F., 1-7-16.

EASTWOOD — John Edgar, *b* Middleton, Manchester, *e* Manchester, 7182, Cpl., d. of w., Home, 13-8-16.

EATON — Samuel, *b* Salford, Lancs., *e* Manchester (Salford), 12908, Cpl., k. in a., F. & F., 28-4-18.

ECKERSALL — Thomas, *b* Stalybridge, Cheshire, *e* Chester (Stalybridge), 252946, Pte., k. in a., F. & F., 29-10-18, formerly 267745 R. Fus.

ECKERSLEY — William Elderton, *b* Salford, Lancs., *e* Manchester (Salford), 7370, L/Cpl., k. in a., F. & F., 13-2-16.

EDGE — George, *b* Withington, Manchester, *e* Manchester (Heaton Mersey, Manchester), 6240, Pte., d. of w., F. & F., 3-7-16.

EDWARDS — Harry, *b* Bunbury, Cheshire, *e* Crewe, Cheshire (Tarporley, Cheshire), 54691, Pte., k. in a., F. & F., 21-3-18.

EDWARDS — John, *b* Salford, Lancs., *e* Manchester (Salford), 27185, Pte., k. in a., F. & F., 23-4-17.

ELLIOTT — Colin, *b* Longsight, Manchester, *e* Manchester, 6607, L/Cpl., k. in a., F. & F., 1-7-16.

ELLIS — Albert, *b* Manchester, *e* Ardwick, Manchester, 35594, L/Cpl., k. in a., F. & F., 31-7-17.

ELSWORTH — Horace, *b* Manchester, *e* Manchester, 7345, L/Sgt., k. in a., F. & F., 25-4-18, M.M.

EMERTON — Albert Oliver, *b* Chelgrave, Bedford., *e* Luton, Bedford. (Tebworth, Bedford.), 41823, Pte., k. in a., F. & F., 23-4-17, formerly 144506 R.F.A.

ENGLAND — Dyson Sidney, *b* Norwich, *e* London (Willesden, Middlesex), 41858, Pte., d. of w., F. & F., 16-8-17, formerly 4007 E. Surrey R.

ENSTONE — Charles, *b* St. John's, Manchester, *e* Manchester, 6986, L/Cpl., k. in a., F. & F., 1-7-16.

ENTWISTLE — Joseph Silvester, *b* Weaste, Manchester, *e* Manchester (Pendleton, Lancs.), 6488, L/Cpl., k. in a., F. & F., 1-7-16.

ESTILL — Charles Henry, *b* Manchester, *e* Newton Heath, Manchester (Harpurhey, Manchester), 23082, Pte., k. in a., F. & F., 23-4-17.

EVANS — Walter, *b* Withington, Manchester, *e* Manchester, 6739, Pte., k. in a., F. & F., 1-7-16.

FAGAN — John Henry, *b* St. Patrick's, Manchester, *e* Manchester, 7294, Pte., d. of w., F. & F., 8-11-17.

FALLON — Edward, *e* Manchester (Rusholme, Manchester), 250790, Pte., d., F. & F., 24-11-18.

FALLON — Thomas, *b* St. Helens, Lancs., *e* Earlstown, Lancs. (Netherfield, Notts), 64523, Pte., k. in a., F. & F., 11-10-18, formerly 77844 Welch R.

FARNWORTH — Thomas, *b* Wigan, Lancs., *e* Ashton-u-Lyne, Lancs. (Wigan), 35496, Pte., k. in a., F. & F., 14-10-16.

FARRELL — Daniel, *b* Liverpool, *e* Manchester (Salford, Lancs.), 23960, Pte., k. in a., F. & F., 21-3-18.

FIELDING Frank, *b* Marsden, Yorks., *e* Manchester (Marsden), 27115, Pte., k. in a., F. & F., 1-7-16.

FISH John, *b* Failsworth, Lancs., *e* Oldham, Lancs. (Failsworth), 54699, Pte., d. of w., F. & F., 1-4-18.

FISHER Thomas, *b* Northallerton, Yorks., *e* Manchester (Weaste, Manchester), 6611, L/Cpl., k. in a., F. & F., 1-7-16.

FITTERS Harry, *b* Hulme, Manchester, *e* Manchester, 6868, Pte., k. in a., F. & F., 9-7-16.

FITTON Tom, *b* Whitefield, Manchester, *e* Manchester, 11543,, Pte. k. in a., F. & F., 21-3-18, M.M.

FITTON William, *b* West Gorton, Manchester, *e* Manchester, 6742, Pte., d. of w., F. & F., 5-7-16.

FLETCHER Joseph, *b* St. Paul's, Manchester, *e* Manchester (Burto-n on-Trent), 6245, L/Cpl., k. in a., F. & F., 1-7-16.

FLINT Mark, *b* Wirksworth, Derby., *e* Wirksworth, 40907, Pte., d. of w., F. & F., 25-4-17, formerly 2178 Notts & Derby R.

FORGHAM Joseph William, *b* Crewe, Cheshire, *e* Manchester, 7358, Pte., k. in a., F. & F., 1-7-16.

FOSBROOKE John James, *b* St. John's, Broughton, Manchester, *e* Manchester (Higher Broughton), 6743, Pte., k. in a., F. & F., 23-4-17.

FOX George, *e* Wellington, Salop (Horsehay, Salop), 64524, Pte., d. of w., Home, 11-11-18, formerly 19469 Shrops. L.I.

FRASER Harry Clegg, *b* Hulme, Manchester, *e* Manchester, (Chorlton-cum-Hardy, Lancs.), 6613, Cpl., k. in a., F. & F., 30-7-16.

FROST Harold, *b* Ardwick, Manchester, *e* Manchester, 276724, Pte., k. in a., F. & F., 21-3-18.

FULCHER John, *b* St. Thomas's, Ardwick, Manchester, *e* Heaton Park, Manchester (Longsight, Manchester), 7314, Sgt., k. in a., F. & F., 9-7-16.

FURBER Reginald, *b* Llandudno, Carnarvon, *e* Llandudno, 42294, Pte., d. o w., F. & F., 26-9-17, formerly 29422 R. Welch R.

GALE Sydney Charles, *b* Westbourne Park, London, *e* Salford, Lancs. (Seedley, Manchester), 302982, Pte., d. of. w, F. & F., 15-6-17.

GARDINER Alfred Robert, *b* Tooting, Surrey, *e* Walton-on-the-Hill, Surrey (Tooting), 41828, Pte., k. in a., F. & F., 23-4-17, formerly 32768 E. Surrey R.

GARNER John, *b* Manchester, *e* Manchester, 34850, Pte., k. in a., F. & F.. 16-6-17.

GARNER William, *b* Stockport, Cheshire, *e* Chester, Cheshire (Stockport), 245106, Pte., k. in a. F. & F., 27-7-17, formerly, 265092 King's Own Royal Lancaster R.

GARRETT Alexander, *b* Farnworth, Lancs., *e* Sandycroft, Flint (Oldham, Lancs.), 48649, Pte., d. of w., F. & F., 16-6-17.

GAYNON Edward, *e* Oldham, Lancs. (Failsworth, Lancs.), 39634, Sgt., k. in a., F. & F., 23-4-17.

GENT Herbert, *b* Nottingham, *e* Nottingham, 43065, Pte., k. in a., F. & F., 23-4-17, formerly 22731 Notts & Derby R.

GEORGE Alfred, *b* St. Martin's, Birmingham, *e* Birmingham, 43076, L/Cpl., k. in a., F. & F., 30-7-17, formerly 11378 Oxf. and Bucks L.I.

GIBSON Frederick, *b* St. Helens, Lancs., *e* Manchester, 7653, Pte., k. in a., F. & F., 1-7-16.

GIBSON Henry, *b* Clitheroe, Lancs., *e* Manchester (Liverpool), 27128, L/Cpl., k. in a., F. & F., 23-4-17.

GIBSON	William, *b* Manchester, *e* Manchester (Hulme, Manchester), 245105, Pte., k. in a., F. & F., 31-7-17, formerly 51244 R.W. Fus.
GIBSON	William, *b* Nantwich, Cheshire, *e* Manchester (Harpurhey, Manchester), 32539, Pte., k. in a., F. & F., 30-7-16.
GILBERT	Albert David, *b* Southwark, Surrey, *e* Camberwell, Surrey (Southwark), 41826, Pte., k. in a., F. & F., 31-7-17, formerly 4441 E. Surrey R.
GILMAN	Arthur Ivan, *b* Hoxne, Suffolk, *e* York (Tadcaster, Yorks.), 377029, Pte., k. in a., F. & F., 21-3-18, formerly 22622 Yorks. L.I.
GLEAVE	Joseph Henry, *b* Newcastle-on-Tyne, *e* Manchester (Newcastle-on-Tyne), 7359, Pte., k. in a., F. & F., 30-2-16.
GLOVER	Anthony, *b* Accrington, Lancs., *e* Accrington, 54706, Pte., k. in a., F. & F., 21-3-18.
GODFREY	William Alfred, *b* Beccles, Suffolk, *e* Stratford, Essex (Walthamstow, Essex), 41862, Pte., d. of w., F. & F., 26-11-17, formerly 4227 E. Surrey R.
GOULD	Henry, *b* St. Pancras, Middlesex, *e* Wirksworth, Derby, 40914, Pte., d. of w., F. & F., 30-10-16, formerly 2926 Notts and Derby R.
GOULDING	Albert, *b* Salford, Lancs., *e* Salford (Beswick, Manchester), 49356, Pte., d. of w., F. & F., 11-4-18.
GRATRIX	Thomas, *e* Manchester (Salford, Lancs.), 250329, L/Cpl., d. of w., F. & F., 28-3-18.
GRAY	Albert, *b* Hulme, Manchester, *e* Manchester, 27165, Pte., d. of w., F. & F., 4-5-17.
GREEN	Obadiah, *b* Burslem, Staffs., *e* Burslem, 42295, Pte., k. in a., F. & F., 31-7-17, formerly T/260141 R.A.S.C.
GREEN	Oswald, *b* Wigan, Lancs., *e* Wigan, 27307, L/Cpl., k. in a., F. & F., 21-3-18.
GREEN	Stanley Edmund, *b* Birkdale, Lancs., *e* Manchester (Ashton-in-Makerfield, Lancs.), 6877, L/Cpl., k. in a., F. & F., 1-7-16.
GREENFIELD	Albert, *b* Hunslet, Yorks., *e* Manchester, 25268, Pte., d., F. & F., 25-3-18.
GREENHALGH	Charles, *b* Bury, Lancs., *e* Bury, 245111, Pte., d., F. & F., 13-10-18, formerly 42731 R. Lancs. R.
GRESTY	Eric, *b* Moss Side, Manchester, *e* Manchester (Urmston, Lancs.), 7449, Pte., k. in a., F. & F., 5-5-16.
GRIFFIN	Michael, *e* Manchester (Patricroft, Manchester), 7221, Pte., k. in a., F. & F., 31-7-17.
GROVER	Alfred Charles, *b* Hampstead, Middlesex, *e* Kilburn, Middlesex, 51028, Pte., k. in a., F. & F., 31-7-17, formerly G/19261 Middlesex R.
GUILFORD	John Charles, *b* Manchester, *e* Manchester (Moston, Manchester), 25959, L/Cpl., d., F. & F., 1-4-17.
GUNN	Alfred Edward, *b* Hoxton, Middlesex, *e* Wimbledon, Surrey (Stratford, Essex), 41856, Pte., k. in a., F. & F., 23-4-17, formerly 3124 E. Surrey R.
GUNN	Thomas Stanley, *b* Hoxton, Middlesex, *e* Wimbledon, Surrey (Stratford, Essex), 41825, Pte., d., F. & F., 6-5-17, formerly 2519 E. Surrey R.
HADFIELD	Douglas Duncan, *b* Prestwich, Lancs., *e* Manchester (Prestwich), 6496, L/Cpl., k. in a., F. & F., 12-10-16.
HALL	John Willie, *b* Moorside, Oldham, Lancs., *e* Oldham, 28248, Cpl., k. in a., F. & F., 21-3-18.

HALL — Joseph, *b* Blackburn, Lancs., *e* Lancaster, 245155, Pte., k. in a., F. & F., 31-7-17, formerly 265527 R. Lancs. R.

HALLIDAY — Anthony, *b* Runcorn, Cheshire, *e* Manchest.r, 27045, Pte., k. in a., F. & F., 23-4-17.

HALLIGAN — John Henry, *b* Liverpool, *e* Birkenhead, Cheshire, 42146, Pte., d. of w., F. & F., 3-8-17, formerly T/4159889 R.A.S.C.

HALSALL — Sidney Ashton, *b* Heaton Chapel, Cheshire, *e* Manchester (Levenshulme, Manchester), 6621, Pte., k. in a., F. & F., 1-7-16.

HAMER — John, *b* Bolton, Lancs., *e* Bury, Lancs. (Bolton, Lancs.), 377795, Pte., k. in a., F. & F., 22-9-17, formerly 4468 Lancashire F.

HAMER — Willie, *b* Burnley, Lancs., *e* Burnley, 245116, Pte., d., F. & F., 16-10-18, formerly 4132 E. Lancs. R.

HAMSHAW — William Henry, *b* Bethnal Green, Middlesex, *e* Southall, Middlesex, 51035, Pte., k. in a., F. & F., 30-7-17, formerly G/19323 Middlesex R.

HANCOCK — James Craven, *b* Leeds, *e* Manchester (Salford, Lancs.), 303011, Pte., k. in a., F. & F., 15-6-17.

HARDING — Albert, *b* Bradford, Lancs., *e* Manchester (Bradford), 4914, Sgt., d. of w., F. & F., 29-3-18.

HARDMAN — John Edward, *b* Birmingham, *e* Birmingham, 43080, Sgt., k. in a., F. & F., 23-4-17, formerly 23459 Worc. R.

HARLING — John Thomas, *b* Gorton, Manchester, *e* Manchester (Failsworth, Lancs.), 6750, Pte., k. in a., F. & F., 1-7-16. M.M.

HARRISON — Albert, *b* Chorlton-on-Medlock, Lancs., *e* Manchester (Withington, Manchester), 6381, Pte., k. in a., F. & F., 1-7-16.

HARRISON — Henry, *b* Flimby, Cumb'land, *e* Workington, Cumb'land (Flimby), 43025, Pte., k. in a., F. & F., 23-4-17, formerly 15379, Border R.

HARRISON — John, *b* Hulme, Manchester, *e* Manchester, 26728, L/Cpl., k. in a., F. & F., 22-9-17.

HART — William Robert, *b* Walworth, Surrey, *e* Camberwell, Surrey (Herne Hill, Surrey), 41867, L/Cpl., k. in a., F. & F., 31-7-17, formerly 4189 E. Surrey R.

HATTON — John, *b* Oldham, Lancs., *e* Ashton-u-Lyne, Lancs. (Oldham), 47897, Pte., k. in a., F. & F., 8-5-18.

HAWLEY — John George, *b* Gorton, Manchester, *e* Manchester (Gorton), 6252, Pte., k. in a., F. & F., 30-7-16.

HAWORTH — Robert, *b* Blackburn, Lancs., *e* Blackburn, 245131, Pte., k. in a., F. & F., 31-7-17, formerly 265887, E. Lancs. R.

HAWXBY — Harold, *b* Flixton, Lancs., *e* Manchester (Ainsdale, Southport, Lancs.), 7115, A/C.S.M., k. in a., F. & F., 9-7-16.

HEALD — Ernest, *b* Manchester, *e* Manchester, 27120, Pte., k. in a., F. & F., 30-7-16.

HEAP — Hargreaves, *b* Burnley, Lancs., *e* Burnley, 42297, Pte., k. in a., F. & F., 31-7-17.

HEATHCOTE — Harold, *b* Manchester, *e* Manchester, 21412, Cpl., k. in a., F. & F., 24-3-18.

HENDERSON — John Hall, *b* Heaton Chapel, Cheshire, *e* Manchester (Hale, Cheshire), 46701, L/Cpl., k. in a., F. & F., 21-3-18.

HENRY — Ellis, *b* Tonge Moor, Bolton, Lancs., *e* Manchester (Harpurhey, Manchester), 7001, Pte., k. in a., F. & F., 1-7-16.

HEWITT	Edward Thomas, *b* Ardwick, Manchester, *e* Manchester (Bury, Lancs.), 7303, Pte., k. in a., F. & F., 9-7-16.
HICKEY	Edward, *b* Nottingham, *e* Manchester (Nottingham), 47489, Pte., k. in a., F. & F., 23-4-17.
HIGHAM	Frederick, *b* Blackburn, Lancs., *e* Blackburn, 245129, Pte., d. of w., F. & F., 5-8-17, formerly 3707 East Lancs. R.
HILL	Rowland, *b* All Saints, Manchester, *e* Manchester (Seedley, Manchester), 6503, Cpl., k. in a., F. & F., 1-7-16.
HILL	Rowland, *b* Salford, Lancs., *e* Manchester, 6628, Pte., k. in a., F. & F., 12-10-16.
HILTON	Robert, *b* Royton, Lancs., *e* Royton, 32942, Pte., d. of w., F. & F., 12-10-16.
HINDLEY	George, *b* Leigh, Lancs., *e* Ashton-u-Lyne, Lancs. (Leigh), 25227, Pte., k. in a., or d. of w., F. & F., 23-4-17.
HOBSON	Frank Herbert, *b* Northwich, Cheshire, *e* Manchester (Northwich), 6389, L/Cpl., k. in a., F. & F., 1-7-16.
HOCKADAY	Fred Lee, *b* Longsight, Manchester, *e* Manchester, 17652, Pte., k. in a., F. & F., 23-4-17.
HOCKNEY	James, *b* Durham, *e* Manchester, 31211, Pte., k. in a., F. & F., 21-3-18.
HODGSON	Percy, *b* Leeds, *e* Winbourne, Dorset, 41865, Cpl., k. in a., F. & F., 25-4-18, formerly 4001 E. Surrey R., M.M.
HOLMES	Fred, *b* Frampton, Leeds, *e* Northampton, 51039, Pte., d. of w., F. & F., 30-7-17, formerly G/86542 Middlesex R.
HOLT	Samuel Ashmore, *b* Old Trafford, Manchester, *e* Manchester, 6888, Pte., k. in a., F. & F., 1-7-16.
HOPKINSON	Alfred Holt, *e* Oldham, Lancs. (Shaw, Lancs.), 46817, Pte., k. in a., F. & F., 21-3-18, M.M.
HORNBY	Luke, *b* Preesall, Lancs., *e* Fleetwood, Lancs. (Whalley, Lancs.), 245128, Pte., k. in a., F. & F., 31-7-17, formerly 265316 R. Lancs. R.
HORROCKS	Robert, *b* Warrington, Lancs., *e* Manchester (Warrington), 27034, Pte., k. in a., F. & F., 22-7-17.
HOUGHTON	Gerald Leighton, *b* Port Sunlight, Cheshire, *e* Manchester (Northwich, Cheshire), 6385, Pte., k. in a., F. & F., 3-5-16.
HOWARTH	Albert Edward, *b* Leigh, Lancs., *e* Heaton Park, Manchester (Warrington, Lancs.), 7300, L/Cpl., k. in a., F. & F., 9-7-16.
HOWARTH	Harry, *b* St. Annes-on-the-Sea, Lancs., *e* Blackpool, Lancs. (St. Annes-on-the-Sea), 39238, Pte., k. in a., F. & F., 31-7-17, formerly 6/28430 Cameron Highlanders.
HOWARTH	James, *b* Chadderton, Lancs., *e* Oldham, 33193, Pte., k. in a., F. & F., 23-11-16.
HOWELLS	Alec, *b* Chorlton-on-Medlock, Lancs., *e* Manchester, 7121, Pte., k. in a., F. & F., 1-7-16.
HOYE	Archer, *b* Hulme, Manchester, *e* Manchester, 6630, Sgt., k. in a., F. & F., 21-3-18.
HUGHES	Frank, *b* Heaton Mersey, Lancs., *e* Manchester (Heaton Mersey), 6509, L/Cpl., k. in a., F. & F., 3-6-16.
HUGHES	Herbert, *b* Manchester, *e* Manchester, 7391, Pte., d. of w., F. & F., 29-1-16.
HUGHES	Joseph, *b* Heaton Mersey, Lancs., *e* Manchester, 6760, Pte., k. in a., F. & F., 1-7-16.
HUGHES	Richard, *b* Manchester, *e* Manchester, 7465, Pte., k. in a., F. & F., 1-7-16.

HUGHES Robert James, *b* Southport, Lancs., *e* Fleetwood, Lancs., 245126, Pte., k. in a., F. & F., 31-7-17, formerly 265580 R. Lancs. R.

HUMPHREY Frederick, *b* Hildenborough, Kent, *e* Tonbridge, Kent (Stoke-on-Trent, Staffs.), 51034, Pte., k. in a., F. & F., 2-8-17, formerly G/19315 Middlesex R.

HUNT Harry, *e* Oldham, Lancs. (Shaw, Lancs.), 46819, Pte., d. of w., F. & F., 26-4-17.

HYDE Robert, *b* Manchester, *e* Manchester (Didsbury, Lancs.), 7168, Pte., k. in a., F. & F., 9-7-16.

JACKSON Ernest, *b* Manchester, *e* Ashton-u-Lyne, Lancs.(Cheetham, Manchester), 35688, L/Cpl., k. in a., F. & F., 21-3-18.

JELLY Frederick, *b* St. Andrew's, Manchester, *e* Manchester, 7011, Pte., d. of w., F. & F., 4-2-16.

JESSOP Charles Oswald, *b* Sale, Cheshire, *e* Manchester (Sale), 7013, L/Cpl., k. in a., F. & F., 9-7-16.

JOHNSON Ben, *b* Hale, Cheshire, *e* Manchester (Bowdon, Cheshire), 6511, Pte., k. in a., F. & F., 9-7-16.

JOHNSON Charles, *b* Cheetham Hill, Manchester, *e* Manchester (Bradford, Lancs.), 43917, Pte., k. in a., F. & F., 21-3-18.

JOHNSON Charles Stanley *b* Cheetham, Manchester, *e* Manchester, 6263, L/Cpl., k. in a., F. & F., 5-5-16.

JOHNSON Harold, *b* Manchester, *e* Manchester (Kearsley, Bolton, Lancs.), 7578, Sgt., k. in a., F. & F., 31-7-17.

JOHNSON Harry Hindley, *b* Bury, Lancs., *e* Heaton Park, Manchester (Higher Broughton, Manchester), 7435, Pte., k. in a., F. & F., 30-7-16.

JONES Arthur, *b* Swinton, Lancs., *e* Swinton, 302879, Pte., k. in a., F. & F., 31-7-17.

JONES Ellis, *b* Rhyl, Flint., *e* Wrexham (Rhyl), 245141, Pte., d. of w., F. & F., 18-8-17, formerly 51234 R. W. Fus.

JONES Vaughan, *b* Flint, *e* Manchester (Holywell, Flint), 6766, Pte., d. of w., F. & F., 15-10-16.

JONES William Christmas, *b* Abererch, Carnarvon, *e* Manchester, 7339, Pte., d. of w., F. & F., 12-9-17.

JOYCE John Joseph, *b* Manchester, *e* Manchester, 49421, Pte., k. in a., F. & F., 21-3-18.

KAY Martin, *b* Lancaster, *e* Manchester (Bradford, Manchester), 49601, Pte., k. in a., F. & F., 21-3-18.

KEANE Francis, *b* Manchester, *e* Manchester, 35048, Pte., k. in a., F. & F., 15-9-16.

KEEGAN Alfred, *b* Manchester, *e* Manchester, 35593, Pte., k. in a., F. & F., 15-10-16.

KEELING George Henry, *b* Salford, *e* Manchester, 7388, Pte., k. in a., F. & F., 5-3-16.

KEELING Samuel, *b* Chorlton-on-Medlock, Lancs., *e* Manchester, 6638, Pte., d. of w., F. & F., 31-7-16.

KELLY Cecil Hartley, *b* Harpurhey, Lancs., *e* Manchester (Blackley, Manchester), 6266, L/Cpl., k. in a., F. & F., 3-2-16.

KEMP Frederick, *b* Turton, Bolton, Lancs., *e* Manchester (Seedley, Manchester), 49174, Pte., k. in a., F. & F., 13-1-18.

KENWORTHY Fred, *b* Oldham, Lancs., *e* Ashton-u-Lyne, Lancs. (Oldham), 57330, Pte., d. of w., F. & F., 2-5-18.

KENYON George, *b* Manchester, *e* Manchester, 27351, Pte., k. in a., F. & F., 30-7-16.

KEWER	Henry John, *b* Streatham, Surrey, *e* Wimbledon, Surrey (Streatham), 41838, Pte., k. in a., F. & F., 28-3-17, formerly 32786 E. Surrey R.
KEWLEY	Thomas, *b* Manchester, *e* Manchester, 277099, Pte., d. of w., F. & F., 30-3-18.
KILDING	Allan, *b* Ripon, *e* Manchester (Ripon), 6517, Pte., k. in a., F. & F., 9-7-16.
KILGOUR	Ralph, *b* Manchester, *e* Manchester, 302903, Pte., d. of w., F. & F., 26-6-17.
KIMPTON	Frederick Arthur, *b* Bedford, *e* Leicester, 41040, L/Cpl., k. in a., F. & F., 21-3-18., formerly 5485 Leicester R.
KINDLEYSIDES	Henry James, *b* Skirwith, Cumb'land, *e* Shap, West'land (Cliburn, West'land), 43029, L/Cpl., k. in a., F. & F., 21-3-18, formerly 17545 Border R.
KNOWLES	Albert, *b* Salford, Lancs., *e* Manchester, 6898, Pte., d. of w., F. & F., 15-10-16.
KNOWLES	James, *b* Hyde, Cheshire, *e* Manchester (Hyde), 7614, Pte., k. in a., F. & F., 1-7-16.
LAIT	Clifford Sargeant, *b* Tendring, Essex, *e* Holloway, Middlesex (Brereton, Staffs.), 43015, Pte., d. of w., F. & F., 13-10-16, formerly 10822 Essex R.
LAMB	Crispin, *b* Hollinwood, Lancs., *e* Hollinwood, 37814, Pte., d. of w., F. & F., 23-3-18.
LAMB	William Arthur, *b* Glodwick, Oldham, Lancs., *e* Oldham, 14527, Pte., k. in a., F. & F., 27-4-18.
LAMBERT	Joseph, *b* Ardwick, Manchester, *e* Manchester (Stockport, Cheshire), 6269, Pte., k. in a., F. & F., 1-7-16.
LANCASTER	Cornelius, *b* Pemberton, Lancs., *e* Wigan, Lancs. (Ince, Wigan), 29431, L/Cpl., d. of w., F. & F., 7-8-17.
LANCASTER	John, *b* Failsworth, Lancs., *e* Hollinwood, Lancs. (Failsworth), 34709, Pte., k. in a., F. & F., 23-4-07.
LANDERYON	Henry John, *b* St. Pancras, Middlesex, *e* St. Pancras (Kentish Town, Middlesex), 57341, Pte., k. in a., F. & F., 3-5-18, formerly 36373 N. Lancashire R.
LAUD	Charles Reginald, *b* Brackley, Northants, *e* Worksop, Notts. (Welbourn, Lincoln), 40816, Pte., k. in a., F. & F., 24-12-16, formerly 33729 Notts and Derby R.
LAWRENSON	Frederick Joseph, *b* New Cross, Manchester, *e* Manchester, 6769, Sgt., k. in a., F. & F., 30-7-17.
LAWSON	John, *b* Newcastle-on-Tyne, *e* Manchester (Reddish, Cheshire), 6639, Pte., k. in a., F. & F., 30-7-16.
LEATHER	Alfred, *b* Cheadle Hulme, Cheshire, *e* Manchester (Cheadle Hulme), 6270, Pte., k. in a., F. & F., 1-7-16.
LEE	Stephen, *b* Manchester, *e* Manchester, 27002, Pte., k. in a., F. & F., 27-1-16.
LEESON	John, *b* Manchester, *e* Manchester, 27043, Pte., k. in a., F. & F., 30-7-16.
LEIGHTON	James, *b* Manchester, *e* Manchester, 202960, Pte., k. in a., F. & F., 21-3-18.
LEVEY	Isaac, *b* Manchester, *e* Salford, Lancs., 46652, Pte., k. in a., F. & F., 5-4-17.
LILLEY	John, *b* Stockport, Cheshire, *e* Oldham, Lancs., 27232, Pte., k. in a., F. & F., 15-6-17.
LITTLE	William, *b* Arlecdon, Cumberland, *e* Manchester (Cleator, Cumberland), 35804, Pte., k. in a., F. & F., 18-10-16.
LITTLEJOHN	James, *b* St. John's, Glasgow, *e* Manchester, 6772, Pte., k. in a., F. & F., 30-7-16.

LITTLER John Laurence, *b* Witton, Cheshire, *e* Manchester (Northwich, Cheshire), 6400, L/Cpl., k. in a., F. & F., 18-10-16.

LLOYD William, *b* Mossley Common, Lancs., *e* Leigh, Lancs. (Boothstown, Lancs.), 32622, Pte., d. of w., F. & F., 21-8-17.

LODGE Alfred Mark, *b* Ashted, Warwick, *e* Birmingham, 43081, Pte., k. in a., F. & F., 23-4-17, formerly 17121 Oxf. and Bucks L.I.

LORD Tom, *e* Bury, Lancs., 352937, Pte., k. in a., F. & F., 21-3-18, formerly 4569 Lancashire Fus.

LOW Charles, *b* Dundee, *e* Ashton-u-Lyne, Lancs. (Urmston, Lancs.), 39972, Pte., k. in a., F. & F., 21-4-17.

LOYNDS Harold, *b* Dukinfield, Cheshire, *e* Manchester (Dukinfield), 12403, L/Sgt., k. in a., F. & F., 31-7-17.

LUCKHAM Ernest Henry, *b* Edmondsham, Dorset, *e* Sherborne, Dorset (Blandford, Dorset), 41876, Pte., k. in a., F. & F., 23-4-17, formerly 32829, E. Surrey R.

LUCKINGS Frederick, *b* Battersea, Surrey, *e* Kingston-on-Thames, Surrey (Tooting, Surrey), 50962, Pte., k. in a., F. & F., 27-4-18, formerly G/86599 Middlesex R.

LUCKMAN Frank Abraham, *b* Liverpool, *e* Manchester (Chorlton-on-Medlock, Lancs.), 6643, Sgt., k. in a., F. & F., 10-2-16.

MAHER Joseph Francis, *b* Hulme, Manchester, *e* Manchester, 6405, Pte., k. in a., F. & F., 1-7-16.

MAINWARING Ernest, *b* Ancoats, Manchester, *e* Manchester, 7541, Pte., k. in a., F. & F., 1-7-16.

MALEY Thomas, *b* St. Helens, Lancs., *e* Manchester (St. Helens), 6775, L/Cpl., d. of w., F. & F., 24-7-16.

MALLALIEU Leo Sebastian, *b* Denton, Manchester, *e* Manchester, 7393, Pte., k. in a., F. & F., 1-7-16.

MALLARD John Edward, *b* Ancoats, Manchester, *e* Manchester, 6648, L/Cpl., k. in a., F. & F., 30-7-16.

MALLINSON Robert Henry, *b* Levens, West'land, *e* Kendal, West'land, 43031, L/Cpl., d. of w., F. & F., 25-9-17, formerly 16336 Border R.

MARKS Henry, *b* Bow, Middlesex, *e* Poplar, Middlesex, 42302, Pte., k. in a., F. & F., 27-4-18, formerly T/4/276097 R.A.S.C.

MARSH Osborne George, *b* Hulme, Manchester, *e* Manchester, 11604, Sgt., k. in a., F. & F., 31-7-17, M.M.

MARTIN Fred, *b* Hadfield, Derby, *e* Manchester (Hadfield), 6524, Cpl., d. of w., F. & F., 18-10-16.

MARTIN Sidney Bert, *b* Wolverhampton, *e* Wolverhampton, 59213, Pte., k. in a., F. & F., 21-3-18, formerly S4/218685 R.A.S.C.

MASON Christopher, *b* Chorlton, Manchester, *e* Manchester, 6276, Pte., d. of w., F. & F., 12-10-16.

MASON James, *b* Manchester, *e* Manchester (Wigan, Lancs.), 26164, Pte., d. of w., F. & F., 16-4-18.

MASON Thomas, *b* Clayton-le-Moors, Lancs., *e* Accrington, Lancs. (Clayton-le-Moors), 64579, Pte., d. of w., F. & F., 29-10-18, formerly 82208 Liverpool R.

MASSEY Emmanuel, *b* Manchester, *e* Manchester, 35643, Pte., k. in a., F. & F., 21-3-18.

MASTERS William Henry, *b* West Cocker, Somerset, *e* Weymouth, Dorset (Crewkerne, Somerset), 41878, L/Cpl., d. of w., F. & F., 21-3-18, formerly 32831 E. Surrey R.

MATHER	Leonard, *b* Pendleton, Lancs., *e* Manchester (Seedley, Mancheters), 6275, Pte., k. in a., F. & F., 9-7-16.
MAYORS	James, *b* Salford, Lancs., *e* Manchester (Salford), 6403, Pte., k. in a., F. & F., 23-4-17.
McDONOUGH	John James, *b* Hulme, Manchester, *e* Manchester, 6779, Pte., k. in a., F. & F., 1-7-16.
McDOUGALL	Frank, *b* Salford, Lancs., *e* Gorton, Manchester, 35658, L/Cpl., k. in a., F. & F., 23-4-17.
McELHINNEY	Joseph, *b* Rusholme, Manchester, *e* Manchester, 6777, L/Cpl., k. in a., F. & F., 14-10-16.
McGOW	John George, *b* St. John's, Carlisle, *e* Manchester (Hebburn-on-Tyne, Durham), 6778, Pte., k. in a., F. & F., 1-7-16.
McKENNA	John, *b* Ancoats, Manchester, *e* Manchester, 6780, Pte., k. in a., F. & F., 15-5-16.
McKIERMAN	Arthur, *b* Manchester, *e* Manchester, 27378, Pte., d. of w., F. & F., 13-8-16.
McMINN	William James, *b* Chorlton-on-Medlock, Manchester, *e* Manchester (Withington, Lancs.), 6646, Sgt., k. in a., F. & F., 31-7-17.
McSPIRIT	John, *b* Greenheys, Manchester, *e* Manchester, 6781, Pte., k. in a., F. & F., 27-4-18.
MEARS	Samuel Frith, *b* Northwich, Cheshire, *e* Manchester (Northwich), 7420, Pte., k. in a., F. & F., 1-7-16.
MEASHAM	Eric, *b* Marple, Cheshire, *e* Manchester (Holmes Chapel, Cheshire), 7624, L/Cpl., k. in a., F. & F., 9-7-16.
MEDLEY	James Holland, *b* Swanage, Dorset, *e* Manchester (Lower Kersal, Lancs.), 7674, Pte., k. in a., F. & F., 1-7-16.
MEIN	William, *b* Dalston, Cumb'land, *e* Manchester (Stockport, Cheshire), 6527, L/Cpl., k. in a., F. & F., 1-7-16, M.M.
MERCER	John, *b* Liverpool, *e* Liverpool (Speke, Lancs.), 401042, Pte., k. in a., F. & F., 21-3-18.
MERRIMAN	Arthur Preston, *b* Penge, Kent, *e* Peckham, Surrey (West Croydon, Surrey), 41839, Pte., k. in a, F. & F., 31-7-17, formerly 32790 E. Surrey R.
MILLS	Richard, *b* Oldham, Lancs., *e* Oldham, 48590, Pte., k. in a., F. & F., 21-3-18.
MILLS	Reuben, *e* Worksop, Notts (Bulwell, Notts), 40824, Pte., k. in a., F.& F., 31-7-17, formerly 3832 Notts and Derby R.
MILLS	Stanley Christopher, *b* Oldham, Lancs., *e* Oldham, 33356, Pte., k. in a., F. & F., 31-7-17.
MILLS	William, *b* Queen's Park, Manchester, *e* Manchester (Sale, Cheshire), 6655, L/Cpl., k. in a., F. & F., 23-4-17.
MILSOM	Henry James, *b* St. Luke's, Manchester, *e* Manchester, 6654, L/Cpl., k. in a., F. & F., 1-7-16.
MITCHELL	James, *b* Ardwick, Manchester, *e* Manchester, 7028, Sgt., k. in a., F. & F., 1-7-16.
MITCHELL	John, *e* Manchester (Bradford, Manchester), 277708, Pte., k. in a., F. & F., 27-4-18.
MONTEVERDE	Edwin, *b* Manchester, *e* Manchester, 33895, Pte., d. of w., F. & F., 3-1-18.
MOONEY	Edward John, *b* Liverpool, *e* Liverpool, 400980, Pte., k. in a., F. & F., 27-4-18.
MOORE	Harry, *b* Manchester, *e* Manchester, 27320, Pte., k. in a., F. & F., 12-10-16.
MOORE	William, *b* Oldham, Lancs., *e* Royton, Lancs. (Oldham), 33450, Pte., k. in a., F. & F., 9-7-16.

MOORES John, *b* Chadderton, Lancs., *e* Chadderton (Middleton Junction, Lancs.), 37980, Pte., k. in a., F. & F., 23-4-17.

MOOREWOOD Edward Hugh, *b* Crewe, Cheshire, *e* Ashton-u-Lyne, Lancs. (Denton, Lancs.), 46835, Pte., d. of w., F. & F., 28-3-17.

MORAN Fred, *b* Salford, Lancs., *e* Salford, 377948, Pte., k. in a., F. & F., 21-3-18.

MORGANS John, *b* Morriston, Glam., *e* Llanelly, Carmarthen (Langhor, near Swansea, Glam.), 42304, Pte., k. in a., F. & F., 31-7-17, formerly 160829 R.F.A.

MORRIS Sidney, *b* Harpurhey, Lancs., *e* Manchester (Harpurhey), 7035, Pte., k. in a., F. & F., 1-7-16.

MORTON Sydney, *b* Leeds, *e* Leeds, 40830, Pte., d., F. & F., 21-2-17, formerly 1853 W. Yorkshire R.

MOSCROP Ernest Arthur, *b* Clapham, Surrey, *e* Croydon, Surrey (Thornton Heath, Surrey), 51195, Pte., k. in a., F. & F., 31-7-17.

MOTTERSHEAD George, *b* Manchester, *e* Manchester (Chorlton-on-Medlock, Lancs.), 27144, Pte., k. in a., F. & F., 5-5-16.

MULLEADY John, *b* Manchester, *e* Manchester (Beswick, Lancs.), 7516, Pte., k. in a., F. & F., 30-7-16.

MULVANNEY Henry, *b* Manchester, *e* Stockport, Cheshire (Edgeley, Liverpool), 64516, Pte., k. in a., F. & F., 22-9-18, formerly 77853 R.W. Fus.

MURDOCK Andrew, *b* St. Peter's, Manchester, *e* Ashton-u-Lyne, Lancs. (Salford, Lancs.), 7384, Pte., k. in a., F. & F., 22-4-17.

MURPHY Edward, A. *b* Liverpool, *e* Liverpool, 61113, Pte., k. in a., F. & F., 21-3-18.

MYERS Thomas, *b* Hulme, Manchester, *e* Manchester (Hulme), 6914, Pte., k. in a., F. & F., 8-5-18.

NASH John, *b* Cheetham, Manchester, *e* Heaton Park, Manchester (Lower Crumpsall, Manchester), 7637, Pte., k. in a., F. & F., 1-7-16.

NAYLOR Herbert, *b* Bradford, Yorks., *e* Manchester (West Didsbury, Manchester), 6660, Sgt., k. in a., F. & F., 12-10-16.

NEILD Francis Albert, *b* St. George's, Manchester, *e* Manchester, 6282, Pte., k. in a., F. & F., 1-7-16.

NEWELL James, *e* Eccles, Lancs., (Walkden, Lancs.) 201517, Cpl., k. in a., F. & F., 31-7-17.

NICOL Peter, *b* Peterhead, Aberdeen, *e* Manchester (Clayton, Manchester), 37937, Pte., d., home, 22-12-17.

NORRIS John, *b* Newton Heath, Manchester, *e* Manchester, 8916, Pte., k. in a., F. & F., 14-6-16.

OATES Benjamin, *b* St. George's, London, *e* Stratford (Shadwell, Middlesex), 43058, A/Cpl., k. in a., F. & F., 18-10-16, formerly 3451 R. Lancashire R.

O'BRIEN John, *b* Manchester, *e* Manchester, 11273, Pte., k. in a., F. & F., 1-7-16.

ODELL Arthur Charles, *b* Newport Pagnell, Bucks., *e* Pottersbury, Northants, (Winslow, Bucks.), 51055, Pte., d. of w., F. & F., 30-4-18, formerly G/86552 Middlesex R.

OGDEN Arthur, *b* Manchester, *e* Manchester (Irlam, Lancs.), 31066, Pte., k. in a., F. & F., 31-7-17.

OGDEN Frederick Ebern, *b* Ascension, Manchester, *e* Manchester (Prestwich, Manchester), 6286, L/Cpl., k. in a., F. & F., 1-7-16.

OGDEN — Harry, *b* Manchester, *e* Manchester (Collyhurst, Lancs.), 27349, Pte., k. in a., F. & F., 22-4-17.

OGDEN — Thomas, *b* Oldham, Lancs., *e* Hollinwood, Lancs. (Oldham), 28457, L/Cpl., k. in a., F. & F., 3-12-17.

OLDFIELD — William Henry, *b* Manchester, *e* Manchester, 35697, Pte., k. in a., F. & F., 27-3-17.

OLIVER — Joseph Stanley, *b* Stockport, Cheshire, *e* Stockport, 54919, Pte., k. in a., F. & F., 27-4-18.

O'NEILL — Charles, *e* Ashton-u-Lyne, Lancs. (Preston, Lancs.), 352329, Pte., k. in a., F. & F., 21-3-18.

ORMROD — Samuel Morgan, *b* All Saints, Manchester, *e* Manchester, 7177, Pte., k. in a., F. & F., 1-7-16.

OWEN — Richard, *b* Harpurhey, Lancs., *e* Manchester, 9235, L/Cpl., k. in a., F. & F., 21-3-18.

PADGHAM — Gilbert Arthur, *b* Kentish Town, Middlesex, *e* Tottenham, Middlesex, 51056, Pte., d. of w., F. & F., 28-11-17, formerly G/19266, Middlesex R.

PARKER — Albert Edwin, *b* Gorton, Manchester, *e* Manchester, 7361, Pte., k. in a., F. & F., 1-7-16.

PARKER — Ernest, *b* Coppull, Lancs., *e* Ashton-u-Lyne, Lancs. (Worthington, Wigan, Lancs.), 401217, Pte., d., F. & F., 12-5-18.

PARKES — Frederick, *b* Northwich, Cheshire, *e* Northwich, 32546, Pte., k. in a., F. & F., 30-7-16.

PARKES — Herbert, *b* Pemberton, Lancs., *e* Ashton-u-Lyne, Lancs. (Wigan, Lancs.), 35503, L/Cpl., k. in a., F. & F., 18-6-17.

PARKIN — Frederick William, *b* Oldham, Lancs., *e* Oldham, 37809, Pte., d. of w., F. & F., 24-4-17.

PARKIN — John, *b* Radford, Notts., *e* Mansfield, Notts. (Sutton-in-Ashfield, Notts.), 40847, Pte., d. of w., F. & F., 25-4-17, formerly 1629 Notts and Derby R.

PARKINSON — Francis, *b* Salford, Lancs., *e* Manchester (Salford), 27047, Pte., k. in a., F. & F., 12-10-16.

PATRICK — George, *b* Collyhurst, Manchester, *e* Manchester, 6540, L/Cpl., k. in a., F. & F., 30-7-16.

PEARCE — Arthur, *b* Limerick, *e* Colchester, Essex, 1248, L/Sgt., k. in a., F. & F., 23-4-17.

PEARSON — Joseph Palister, *b* Loftus, York, *e* Manchester (East Loftus), 25899, Pte., k. in a., F. & F., 31-7-17.

PEAT — Charles, *b* Bermuda, *e* Manchester (Collyhurst, Manchester), 251621, L/Cpl., k. in a., F. & F., 28-3-18.

PEMBERTON — Jesse Edwin, *b* Glossop, Derby, *e* Manchester, 33704, Cpl., k. in a., F.& F., 21-3-18.

PETERSON — Samuel, *b* Widnes, Lancs., *e* Manchester (Widnes), 26484, L/Cpl., k. in a., F. & F., 22-4-17.

PETTIT — Herbert, *e* Northampton, 51059, Pte., d. of w., F. & F., 6-8-17, formerly G/86583 Middlesex R.

PHILLIPS — William, *b* Horwich, Lancs., *e* Manchester (Lostock, near Bolton, Lancs.), 7421, Pte., k. in a., F. & F., 1-7-16.

PICKERING — Edwin, *b* Manchester, *e* Manchester, 21615, Pte., k. in a., F. & F., 27-4-18.

PICKERING — Horace, *b* Winnington, Cheshire, *e* Manchester (Winnington), 6418, L/Cpl., k. in a., F. & F., 5-5-16.

PICKERING — John Wasley, *b* Clayton Bridge, Lancs., *e* Ashton-u-Lyne, Lancs. (Oldham, Lancs.), 37648, Pte., k. in a., F. & F., 21-3-18.

PLATT James, *b* Mossley, Manchester, *e* Ashton-u-Lyne, Lancs. (Dukinfield, Cheshire), 39993, Pte., k. in a., F. & F., 22-4-17.

POINTON Trevor, *b* Shrewsbury, Shrops., *e* Manchester (Moston, Manchester), 6793, Pte., d. of w., F. & F., 26-2-16.

POLLITT George, *b* Collyhurst, Manchester, *e* Manchester, 6921, Pte., d. of w., F. & F., 20-2-16.

POWER Lawrence, *b* Rensgrave, Co. Wexford, *e* Manchester (Arthurstown, Co. Waterford), 54101, Pte., k. in a., F. & F., 3-4-17.

POYNTON Herbert, *b* Manchester, *e* Manchester (Salford, Lancs.), 7528, Pte., d., F. & F., 4-3-17.

PRESTON Frederick, *b* Liverpool, *e* Liverpool (Wavertree, Lancs.), 61126, Pte., d., F. & F., 6-10-18.

PRICE Charles Frederick Tempest, *b* Brooklands, Cheshire, *e* Manchester (Sale, Cheshire), 7180, Pte., k. in a., F. & F., 15-6-16.

PRIESTNER William Henry, *b* Handforth, Cheshire, *e* Manchester (Handforth), 10260, Pte., k. in a., F. & F., 15-6-17.

PULLEN Nelson Arthur, *b* Manchester, *e* Manchester (Knighton, Radnor), 26388, Pte., k. in a., F. & F., 1-7-16.

PYE John Samuel, *b* Lowestoft, Suffolk, *e* Lowestoft, 57357, Pte., d., F. & F., 7-10-18, formerly 21364 Suffolk R.

QUALEY Patrick, *b* Wigan, Lancs., *e* Ashton-u-Lyne, Lancs. (Wigan), 35442, Pte., k. in a., F. & F., 31-7-17.

QUANN James, *b* Waterford, Ireland, *e* Manchester, 27093, L/Cpl., k. in a., F. & F., 28-9-17.

QUINLIVAN Joseph, *b* Fulleage, Burnley, Lancs., *e* Ashton-u-Lyne, Lancs. (Burnley), 1667, Sgt., k. in a., F. & F., 21-3-18.

RAE Thomas, *e* Manchester (Hulme, Manchester), 7618, Pte., d. of w., F. & F., 17-12-16.

RAMSDEN Herbert William, *b* Cheetham, Manchester, *e* Manchester, 7434, Pte., k. in a., F. & F., 3-5-16.

RANDALL George, *e* Mansfield, Notts. (Pleasley, near Mansfield), 40858, Pte., k. in a., F. & F., 12-9-17, formerly T34410, Notts and Derby R.

RANKIN Edwin, *e* Manchester (Ancoats, Manchester), 7525, Pte., k. in a., F. & F., 28-7-16.

RATHBONE George, *b* Manchester, *e* Manchester, 29900, Pte., k. in a., F. & F., 22-4-17.

RAVENSCROFT Samuel, *b* Ardwick, Manchester, *e* Manchester, 7252, L/Cpl., k. in a., F. & F., 1-7-16.

RAWCLIFFE Wilfred, *b* Macclesfield, Cheshire, *e* Hollinwood, Lancs. (Failsworth, Lancs.), 33644, Pte.,k. in a., F. & F., 31-7-17.

REDDY James, *b* Hulme, Manchester, *e* Manchester, 7045, C.S.M., d. of w., F. & F., 6-7-16.

REDFERN James, *b* Hulme, Manchester, *e* Manchester, 7142, Pte., d., F. & F., 20-6-16.

REDFERN William Henry, *b* Ancoats, Manchester, *e* Manchester, 12744, Pte., k. in a., F. & F., 31-7-17.

REEVE Ernest Edward, *b* Needham, Norfolk, *e* Fressingfield, East Suffolk (Harleston, Norfolk), 51062, Pte., k. in a., F. & F., 25-11-17, formerly G/19329 Middlesex R.

RICHARDSON Charles Clement, *b* Runcorn, Cheshire, *e* Manchester (Ardwick, Manchester), 7515, Pte., k. in a., F. & F., 30-7-16.

RICHARDSON George, *e* Ashton-u-Lyne, Lancs., 401099, Pte., k. in a., F. & F., 21-3-18, formerly 18781 Cheshire R.

RICK Charles, *b* Newark, Notts., *e* Newark (Grimesthorpe, Sheffield), 40850, Pte., k. in a., F. & F., 21-3-18, formerly 4022 Notts and Derby R.

RIDGWAY Alfred, *b* Manchester, *e* Salford, Lancs. (Clayton, Manchester), 35587, Pte., k. in a., F. & F., 23-4-17.

ROBERTS Ernest Walker, *b* Prestwich, Lancs., *e* Manchester (Prestwich), 6298, Pte., k. in a., F. & F., 1-7-16.

ROBERTS George Herbert, *b* Hanley, Staffs., *e* Salford, Lancs. (Fulham, Middlesex), 36952, L/Cpl., d. of w., F. & F., 27-11-17.

ROBERTS Thomas Herbert, *b* St. Stephen's, Manchester, *e* Manchester, 6672, Cpl., d. of w., F. & F., 6-7-16.

ROBINSON Arnold, *b* Weaverham, Cheshire, *e* Manchester (Weaverham), 6427, Pte., k. in a., F. & F., 1-7-16.

ROBINSON Henry, *b* Kendal, West'land, *e* Manchester (Kendal), 6797, Pte., k. in a., F. & F., 1-7-16.

ROBINSON Jack, *e* Kettering, Northants, 51061, Pte., k. in a., F. & F., 27-7-17, formerly G/19296 Middlesex R.

ROBINSON Thomas William, *b* St. Stephen's, Manchester, *e* Manchester, 6430, L/Cpl., k. in a., F. & F., 9-7-16.

ROE George, *b* Rusholme, Manchester, *e* Manchester (Rusholme), 7143, Pte., k. in a., F. & F., 25-4-18.

ROSE Francis William, *b* Liverpool, *e* Manchester (Seedley, Manchester), 27073, Pte., k. in a., F. & F., 9-7-16.

ROSEWARREN Thomas, *b* Eccles, Lancs., *e* Wigan, Lancs. (Patricroft, Lancs.), 43783, Pte., k. in a., F. & F., 21-3-18.

ROSS Harold, *b* Salford, Lancs., *e* Manchester (Salford), 6925, Pte., k. in a., F. & F., 1-7-16.

ROUSE Bernard, *b* Matlock, Derby, *e* Manchester (Matlock), 2354, Pte., k. in a., F. & F., 21-3-18.

ROUSE Samuel, *b* Winster, Derby, *e* Manchester (Winster), 31411, Pte., k. in a., F. & F., 30-7-16.

ROYLE Albert, *b* Manchester, *e* Manchester, 19244, Pte., k. in a., F. & F., 21-4-17.

ROYLE Leonard, *b* Blackley, Manchester, *e* Manchester, 39442, Pte., k. in a., F. & F., 21-3-18.

ROYLE Thomas Melbourne, *b* Knott Mill, Manchester, *e* Manchester, 27095, Pte., d. of w., Home, 3-4-17.

ROYLE William, *b* Bent Lane, Lancs., *e* Manchester (Urmston, Lancs.), 7256, Pte., d. of w., F. & F., 21-3-18.

RUBERY Luke, *b* St. Mary's, Worcester, *e* Worcester, 41893, Pte., k. in a., F. & F., 31-7-17, formerly 4152 E. Surrey R.

RUSHTON John, *e* Manchester (Wilmslow, Cheshire), 250746, Pte., d. of w., F. & F., 9-8-17.

RUSSELL Charles Archibald, *b* Heaton Mersey, Cheshire, *e* Manchester (Didsbury, Lancs.), 7144, Pte., d. of w., F. & F., 5-8-16.

RYAN Albert Edward, *b* Oldham, Lancs., *e* Oldham, 38700, Pte., d. of w., F. & F., 25-3-17.

RYCROFT Alfred Bertie, *b* Peterborough, Northants, *e* Peterborough, 51063, Pte., d. of w., F. & F., 31-7-17, formerly G/86538 Middlesex R.

RYDER John, *b* Old Trafford, Manchester, *e* Manchester, 46650, Pte., k. in a., F. & F., 21-3-18.

SANDERS John Edward, *b* Salford, Lancs., *e* Manchester (Morecambe, Lancs.), 7481, Pte., k. in a., F. & F., 9-7-16.

SANDHAM Thomas, *b* Skerton, Lancs., *e* Manchester (Newton Heath, Manchester), 18027, Pte., k. in a., F. & F., 23-4-17.

SANDIFORD Thomas Riley, *b* Hollinwood, Oldham, *e* Oldham, Lancs., 27470, Cpl., k. in a., F. & F., 21-4-17.

SCHAEFER Carl, *b* Sale, Cheshire, *e* Manchester, 6802, L/Sgt., k. in a., F. & F., 31-7-17.

SCHAEFER Herman, *b* Moss Side, Manchester, *e* Ardwick, Manchester, 44112, Pte., k. in a., F. & F., 21-3-18.

SCHOFIELD William Edward, *b* Beswick, Manchester, *e* Newton Heath, Manchester, 35554, Pte., k. in a., F. & F., 23-4-17.

SCHOLES Walter, *b* St. Michael's, Manchester, *e* Manchester, 6926, Pte., d., F. & F., 11-10-18.

SCOWCROFT John, *b* Harwood, Bolton, Lancs., *e* Manchester (Harwood), 6303, L/Cpl., k. in a., F. & F., 1-7-16.

SEDDON Herbert, *b* Salford, Lancs., *e* Salford, 36287, Pte., k. in a., F. & F., 21-3-18.

SERMON Adam, *b* Ancoats, Manchester, *e* Ashton-u-Lyne, Lancs. (Stockport, Cheshire), 43112, L/Cpl., d. of w., F. & F., 4-5-17, formerly 5516 Lancashire Fus.

SHAW George Frederick, *b* Eccles, Manchester, *e* Manchester, 51268, Pte., k. in a., F. & F., 31-7-17, formerly S4/125640 R.A.S.C.

SHAW George Thomas Louis, *b* Great Strickland, Cumb'land, *e* Appleby, West'land (Great Strickland), 43036, L/Cpl., d. of w., F. & F., 4-12-17, formerly 19702 Border R.

SHAW John, *b* Hollinwood, Lancs., *e* Failsworth, Lancs. (Hurts Brook, Ashton-u-Lyne, Lancs.), 39921, Pte., k. in a., F. & F., 23-4-17.

SHEARD George, *b* Old Trafford, Manchester, *e* Ardwick, Manchester, 6676, Cpl., k. in a., F. & F., 23-4-17, **M.M.**

SHELDON Ernest, *b* Ancoats, Manchester, *e* Ardwick, Manchester, 300031, L/Cpl., d., F. & F., 30-10-18.

SHENTON Harry, *b* Ardwick, Manchester, *e* Manchester, 7482, Pte., k. in a., F. & F., 9-7-16.

SHEPHERD Fred, *b* Manchester, *e* Manchester (Abington, Berks.), 35696, Pte., k. in a., F. & F., 21-3-18.

SHERRY John, *b* Manchester, *e* Manchester (Salford, Lancs.), 302987, Pte., k. in a., F. & F., 29-11-17.

SHORE William, *b* Sandbach, Cheshire, *e* Manchester, 25396, Pte., k. in a., F. & F., 23-4-17.

SIMMONS Edward, *e* Ardwick, Manchester (Bradford, Manchester), 47470, Pte., k. in a., F. & F., 31-7-17.

SINGLETON Arthur, *b* Blackpool, Lancs., *e* Manchester (Prestwich, Lancs.), 6556, Sgt., k. in a., F. & F., 30-7-16.

SKELTON Arthur, *b* Pendleton, Lancs., *e* Salford, Lancs., 43068, L/Cpl., k. in a., F. & F., 27-4-18, formerly 20562 Lancashire Fus.

SLATER Frederick, *b* St. Paul's, Pendleton, Lancs., *e* Manchester (Seedley, Manchester), 6929, Pte., d., F. & F., 31-1-16.

SMALLEY James, *b* Broughton, Lancs., *e* Manchester, 23185, Pte., k. in a., F. & F., 23-4-17.

SMITH Arthur Alfred, *b* Sheffield, *e* Hollinwood, Lancs. (Oldham, Lancs.), 36833, Pte., k. in a., F. & F., 28-7-17.

SMITH Frederick Rowland, *b* Leicester, *e* Manchester (Leicester), 6307, L/Cpl., k. in a., F. & F., 9-7-16.

SMITH Harry, *b* Leicester, *e* Leicester, 40943, Pte., k. in a., F. & F., 31-7-17, formerly 3676 Leicester R.

SMITH	Herbert Frederick, *b* Cheetham Hill, Manchester, *e* Manchester, 7056, L/Cpl., d. of w., F. & F., 13-8-17.
SMITH	James Archibald, *b* Boro, Middlesex, *e* Bethnal Green, Middlesex, 47540, L/Cpl., k. in a., F. & F., 21-3-18, formerly R/28815 K.R. Rifle C.
SMITH	James Frederick, *b* Manchester, *e* Manchester, 19513, Pte., d. of w., F. & F., 29-11-17.
SMITH	Michael, *b* Liverpool, *e* Liverpool, 49225, Pte., k. in a., F. & F., 31-7-17.
SMITH	Roger, *b* Walmersley, Bury, Lancs., *e* Manchester (Glossop, Derby), 6683, Sgt., k. in a., F. & F., 15-10-16, **M.M.**
SMITH	William, *b* Liverpool *e* Liverpool, 400966, Pte., k. in a., F. & F., 21-3-18.
SMITH	William Vincent, *b* Walkden, Manchester, *e* Manchester (Worsley), 6558, Pte., d., F. & F., 26-10-18.
SMULLEN	Abraham, *b* Belfast, *e* Manchester (Cheetham, Manchester), 33847, Pte., k. in a., F. & F., 1-3-18.
SNOWDEN	Frank, *b* East Retford, Notts., *e* Newark, Notts. (Retford), 40861, L/Sgt., k. in a., F. & F., 21-3-18, formerly 4045 Notts and Derby R., **D.C.M.**
SOUTH	Harold, *b* Blackley, Manchester, *e* Manchester, 6805, Pte., k. in a., F. & F., 1-7-16.
SOUTHWORTH	Bernard, *e* Leigh, Lancs. (Bolton, Lancs.), 202875, Pte., k. in a., F. & F., 21-3-18.
SPENCER	Wilfred Reginald, *b* Bethnal Green, Middlesex, *e* Stratford, Essex (Bow, Middlesex), 1247, Pte., k. in a., F. & F., 23-4-17
STABLER	William, *b* Salford, Lancs., *e* Manchester, 7485, Pte., k. in a., F. & F., 9-7-16.
STAFFERTON	William Charles, *e* Northampton, 51067, Pte., k. in a., F. & F., 12-9-17, formerly G/86574 Middlesex R.
STAFFORD	Frank Robert, *b* Manchester, *e* Manchester, 35566, Pte., k. in a., F. & F., 18-10-16.
STALKER	James, *b* Plumpton, Cumb'land, *e* Kirby Stephen, Westmorland, 43094, L/Sgt., k. in a., F. & F., 21-3-18, formerly 5965 Border R.
STANTON	Harry, *b* Birmingham, *e* Warwick (Selly Park, Birmingham), 64507, Pte., k. in a., F. & F., 22-10-18, formerly 39505 R. Warwick R.
STARKEY	William, *b* Altrincham, Cheshire, *e* Manchester (Altrincham), 7587, Pte., k. in a., F. & F., 1-7-16.
STEARNS	Walter Ryder, *b* Rusholme, Manchester, *e* Manchester, 6931, Pte., k. in a., F. & F., 9-7-16.
STEEL	Samuel, *b* Oldham, Lancs., *e* Chadderton, Lancs. (Oldham), 302736, Pte., k. in a., F. & F., 21-3-18.
STEVENS	Charles Alfred, *b* Clapham, Surrey, *e* Ashton-u-Lyne, Lancs. (Chorlton-on-Medlock, Manchester), 723, Pte., k. in a., F. & F., 23-4-17.
STIRLAND	William, *e* Kimberley, Notts, 40866, L/Cpl., d. of w., F. & F., 7-8-17, formerly 3827 Notts and Derby R.
STONE	Reuben, *b* Manchester, *e* Manchester, 33502, Pte., k. in a., F. & F., 23-4-17.
STONEHEWER	Richard Alfred, *b* Crewe, Cheshire, *e* Manchester (Stockport), 6808, L/Cpl., k. in a., F. & F., 23-4-17.
STUTTARD	Charles Alwyne, *b* Middlesborough, *e* Manchester, 7154, Sgt., k. in a., F. & F., 30-7-17.
STUTTER	William, *b* Stockport, Cheshire, *e* Bury, Lancs. (Manchester), 51286, Pte., k. in a., F. & F., 31-7-17, formerly 4500 Lancashire Fus.

TASSELL — William James, *b* Kensington, Middlesex, *e* Camberwell, Surrey (Peckham, S.E.), 57350, Pte., k. in a., F. & F., 3-5-18, formerly 36555 N. Lancs. R.

TATTERSALL — Ernest, *b* Salford, Lancs., *e* Manchester (Manchester), 6689, Pte., k. in a., F. & F., 1-7-16.

TAYLOR — Charles, *b* Manchester, *e* Manchester, 27362, Pte., d. of w., F. & F., 31-7-16.

TAYLOR — Daniel, *b* Wigan, Lancs., *e* Wigan, 27306, Pte., k. in a., F. & F., 30-7-16.

TAYLOR — George Henry, *b* Liverpool, *e* Manchester (Crumpsall, Manchester), 9190, L/Cpl., d. of w., F. & F., 8-4-18.

TAYLOR — Leonard Wilfred, *b* Stratford, Essex, *e* Tottenham, Middlesex, 51068, Pte., k. in a., F. & F., 31-7-17, formerly G/19270 Middlesex R.

TAYLOR — Major, *b* St. Simon's, Salford, Lancs., *e* Manchester (Salford), 6934, Pte., k. in a., F. & F., 1-7-16.

TAYLOR — Owen, *b* Golborne, Lancs., *e* Ashton-u-Lyne, Lancs. (Moston, Manchester), 32608, Pte., k. in a., F. & F., 20-6-17.

THOMAS — Edward, *b* Preston, Lancs., *e* Manchester, 6563, L/Cpl., d., F. & F., 3-3-16.

THOMAS — Reginald Clifton, *b* Blackpool, Lancs., *e* Manchester (Harpurhey, Lancs.), 303307, Pte., k. in a., F. & F., 21-3-18.

THOMPSON — Albert, *b* Manchester, *e* Manchester (Lower Broughton, Manchester), 18737, Pte., k. in a., F. & F., 23-4-17.

THOMPSON — Richard Samuel, *b* Manchester, *e* Manchester, 7287, Pte., k. in a., F. & F., 30-7-16.

THOMPSON — William, *b* Failsworth, Lancs., *e* Manchester, 29617, L/Cpl., k. in a., F. & F., 21-3-18, **M.M.**

THORNTON — Thomas, *b* Manchester, *e* Manchester, 4543, Pte., k. in a., F. & F., 24-8-16.

TINGEY — Thomas, *b* Sheffield, *e* Cambridge, 57358, Pte., d., F. & F., 17-10-18, formerly 18047 Suffolk R.

TOLLEY — William, *e* Arnold, Notts. (Daybrook, Notts.), 40871, Pte., k. in a., F. & F., 31-7-17, formerly 3876 Notts and Derby R.

TOWNSEND — Benjamin, *b* Tideswell, Derby, *e* Manchester (Tideswell), 27140, Pte., d. of w., F. & F., 2-7-16.

TUFFS — Frederick, *e* Manchester (Gorton, Manchester), 49405, Pte., k. in a., F. & F., 21-3-18.

TURNER — Ephraim, *b* Stockport, Cheshire, *e* Bury, Lancs. (Stockport), 43067, L/Cpl., k. in a., F. & F., 21-3-18, formerly 468 Lancashire Fus.

TURNER — George, *b* Coventry, *e* Coventry, 57334, Pte., k. in a., F. & F., 24-3-18, formerly M/286440 R.A.S.C.

TURNER — Herbert Frederick, *b* Barnsbury, Middlesex, *e* Peterborough (Hackney, Middlesex), 51069, Pte., k. in a., F. & F., 31-7-17, formerly G/19291 Middlesex R.

TWIGG — Richard, *b* Hulme, Manchester, *e* Manchester, 6813, Sgt., k. in a., F. & F., 30-7-16.

VALENTINE — Henry, *e* Manchester (Old Trafford, Manchester), 251339, Pte., k. in a., F. & F., 21-3-18.

WADE — George Frederick, *e* Northampton, 51080, Pte., k. in a., F. & F., 31-7-17, formerly G/86576 Middlesex R.

WALKER — Albert, *b* Salford, Lancs., *e* Manchester (Salford), 6442, Sgt., d. of w., F. & F., 8-4-18, **M.M.**

WALKER George Woodburn, *b* St. George's, Wolverhampton, *e* Manchester (Heaton Moor, Stockport, Cheshire), 7293, Pte., d. of w., F. & F., 7-8-17.

WARD Harry, *b* St. Albans, Herts., *e* Manchester, 23199, Pte., k. in a. F. & F., 15-6-17.

WARD William Alfred, *e* Northampton, 51081, Pte., k. in a., F. & F., 27-7-17, formerly G/86554 Middlesex R.

WARD William Nelson, *b* Salford, Lancs., *e* Manchester (Weaste, Lancs.), 6443, L/Cpl., d. of w., F. & F., 18-10-16.

WARDLE Percy, *b* Beswick, Manchester, *e* Manchester (West Gorton, Manchester), 7483, Pte., d. of w., F. & F., 4-8-16.

WATSON Harry, *b* Leigh, Lancs., *e* Leigh, 32118, Pte., k. in a., F. & F., 31-7-17, formerly 112992 R.F.A.

WEBSTER William, *b* Wigan, Lancs., *e* Wigan, 202674, Pte., k. in a., F. & F., 27-4-18.

WEILDING Charles, *b* Hulme, Manchester, *e* HeatonPark, Manchester, 7336, Pte., k. in a., F. & F., 29-7-16.

WELCH Thomas Edwin, *b* Hulme, Manchester, *e* Manchester, 6320, Sgt., k. in a., F. & F., 1-7-16.

WHITE James, *b* St. Mark's, Manchester, *e* Manchester, 6446, Pte., d. of w., F. & F., 14-6-16.

WHITEHEAD Frederick, *e* Northampton, 51078, Pte., d. of w., F. & F., 24-3-18, formerly G/86544, Middlesex R.

WHITEHEAD Laurence, *b* St. Luke's, Manchester, *e* Manchester, 6322, Sgt., k. in a., F. & F., 30-7-16.

WHITFIELD Charles, *b* Manchester, *e* Manchester, 32511, Pte., k. in a., F. & F., 30-7-16.

WHITTAKER William, *b* Salford, Lancs., *e* Salford, 37755, Pte., d. of w., F. & F., 25-6-17.

WHITWORTH Edward, *b* Oldham, Lancs., *e* Oldham, 32959, L/Cpl., k. in a., F. & F., 15-6-17.

WIGGINS Frederick, *b* St. Mary's, Manchester, *e* Manchester, 6943, L/Cpl., k. in a., F. & F., 1-7-16.

WILD Ben, *b* Failsworth, Lancs., *e* Manchester (Failsworth), 31310, Pte., d. of w., F. & F., 30-12-17.

WILDE Ernest, *b* Stalybridge, Cheshire, *e* Manchester (Stalybridge), 7175, L/Cpl., k. in a., F. & F., 1-7-16.

WILDE Joseph, *b* Hyde, Cheshire, *e* Heaton Park, Manchester (Hyde), 7410, Pte., k. in a., F. & F., 9-7-16.

WILKINS George, *b* Preston, Lancs., *e* Manchester (Patricroft, Lancs.), 7273, Pte., k. in a., F. & F., 9-7-16.

WILKINSON Alfred, *b* St. Mark's, Manchester, *e* Manchester, 6448, Pte., k. in a., F. & F., 30-7-16.

WILLCOCKS Leonard, *b* New Cross, Manchester, *e* Manchester, 6701, L/Cpl., k. in a., F. & F., 9-7-16.

WILLIAMS Arthur, *b* Manchester, *e* Manchester, 48397, Pte., k. in a., F. & F., 21-3-18.

WILLIAMS Frank Arthur, *b* Chatham, Kent, *e* Chatham, 51074, Pte., k. in a., F. & F., 31-7-17, formerly G/19301 Mid'sex R.

WILLIAMS Walter, *b* Withington, Manchester, *e* Manchester, 6326, Sgt., d. of w., Home, 17-7-16.

WILLMER Dudley, *e* Wigan, Lancs. (Leek, Staffs.), 47159, Pte., d., Home, 30-11-17.

WILSON Harry, *b* Kilburn, Middlesex, *e* Manchester (West Hampstead, London), 6572, Sgt., k. in a., F. & F., 1-7-16.

WILSON Norman Fowler, *b* Werneth, Lancs., *e* Manchester, 6819, Pte., k. in a., F. & F., 1-7-16.

WILSON Robert, *b* Barton-on-Irwell, Lancs., *e* Manchester (Patricroft, Lancs.), 7274, Pte., k. in a., F. & F., 18-10-16.

WILSON Robert, *b* Northwich, Cheshire, *e* Manchester (Northwich), 9203, L/Cpl., k. in a., F. & F., 21-3-18.

WILSON Walter, *b* Whitchurch, Shrops., *e* Manchester (Bradford, Manchester), 7576, Pte., k. in a., F. & F., 30-7-16.

WILSON Watkin, *b* Shrewsbury, *e* Manchester (Gorton, Manchester), 6329, L/Sgt., d. of w., F. & F., 27-3-18.

WINSTANLEY Gerald, *b* Hale, Cheshire, *e* Altrincham, Cheshire (Hale), 48013, Pte., k. in a., F. & F., 12-10-16, formerly 23919 Border R.

WITHINGTON William Henry, *b* Miles Platting, Manchester, *e* Manchester, 17269, Pte., k. in a., F. & F., 21-3-18.

WOLSTENCROFT Stanley, *b* Platt Church, Rusholme, Manchester, *e* Manchester, 252213, C.S.M., d. of w., F. & F., 27-3-18.

WOOD Harry George, *b* Drambury, New York City, U.S.A., *e* Manchester (Heaton Moor, Stockport, Cheshire), 12699, L/Cpl., k. in a., F. & F., 31-7-17.

WOOD Percy Harold, *b* Swinton, Manchester, *e* Manchester (Didsbury, Lancs.), 6706, Pte., d. of w., Home, 27-7-16.

WOODCOCK Ernest, *b* March, Cambs., *e* March, 51226, Pte., k. in a., F. & F., 31-7-17.

WOODS Edward, *b* Openshaw, Manchester, *e* Manchester (Barton, Lancs.), 7275, Pte., d., F. & F., 21-7-18.

WOORE Percival Ernest, *b* Wilmslow, Cheshire, *e* Manchester (Wilmslow), 11973, Cpl., k. in a., F. & F., 31-7-17.

WORSLEY Samuel, *b* Liverpool, *e* Manchester, 7556, L/Cpl., k. in a., F. & F., 23-4-17.

WRIGHT Herbert, *b* Salford, Lancs., *e* Manchester (Salford), 27048, Pte., k. in a., F. & F., 1-7-16.

WRIGLEY Thomas, *b* St. Matthew's, Ardwick, Manchester, *e* Ardwick, 44107, Pte., d., F. & F., 27-10-18.

WYATT William, *b* Ludlow, Shrops., *e* Manchester (Ludlow), 27114, Pte., k. in a., F. & F., 23-4-17.

WYCHERLEY Harry, *b* Chorlton-cum-Hardy, Manchester, *e* Manchester, 7071, Pte., k. in a., F. & F., 30-7-17.

YARWOOD Ralph, *b* Macclesfield, Cheshire, *e* Oldham, Lancs., 48566, Pte., d. of w., F. & F., 13-8-17.

YARWOOD Thomas, *b* Heaton Mersey, Manchester, *e* Manchester, 7167, Pte., k. in a., F. & F., 21-3-18.

YATES James, *b* St. George's, Darwen, *e* Manchester (Cleveleys, Blackpool, Lancs.), 6709, Pte., k. in a., F. & F., 1-7-16.

YATES Thomas, *b* Leigh, Lancs., *e* Leigh, 203846, Pte., k. in a., F. & F., 21-3-18.

17TH

CONTENTS

APPENDIX

CHAPTER I.

FORMATION AND TRAINING

WHEN Great Britain declared war on 4th August, 1914, a new army of 100,000 was at once called for, and the answer was so immediate that Lord Kitchener asked for a further 500,000. The matter as regards Manchester was taken up vigorously by the Lord Mayor and Corporation, with the valuable assistance of the Earl of Derby. The original purpose was to raise one City Battalion, but recruiting proceeded so briskly that sanction was asked for, and obtained, to raise a City Brigade.

The 17th (Service) Battalion, at first known as the 2nd City Battalion, was recruited entirely on the 2nd and 3rd September, 1914: the official date of the raising of the Battalion being August 28th. Lieut.-Col. Johnson, late in command of the 14th Battalion, was gazetted to the command 1st September, 1914.

Much organising work was necessary and was most efficiently done by Councillor Taylor (afterwards Staff-Captain to the Brigade), Messrs. E. Tootal Broadhurst, Kenneth Lee, Vernon Bellhouse and A. H. Dixon (President of the Committee formed to control financial arrangements) and Major Sington, R.E. It was arranged that the Battalion should go into Heaton Park, and while arrangements were being made, the men received their first instruction in drill at the Manchester Artillery Drill Hall, where they were divided into companies and platoons by Captain Walkley, the chief recruiting officer.

On the 19th September, 1914, the Battalion marched to Heaton Park, where it remained for seven months, at first under canvas, and later in temporary hutments. It was fortunate in obtaining an efficient Quartermaster in Lieut. (later Captain) E. Lloyd, late 2nd Battalion Manchester Regiment. The principal difficulty in the early days was the lack of officers—the Colonel only was gazetted—and experienced N.C.O.'s, and in this matter the Battalion owes much to the energy and ability of its first Sergeant-Major (afterwards Captain) A. Harrey, late South Staffordshire Regiment. A further trouble was the great shortage of rifles. Captain Caswell, late

Sherwood Foresters, acted for a time as temporary Adjutant, and was later gazetted Major and Second-in-Command. On December 11th, however, Captain L. de H. Larpent, of the Connaught Rangers, who had returned wounded from France took up the duties of Adjutant, remaining with the Battalion until the 10th June, 1915. The value of his work is fittingly expressed in Battalion Orders of that date.

"On the departure of Captain L. de H. Larpent (Connaught Rangers) the C.O. wishes to place on record his high appreciation of the services rendered by this officer during the time he has acted as temporary Adjutant to the Battalion. The C.O. feels that the general efficiency of the Battalion, as regards its interior economy, discipline, and the system of training inaugurated for N.C.O.'s and men, is due to the energetic and painstaking way in which Captain Larpent has worked. He much regrets that he is losing the services of this officer."

Whilst at Heaton Park the Battalion, together with the 1st City Battalion (16th Manchesters) was reviewed on the 24th November, 1914, by the Lord Mayor of Manchester; and on the 1st December by General Sir Henry Mackinnon, G.O.C. Western Command. In January, 1915, the Brigade received its Staff, and was fortunate in obtaining as Brigadier a former Colonel of the 2nd Battalion Manchester Regiment, Lieut.-Col. H. C. E. Westropp, then commanding the 12th Battalion Manchester Regiment. The Brigade was then known as the 111th Brigade, Fifth Army, but later became the 90th Brigade, Fourth Army.

Previous to this, in December, 1914, the formation of a reserve company was authorised. Recruits, however, came forward in such numbers that a Second Manchester City Brigade was formed. Consequently as recruits for the reserve company were scarce, a campaign was organised by Lieut. Etchells in February, 1915, with the result that the company was completed in a week.

Before leaving Manchester the two Brigades with other locally-raised units marched past Lord Kitchener, in Albert Square, on the 21st March, 1915.

On 24th April, 1915, the Battalion, less its Depôt Company, moved to Belton Park, Grantham. The Depôt Companies of the Brigade subsequently formed the 25th (Reserve) Battalion Manchester Regiment. At Grantham the various units of the 30th Division were brought together under Major-General W. Fry, C.B., C.V.O.

The work carried out consisted chiefly of battalion training, musketry, and entrenching, with some brigade training. Whilst at Grantham the Division was inspected by General Sir Archibald Murray, afterwards Chief of the General Staff. Brigadier-General

Westropp was prevented by the recurrence of an old complaint from continuing in command of the Brigade, and his place was taken by Lieut.-Col. C. J. Steavenson, King's Liverpool Regiment. The Battalion was formally taken over by the military authorities on the 10th August, 1915.

On 7th September, 1915, the Division moved to Lark Hill, Salisbury Plain, to complete its training. Brigade training was carried out and the musketry courses completed. On 4th November, 1915, the Division was inspected by the Earl of Derby, and by General Sir A. H. Paget, G.O.C. Salisbury Training Centre.

The following is the Roll of Officers who subsequently embarked with the Battalion for France :—

Headquarters : Lieut.-Col. H. A. Johnson, *C.O.* ; Major J. J. Whitehead ; Captain C. L. Macdonald, *Adjutant* ; Lieut. T. A. Yarwood, *Quartermaster.*

" A " Company : Capt. E. Lloyd, *O.C.* ; Capt. E. Fearenside, Lieut. J. N. W. Sidebotham (*Lewis Guns*), Sec.-Lieut. W. R. Tonge, Sec.-Lieut. R. F. Mansergh, Sec.-Lieut. J. D. Kirkwood.

" B " Company : Capt. J. V. Williams, *O.C.* ; Capt. R. J. Ford, Lieut. L. B. Humphreys, Sec.-Lieut. A. G. Cameron, Sec.-Lieut. J. F. Cotterell, Sec.-Lieut. R. L. Johnston (*Transport*).

" C " Company : Capt. E. J. Malim, *O.C.* ; Capt. J. G. Madden, Lieut. E. L. Heyworth, Sec.-Lieut. C. R. Stevens, Sec.-Lieut. E. E. Elwell, Sec.-Lieut. J. Orford.

" D " Company : Capt. S. Kenworthy, *O.C.* ; Capt. N. Vaudrey, Lieut. F. J. G. Whittall, Lieut. E. Wigley, Sec.-Lieut. G. F. Potts (*Signals*).

CHAPTER II

IN THE MARICOURT SECTOR

FIFTEEN months of hard training gave place to grim reality on November 8th, 1915, when the Battalion, less three officers—Major Whitehead, Lieut. Sidebotham and Sec.-Lieut. Johnston—and 109 men with regimental transport, who had crossed via Southampton and Havre the previous day, left Amesbury, via Folkestone, for service overseas. The first night on French soil was spent at Boulogne.

It was not until December 9th, however, that the Seventeenth reached the front-line trenches. The intervening month was largely one of travel. Leaving Boulogne on November 9th the Battalion moved, via Pont Remy, to Domqueur, where it remained from the 11th to 17th November. On this latter date Vignacourt was reached, and the next day the Battalion was at Bertangles, where a stay was made until the 28th. A ten miles' march on this date over roads hard with frost brought the Battalion to Montrelet, and on December 7th, after a seventeen miles' tramp, the Seventeenth reached Covin. Here for the next seven days officers and men were given practical tuition by the 143rd Brigade in trench warfare, under most realistic conditions, the camp being deep in mud. All this was a means to an end. On the 9th " A " and " B " Companies took a spell in the line at Fonquevillers, in a sector held by a Battalion of the Warwickshire Regiment, to whom the Seventeenth were attached for instruction. On the 11th " C " and " D " Companies relieved their comrades.

As the trenches were in a very wet condition, and accommodation was limited, the H.Q. of the Seventeenth were billeted in the Château de la Haye, which was practically untouched by shell-fire, although it was not more than a mile distant from the front-line trenches. These were reached by a long communication-trench, known as " La Haye Cut," which was, however, in such a bad condition that unless circumstances made it imperative the road was generally used.

The Battalion suffered its first casualty on the 13th, Sec.-Lieut. R. L. Johnston, who was in command of the transport at Bayencourt, being killed by an anti-aircraft shell. On the 14th the Battalion marched to Couin, and after a night spent under canvas arrived back at Montrelet, where it remained in billets over Christmas and New Year. On the 9th January it reached Suzanne, via Naours, Pont Nuyelles and Sailly Laurette. Whilst in Suzanne heavy shelling was experienced, and one man was killed and five wounded. On the following day the Battalion relieved the 16th Manchesters in A. 3 sub-sector, to the west of Maricourt Wood; having the 2nd Bedfords on its right and the 17th King's Liverpools on the left. Sec.-Lieut. W. R. Tonge was killed in the trenches on this date, being picked off by a sniper in a little-used part of the fire trench of the right sector, where the mud was so bad that it was impossible to remove him and he was buried in the trench.

A. 3 sub-sector was part of a trench system known as "Maricourt Defences," a second line for the defence of the village. In the centre of the system was a series of strong points with dug-outs, machine gun emplacements commanding special points, bombing islands, bomb and water stores, &c. These trenches were not under observation, but care had to be taken in the outlying parts that working parties were not too markedly conspicuous.

Z. 3 sub-sector, which reached from the north-east corner of Maricourt Wood to the Maricourt-Peronne Road, was an old French line and had fallen into such disrepair that only parts of the original front line could be used. "Gum-boots," thigh high, were essential. The mud in places was knee deep. Two communication trenches ran from Maricourt village to the front line; one from the north end of the main street through Maricourt Wood, past Headquarter's dug-out and dressing station, to "Piccadilly Circus," where it divided, the left branch leading to one company front along the edge of the Wood, the right branch to another company just outside the Wood. The second communication trench roughly followed the Peronne Road to a third company. The other company was usually in reserve.

Y. 3 sub-sector extended from the Peronne Road to Fargny Mill. Battalion Headquarters were in dug-outs in the Suzanne-Maricourt valley, from where a long communication trench, known as "Fargny Wood Avenue," led up to the right of the position. Another communication trench from the Peronne Road led up to the left, and both trenches were very bad going, being old French trenches as in Z. 3 sub-sector. The whole of the front line in this case was passable, though in places not good, and the field of fire was very limited—about fifty yards in some places.

On the left the German trenches in "Y" Wood, were in dead ground, so listening-posts were made. The enemy was evidently possessed with the same idea for he sapped out towards our right centre and established a post within fifteen yards. The extreme right trench overlooked the Somme Marshes, and any movement in Curlu could be plainly seen. It proved an excellent position for the Battalion snipers, and they did some good shooting with telescopic sights. From Y. 13 a steep ladder-like cut led down to the level of the Somme and from thence a track ran to Fargny Mill. This, usually held by one company, was in the nature of an advanced post, and was in full view of the Hun bombing post, "Chapeau de Gendarme."

The trenches, such as they were, were built in the broken foundations of the houses, and in some places took the form of sandbags, as the ground was too wet and marshy for digging purposes. The position could not be approached unobserved by day, and the Hun snipers were usually busy on the exposed portion of the approach. A causeway led across the river to a large, flat, horse-shoe shaped piece of ground, formed by the bend of a river, and known as "Trafford Park." This was patrolled at night from Vaux village, and sometimes from Fargny Mill.

Rations, letters, R.E. stores, &c., came up from Suzanne at night as part of the road was under enemy observation during daylight. There was, however, communication with Suzanne and Brigade Headquarters in the White Château there, by means of a track in the valley which followed the line of the road. The roads in Maricourt village were not as a rule under observation and could be used freely by day, but trenches ran beside those most frequently in use and in the event of shelling proved extremely serviceable.

The straggling village of Maricourt was the centre of an important salient which formed the extreme right of the British front, and for six months or so the Seventeenth remained in this Maricourt-Suzanne area, generally relieving the 16th Manchesters in the trenches, in spells of two to four days.

On the 28th January there was a violent bombardment of Maricourt. The 17th King's Liverpools were rushed up to man the Maricourt defences. In addition there was a call for one and a half Companies of the 17th Manchesters to reinforce. Capt. Williams was despatched with "B" Company, and two platoons of "C" Company under Lieut. E. L. Heyworth. This party moved up to Maricourt by Valley Road, under heavy shell fire, and came under the orders of Lieut.-Col. Fairfax, 17th King's Liverpool Regiment.

Two men were killed and six wounded in this movement. On the same date an order was received for two platoons to reinforce the 18th Manchesters in Battle Dug-outs, Vaux Wood, and Capt. Kenworthy answered the call with two platoons of " D " Company. This party moved up by a trench deep with mud, and was heavily shelled by lachrymatory shells. Gas helmets had to be worn.

This trying move was successfully accomplished by 5-15 p.m. The detachment spent the night and the following day in Battle Dug-outs, under the orders of Lieut.-Col. Fraser, commanding 18th Manchesters.

On the night of the 29th Capt. Kenworthy's party were sent into Vaux Wood to replace " C " Company, 18th Manchesters, who had been despatched to Fargny Mill. Furthermore, Lieut.-Col. Johnson was instructed to send one company to reinforce the right of the 18th Manchesters at Royal Dragon's Wood, lying to the south of Vaux, and Capt. Ford with " A " Company was sent for this purpose.

Half Companies of " C " and " D " meanwhile remained in reserve at Suzanne. And a most uncomfortable time they had, for the village was shelled all day with H.E. and lachrymatory shells. There were two casualties, and the Headquarter's Mess was struck by shell.

At 8-30 p.m. on the 29th, order was received for these two half Companies to proceed to Eclusier and report to the French Commander at that point. Capt. Malim took command, and the move was completed by 9-15 p.m. This column was quickly on the move for the men had been sleeping in full marching order. The route taken was the Suzanne-Vaux-Eclusier Road. No untoward incident occurred until Royal Dragon's Wood was passed, but when the column had reached the road across the Somme to Eclusier Corner (immediately below the Wood) the point was very heavily shelled—luckily without any casualties to " D " Company, who were in the rear. On reaching Eclusier Capt. Malim reported to the French Commandant, who, although greatly surprised that troops had been sent to his support, ordered the detachment to man a support trench behind Eclusier village. Capt. Malim found it to be, on inspection, cut no more than a foot deep in the chalk.

Parties were thereupon sent to Dragon's Wood for picks and shovels, but by the time they returned dawn was breaking and it was manifestly impossible to get a trench cut before daylight. It was, therefore, decided to remain on the road and dig in, but this intent was frustrated, for water was reached at one foot below the surface. The troops, in consequence, had to seek cover in the neighbouring hedgerows. Subsequently the detachment was withdrawn, in small parties, and returned to Suzanne.

Whilst part of the detachment was lying hidden in the buildings and garden of a small farm by Eclusier bridge—the only building in the village which had not been destroyed—the O.C. chanced to meet a French Sergeant who, before the war, had been chef at a well-known London restaurant which he had been in the habit of patronising.

February passed uneventfully, and during March the Battalion received a number of officer reinforcements—Sec.-Lieuts. Ilett, Haslam, Calvert, Wain, Jensen and Kerr.

On March 18th the Battalion was relieved by the 7th Buffs, and proceeded across country in bright moonlight to Grovetown Camp, near Bray. On the 28th Lieut.-Col. Johnson was admitted sick to hospital, and Major J. J. Whitehead assumed command during his absence. The Battalion on the 29th proceeded in detachments to Bonnay, Heilly, and Morlancourt, and from these places the men took over working shifts from the 89th Brigade.

Lieut.-Col. Johnson rejoined from Base Hospital on April 10th. Two days later the Battalion moved to Cardonnette, and from the 13th to 29th the Seventeenth were at St. Sauveur, where Battalion Sports were held. On the latter date a move was made to Corbie, and on the following day to Bray.

On May 1st the Seventeenth were back in their old positions, relieving the 8th East Surreys in Vaux Wood and village, and in Royal Dragon's Wood. Here they remained until June 1st. Sec.-Lieut. T. H. Clesham joined on 9th May, and there were two drafts of men during the month. Sec.-Lieut. C. T. Jensen was killed in action on the 10th.

On June 1st the Battalion was relieved by the 1st Battalion 37th French Infantry Regiment. The dividing line between the French and British armies then became a line running approximately north and south through the centre of Maricourt village. The handing over of the sector to the French was carried through without a hitch. Upon relief the Battalion marched to Bois Celestins, where it encamped in huts, and provided working parties for the 30th Division and 13th Corps, quarrying, unloading barges, making roads, &c. From the 8th to 11th June the Battalion was billeted at Bray, and carried on similar work. On the last-named date the Manchesters moved via Bronfay Farm to Maricourt defences, and divided the Maricourt defences with the French—the latter having charge of the eastern half. Whilst here they were kept hard at work unloading and carrying stores and ammunition, and carrying for the tunnelling companies. Not very exciting work, but a soldier's duties are many. On the night of the 14th June the village was bombarded, and the

Battalion had six casualties. A relief was effected on the 18th by the 17th K.L.R. (89th Brigade), and the Seventeenth marched to Etinehem Camp. After a few hours rest the journey was resumed to the railhead at Heilly, where the Battalion entrained for Ailly-sur-Somme, and by march-route to Briquemesnil. Here Brigade training was carried out until June 26th, when the Battalion marched to Ailly, and entrained for Mericourt-sur-Somme, journeying thence to Etinehem. Here final preparations were made for the opening of the Somme battle. On the night of the 30th the Battalion took up its position in assembly trenches, south of Cambridge Copse, a little to the north-west of Maricourt village.

CHAPTER III

THE BATTLE OF THE SOMME

MONTAUBAN TRONES WOOD GUILLEMONT

THE Battalion reached the point of Assembly about 10 p.m. and spent the rest of the night of the 30th June there, "zero" being 7 a.m. next morning. At this hour the artillery bombardment, which had been in progress for about a week, became intense, and was concentrated on the German front-line and communication trenches.

The assembly trenches had been dug in two lines on the reverse slope of a slight rise and were, therefore, in dead ground, the men being out of rifle and machine-gun fire until the ridge immediately in front had been crossed. "A" and "B" Companies occupied the first line and "C" and "D" Companies the second. The advance was carried out in four waves, the first consisting of two platoons each of "A" and "B" Companies, and the second of two further platoons of the same Company. "A" Company's platoons supported their own Company, and "B" platoons acted similarly. The third and fourth waves were made up in the same manner of "D" and "C" Companies. "C" Company supporting "B" (the right hand Company) had their left resting on the Maricourt-Montauban Road, and the advance was in "Blob" formation, so as to offer a smaller target to the artillery. The advance was carried out at a slow walk, no other pace being possible owing to the distance of the objective (about 3,000 yards), and the quantity of material it was necessary to carry. In addition to his ordinary equipment each man carried an extra 250 rounds S.A.A., two Mills' bombs, rations, pick and shovel, and canvas bucket containing ten Mills' bombs. Those who did not carry the bucket of bombs carried either a trench ladder or rolls of barbed wire. Each man had a bright yellow patch on his back in order that the artillery observers might be able to locate the progress of the advance. In addition every tenth man bore a bright square of metal on his back for the same purpose. The ground was very badly cut up and the going difficult, but as the German trenches were so battered the scaling ladders were hardly required, as most of the wire entanglements had already been cut by the artillery. The advance was so rapid that the infantry was obliged to wait nearly three-quarters of an hour behind their own barrage till it lifted to the north side of the village. "C" Company retained their "Blob" formation as far as the Glatz Redoubt, then extended to cross the ridge immediately north of it, where they had heavy casualties by machine-gun fire from the direction of Mametz. The advance from Carnoy did not seem to be moving quite so fast, though a great number of prisoners could be seen pouring down the valley by Valley Trench and Breslau Point towards our lines.

The first two waves were by now very much thinned, and as the first party of "C" Company got over the ridge they came up with what remained of "B" Company, and entered Montauban at the south-east corner in extended order, moving directly through the orchard there to line its northern edge. From this position parties of the enemy could be observed retreating in disorder towards Longueval and Bazentin-le-Grand.

The advance had been rehearsed so exhaustively on a specially selected piece of ground behind the lines that the movements had become stale with repetition. Consequently, on finally reaching the objective a platoon humorist, bowed under his heterogeneous assortment of burdens, was heard to remark: "Now we'll go back and do it all over again before tea!"

For purposes of defence the village was divided up amongst Battalions in a series of strong points. The right of the Seventeenth was an old German trench line through the orchard east of the village, and their left the church and a road running north. "A" and "B" Companies, now under the command of Lieuts. Humphreys and Mansergh, occupied the orchard trench—on the right facing Bernafay Wood. Captain Ford ("A" Company) had been killed near the German front line, and Captain Vaudrey ("B" Company) in the Glatz Redoubt. No. 9 Platoon ("C" Company), under Lieut. E. L. Heyworth, was on the left of "A" and "B" Companies, and faced Longueval, and here a new trench was constructed, under heavy rifle fire, just inside the orchard. No. 10 Platoon (Lieut. Sproat) held the next section, where it was necessary to dig a trench in the open to obtain a better field of fire towards Bernafay Wood, from which direction a counter-attack was expected. This working party was, however, observed by the enemy gunners and shelled out, suffering heavy casualties, including Lieut. Sproat who was killed.

The remaining two platoons of "C" Company (Lieut. Stevens) consolidated a strong point at the extreme end of the village.

Capt. Madden ("C" Company), the only surviving Company-Commander, established his Headquarters near the right of No. 9 Platoon's position. Digging was very difficult at the point where Lieut. Stevens was on account of the foundations of ruined buildings, but sufficient protection was constructed to accommodate the numbers available. Meanwhile, one platoon was sent to an old German dug-out to rest and act as local reserve. A Lewis gun post, established on the sunken road, a little to the left of the position held by No. 9 and No. 10 Platoons, was destroyed, and Sergeant Wilkinson and his crew wiped out. A second Lewis gun operated in the open between "C" and "A" Companies, firing in the direction of Longueval and Bernafay Wood. This gun remained in action until after the Battalion was relieved and did good work. The crew were Privates Clough, Evans, Gordon, Worthington and Wright. A third gun, operating about the centre of "B" Company's line, under Corporal Allison, and a fourth under Private P. Worthington on "B" Company's right, were both directed towards Bernafay Wood.

The C.O., Lieut.-Col. H. A. Johnson, having been wounded during the advance, the command was taken over by the Adjutant, Major C. L. Macdonald, who established his Headquarters in an old German dug-out, near the cross roads, and had "D" Company as Battalion reserve. This Company was now in charge of Lieut. Whittall, Capt. Kenworthy having been killed during the advance.

Capt. Madden took over "A" and "B" Companies, and Lieut. Heyworth commanded "C" Company. No. 9 Platoon ("C" Company) was taken over by Sergeant Smith. "C" Company's position, after being harassed by snipers, ultimately became the mark of the German artillery, with disastrous results. The dug-out with the reserve platoon was first hit, and a runner, reporting that it was badly shaken and did not look safe, received orders that the platoon was to come out into the fire trench. Before he got back, however, the dug-out was again hit and the roof smashed in. Fortunately, the N.C.O.'s got out a number of the men, and a few more managed to extricate themselves from the wreckage, among these being Glennie, one of the signallers, who though badly burnt about the face and eyes went back to look for the other operator. A party of Engineers was sent up, but only a runner, Private Beasley, was eventually dug out.

The northerly strong point itself was next heavily shelled. Headquarter's, therefore, decided to abandon it, and take up a fresh position a little further back, on an oblique line running up from the strong point to the left of No. 9 Platoon's position. This was on rising ground with a good field of fire north and north-east. A couple of ranging shells came over when the work of digging-in began, and it was strongly impressed upon the men that it was essential to get under ground before shelling began in earnest. They fully realised this and by evening when the bombardment began again they were well under cover and no further casualties occurred. No counter-attack reached the village, and the battered Seventeenth was relieved in the early hours of July 3rd by the 12th Royal Scots, of the 9th Division, and moved off down the valley towards Carnoy. At Bronfay Farm, where the rolls were called, it was then found that the casualties amounted to eight officers and three hundred and fifty other ranks, out of a total of about nine hundred who went over on the 1st. The Battalion then proceeded to a bivouac camp at Happy Valley—off the Bray-Albert Road—for rest and reorganisation.

After the gruelling it had received in the Montauban attack it was generally supposed that the Seventeenth would leave the latter zone to reorganise, especially as its numbers had dwindled to not more than about four hundred and fifty of all ranks. Contrary to expectations, however, orders were received on July 7th to make up the complement of bombs and equipment and to be ready to move at a moment's notice. The weather conditions too, at this time, were vile, owing to the heavy rain which flooded the men out of their bivouacs. At noon of July 8th orders came for the Battalion to move into assembly trenches at Oxford Copse, Maricourt, under the command of Major Whitehead, and here it arrived about 4 p.m. Nothing was known at the time regarding the Battalion's destination, but the general opinion pointed to it taking over a portion of the line in the neighbourhood of Trones Wood. The Battalion remained at Oxford Copse until 1 a.m. on July 9th, at which hour it moved by communication trenches across the old " no man's land " to Glatz Redoubt, where orders were received for the Battalion to proceed to Briqueterie with all speed. By the time all the Companies had reached that rendezvous it was already daylight, and everyone was worn out with fatigue. Nevertheless, an attack was ordered on the northern half of the Wood within an hour. Accordingly officers and N.C.O.'s were summoned to a hasty conference. Plans were discussed and arrangements settled. " A " Company was specially detailed to link up with a South African Company which was holding the western half of a trench running from the north-east of Bernafay Wood to the north-west of Trones Wood. But difficulties were made to be surmounted, and it is on occasions such as this that a man's mettle is revealed. Despite fatigue, and the short time for preparation, the Battalion worried through to its positions.

The line in this sector ran as follows: north of Montauban—Bernafay Wood, southern end of Trones Wood—Maltzhorn Farm.

On the preceding day a footing had been gained in the southern portion of the Wood by the 2nd Wilts. The Seventeenth were to approach their objective from the south of Bernafay Wood and move in a north-easterly direction towards Trones, with their centre on the railway—a distance of about six hundred yards. Unobserved by the enemy, Companies got into artillery formation south of Bernafay Wood and moved off in good parade-ground order—" B " and " D " leading, with " A " and " C " in support. The first two hundred yards was traversed without incident—the enemy apparently not expecting any attack. This supposition was probably strengthened by the fact that it was now 6-40 a.m. and a bright summer morning. But the Hun quickly bestirred himself. The Battalion came under heavy shell fire from the front of the Wood, but this sudden activity could not hold up the attack, and our men covered the remaining distance in good order, entering the Wood with a rush. The enemy had been holding an irregular shallow trench along the western edge. This they quickly evacuated with our men in chase, some escaping, though a considerable number were either killed or captured.

The Seventeenth pushed ahead and endeavoured to consolidate the north and eastern sides, but the enemy put down a terrific 5·9 barrage, and the place became an absolute inferno. " It seemed as if," writes an officer, " every gun in the sector had been switched on to this one small area." The worst place in the Wood was a wide communication trench in the centre, running north and south. This proved a veritable death-trap, in that it gave apparent shelter to many men, and served as an attractive target. Owing to the great number of casualties sustained during the bombardment it was found impossible to hold the entire length of the Wood, and it was, therefore, decided that the north-eastern and north-western ends only—where there were already some trenches dug—should be consolidated. About three officers and fifty N.C.O.'s and men gallantly fought their way to the north-western end of the Wood, and consolidated and reversed the Hun trenches.

Lieut. McCardle and about six men meanwhile endeavoured to connect up with the South Africans who were supposed to be holding the trench that linked up the northern ends of Bernafay and Trones Woods. This was according to plan, but instead of meeting the South Africans as they had anticipated they encountered a small body of the enemy, three members of which were killed and the rest dispersed. Lieut. McCardle and his six men got back safely. Probably the only survivor from the northern portion of the Wood was Sergeant Bingham, and he was wounded. Owing to the denseness of the Wood it was difficult to reorganise the various Companies. They were scattered about over a distance of a half-mile and as, in many places, there were no trenches, it occupied an hour or so in covering a few hundred yards owing to the fallen timber and thick undergrowth. The Germans launched a counter attack from the south-eastern edge of the Wood, but about 2 p.m. the position was nevertheless established with Brigade Headquarters at Briqueterie. Battalion Headquarters was in the centre communication trench lying to the south of the Wood. On the north-western edge were some fifty men of " A " and " B " Companies, with " D " on the north-east, and " C " further back. The shell-fire increased rather than abated and the losses continued to be heavy, whilst circumstances were not improved by the fact that a blazing sun was beating down on the position, which raised a thirst which gallons only could have slaked.

In view of the heavy casualties, which rendered it impossible to hold so much ground, orders were issued for the entire evacuation of the Wood. This movement had barely been carried out when the Germans attacked in force at 4-15 p.m. They quickly occupied the entire Wood, and succeeded in cutting off the detachments of " A " and " B " Companies occupying the north-western edge. The order to withdraw had not reached them, and the enemy occupying the Wood behind swept down upon them before any aid could be sent. These gallant lads hung on as long as was humanly possible, but were eventually bombed out. A few who tried to get away across the open were cut off by the enemy occupying a rear trench. None returned. All were either killed or captured.

Tactically, Trones Wood was of great importance. Until it was taken no attack could be launched against Guillemont, which lay about eight hundred yards to the eastward, and constituted a distinct stronghold in the German second line system. Consequently the whole Somme front was held up until this position was taken.

The action just described is thus referred to in Doyle's " 1916 Campaign " :—

" Upon July 9th at 6-40 a.m. began the third attack upon Trones Wood, led by the Seventeenth. They took over the footing already held, and by 8 o'clock they had extended it along the eastern edge, practically clearing the Wood of German infantry. There followed, however, a terrific bombardment, which caused such losses that the Seventeenth and their comrades of the 18th were ordered to fall back once more, with the result that the Scots Fusiliers had to give up the northern end of their Maltzhorn trench."

The Manchesters casualties in this engagement amounted to ten officers and one hundred and ninety-six other ranks. The 89th Brigade relieved on the 11th, and the Manchesters withdrew, first towards the British old front line trenches, east of Machine Gun Wood, and later to Bois Celestins. Here the Battalion received drafts amounting to 569 N.C.O.'s and men. On the 13th the

Battalion went into billets at Daours and Vecquemont, where for some days it was engaged in reorganising. Further drafts amounting to 144 were received.

Lieut.-Col. Grisewood took over the command from the 15th. On the 19th the Battalion was back at Bois Celestins, and on the following day marched to the Happy Valley bivouac. On the 22nd the Battalion marched to Mansel Copse bivouacs, and, on the 24th, assembled at Cambridge Copse at 1 a.m., moving to the British old line system east of Talus Boise at 10 a.m.

From the 24th to 29th the Battalion worked on assembly trenches, between Bernafay and Trones Wood, and made final preparations for the attack on Guillemont. The projected frontal advance upon Guillemont from the direction of Trones Wood would appear to have been about as difficult an operation as could well be conceived in modern warfare. Everything helped the defence and nothing favoured the attack. The approach has a glacis some 700 yards in width, which was commanded by the guns of the village, and also by those placed obliquely to north and south. There was no cover of any kind. To conform, however, with the plans of the French it was necessary that the attack should be attempted. The attack had been arranged for the morning of July 30th, and it was launched in spite of the fact that during the earlier hours the fog was so dense that it was difficult to see more than a few yards.

The 98th Brigade advanced upon the right and the 90th upon the left, the latter's objective being the village itself. The two leading Battalions, the 2nd Scots Fusiliers and the 18th Manchesters, reached it and established themselves firmly in its western suburbs ; but the German barrage fell so thickly that no help could reach them. The Seventeenth were detailed to support, and the following particulars regarding their share in the attack are given by an officer who was present :

" Our orders were that " A " Company was to support the 2nd Royal Scots Fusiliers who were to attack the village from the east side of Trones Wood, the edge of which constituted the British front line. Other Companies of the 17th Manchesters were to follow if necessary.

" On the evening of the 29th we were in the old British front line, north of Maricourt, and began to move up the assembly trenches at about 9-30—which trenches had been dug by our Battalion between Bernafay and Trones Woods. 'Zero' hour was 3-45 a.m. and we had to be in position by 2-30. Our troubles began early. When my Company got as far as Glatz Redoubt (half-mile south of Bernafay Wood) about 10 o'clock the enemy commenced a very heavy bombardment with phosgene gas shells, the first occasion I believe on which they were used. Gas helmets of the old type were speedily put on. We were plunged into darkness, and nearly suffocated in our gas-helmets. We sustained a number of casualties but finally arrived at the Assembly trenches at 2-45. The gas shelling had now ceased, and we were thankful to remove our gas helmets. Lieut. M. Miller having been killed I took charge of the left half-company deployed on the north side of the Montauban-Guillemont Road ready to advance on the village. The right half-company was to carry out the same movement on the south side of the road. We had, however, about three-quarters of an hour to wait before we were due to move forward, when we were informed that an aeroplane had observed Huns massing in the sunken road running north and south behind the village, and that our attack was to begin at once. Dawn was just breaking, but there was thick mist everywhere. Our Company moved forward in artillery formation, round the southern end of Trones Wood, and then slightly to the north, till we reached the road. Here the Company extended on both sides of the road and then moved forward in extended order towards the village, which would be about 1,000 yards away. We moved forward till we arrived at a thick barrier of wire lining the western bank of sunken road, which we found impossible to penetrate. We, therefore, moved along it to the right until we came to the opening where the Montauban-Guillemont Road cuts through it. Here we found the other half-company who had been obliged to follow the same method. Our artillery meanwhile was concentrating on the far side of the village, and we now began to be subjected to hostile rifle and machine-gun fire. We could see nothing of the Royal Scots Fusiliers, but at the corner of the cross roads we found a machine-gun manned by two men of the Machine Gun Corps, in charge of a badly-wounded officer. He was unable to supply us with any definite information, but believed that some of the R.S.F.'s were on the other side of the village. This was the only machine gun operating out of twenty-eight which had been sent up for the attack. We experienced considerable attention from the enemy, rifle fire being opened on us at quite short range. I took a bombing-party forward, but had not proceeded far when the Germans counter-attacked and caused us to fall back. The other Companies, under Major Macdonald, on the east of Trones Wood, also met with stubborn opposition.

"We were relieved just before daybreak and proceeded to the Battalion assembly point, near Maricourt. Later the Seventeenth marched to Happy Valley, where we entrained for Berguette and a month's well-earned rest."

The attack on Guillemont, unfortunately, proved a costly failure. "Two Companies of the 17th Manchesters," says Doyle, "made their way with heavy loss through the fatal barrage but failed to alleviate the situation. It would appear that in the fog the Scots were entirely surrounded, and they fought, as is their wont, while a cartridge lasted."

CHAPTER IV

THE FLERS ATTACK

THE 17th Manchesters casualties in the attack on Guillemont amounted to five officers and two hundred and seventy-four other ranks.

On August 2nd the Battalion, which had received the following officer reinforcements—Sec.-Lieuts. G. B. Shapland, H. Wilks and T. Cartman—marched to Grovetown Camp, and there entrained for Longpré. The next move was to Airaines. On the 5th the Battalion was at Berquette. Béthune was reached on the 11th, and here a stay was made until September 3rd. Lieut.-Col. Grisewood having transfererd to the 96th F.A., Major J. J. Whitehead took over the command. From September 3rd to 8th the Manchesters were in Brigade reserve at Le Touret. On the latter date the Battalion relieved the 16th Manchesters in the Festubert right sector, remaining there until the 14th, when it moved into the Festubert village line.

The 94th Brigade took over two days later, the 17th Manchesters being relieved by the 12th Yorks and Lancs. A move was made to Le Hamel and Essars and on the 17th the Battalion was at Gonnehem, whence it moved, via Chocques, Candas and Beuval, to Montonvillers, which place was reached on the 21st. Here the Battalion remained until the 4th October, when it moved by way of Flesselles and Dernancourt to Buire. On the 6th Fricourt Camp was reached.

A further attack being imminent Fricourt was quitted at 6-15 a.m. on the 10th and the Battalion relieved the 26th Royal Fusiliers and 12th K.R.R. north of Flers about midnight. The next night the Manchesters took over the line from the 2nd Bedfordshires, on the left of the Brigade front.

The attack was to be delivered upon a system of trenches in advance of Flers. On the morning of the 12th October the 17th Manchesters took over the front line which had been occupied for two days by the 16th. "B" and "D" Companies occupied the left sector, "A" and "C" the centre, and two Companies of the

R.S.F. the right. The 18th Manchesters were in support to the 17th Battalion, and the remaining two Companies of the R.S.F. supported their own Battalion. The attack took place at 2-5 p.m. without artillery preparation, until five minutes before "zero," when an intense bombardment opened. The enemy's line was a complicated network of trenches, some of which had been completely demolished. There was no unusual movement on the part of the enemy until our artillery opened. Then, as if the Germans had been forewarned, they dropped a heavy artillery barrage between our first and second lines.

"Practically no shells dropped either in or in front of our advanced line," writes an N.C.O. who took part in the attack, "but as their artillery barrage commenced a machine-gun barrage was also put up. So heavy was it that I can only compare the sound of the bullets striking our parapet to the rattle of a side-drum. Our men went over in four waves, but they were at once checked by the machine-gun fire, and I think none of them got beyond twenty yards from our line. Each wave seemed to be swallowed up in turn as it went over. Only a few wounded got back before dark.

"During the action all the officers of the Battalion became casualties, except Major Whitehead and Lieuts. Cartman and Faux. Consequently, W.O.'s took command of Companies as below:

"A" Company, C.S.M. Ham; "B" Company, R.S.M. Coates; "C" Company, C.S.M. Bingham; "D" Company, C.S.M. Jacques.

"The 18th Battalion supporting us were caught in the artillery barrage, and very few reached us. Such as did formed up with our second and third waves, and went on. The fourth wave was stopped before it went over, and these two platoons together with a few machine guns and the 18th's Lewis guns remained in the line until late in the evening, when the 16th again took over. "B" and "D" Companies managed to reach their objectives, but had to withdraw on account of the number of casualties. The Royal Scots Fusiliers got no farther forward than we did, and also withdrew at dusk."

The Flers attack, though gallantly carried out, was a confessed failure. Very little ground was gained and the casualties heavy, the Seventeenth's loss being twelve officers and 213 other ranks.

On the following day the Battalion was in support, and on the 15th was relieved by the 2nd R.S.F. The next day the Seventeenth moved to Pommern Redoubt, where it remained in bivouac until the 22nd, when it marched to Ribemont. Major J. J. Whitehead was appointed Temporary Lieut.-Col., and Sec.-Lieut. V. E. Rallison joined the Battalion. Three drafts of men were received, numbering altogether one hundred and forty-two.

On the 26th the Battalion entrained at Mericourt for Doullens, and marched on the following day to billets at Le Souich, where it received strong officer reinforcements. Lieuts. J. H. Chadwick, J. Duncan and J. E. Lightburn, and Sec.-Lieuts. N. Butterworth, R. J. Jackman, B. H. Mills and H. J. Robinson joined on the 27th, and the next day the following officers were drafted from the 3rd Manchesters: Capt. H. T. Pomfret, Sec.-Lieuts. F. E. Clayton, H. J. Cole, F. E. Holmes, F. A. Orritt, T. Longworth, W. H. Palmer, R. W. L. Wain (who subsequently won the V.C. in the Tank Corps) and E. G. Woodward. On the 29th the Battalion marched to huts at Bavincourt, and from the 30th October to 6th November it was in Divisional reserve at Bailleulval. The Battalion relieved the 2nd Royal Scots Fusiliers in the right sub-sector at Bellacourt on November 6th, and after six days in the line went into Brigade reserve. On the 18th it again relieved the 2nd Royal Scots Fusiliers in the line. Meanwhile, there had been some changes in the personnel, Capt. E. Fearenside, D.S.O., temporarily left the Battalion on October 10th, and Sec.-Lieuts. F. A. Rayner and C. S. Miles were taken on the strength on November 7th and 10th respectively.

Lieut.-Col. J. J. Whitehead proceeded on leave on the 14th November, and Capt. H. T. Pomfret took over the temporary command in September, whilst Major (Temporary Lieut.-Col.) C. L. Macdonald left the Battalion to take command of the 30th Division School. The Manchesters were again in Divisional reserve at Bailleulval from the 24th to 30th, when they again took over the line at Bellacourt.

This was an extraordinarily quiet sector and relief took place in broad daylight. The Divisional front was extremely lengthy and each Battalion had much larger expanse of trench to man than usual. This was accomplished by the establishment of posts at intervals. " No man's land " consisted of a shallow depression densely packed with wire, and the nearest German post to our front line was the head of a sap, known as the Talus. Just after Christmas it was the intention of the Battalion to raid this sap-head for identification purposes. Lieut. Woodward and Sec.-Lieut. Miles were in charge of the raiding party, but owing to a last minute hitch the attempt was never made. The original intention had been to blow a gap through the German wire by means of a Bangalore Torpedo—a steel tube filled with T.N.T. and detonated. This harpoon-shaped instrument, 35 feet long, was duly carried over the top by a party of twenty-five men in charge of Sec.-Lieut. T. Longworth and C.S.M. Jacques, of " D " Company, but the scheme did not progress far enough for use to be made of it. As usual on such an occasion it rained in torrents and the trenches in places were over knee deep in water and mud.

A peculiarity about this part of the British front was that the three villages immediately behind the Battalion front were, when the Seventeenth arrived, almost undamaged by shell fire, and village-life was carried on much as usual. It was reported that an officer bought the Continental Edition of a well-known English daily paper at the end of Church Street, by which name the main communication trench was known. Trench life was not at all comfortable, for the weather towards the end of the year was very bad and a portion of the Battalion's right front had to be evacuated in consequence of the uninhabitable conditions. A singular feature of the Battalion's stay in this " cushy " sector was that German shelling invariably occurred on relief days, suggesting that the enemy could either overlook our positions or that he was well informed. After the Hun retired in the early part of 1917 it was discovered that he had a reinforced-concrete observation tower in a ruined building at Blairville, a village directly in front of the Seventeenth's position, which was subsequently found to be undermined with vast tunnels capable of holding at least a couple of battalions.

Exchanges continued every few days until January 6th, 1917, when the Battalion marched to Bavincourt, and on the following day to Corps reserve at Sus St. Leger. Capt. W. B. Orr joined the Battalion and took command of " B " Company, and Capt. E. Fearenside, D.S.O., rejoined and took command of " A " Company. Sec.-Lieuts. J. Broadbent, D. H. Budenberg, L. Rathbone and F. Thorp were also added to the strength and there were two small drafts of men during the month. Lieut.-Col. J. J. Whitehead rejoined on the 15th and Capt. E. Fearenside, D.S.O., was appointed Second-in-Command on the 23rd.

The Battalion continued various forms of training at Sus St. Leger until February 4th, when it moved to billets at Pommern. Whilst here Capt. Fearenside took over temporary command, and Sec.-Lieuts. A. C. Carter, H. V. Hobbs and W. F. Swift joined from base. Until March 20th, when the Battalion relieved the 2nd Bedfords in the line in front of Agny and south of Mercatel, they were busily engaged on railway work preparatory to the battle of Arras which opened on Easter Monday.

For some time the Germans had been gradually falling back from the Somme to Arras, and when the Seventeenth took over from the Bedfords they became engaged in quite a new mode of warfare in sapping forward each night and keeping touch with the enemy. During one of these nightly patrols the Seventeenth had the misfortune to lose two officers, Sec.-Lieuts. V. E. Rallison and H. V. Hobbs, and four men. They encountered the enemy in a ruined mill and were thrown off their guard in consequence of being challenged in English.

The 2nd Royal Scots Fusiliers relieved on the 23rd and the Battalion moved back into Madeleine Redoubt, an old German strong point, where they were heavily shelled and sustained many casualties. Whilst here working parties went out nightly to dig communication trenches to the front line of the Brigade sector.

From March 27th to April 3rd the Battalion was billeted in the tunnels at Blairville, still providing working parties under R.E. It was later in Brigade reserve south of Mercatel.

On April 13th the Seventeenth marched, via Berles and Beinvillers, to billets at St. Amand, but five days later it was back in the Mercatel area.

CHAPTER V

IN THE ARRAS SECTOR AND AT YPRES

THE Battalion left St. Amand at noon on the 18th April, arriving at the Hindenburg system of trenches near Neuville-Vitasse at 4 a.m. on the 19th, and on the following day relieving a Battalion of the London Regiment in the hurriedly-dug trenches in front of Héninel, and facing Cherisy. Prior to the morning of the 23rd, when the continuance of the Arras advance was due, the Battalion sustained a number of casualties in consequence of the heavy hostile shelling, Lieut. F. E. Holmes and thirteen men being wounded and six men killed. At 4-45 a.m. on the morning of the 23rd the Battalion moved to the attack under the command of Lieut.-Col. Whitehead and the following officer personnel :—

Headquarters : Capt. F. Duncan (*Adjutant*) ; Lieut. G. F. Potts ; Sec.-Lieut. T. Longworth (*Intelligence Officer*).

" A " Company : Lieut. A. T. G. Holt ; Sec.-Lieut. W. H. Palmer.

" B " Company : Capt. T. Cartman ; Sec.-Lieut. D. H. Budenberg ; Sec.-Lieut. F. A. Raynor.

" C " Company : A/Capt. H. J. Cole ; Sec.-Lieut. F. A. Orritt ; Sec.-Lieut. B. H. Mills.

" D " Company : Capt. J. H. Chadwick ; Sec.-Lieut. R. I. Jackman ; Sec.-Lieut. L. Rathbone ; Sec.-Lieut. J. Broadbent.

The Battalion took up an advanced position, and dug themselves in, but at 9 a.m. the enemy launched a counter-attack of great violence which, owing to the gallantry of the defenders, was repulsed and the position maintained. At 2 p.m. a further enemy attack was made and the Battalion suffered many casualties. At nightfall it was withdrawn with a strength of 260 men out of 650 who went over the top. Lieut. G. F. Potts and Sec.-Lieuts. W. H. Palmer and B. H. Mills were killed in action, and Capt. J. H. Chadwick, Capt. T. Cartman, A/Capt. H. J. Cole and Sec.-Lieuts. F. A. Orritt, R. J. Jackman, F. A. Raynor and J. Broadbent were wounded. Lieut. A. T. S. Holt was taken prisoner.

R.S.M. H. Coates performed excellent work in bringing in wounded under heavy shell and machine gun fire. There being no stretcher-bearers at hand he organised a party from Headquarters' Company and assisted in bringing in the wounded, among them being Capt. J. H. Chadwick and Sec.-Lieut. F. A. Orritt. He attended Lieut. G. F. Potts when that officer was mortally wounded, finding him cover in a shell hole. Further, when news of a counter-attack was received, he organised Headquarters' Company to defend the front-line trench.

Upon being relieved the Battalion marched back to the Hindenburg line, near Neuville-Vitasse, remaining there until the 27th. Upon this date it moved by march-route to Arras; trained thence to St. Pol; finally moving again by march-route to billets at Heriçourt. Here Lieut.-Col. H. A. Johnson rejoined and took over the command from Major Whitehead. The Battalion remained at Hericourt until May 3rd, receiving drafts and training. On this date it moved, via Guinecourt, Linzen and Fillieyres, to Cherienne, where reorganisation was commenced.

For Distinguished Gallantry in the attack of April 23rd the following awards were made :—

D.S.O., Major J. J. Whitehead; *M.C.'s*, Capt. T. Cartman, Lieut. A. T. S. Holt, R.S.M. H. Coates; *D.C.M.'s*, R.S.M. H. Bingham, Private W. Flaherty.

While Military Medals were awarded to the undermentioned :— Privates S. Ackerley, J. E. Fielden, J. Farmer, J. Helsby, J. N. Roberts, W. R. Spratley, J. Ward.

On May 20th the Battalion was again on the move, proceeding by march-route to Blangerval. It was now heading north for the Ypres area, proceeding by way of Hericourt, Croisette, St. Pol and Wavrans to billets at Monchy Cayeux. On the 24th it was at Guarbecque, and on the following day in billets a little to the north of Le Brearde, where two days were spent. The last day of the month found the Battalion at Zoufques. Here it received drafts, remaining until June 6th. On that date it proceeded by route-march to St. Omer, entrained for Poperinghe, and proceeded thence to St. Lawrence Camp.

On June 9th the Manchesters moved into the forward area, in reserve to the 2nd R.S.F.'s, and on the following day took over the front line. The 1st Worcesters relieved on the 14th and the Seventeenth fell back to Zillebeke Bund and Château Segard. From here the Battalion supplied working parties to the 2nd Canadian Tunnelling Company.

During the spell in the Ypres Salient, in the Zillebeke area, Sec.-Lieut. S. A. Knowles led a raid on the German line which resulted in the capture of two prisoners without any loss to ourselves. This was a notable achievement inasmuch as it secured the first identification that had been obtained on the Ypres front for some time.

Lieut.-Col. H. A. Johnson proceeded on home leave on June 17th, when Major J. J. Whitehead, D.S.O., took temporary command, with Major E. Fearenside, D.S.O., as second-in-command. The remainder of the month of June was passed chiefly at Micmac and Palace Camps.

From July 1st to 5th the Battalion provided working parties on Cable trench, near Zillebeke. On the latter date a move was made by march-route to Reninghelst, thence by train to Watten, and again by march-route to Nielles-les-Ardres. From then on, until the 30th, several moves were made—Dallington Camp (Wippenhoek area), Steenvoorde and Château Segard. During this time intensive training proceeded, reinforcements were received, and preparations made for the July attack at Ypres. On the night of the 30th the Battalion moved into assembly positions in " no man's land " and at 3-50 a.m. on the following morning went into action in front of Ypres with the following strength :—

Lieut.-Col. J. J. Whitehead, D.S.O., Capt. W. J. C. Faux, Lieuts. J. Duncan, E. G. Woodward, Sec.-Lieuts. D. H. Budenberg, A. C. Carter, J. L. Clayton, H. G. Frith, T. F. Goldsmith, R. Halliday, P. Shenton, J. Hillian, S. A. Knowles, A. N. Marchant, W. R. M. Parry, R. F. Richardson, R. Sant, W. H. Smith, E. H. Southcombe, P. Ward.

Capt. H. T. Pomfret acted as Liaison Officer at advanced Divisional Headquarters ; Sec.-Lieut. C. S. Miles, Brigade Observation Officer ; Sec.-Lieut. B. R. Cobley was in charge of Brigade Mobile Dump. Other ranks numbered 547.

The 16th and 18th Manchesters having attained the first objective of the attack the 17th Battalion passed through the 16th and consolidated just short of the second objective, owing to the very heavy machine-gun fire which held up the attack. Sec.-Lieuts. Frith and Southcombe were killed ; Capts. Faux and Orr, and Sec.-Lieuts. Halliday, Marchant, Parry, Sant and Shenton wounded, and Sec.-Lieut. Richardson wounded and missing. Of other ranks 19 were killed, 112 wounded and 34 missing.

The Battalion was withdrawn in the early morning of August 1st, and proceeded to rendezvous at Zillebeke, removing later during the same day to the Château Segard area. Later movements during the month were to Wippenhoek, St. Sylvestre-Cappel, Merris, Berthen and finally to the Kemmel area.

Lieut.-Col. J. J. Whitehead, D.S.O., having proceeded on ten days' leave on the 16th, Major E. Fearenside, D.S.O., took over the command.

For gallant conduct in the attack of July 31st the following awards were made :—

M.C., Capt. W. B. Orr; *D.C.M.'s*, Sergeant F. Cowman, Private P. Duffy; *M.M.'s*, Corporal W. Fearnley, Privates A. E. Hare, R. Armstrong, J. Murphy.

The Battalion relieved the 14th Australian Battalion, south of Messines, on the 28th August, being in reserve to the 4th Australian Brigade. The next night it relieved the 52nd Australian Battalion in the line, in the sector north of the river Douve. The tour lasted until September 3rd, when the Manchesters were relieved by the 5th Oxford and Bucks L.I., and marched to Kia-Ora Camp, Kemmel area. Whilst there the Battalion provided working-parties in the line, under supervision of the R.E.

On September 12th the Manchesters relieved the 2nd Royal Scots Fusiliers as support Battalion at Torreken Farm, right Brigade area, and moved into the line on the 22nd, relieving the 2nd Bedfords in the Hollebeke area. During the month Capt. A. C. Carter was severely wounded, and the Battalion had eleven men killed in action and nineteen wounded.

October 1st found the Battalion still at Hollebeke in the left sub-sector, but the 2nd Bedfords relieved the same night, and the Manchesters went into Divisional reserve at Vrolandhoek Camp. Sec.-Lieuts. F. V. Harrison, H. Owens, H. T. Prentis, F. C. Sturman, J. A. Woollam, and K. Yorke-Jones joined from the base. Lieut.-Col. J. J. Whitehead was granted extended leave, on medical grounds, and Major E. Fearenside, D.S.O., was promoted A/Lieut.-Col. during his absence.

Subsequently the following officers joined from base :—

Sec.-Lieuts. G. R. Barnes, F. Dunn, J. E. Hatton, W. M. Harrison, C. E. Hope.

The Battalion had been temporarily attached to the 8th Corps, but on October 18th it was transferred to the Canadian Corps for railway work, and moved by 'bus to the neighbourhood of Goldfish Château, near Ypres. On the 31st it rejoined the 8th Corps, and moved to a camp near Kemmel. November 8th found the Battalion at Daylight Corner Camp, near Lindenhoek. On the 11th it was in the Strazeele area, and on the 14th proceeded by 'bus to the east of Steenvoorde. On the 24th the Battalion was at Chippawa Camp, near Reninghelst; next day at Tor Top Tunnels; and on the 30th it took over the Brigade left sub-sector south of Polderhoek.

A/Lieut.-Col. Fearenside proceeded on leave to England, and Major W. H. Colley, of the Yorkshire Regiment, took over the command.

On the 30th November the Manchesters were in the line astride the Menin Road, with the Anzacs on their immediate left, when they attacked Polderhoek Château. In this attack "B" Company had over twenty casualties. The position was held until the night of December 3rd, when the 17th King's Liverpool Regiment relieved, and the Manchesters returned to Chippawa Camp, near Reninghelst, remaining there until the 12th. On the latter date the Battalion was back in support to the line. The enemy attacked on the 14th in front of Polderhoek and regained about 300 yards frontage of the line gained by the Anzacs on the 3rd. "C" and "B" Companies of the Seventeenth were sent up to reinforce the 18th Manchesters. This movement was carried out in daylight, and happily, without casualties. Jericho Pill-box and a portion of the trench evacuated by the 18th Manchesters were occupied by these Companies. From the 18th to 24th the Seventeenth were again at Chippawa Camp.

Corporal Giblin ("B" Company) and Private Preston ("C" Company) were awarded the Military Medal.

As the Battalion was due back in the line across the Menin Road on Christmas Eve the festive season was celebrated in advance. The 30th Division Concert Party—the "Blue Birds"—gave an entertainment on the 21st, and Christmas dinner was served by officers in the huts at Chippawa Camp on the 23rd.

The Seventeenth remained in the line until the 30th, when it moved into Brigade reserve at Tor Top Tunnels. Subsequently a move was made by route-march on the 30th to Sivan Château, where Lieut.-Col. Fearenside rejoined and took over command.

Sec.-Lieut. K. Yorke-Jones was killed in action on the 26th, Sec.-Lieut. P. Ward on the following day, and during the month the Battalion had eleven men killed and twenty-six wounded.

CHAPTER VI

THE LAST YEAR: BATTLE OF ST. QUENTIN AND LATER

JANUARY 1st, 1918, found the Battalion billeted at Swan Château and supplying working-parties for the Ypres sector front line. On the 5th the Battalion proceeded to Dickebusch, thence by train to Blaringhem, and by route-march to Ebblinghem. The next move was by train from Steenbecque to Longeau (Amiens), thence to La Neuville (Corbie), which place was reached on the 8th and a stay made until the 13th.

Lieut.-Col. J. J. Whitehead, D.S.O., rejoined on the 6th. Major H. T. Pomfret also rejoined, and Major W. H. Colley transferred to the 2nd Battalion Yorkshire Regiment.

Harbonnieres was reached on the 14th and a move was made to Gruny on the same day, where the Battalion remained until the 19th. From this date until the 26th it was at Moyencourt. Two days were spent at Montescourt in the St. Quentin area. During the 27th to the 28th the Battalion was billeted in sections at Sinceny, Autreville and Marisel. Then it took over the line in the Brigade left sub-sector (Aurigny Rouy) from 29th Dragoons, 5th French Cavalry Division. The position was the extreme right flank of the British line.

Matters were so quiet at this period that a chapel was established at Headquarters. In the front line the men slept in beds, left by the French, and enjoyed hot meals daily. Somewhere about this period the Croix de Guerre was awarded to C.S.M. F. H. Silcock and Sergeant G. Royle. Further, a draft was received from the 19th Manchesters of a number of officers and 281 other ranks.

The Battalion remained in the line until February 9th, when it was relieved by the 7th Londons, and moved to billets at Chauny. On the 10th it was billeted at Guiscard, and on the following day at Freniches, where it remained until the 17th. Next day it was at Chaulnes, where a stay was made until the 28th, when the Battalion moved by march-route to Dury. From the 7th to the 10th March it was billeted at Etreillers, where general training and the manning of battle-positions was carried out. On the last-named date the Battalion relieved the 2nd Yorkshires in the left sector of the line before St. Quentin. This tour lasted until the 18th, when the 16th Manchesters relieved, and the Seventeenth was billeted partly at Savy Dug-outs and at Vaux.

The long-expected enemy attack opened at 4-50 a.m. on the 21st, and the Battalion immediately took up its battle-positions as follows:—

"D" on right front; "B" on left front; "C" for counter attack; "A" in reserve.

On the Battalion's right flank were the 2nd Yorkshires, with the 2nd Bedfords on the left, and the 2nd Royal Scots Fusiliers in Etreillers defences.

It should be noted that the Seventeenth was in the rear of the 16th Manchesters, who under Lieut.-Col. W. Elstob were holding forward battle-positions. The story of the wonderful defence of Manchester Hill until late in the afternoon has been told elsewhere.

Until noon on the morning of the 21st observation was impossible although the Battalion had a signalling station in a tree-top near the Goodman Redoubt. Visibility was bad until the afternoon when the enemy's movements were clearly established. Communication was, however, kept up with the forward Company by the excellent work of the signallers and when night fell the Seventeenth's position was still intact, although the enemy were massing in front. Dawn on the 22nd was also enshrouded in dense mist. Early on the enemy entered the Quarry at Savy, but a smart attack, led by Sec.-Lieut. F. V. Harrison of "B" Company (Capt. Cottrell), drove out the Germans and resulted in the capture of 31 prisoners and the release of several men belonging to another unit. Towards the afternoon the Germans gradually encroached upon the flanks, and this advance was assisted by low-flying aeroplanes that constantly harassed the defenders. Brigade Headquarters moved back, and in maintaining communication across a shell-strewn area several runners were killed. S.O.S. was asked for both by runner and pigeon, but there was no artillery reply. It looked like fighting to the last man, and everyone seemed to be aware of the fact.

Preceded by a heavy bombardment the enemy attacked about 4 p.m. and after heavy fighting succeeded in surrounding "B," "D" and "C" Companies' keeps, which after the last round of ammunition had been expended fell into the enemy's hands. "A" Company and Headquarter's position, Goodman Redoubt, was evacuated an hour after the enemy had gained a footing it in. Here too all ammunition had been expended and the Redoubt was now surrounded. Yet notwithstanding heavy machine-gun, rifle, and artillery fire the survivors of the Battalion managed to extricate themselves and were withdrawn, first to the Villeque line, near Bunny Wood, where they were reorganised. Owing, however, to the enemy closing in on both flanks the Battalion was further withdrawn to Muille Villette.

Amongst officers and men who especially distinguished themselves by their gallantry in this engagement the following should be named :

Capt. Ince and Capt. Keefe, Sec.-Lieut. Miles, Sec.-Lieut. F. V. Harrison, C.S.M. Rhodes and Private Coleman.

At 5 a.m. on the 23rd the Battalion marched to Moyencourt, where during the morning it took up a position in reserve at Lannoy Farm. At 9 p.m. it moved to defensive positions east of Esmery Hallon.

The enemy attacked again at 9 a.m. on the 24th, when owing to both flanks having been withdrawn the Battalion was compelled to fall back and new positions were taken up on the canal bank east of Moyencourt. On the following day enemy attacks were broken up by our rifle and artillery fire and heavy casualties inflicted. At 4-15 p.m. orders were received to withdraw from the canal bank, the enemy being well round on both flanks. The 2nd Bedfords, 2nd Royal Scots Fusiliers and 16th and 17th Manchesters held the Brigade sector intact, under the command of Lieut.-Col. J. J. Whitehead, D.S.O., until this order was received. The Battalion was then withdrawn to Roiglise, and on receipt of further orders moved to Ercbes. On the 26th the Battalion manned reserve defences to Folies. Lieut.-Col. Whitehead was admitted to hospital, and Capt. R. C. M. Keefe, M.C., took over temporary command.

At noon on the 27th the enemy again launched an attack in force. The front line fell back through the Battalion's lines and, owing to the withdrawal of the flanking Battalions, the Seventeenth were compelled to fall back. A position 1,000 yards in rear was then taken up.

The C.O., Capt. Keefe, M.C., was killed at 2 p.m., and Capt. and Adjutant J. Duncan took over the command. During the forenoon of the 28th the enemy drove in the flanking Battalions and attempted to surround the Brigade sector. At noon information was received that the French had taken over, and the Battalion was ordered to withdraw. This was carried out under heavy hostile machine-gun and rifle fire, and the Battalion marched to billets at Rouvres, west of Moreuil, which place was reached at 8 p.m. On the following day a composite Battalion was formed of men of the 17th Manchesters, 2nd Yorks and 2nd Wilts, and this Battalion was attached to the 4th French Reserve Cavalry Division

On the 31st March the Battalion and transport moved to the St. Valery-sur-Somme area, and was billeted at Estraboeuf. Major H. T. Pomfret rejoined from 18th Corps and took over command.

The casualties for the month were as follows :—

Killed in action : Capt. R. C. M. Keefe ; Sec.-Lieut. C. E. Hope ; 39 other ranks. Wounded in action : Capt. N. S. Ince, M.C. ; Lieut. J. F. Cottrell ; Sec.-Lieut. H. A. Arnold ; Sec.-Lieut. H. Owens ; Sec.-Lieut. J. E. Hatton ; 100 other ranks. Wounded and Missing : Capt. J. L. Clayton ; 20 other ranks. Killed : A/Capt. H. Taylor, M.C. ; Sec.-Lieut.-F. Cartwright ; Missing : Capt. E. G. Woodward ; Lieut. T. Longworth ; Sec.-Lieut. G. Dunscombe ; Sec.-Lieut. F. V. Harrison ; Sec.-Lieut. S. A. Jackson ; Sec. Lieut. C. S. Miles ; 281 other ranks.

The Battalion remained in billets at Estraboeuf until April 5th, during which period reorganisation was carried out. On this date it marched to Woincourt, entrained for Proven, and marched thence to camp in the St. Sixte area, where training was continued. On April 9th the Battalion marched to White Mill Camp, Elverdinghe, and whilst here provided working-parties under R.G.A. for moving shells in forward area. Major Fearenside, D.S.O., rejoined on the 16th and took over command. Capt. T. Cartman, M.C., also re-joined and took over command of "B" Company. The Battalion marched to Scottish Camp, Busseboom, on the 18th, being transferred from 2nd Corps to 22nd Corps, and was warned to be prepared to move at short notice. "A" and "B" Companies were fused to form "C" Company, 16th Manchesters, and "C" and "D" to constitute "D" Company in the same Battalion. On the 20th Headquarters moved to Buysscheure in the Lederzeele area.

The remains of the Battalion now forming two Companies of the 16th Manchesters, under their Headquarters marched to the front line near Spoil Bank and Lock 8. On the 25th the enemy made a renewed attack and forced back the line south of Ypres-Comines Canal. "C" and "D" (Composite Company) gallantly led by Sec.-Lieut. D. H. Budenberg, who was killed in the advance, counter-attacked and restored the situation on this front.

The remaining Composite Company, under Sec.-Lieut. F. Ruddy, D.C.M., successfully formed a defensive flank, which enabled the Battalion to maintain its position.

In thick mist on the 26th the enemy broke through the line held by the Battalion on the Manchester's left, and completely enveloped "C" and "D" Composite Company.

The survivors of the other Company were subsequently withdrawn after hard fighting, to the north bank of the Canal, Lock 8, suffering heavy casualties during withdrawal. Here a line was formed and held during two days' fighting.

On the 29th the Battalion was relieved, and withdrawn to Scottish Camp, Busseboom, where the survivors of the 16th and 17th Manchesters were formed into one Composite Company and attached to the 2nd Yorkshire Regiment. This Company proceeded to man trenches near Ouderdom.

In addition to Sec.-Lieut. D. H. Budenberg killed in action, Sec.-Lieut. F. P. Leybourn was wounded and the following officers were found to be missing :—

Sec.-Lieuts. S. W. Cannon, J. Hillian, G. Leach, M.M., C. T. Marshall, H. T. Prentis, L. Rathbone, W. H. Smith, J. A. Woollam. There were besides 212 other ranks casualties.

Lieut. J. F. Cottrell and Sec.-Lieut. H. Heywood were awarded the Military Cross; Sergeant W. Brookes, Private R. Allen, the Distinguished Conduct Medal; and Privates E. Hurley and J. J. Pickavance, and Lance/Corporals F. Stafford and C. Turner the Military Medal.

On May 1st Capt. T. Cartman, M.C., and Sec.-Lieuts. F. Ruddy, D.C.M., and C. Hill returned to the Seventeenth's Headquarters at Buysscheure, where they were joined by the rest of the Composite Battalion on the 9th. On the 13th Lieut. D. E. Morgan and 33 other ranks (Transport personnel) proceeded to Transport Disbandment Camp. The following day Sec.-Lieut. F. Halliwell and 155 other ranks proceeded to base for redrafting.

On the 15th what personnel remained was formed into a training cadre for the purpose of training American troops. The cadre consisted of Major E. Fearenside, D.S.O., Capt. and Adjutant J. Duncan, Lieut. and Quartermaster G. F. V. Dalley, Major H. T. Pomfret; Captains T. Cartman, M.C., and C. Sadler; Sec.-Lieuts. R. Halliday, C. Hill and F. Ruddy, D.C.M.; and 54 other ranks. This cadre, together with the band, entrained at Audruicq, for Woincourt, and marched thence to billets at Guerville, near Eu. Here it was affiliated with the 2/140th U.S. Infantry Regiment. Training commenced on the 20th May—tactical work, specialists, Lewis gunners, bombers, and lectures each evening.

Later the cadre was split up and one part under Major H. T. Pomfret proceeded to La Haie Château to assist in training the 3/140th U.S. Infantry Regiment.

During the month the following honours were awarded :—

Military Cross: Sec.-Lieut. F. Ruddy, D.C.M.; Sec.-Lieut. C. Hill. *Military Cross and Bar:* Sec.-Lieut. T. F. Goldsmith (attached 90th T.M.B.). *Distinguished Conduct Medal:* C.S.M.

G. Green; Private C. F. Carter. *Military Medal:* Lance/Corporal H. Hodson; Private T. W. Walker. *Bar to Military Medal:* Corporal J. Helsby, M.M.; Private E. Hurley, M.M.

The following were also mentioned in despatches:—

Capt. and Adjutant J. Duncan; Capt. C. S. Miles; R.Q.M.S. J. Wood.

On July 21st the two American Battalions left Guerville and Le Haie and were replaced by the 1/132nd and 2/132nd U.S. Infantry Regiments. On this date the Cadre and 132nd Infantry Regiment moved by bus to Molliens-au-Bois, remaining until the 27th.

During this tour the Vadeni line was occupied for twenty-four hours. On the 27th the Cadre marched to Bertaucourt, and on the following day to Pont-Remy, where it was affiliated to the 123rd Machine Gun Battalion (U.S.A.)

On July 3rd the Cadre moved to Yaucourt-Bussus, and on the 20th to Cocquerel. The next move was to Haudricourt on the 23rd, where two days later orders for disbandment were received. The Cadre was disbanded on July 30th, when the personnel—less Lieut.-Col. E. Fearenside, D.S.O., Major H. T. Pomfret, Lieut. and Quartermaster G. E. V. Dalley, and seven other ranks—was transferred to the 13th Manchesters.

The remainder proceeded to base.

Later Honours: Major H. T. Pomfret, M.C., November 1918; Capt. C. Sadler, M.C., June 1919; Capt. E. G. Woodward, M.C., July 1919; Capt. C. S. Miles, M.C.; Sec.-Lieut. F. V. Harrison, M.C.; Lieut.-Col. E. Fearenside, D.S.O., O.B.E. and "Mention," June 1919.

Appendix I
HONOURS

DISTINGUISHED SERVICE ORDER

Name	*Rank*	*Place and date of deed*	*Gazetted*
FEARENSIDE, Edmund ..	T/Capt.		26-9-16
MACDONALD, Charles Leslie	Capt. T/Maj.		1-1-17
„ „ (*Bar*) ..	T/Lieut.-Col.	Ypres, 1917 ..	26-9-17
(*Attached* 19*th*)			9-1-18
MADDEN, John Greville ..	T/Capt.		25-8-16
WHITEHEAD, John James	T/Major (A/Lt.-Col.)		4-6-17
RAE, Geo. Bantham Leathart (10th B. Liv. R.) *attached* 17th	Major	France & Flanders..	3-6-19

MILITARY CROSS

Rank	*Name*	*Gazetted*	*Remarks*
T/Lt. (A/Cpt.)	CARTMAN, Thomas ..	18-6-17	
17/9369 S.M.	COATES, Henry	18-6-17	
T/Sec.-Lieut.	GOLDSMITH, Thomas Fredk.	16-9-18	
„	„ „ (*Bar*) ..	Same date	
T/Sec.-Lieut.	HEYWOOD, Norman ..	26-7-18	
T/Lieut.	COBLEY, Benjamin Repington (*Attached 2nd Batt.*)	15-2-30 30-7-19	Fonsomme Line, 1/2-10-18
T/Sec.-Lieut.	HOLT, Alan Thomas Selbourne	18-6-17	
T/Lieut.	MANSERGH, Robert Forbes	26-9-16	
T/Sec.-Lieut.	RUDDY, Fred .. .. D.C.M. (in R. Fus., 25-11-16)	16-9-18	
Capt. T/Maj.	POMFRET, Hugh Tunbridge	1-1-19	France & Flanders
T/Capt.	SADLER, Charles	3-6-19	France & Flanders
T/Sec.-Lieut.	TAYLOR, Harry	26-5-17	K. in a., 22-3-18
T/Lt. (A/Cpt.)	WOODWARD, Ernest George	30-1-20	To date 5-5-19
T/Lieut.	WHITTALL, Frederick John Gordon	26-9-16	
T/Sec.-Lieut.	DAWSON, William Harrington Hulton	10-1-17	

DISTINGUISHED CONDUCT MEDAL

No.	*Name*	*Rank*	*Place and date of deed*	*Gazetted*
27318.	ALLEN, R. ..	Pte.	Spoil Bk., Ypres, 30-4-18	3-9-18
8066.	BINGHAM, H. ..	C.S.M.	Héninel, 23-4-17 ..	4-6-17 9-7-17
11760.	BROOKES, W. ..	Sgt.	Spoil Bk., Ypres, 30-4-18	3-9-18
17/9323.	CARTER, C. F. ..	L/Cpl.	Guerville, 31-5-18 ..	3-9-18
17/8501.	COWMAN, F. ..	Sgt.	Ypres, 31-7-17	22 10-17 26-1-18
38544.	CURRAN, —, M.M.	Sgt.	5-6-18	3-10-18
28259.	DUFFY, P. ..	Pte.	Ypres, 31-7-17	22-10-17 26-1-18
24357.	DUNN, J.	Pte.		3-6-18 21-10-18
33875.	DUNN, T.	Pte.	Ypres, 15-9-17	22-10-17 26-1-18
2729.	FLAHERTY, W.	Pte.	Héninel, 23-4-17 ..	18-6-17
51920.	GREEN, B. ..	C.S.M.	Guerville, 31-5-18 ..	3-9-18

DISTINGUISHED CONDUCT MEDAL—*continued*

No.	*Name*	*Rank*	*Place and date of deed*	*Gazetted*
17/1686.	HALL, A.	Pte.		26-9-16
302534.	JONES, J. ..	L/Cpl.		1-1-18 17-4-18
8781.	OVERTON, C. E.	Pte.		26-5-17
43143.	PASCOE, C. F. ..	Pte.	Ypres, 15-9-17	22-10-17 26-1-18
17/9014.	ROYLE, G. ..	Cpl. (L/Sgt.)	Since Nov. 1915 notable in mending roads in La Douve and Menin Rd. Sectors; and at St. Quentin March 18th.	1-1-19 3-9-19
17/8323.	WALLWORK, E.	Sgt.		26-9-16
43403.	YOUNG, J. E. ..	C.S.M.		3-6-18 21-10-18

MILITARY MEDAL

No.	*Name*	*Rank*	*Place and date of deed*	*Gazetted*
8046.	ACKERLEY, S. ..	Pte.	Héninel, 23-4-17 ..	9-7-17
2271.	ARMSTRONG, R.	Pte.	Ypres, 31-7-17	22-9-17
26256.	BENNETT, H. ..	Pte.		16-11-16
17/9126.	BLADES, M. ..	Cpl.		16-11-16
17/8079.	BLAKELEY, F. ..	Pte.		21-10-16
17/8409.	BOLT, W. N. ..	Pte.		16-11-16
17/9500.	BOWER, A. ..	Pte.		16-11-16
9227.	CHRICHTON, N. D.	Sgt.		30-1-20
17/8543.	ENTWISTLE, N.	L/Cpl.		16-11-16
9313.	FARMER, J. ..	Pte.	Héninel, 23-4-17 ..	9-7-17
47423.	FEARNLEY, W.	L/Cpl.	Ypres, 31-7-17	28-9-17
46461.	FIELDEN, J. E. ..	Pte.	Héninel, 23-4-17 ..	9-7-17
17/11186.	FRAWLEY, J. C.	Pte.		21-9-16
17/26327.	GUTHRIE, H. S.	L/Cpl.		23-8-16
43344.	HARE, A. E. ..	Pte.	Ypres, 31-7-17	28-9-17
47427.	HELSBY, J. ..	Pte.	Héninel, 23-4-17 ..	9-7-17
"	" (*Bar*) ..	(Cpl.)	Guerville, 31-5-18 ..	13-9-18
3186.	HODSON, G. H. ..	L/Cpl.		29-8-18
50002.	HURLEY, E. ..	Pte.	Ypres, 30-4-18	27-6-18
"	" (*Bar*) ..	Pte.	Guerville, 31-5-18 ..	29-8-18
10286.	KENYON, T. ..	Pte.		22-1-17
8742.	MOXON, F. W. ..	Sgt.		11-11-16
21073.	MURPHY, J. ..	Pte.	Ypres, 31-7-17	28-9-17
33403.	PICKAVANCE, J. J.	Pte.	Spoil Bk., Ypres, 30-4-18	27-6-18
240185.	PRESTON, E. ..	Pte.	Ypres, 16-12-17	13-3-18
8827.	ROGERS, H. ..	Pte.		11-11-16
17/8875.	SCHOLEY, C. ..	Pte.		21-9-16
17/8855.	SCOTT, J.	Cpl.		22-1-17
43337.	SPRATLEY, W. R.	Pte.	Héninel, 23-4-17 ..	9-7-17
2702.	STAFFORD, G. W.	Pte.	Spoil Bank, Ypres, 30-4-18	27-6-18
47317.	TURNER, C. ..	L/Cpl.	Spoil Bank, Ypres, 30-4-18	27-6-18
203202.	WALKER, J. W.	Pte.	Guerville, 31-5-18 ..	13-9-18
17/8976.	WILKINSON, A.	Pte.		22-1-17
17/8935.	WORTHINGTON, F.N.	Pte.		16-11-16
17/8955.	WRIGHT, L. W. ..	Cpl.		16-11-16
2163.	GIBLIN, A. ..	Cpl.	Ypres, 16-12-17.. ..	13-3-18
8818.	ROBERTS, J. ..	Pte.	Héninel, 23-4-17 ..	9-7-17

MERITORIOUS SERVICE MEDAL

No.	Rank	Name	Gazetted
11760.	Sgt. ..	BROOKES, W. (D.C.M.)	29-8-18
43274.	Sgt. ..	PACKER, W. A.	17-6-18
7/9310.	L/Cpl. ..	YOUNG, G.	17-6-18

FOREIGN DECORATIONS

BELGIUM—CROIX DE GUERRE

No.	Rank	Name	Gazetted
8852.	Sgt.	ROYLE, George	12-7-18
8295.	C.S.M.	SILCOCK, Frank Howard	12-7-18

APPENDIX II
OFFICERS KILLED
(IN ORDER OF DATE)

OFFICERS KILLED (in order of date)

Rank	*Name*	*Date*	*Place*
T/Sec.-Lt.	JOHNSTON, Robert London ..	13-12-15	Bayencourt
T/Sec.-Lt.	TONGE, William Russell	12-1-16	Suzanne
T/Sec.-Lt.	CLESHAM, Thomas Henry ..	1-7-16	
Capt.	VAUDREY, Norman	1-7-16	Montauban
T/Lieut.	SPROAT, Gerald Maitland .. (11th B. Man. R.) *attached*	1-7-16	Montauban
T/Capt.	FORD, Reginald James	2-7-16	Montauban
T/Capt.	KENWORTHY, Stanley	1-7-16	Montauban
T/Sec.-Lt.	CALVERT, Robert Mayson ..	6-7-16	
Sec.-Lieut.	GRIGG, Malcolm Howard .. .. (26th B. Man. R.) *attached*	9-7-16	
Sec.-Lieut.	CALLAN-MACARDLE, Kenneth ..	10-7-16	
T/Lieut.	JENSON, Cyril Thornton .. .. (25th B. Man. R. & T. How. Battery) *attached*	10-5-16	Maricourt
T/-Lieut.	GOODWIN, Eric Lindsey .. .. (13th B. Man. R.) *attached*	12-10-16	
T/Sec.-Lt.	JONES, Walter Teuran	12-10-16	
Capt.	SIDEBOTHAM, James Nasmyth Wedgwood	12-10-16	Maricourt
T/Sec.-Lt.	WILKS, Harold	12-10-16	
T/Capt.	BROWN, Macdonald Warriner ..	12-10-16	
T/Sec.-Lt.	HOBBS, Herbert Victor	7-4-17	
Sec.-Lieut.	RALLISON, Victor Edward .. (— B. Man. R.) *attached*	7-4-17	
T/Sec.-Lt.	PALMER, Walter Harvey ..	23-4-17	Héninel
T/Lieut.	POTTS, Geoffrey Fildes	23-4-17	Héninel
T/Sec.-Lt.	FRITH, Henry George	31-7-17	Ypres
Sec.-Lieut.	SOUTHCOURT, Edward Hamilton (3rd B. Man. R.) *attached*	31-7-17	Ypres
T/Sec.-Lt.	YORKE-JONES, Kenrick	26-12-17	
T/Sec.-Lt.	HOPE, Charles Edward	22-3-18	Savy
Lieut.	TAYLOR, Harry, M.C.	22-3-18	
T/Lieut.	MORGAN, Hubert Hoppin ..	30-3-18	
Sec.-Lieut. (A/Capt.)	BUDENBURG, Donald Harlow .. (4th B. Man. R.) *attached*	25-4-18	Spoil Bk., Ypres
Sec.-Lieut.	PRENTIS, Horace Taylor	27-4-18	
T/Sec.-Lt.	HALLIWELL, Frederick	12-10-18	
T/Sec.-Lt.	LEGBOURN, Frederick Percy ..	1-11-18	
Sec.-Lieut.	DUNSCOMBE, George, ...	6-11-18	D. (P. of W.)
T/Capt.	KEEFE, Ronald Couray Murray, M.C. (19th B. Man. R.) *attached*	27-3-18	Folies

APPENDIX II
continued
W.O.'s, N.C.O.'s
AND MEN
KILLED

ACKERLEY Sydney, *b* St. Ignatius', Salford, Lancs., *e* Manchester (Salford), 8046, L/Cpl., k. in a., F. & F., 22-3-18, **M.M.**

AFFLECK Henry, *b* Liberton, Midlothian, *e* Dalkeith (Edinburgh). 42198, Pte., d. of w., F. & F., 22-7-17, formerly T4/057689 R.A.S.C.

AIKEN Joseph, *b* Hulme, Manchester, *e* Manchester, 8043, Cpl., k. in a., F. & F., 23-4-17.

AKERS Fred, *b* St. Paul's, Preston, Lancs., *e* Preston, 43125, Pte., d. of w., F. & F., 21-4-17, formerly 16409 N. Lancs. R.

ALLAN Charles, *b* Everton, Liverpool, *e* Port Sunlight (Everton), 43204, Cpl., k. in a., F. & F., 30-4-18, formerly W/279 Cheshire R.

ALLEN Robert, *b* Manchester, *e* Manchester (Hyde, Cheshire), 27318, Pte., k. in a., F. & F., 7-5-18, **D.C.M.**

ALMOND Frank, *b* Didsbury, Manchester, *e* Manchester, 8371, Pte., k. in a., F. & F., 30-7-16.

AMOS Percy Alfred, *b* Colchester, Essex, *e* Manchester (Ipswich, Suffolk), 8047, Sgt., k. in a., F. & F., 1-7-16.

ANKERS John, *b* Mossley, Lancs., *e* Mossley, 35527, Pte., k. in a., F. & F., 30-7-16.

APPLEYARD James, *b* Hathersage, Derby, *e* Manchester (Rusholme, Lancs.), 9239, Pte., d. of w., Home, 22-9-16.

ARMSTRONG Adam, *b* Unsworth, Lancs., *e* Manchester (Bury, Lancs.), 9168, Pte., d. of w., F. & F., 18-8-16.

ARNOLD Robert, *b* Greenwich, Kent, *e* London (Walworth, Surrey), 51084, Pte., k. in a., F. & F., 15-9-17, formerly S4/110060 R.A.S.C.

ASHTON Walter, *b* Dukinfield, Cheshire, *e* Manchester (Stalybridge, Cheshire), 8364, Pte., k. in a., F. & F., 10-7-16.

ASHWORTH William, *b* Bury, Lancs., *e* Manchester (Walmersley, Bury, Lancs.), 9110, Pte., k. in a., F. & F., 20-1-16.

ATHERTON Thomas, *b* Ince, Wigan, Lancs., *e* Wigan, 48139, Pte., k. in a., F. & F., 20-4-18.

ATKINS Frederick, *b* Staton Church, Berks., *e* Oxford (Henley-on-Thames, Oxon.), 43277, Pte., k. in a., F. & F., 12-10-16, formerly 16660 R. Berks. R.

ATKINSON John Cecil, *b* St. Martin's, Leeds, *e* Manchester (Leeds), 8050, Pte., k. in a., F. & F., 28-1-16.

ATKINSON Rowland, *b* Chorlton-on-Medlock, Manchester, *e* Manchester, 10337, Pte., k. in a., F. & F., 1-7-16.

ATTEWELL Charles, *b* Bordwell, Barnsley, Yorks., *e* Doncaster, Yorks., 42197, Pte., k. in a., F. & F., 22-3-18, formerly T4/250839 R.A.S.C.

AUSTEN John William, *b* Hurley, Berks., *e* Maidenhead, 43276, Pte., d., F. & F., 28-6-18, formerly 20975 R. Berks. R.

BAGSHAW George Herbert, *b* Miles Platting, Manchester, *e* Manchester, 8432, Pte., k. in a., F. & F., 28-1-16.

BAGULEY John, *b* Hulme, Manchester, *e* Manchester, 8385, L/Cpl., k. in a., F. & F., 30-7-16.

BAILEY Albert James, *b* Smallthorne, Burslem, Staffs., *e* Manchester, 8064, Cpl., k. in a., F. & F., 23-4-17.

BALDING Alfred John, *b* Stalybridge, Cheshire, *e* Manchester (Middleton, Lancs.), 13055, Pte., k. in a., F. & F., 30-6-17.

BAMFORD Gerald, *b* Meltham, Huddersfield, Yorks., *e* Manchester, 8398, Sgt., k. in a., F. & F., 10-7-16.

BARLOW James Henry, *b* St. Stephen's, Salford, Lancs., *e* Manchester, 8389, Pte., k. in a., F. & F., 15-3-16.

BARNES Widmer, *b* St. George's, Bolton, Lancs., *e* Bolton, 43130, Pte., d. of w., F. & F., 28-9-17, formerly 17653 N. Lancs. R.

BARNETT Thomas, *b* Lower Broughton, Manchester, *e* Manchester, 8387, L/Cpl., k. in a., F. & F., 10-7-16.

BARNFIELD Tom, *b* Pendleton, Salford, Lancs., *e* Manchester, 8076, Pte., k. in a., F. & F., 1-7-16.

BARRETT Alfred, *b* Liverpool, *e* Manchester, 8391, L/Cpl., k. in a., F. & F., 1-7-16.

BARRETT William, *b* Tunstall, Staffs., *e* Manchester, 26311, Pte., k. in a., F. & F., 10-7-16.

BARROW Thomas, *b* Bedford Leigh, Lancs., *e* Manchester (Bradford, Manchester), 8058, L/Cpl., k. in a., F. & F., 22-3-18.

BARTON Albert, *e* Birkenhead, Cheshire (Hoylake, Cheshire), 40757, L/Cpl., d., Home, 14-6-17, formerly 2881 Ches. R.

BATE William, *b* Nantwich, Cheshire, *e* Shrewsbury, Shrops. (Nantwich), 42195, Pte., k. in a., F. & F., 30-6-17, formerly 15097 Shropshire L.I.

BAUMBER Alfred, *b* Whitman, Staffs., *e* Ashton-u-Lyne, Lancs. (Flixton, Lancs.), 34820, Pte., k. in a., F. & F., 23-4-17.

BAYLEY Lionel, *b* Mobberley, Knutsford, Cheshire, *e* Knutsford (Mobberley), 9510, Pte., d. of w., F. & F., 4-7-16, formerly 15890 Cheshire R.

BEACH Harold, *b* Wigan, Lancs., *e* Wigan, 32767, Pte., k. in a., F. & F., 22-3-18.

BELLINGER Thomas, *b* Shrivenham, Berks., *e* Fasington, Berks. (Shrivenham), 43281, Pte., k. in a., F. & F., 15-10-16, formerly 20978 R. Berks. R.

BENNET John, *b* St. Jude's, Manchester, *e* Manchester, 8453, Pte., k. in a., F. & F., 10-7-16.

BENNETT Arthur Edward, *b* Denver, Colorado, U.S.A., *e* Manchester, 8392, Pte., k. in a., F. & F., 1-7-16.

BENNETT Edward, *b* Crewe, *e* Manchester, 8393, L/Cpl., k. in a., F. & F., 2-7-16.

BENNISON Richard, *b* Bolton, Lancs., *e* Bolton, 43132, Sgt., k. in a., F. & F., 12-10-16, formerly 16117 N. Lancs. R.

BERRISFORD Charles William, *b* Salford, Lancs., *e* Manchester, 8417, Cpl., k. in a., F. & F., 1-7-16.

BICKERTON Thomas Hilditch, *b* Cheetham, Manchester, *e* Manchester, 8438, L/Cpl., k. in a., F. & F., 1-7-16.

BIRCHALL Harry, *b* Miles Platting, Manchester, *e* Manchester (Ollerton, Knutsford, Cheshire), 8439, Pte., k. in a., F. & F., 10-7-16.

BIRD Fred, *b* Whalley, Baxenden, Lancs., *e* Accrington, Lancs., 43151, Sgt., k. in a., F. & F., 23-4-17, formerly 11/15220 E. Lancashire R.

BLACKBURN Joseph, *b* Manchester, *e* Salford, Lancs. (Pendleton, Manchester), 45164, Pte., k. in a,, F. & F., 22-3-18.

BLAIR Frederick, *e* Manchester, 47429, Pte., k. in a., F. & F., 23-4-17.

BLAKELEY Fred, *b* Prestwich, Manchester, *e* Manchester (Prestwich), 8079, L/Cpl., k. in a., F. & F., 23-4-17, M.M.

BLOOR William, *b* Hulme, Manchester, *e* Manchester, 8442, Pte., k. in a., F. & F., 30-7-16.

BLOUNT Harold, *b* Clayton, Manchester, *e* Manchester, 8080, L/Cpl., k. in a., F. & F., 1-7-16.

BLUNDELL Archie Edgar, *b* Bow, Middlesex, *e* Bow, 43271, Pte., k. in a., F. & F., 12-10-16, formerly 11580 R. Berks R.

BLUNDELL George, *b* Longsight, Manchester, *e* Manchester, 9005, Pte., k. in a., F. & F., 1-7-16.

BOARDMAN James, *b* Miles Platting, Manchester, *e* Manchester (Blackburn, Lancs.), 9022, Pte., k. in a., F. & F., 1-7-16.

BOLITHO Percival, *b* Accrington, Lancs., *e* Accrington, Lancs., 43152, Pte., k. in a., F. & F., 17-10-16, formerly 25046 E. Lancashire R.

BONES Herbert John, *b* Southwark, Surrey, *e* London, 41602, Pte., d. of w., F. & F., 24-3-18, formerly G/15800 R. W. Kent R.

BOOTH Arnold, *b* Hyde, Cheshire, *e* Hyde, 43207, L/Cpl., d., F. & F., 26-6-18, formerly 32970 Cheshire R.

BOOTH Henry Ernest, *b* Newton Heath, Lancs., *e* Manchester, 24867, Pte., k. in a., F. & F., 31-7-17.

BOOTH Thomas, *b* Higher Blackley, Lancs, *e* Manchester, 34439, Pte., k. in a., F. & F., 23-4-17.

BOSELEY Arthur, *b* Tilehurst, Berks., *e* Pangbourne, Berks. (Reading, Berks.), 43280, Pte., d. of w., F. & F., 12-10-16, formerly 20969 R. Berks. R.

BOSTWICK George, *b* Manchester, *e* Manchester, 26465, Pte., k. in a., F. & F., 30-6-17.

BOYLING Arthur, *b* Thornham, Lancs., *e* Royton, Lancs. (Chadderton, Lancs.), 33988, Pte., k. in a., F. & F., 12-10-16.

BRADLEY Archie, *b* Wilmslow, Cheshire, *e* Manchester, 401211, Pte., k. in a., F. & F., 22-3-18.

BRADLEY Thomas Isaac, *b* Bilston, Wolverhampton, *e* Manchester, 9067, Pte., k. in a., F. & F., 30-7-16.

BRADSHAW Richard, *b* Weaste, Salford, Lancs., *e* Manchester (Salford), 8445, Pte., d. of w., F. & F., 28-1-16.

BRAZNELL James, *b* Market Drayton, Shrops., *e* Manchester, 9245, L/Sgt., k. in a., F. & F., 1-7-16.

BRIERLEY Harry, *b* Manchester, *e* Manchester (Winton, Patricroft, Lancs.), 9389, Pte., k. in a., F. & F., 12-7-16.

BRIERLEY John, *b* Greenfield, Yorks., *e* Manchester, 9246, L/Sgt., k. in a., F. & F., 10-7-16.

BRINDLE James, *e* Wigan, Lancs. (Morecambe, Lancs.), 47413, L/Cpl., k. in a., F. & F., 22-3-18.

BRINDLEY Harry, *b* Normacot, Staffs., *e* Dover (Normanton, Staffs.), 44694, C.S.M., k. in a., F. & F., 22-3-18, formerly 13954 R. Fus., M.M.

BRINDLEY Jim, *b* Hurdsfield, Macclesfield, Cheshire, *e* Macclesfield, 43219, Pte., k. in a., F. & F., 23-4-17, formerly 26946 S. Lancashire R.

BROADMEADOW Stephen, *b* Moss Side, Manchester, *e* Manchester (Sale, Cheshire), 8084, L/Sgt., k. in a., F. & F., 10-7-16.

BROWN Herbert, *b* Harpurhey, Manchester, *e* Manchester, 8060, Sgt., k. in a., F. & F., 21-3-18.

BROWNJOHN Lewis Charles, *b* St. Giles', Oxford, *e* Manchester, 9045, Sgt., k. in a., F. & F., 30-7-16.

BRUCKSHAW George, *b* Salford, Lancs., *e* Manchester, 9006, Sgt., k. in a., F. & F., 1-7-16.

BRUNTON James, *b* Carlisle, *e* Preston, Lancs. (Nelson, Lancs.), 43154, Pte., d., F. & F., 20-10-17, formerly 24996 E. Lancashire R.

BRYNE Frank, *b* Rhyl, Flint., *e* Manchester (Rhyl), 9115, Pte., k. in a., F. & F., 1-7-16.

BUCKLEY Arthur, *b* Weaste, Manchester, *e* Manchester, 8073, Pte., k. in a., F. & F., 30-7-16.

BULL Ernest, *b* St. John's, Heaton Mersey, Cheshire, *e* Stockport, Cheshire (Heaton Mersey, Cheshire), 9527, Pte., d. of w., F. & F., 29-7-16, formerly 13581 Cheshire R.

BURNS Henry, *b* Manchester, *e* Manchester, 9464, Pte., k. in a., F. & F., 1-7-16.

BURROWS Edwin, *b* Oxford, *e* Acton, Middlesex, 43278, Pte., k. in a., F. & F., 12-10-16, formerly 19171 R. Berks. R.

BURTON Thomas, *b* Manchester, *e* Manchester, 34826, Pte., k. in a., F. & F., 23-4-17.

BUTLER Robert, *b* Preston, Lancs., *e* Manchester (Preston), 48775, Pte., k. in a., F. & F., 27-12-17.

BUTTERWORTH William Sylvester, *b* St. George's, Bolton, Lancs., *e* Manchester (Bolton), 8418, Sgt., k. in a., F. & F., 1-7-16.

CALDWELL Walter Henry, *b* Chorlton-cum-Hardy, Manchester, *e* Manchester, 12299, Pte., k. in a., F. & F., 22-3-18.

CAREY George, *e* Bolton, Lancs., 43137, A/Cpl., k. in a., F. & F., 20-4-18, formerly 3218 N. Lancs. R.

CARROLL John, *b* Manchester, *e* Manchester, 34955, Pte., k. in a., F. & F., 23-4-17.

CARTLEDGE George Levison, *b* Manchester, *e* Manchester, 26324, Pte., d. of w., F. & F., 15-3-16.

CAWLEY Harry, *b* Collyhurst, Manchester, *e* Manchester, 8110, Pte., k. in a., F. & F., 1-7-16.

CHAMBERS John, *b* Manchester, *e* Manchester, 26297, Pte., k. in a., F. & F., 1-7-16.

CHANT William, *b* Moss Side, Manchester, *e* Manchester, 8461, Pte., d. of w., Home, 24-4-17.

CHARLESWORTH William, *b* Wolverhampton, Staffs., *e* Widnes, Staffs., 43224, Pte., d. of w., F. & F., 8-4-17, formerly 19690 S. Lancashire R.

CHARNOCK Thomas, *b* Goose Green, Wigan, Lancs., *e* Wigan, 47428, Cpl., d., F. & F., 21-12-18.

CHILDS Charles Henry, *b* Acton, Middlesex, *e* Acton, 43353, Pte., k. in a., F. & F., 12-10-16, formerly G/26271 R. Fus.

CHINN Alfred, *b* Liverpool, *e* Liverpool, 51095, Pte., k. in a., F. & F., 19-12-17.

CLARK James, *b* Old Trafford, Manchester, *e* Manchester, 12307, Pte., k. in a., F. & F., 22-3-18.

CLARK Joseph, *b* Newark, Notts., *e* Manchester (Salford, Lancs.), 8472, Pte., k. in a., F. & F., 1-7-16.

CLARKE Edwin, *b* Runwell, Wickford, Essex, *e* Manchester (Bolton-le-Moors, Lancs.), 8101, Pte., k. in a., F. & F., 1-7-16.

CLARKE William, *b* Oldham, Lancs., *e* Oldham, 33998, Pte., k in a., F. & F., 12-10-16.

CLELAND James, *b* Felling-on-Tyne, Northumberland, *e* Manchester (Gateshead-on-Tyne, Durham), 8096, Pte., k. in a., F. & F., 31-7-17.

CLIFF Henry Thomas, *b* Coalville, Leicester, *e* Loughborough, Leicester (Coalville), 41074, Sgt., k. in a., F. & F., 22-3-18, formerly 4149 Leicester R.

COLLINSON Frank, *b* Bradford, Lancs., *e* Manchester (Bradford), 18346, Cpl., k. in a., F. & F., 23-4-17.

COOKE George Edward, *b* Lewes, Sussex, *e* Reading, Berks. (Lewes, Sussex), 43289, Pte., k. in a., F. & F., 25-3-17, formerly 21323 R. Berks. R.

COOKSON Harry, *b* Kirkham, Lancs., *e* Nelson, Lancs. (Brierfield, Lancs.), 43160, Pte., k. in a., F. & F., 30-12-16, formerly 26317 E. Lancashire R.

COOPER Victor, *b* Sunninghill, Berks., *e* Ascot, Berks. (Sunninghill), 43290, Pte., k. in a., F. & F., 8-4-17, formerly 20980 R. Berks. R.

COPPERTHWAITE, William, *b* Henley, Oxon., *e* Reading, Berks., 43288, Pte., k. in a., F. & F., 22-4-17, formerly 21320 R. Berks .R.

COPSEY Harry, *b* Peterborough, Lincoln, *e* Manchester, 8487, Pte., k. in a., F. & F., 13-5-16.

CORNELL Ebenezer James, *b* Lode, Cambs., *e* Colchester, Essex, 41653, Pte., k. in a., F. & F., 31-7-17, formerly G/16261 R. W. Kent R.

COULSON William Bernard, *b* Longsight, Manchester, *e* Manchester, 39404, Pte., d. of w., Home, 18-5-17.

CRAIG Hubert, *b* Walsall, Staffs., *e* Manchester, 8474, Pte., k. in a., F. & F., 12-10-16.

CRANE James, *b* Langham, Norfolk, *e* Oldham, Lancs. (Felthorpe, Norwich), 45052, Pte., k. in a., F. & F., 26-9-17.

CROOK Seth, *e* Burnley, Lancs., 47426, Sgt., d. of w., Home, 6-11-18.

CROOK William, *b* Ince, *e* Wigan, Lancs., 377783, Pte., d. of w., F. & F., 3-12-17.

CROSSLEY William Philip, *b* Levenshulme, Manchester, *e* Manchester, 8489, L/Cpl., d. of w., F. & F., 4-7-16.

CROWE Frederick Guest, *b* Kendal, Westmorland, *e* Manchester, 8466, Pte., d., F. & F., 26-9-16.

CUERDEN Frederick James, *b* Pemberton, Wigan, Lancs., *e* Wigan, 36152, Pte., k. in a., F. & F., 23-4-17.

CULLEN Edward, *e* Dover (Dublin), 24771, Pte., d. of w., F. & F., 22-3-18.

CULSHAW William, *b* Skelmersdale, Liverpool, *e* Manchester (Rainhill, Lancs.), 8467, Pte., k. in a., F. & F., 24-8-16.

DALE Clarence, *b* St. Luke's, Southport, Lancs., *e* Manchester, 8522, Pte., d. of w., F. & F., 13-6-17.

DAVIDSON James, *b* Liverpool, *e* Liverpool, 51103, Pte., k. in a., 31-7-17.

DAVIDSON John Charles, *b* Edge Hill, Lancs., *e* Manchester, 8512, Pte., k. in a., F. & F., 29-2-16.

DAVIES Cyril Edwin, *b* Bungay, Suffolk, *e* Manchester, 9146, Pte., d. of w., F. & F., 22-7-16.

DAVIS Alfred William, *b* Weaste, Manchester, *e* Manchester (Eccles, Lancs.), 8125, Pte., d. of w., F. & F., 3-7-16.

DAWSON Frank, *b* Barrow-in-Furness, Lancs., *e* Manchester, 35104, Pte., k. in a., F. & F., 30-7-16.

DAY James, *b* Congleton, Cheshire, *e* Hollinwood, Lancs. (Chadderton, Lancs.), 28054, L/Cpl., k. in a., F. & F., 3-12-17.

DEAN George, *b* Manchester, *e* Manchester, 9327, Pte., d. of w., Home, 12-9-16.

DICKENSON John, *b* Chorley, Lancs., *e* Chorley, 43133, Pte., k. in a., F. & F., 12-10-16, formerly 14284 N. Lancs. R.

DICKENSON William, *b* Salford, Lancs., *e* Manchester, 12555, C.S.M., k. in a., F. & F., 30-4-18, formerly 5205 Lancashire Fus.

DILLON John Richard, *b* Prescot, Lancs., *e* Liverpool, 401013, Pte., k. in a., F. & F., 22-3-18.

DISLEY Percy, *b* Bacup, Lancs., *e* Manchester, 26578, Pte., d. of w., F. & F., 23-3-18.

DIXON William Baldwin, *b* Burnley, Lancs., *e* Bury, Lancs. (Burnley), 55023, L/Cpl., d., F. & F., 11-7-18, formerly 23320 E. Lancashire R.

DIXON William, *b* Oldham, Lancs., *e* Hollinwood, Lancs. (Oldham), 47052, Pte., d., F. & F., 16-10-18.

DOBSON Walter, *b* Baxenden, Lancs., *e* Accrington, Lancs., 43161, Pte., k. in a., F. & F., 11-10-16, formerly 24439 E. Lancashire R.

DODD John William, *b* St. Peter's, Ashton-u-Lyne, Lancs., *e* Ashton-u-Lyne, 48500, Pte., d., F. & F., 22-10-18.

DODSON Joseph, *b* Salford, Lancs., *e* Sale, Cheshire (Salford), 39525, Pte., d. of w., F. & F., 26-4-17.

DOOLEY Patrick Francis, *b* St. Bartholomew's, Salford, *e* Manchester (Salford), 5387, Pte., k. in a., F. & F., 22-3-18.

DRAKE Henry, *b* Manchester, *e* Manchester, 8511, Pte., d. of w., F. & F., 27-3-18.

DUFF John James, *b* Red Bank, Manchester, *e* Manchester, 18385, Sgt., k. in a,. F. & F., 23-4-17.

DUFFY Patrick, *b* Salford, Lancs., *e* Manchester (Salford, Lancs.), 28259, Pte., d., F. & F., 21-10-18, **D.C.M.**

DUNN William, *b* Collyhurst, Manchester, *e* Manchester, 8121, Pte., k. in a., F. & F., 1-7-16.

DWYER Herbert, *e* Gorton, Lancs., 34008, Pte., k. in a., F. & F., 23-4-17.

EASTWOOD Arthur, *b* Salford, Lancs., *e* Manchester (Ilkeston, Derby), 5379, L/Cpl., k. in a., F. & F., 22-3-18.

EATON Charles William, *b* Altrincham, Cheshire, *e* Manchester (Hale, Cheshire), 8541, Pte., k. in a., F. & F., 1-7-16.

EATON William, *b* Manchester, *e* Manchester, 34264, Pte., k. in a., F. & F., 31-7-17.

ECKERSALL Henry, *b* Heaton Park, Manchester, *e* Manchester (Great Lever, Bolton, Lancs.), 8538, Pte., d. of w., F. & F., 2-2-16.

EDMONDSON Leonard Alfred, *b* Whalley Range, Manchester, *e* Manchester, 8132, Cpl., k. in a., F. & F., 12-10-16.

EDWARDS Alfred, *b* Newbury, Berks., *e* Manchester (Newbury), 31181, Pte., k. in a., F. & F., 23-4-17.

EDWARDS Emerys, *b* Broughton, Manchester, *e* Manchester, 9033, Pte., k. in a., F. & F., 1-7-16.

EFFERT Carl Otto, *b* Eastbourne, Sussex, *e* Brighton, Sussex, 41639, Pte., k. in a., F. & F., 23-4-17, formerly 3028 R.F.A.

ELLIOTT Charles, *b* Hendham Vale, Lancs., *e* Manchester, 9166, Pte., k. in a., F. & F., 1-7-16.

ELLIOTT George Bartlett, *b* Hale, Cheshire, *e* Manchester, 32794, A/Cpl., k. in a., F. & F., 12-10-16.

ELLIOTT George, *b* St. Martin's, Leicester, *e* Leicester, 40961, Pte., k. in a., F. & F., 22-3-18, formerly 4019 Leicester R.

ELLIOTT Reginald Charles, *b* Cheltenham, Glos., *e* Cheltenham, 42135, Pte., k. in a., F. & F., 31-7-17, formerly T4/128596 R.A.S.C.

ELLIS Harold John Henry, *b* Thurlstone, Devon., *e* Kingsbridge, Devon., 42132, Pte., k. in a., F. & F., 22-3-18, formerly 14868 Devon. R.

ELLIS Robert, *b* Salford, Lancs., *e* Manchester, 8134, Pte., k. in a., F. & F., 1-7-16.

ELLISON Thomas Arthur, *b* Moss Side, Manchester, *e* Manchester (Urmston, Lancs.), 8534, Cpl., k. in a., F. & F., 11-7-16.

ENTWISTLE James Henry, *b* Kearsley, Lancs., *e* Swinton, Lancs., 38429, Pte., d., F. & F., 11-7-16.

EVANS Henry Kay, *b* Levenshulme, Manchester, *e* Manchester, 8135, L/Sgt., k. in a., F. & F., 12-10-16.

EVANS Richard, *e* Manchester (Shrewsbury, Shrops.), 33682, Pte., d., F. & F., 5-5-18.

FALLA Ernest, *b* Newton Heath, Manchester, *e* Manchester, 8554, L/Cpl., k. in a., F. & F., 1-7-16.

FALLOWS John Adam, *e* Manchester (Pendleton, Manchester), 42142, Pte., d. of w., F. & F., 21-3-18, formerly T4/159633 R.A.S.C.

FARRELL Joseph, *b* Blackburn, Lancs., *e* Manchester (Stockport, Cheshire), 47219, Pte., k. in a., F. & F., 23-4-17.

FARRELLY John Rupert, *b* Whitefield, Manchester, *e* Manchester (Whitefield), 10276, L/Cpl., d., F. & F., 25-6-18.

FARROW John, *b* Urmston, Lancs., *e* Manchester (Hale, Cheshire), 8138, Sgt., d. of w., F. & F., 5-5-16.

FARTHING Alwyn, *b* Hulme, Manchester, *e* Ashton-u-Lyne, Lancs. (Hulme, Manchester), 39401, Pte., d. of w., F. & F., 6-12-17.

FAULKNER Frederick, *b* Salford, Lancs., *e* Manchester (Blackley, Manchester), 41420, Pte., k. in a., F. & F., 30-4-18.

FAWKES Edward Gladstone, *b* Stockport, Cheshire, *e* Manchester (Stockport), 9036, Pte., k. in a., F. & F., 1-7-16.

FEARN Harry Lewis, *b* Newton Heath, Manchester, *e* Manchester, 8137, Pte., k. in a., F. & F., 30-7-16.

FELSTEAD Charles Robert, *b* Manchester, *e* Manchester, 27321, Pte., k. in a., F. & F., 1-7-16.

FINLOW Frank, *b* Buxton, Derby., *e* Manchester (Buxton), 33626, Pte., d. of w., F. & F., 8-5-17.

FINN Thomas, *b* Bacon, Co. Mayo, *e* Oldham, Lancs., 34903, Pte., k. in a., F. & F., 30-7-16.

FIRTH Job, *b* Deal, Kent, *e* Sandwich, Kent (Deal), 51104, Pte., d., F. & F., 4-5-18, formerly S4/110034 R.A.S.C.

FITTON Joe, *b* Shaw, Lancs., *e* Shaw, 38625, Pte., d. of w., F. & F., 20-5-17.

FITZPATRICK John, *b* Salford, Lancs., *e* Manchester (Salford), 8142, Pte., k. in a., F. & F., 29-2-16.

FLACK James, *b* Chrishall, Essex, *e* Nazeing, Essex, 41662, Pte., k. in a., F. & F., 31-7-17, formerly G/16291 R.W. Kent R.

FLETCHER Joseph, *b* Manchester, *e* Manchester (Bradford, Manchester), 26396, L/Cpl., k. in a., F. & F., 22-3-18.

FLOCKTON John Hine, *b* Hulme, Manchester, *e* Manchester, 26135, L/Cpl., d. of w., Home, 16-6-18.

FLOOD Sydney, *e* Manchester, 21393, Pte., k. in a., F. & F., 22-3-18.

FLOWER Edward Avenell, *b* New Cross, Surrey, *e* Camberwell, Surrey (Deptford, Kent), 41824, L/Cpl., d. of w., F. & F., 24-4-17, formerly 32762 E. Surrey R.

FLOWER Ernest, *b* Leek, Staffs., *e* Manchester (Leek), 8999, Pte., d. of w., F. & F., 1-7-16.

FOAD Henry John Wellard, *b* Minster, Thanet, Kent, *e* Faversham, Kent (Ramsgate, Kent), 51173, Pte., d. of w., F. & F., 10-7-18.

FOALE Ernest, *b* Salford, Lancs., *e* Manchester (Seedley, Manchester), 8140, Sgt., k. in a., F. & F., 12-10-16.

FODEN Harry, *b* Bradford, Manchester, *e* Manchester (Bradford), 8563, Pte., k. in a., F. & F., 5-5-16.

FOSTER Peter Francis, *b* Manchester, *e* Manchester, 33618, Pte., k. in a., F. & F., 22-3-18.

FOX Henry, *b* Manchester, *e* Manchester, 21458, Pte., k. in a., F. & F., 30-4-18.

FRANCIS William G., *b* Salcot, Essex, *e* Colchester, Essex (Witham, Essex), 41658, Pte., k. in a., F. & F., 23-4-17, formerly G/15906 R.W. Kent R.

FREE Robert Malcolm, *b* Hadstock, Cambridge, *e* Worksop, Notts. (Nottingham), 42139, Pte., d. of w., F. & F., 25-9-17, formerly 13100 Notts and Derby R.

FREEMAN Harold Wadsworth, *b* Sherbrooke, Quebec, Canada, *e* Manchester (Southport, Lancs.), 26469, Pte., k. in a., F. & F., 10-7-16.

FRENCH Frederick Charles Camfield, *b* Hove, Sussex, *e* Woolwich, Kent (Greenwich, Kent), 43410, Pte., k. in a., F. & F., 7-5-18, formerly G/8203 R. Sussex R.

FRENCH Hubert, *b* Great Tey, Essex, *e* Southend, Essex (Marks Tey, Essex), 51106, Pte., k. in a., F. & F., 31-7-17, formerly S/4/140163 R.A.S.C.

FRENCH Richard, *b* Manchester, *e* Manchester, 27334, Pte., k. in a., F. & F., 1-7-16.

FROST Richard, *b* Bradford, Manchester, *e* Manchester (Bradford), 8553, Pte., k. in a., F. & F., 29-2-16.

FULLER George Eric, *b* Manchester, *e* Manchester, 8566, Pte., k. in a., F. & F., 31-7-17.

FURBER Cyril, *b* Chester, *e* Chadderton, Lancs. (Oldham, Lancs.), 33414, Cpl., k. in a., F. & F., 12-10-16.

GALE Norman, *b* Manchester, *e* Manchester, 17897, Pte., k. in a., F. & F., 30-7-16.

GARDNER Albert John, *b* Newington, Wallingford, Oxon., *e* Reading (Newington), 43273, L/Cpl., k. in a., F. & F., 12-10-16, formerly 9219 R. Berks. R.

GATLEY James, *b* Wincham, Cheshire, *e* Northwich, Cheshire (Wincham), 43213, Pte., k. in a., F. & F., 31-7-17, formerly 33128 Cheshire R.

GEORGE Horace, *b* Beeston, Notts., *e* Hove, Sussex, 41619, Pte., k. in a., F. & F., 26-9-17, formerly G/15541 R.W. Kent R.

GIBBONS Austin, *b* Manchester, *e* Manchester, 31257, Pte., k. in a., F. & F., 15-3-16.

GIBSON Walter, *b* Long Clawson, Leicester, *e* Manchester, 9499, Cpl., k. in a., F. & F., 30-7-16.

GIBSON William, *b* Newbiggin-by-the-Sea, Northumberland, *e* Newcastle-on-Tyne (Morpeth, Northumberland), 51109, Pte., k. in a., F.& F., 30-4-18, formerly S4/092426 R.A.S.C.

GILL Robert Thomas, *b* Hollinwood, Lancs., *e* Hollinwood, 38479, Pte., k. in a., F. & F., 22-3-18.

GLEAVE John, *b* Collyhurst, Manchester, *e* Manchester (Salford, Lancs.), 8571, Pte., k. in a., F. & F., 30-7-16.

GOADBY Charles, *b* Milford, Derby., *e* Manchester (Swanwick, Derby.), 12636, Pte., k. in a., F. & F., 22-3-18.

GORNER John Frederick, *b* St. Mark's, Manchester, *e* Manchester (Crewe), 8590, Pte., d., F. & F., 22-10-18.

GORNER John Robert, *b* Prestwich, Lancs., *e* Manchester (Salford, Lancs.), 47459, Sgt., d. of w., F. & F., 24-4-17.

GOSLING Frank Herbert, *b* St. Mary's, Stockport, Cheshire, *e* Manchester (Stockport), 8568, Cpl., d., F. & F., 1-7-18.

GOULDSBOROUGH, Walter, *b* Hr. Broughton, Manchester, *e* Manchester, 8144, Pte., k. in a., F. & F., 30-7-16.

GRANGE Joseph, *b* Manchester, *e* Ashton-u-Lyne, Lancs. (Ardwick, Manchester), 36539, Pte., k. in a., F. & F., 23-4-17.

GRAY Bertie, *b* Warwick, *e* Birmingham (Selly Oak, Birmingham), 43297, Pte., k. in a., F. & F., 23-4-17, formerly 21243 R. Berks. R.

GREEN Percy Robert, *b* London, *e* Southport, Lancs. (London), 9520, Pte., k. in a., F. & F., 29-5-16.

GREENHILL John, *b* Hr. Broughton, Manchester, *e* Manchester (Rugeley, Staffs.), 8145, Pte., k. in a., F. & F., 10-7-16.

GRIBBIN Sydney, *b* Liverpool, *e* Liverpool, 54714, Pte., k. in a., F. & F., 22-3-18.

GRIFFITHS William Price, *b* Liverpool, *e* Manchester (Alderley Edge, Lancs.), 9466, Pte., k. in a., F. & F., 1-7-16.

GRIFFITHS Sidney, *b* Ashton-u-Lyne, Lancs., *e* Ashton-u-Lyne, 30036, Pte., d., F. & F., 13-9-18.

GRINDEY Harry, *b* Burslem, Staffs., *e* Liverpool (Milton, Stoke-on-Trent, Staffs.), 51107, Pte., d. of w., F. & F., 4-12-17, formerly S4/184683 R.A.S.C.

GRUNDY Sydney, *b* Walkden, Manchester, *e* Manchester (Little Hulton, Bolton, Lancs.), 8569, Pte., k. in a., F. & F., 30-7-16.

GUEST Charles, *b* Lymm, Cheshire, *e* Ashton-u-Lyne, Lancs. (Hale, Cheshire), 36605, Pte., k. in a., F. & F., 22-3-18.

GUTHRIE Harry Sydney, *b* Newton-le-Willows, Lancs., *e* Manchester, 26327, A/Sgt., k. in a., F. & F., 11-10-16, M.M.

HACKETT Albert, *b* Horley, Surrey, *e* Bognor, Sussex (Newton, near Bognor), 43419, Pte., k. in a., F. & F., 12-10-16, formerly 4933 Middlesex R.

HAGGERTY Thomas, *b* Newcastle-on-Tyne, *e* Newcastle-on-Tyne, 43195, Pte., d. of w., F. & F., 13-10-16, formerly 28135 Northumberland Fus.

HALES Edward, *b* Cottom, Suffolk, *e* Oldham, Lancs. (Bacton, Hereford), 38721, Pte., k. in a., F. & F., 22-3-18.

HALL Albert, *b* Kilburn, Middlesex, *e* London (Watford, Herts.), 43305, Sgt., k. in a., F. & F., 23-4-17, formerly 12078 R. Berks. R.

HALL James, *b* Manchester, *e* Manchester, 43232, Pte., k. in a., F. & F., 23-4-17, formerly 17505 S. Lancashire R.

HALL Sydney, *b* Sandbach, Cheshire, *e* Shrewsbury, Shrops. (Sandbach, Cheshire), 42119, C.S.M., k. in a., F. & F., 28-6-17, formerly 13883 Shropshire L.I.

HALLIWELL William Thomas, *b* Manchester, *e* Ashton-u-Lyne, Lancs. (Newton Heath, Manchester), 34228, Pte., k. in a., F. & F., 22-3-18.

HALLWORTH Arthur, *b* Marsden, Yorks., *e* Manchester (Greenfield, Oldham, Lancs.), 26464, Pte., k. in a., F. & F., 1-7-16.

HAMER Samuel, *b* Stalybridge, Cheshire, *e* Manchester (Rochdale, Lancs.), 9185, Pte., k. in a., F. & F., 23-4-17.

HAMPSON Wallace, *b* Bolton, Lancs., *e* Manchester, 9395, Pte., d., F. & F., 30-1-17.

HANSELL Abraham, *b* Manchester, *e* Manchester, 9444, Pte., k. in a., F. & F., 1-7-16.

HARDING Frederick Sydney, *b* Whitefield, Manchester, *e* Manchester (Whitefield), 8643, Pte., k. in a., F. & F., 1-7-16.

HARDMAN George, *b* Bury, Lancs., *e* Manchester (Bury), 9273, Pte., k. in a., F. & F., 1-7-16.

HARE	Sidney Birks, *b* Pudsey, Yorks., *e* Manchester (Pudsey), 8170, Cpl., k. in a., F. & F., 1-7-16.
HARGREAVES	Robert, *b* Bolton, Lancs., *e* Bolton (Astley Bridge, Bolton), 43231, L/Cpl., k. in a., F. & F., 23-4-17, formerly 18533 S. Lancashire R.
HARRIS	John, *b* Fenton, Staffs., *e* Longton, Staffs. (Fenton, Stoke-on-Trent, Staffs.), 47438, Pte., k. in a., F. & F., 23-4-17, formerly 36162 R.W. Fus.
HARRIS	Leonard, *b* Broomfield, Essex, *e* Clacton-on-Sea, Essex, 41644, Pte., d. of w., F. & F., 10-4-17, formerly G/16274 R.W. Kent R.
HARRISON	Albert Edward, *b* Manchester, *e* Manchester, 11195, Pte., k. in a., F. & F., 1-7-16.
HARVEY	Harry, *b* Wycombe, Bucks., *e* High Wycombe, 41609, Pte., k. in a., F. & F., 23-4-17, formerly G/16894 R.W. Kent R.
HASSALL	Frederick, *b* Hr. Broughton, Salford, Lancs., *e* Manchester, 8166, Pte., k. in a., F. & F., 10-7-16.
HATTON	Frederick, *b* Openshaw, Manchester, *e* Manchester, 9269, Pte., d. of w., F. & F., 14-10-16.
HAYES	Harry, *b* Worsley, Lancs., *e* Manchester (Worsley), 8606, Pte., k. in a., F. & F., 1-7-16.
HAYMES	Arthur, *b* Coventry, *e* Manchester (Blackburn, Lancs.), 9098, C.S.M., d., Home, 1-10-15.
HEAP	James, *b* Hyde, Manchester, *e* Manchester (Heaton Mersey, Cheshire), 8646, L/Cpl., d., F. & F., 29-8-18.
HEARDMAN	Francis, *b* Salford, Lancs., *e* Manchester, 8172, Pte., k. in a., F. & F., 30-7-16.
HENDERSON	Robert, *b* Accrington, Lancs., *e* Manchester (Accrington), 8647, Pte., k. in a., F. & F., 10-7-16.
HERBERT	Harold, *e* Manchester, 25863, Pte., k. in a., F. & F., 31-7-17.
HERBERT	Hugh Fraser, *b* Galashiels, Selkirk, *e* Manchester (Galashiels), 8623, L/Cpl., k. in a., F. & F., 12-10-16.
HEYS	Harry, *b* Lancaster, *e* Preston, Lancs. (Nelson, Lancs.), 43168, Pte., k. in a., F. & F., 12-10-16, formerly 26472 E. Lancashire R.
HEYS	Robert, *b* Rawtenstall, Lancs., *e* Rawtenstall, 43166, Pte., k. in a., F. & F., 12-10-16, formerly 25013 E. Lancs. R.
HEYWOOD	James, *b* Middleton, Lancs., *e* Royton, Lancs., 27242, Pte., d. of w., F. & F., 1-7-16.
HIGGINS	Charles, *b* Eccles, Lancs., *e* Manchester (Eccles), 8178, Pte., k. in a., F. & F., 1-7-16.
HIGGINS	John, *b* Salford, Lancs., *e* Manchester (Salford, Lancs.), 8651, Pte., d., F. & F., 5-7-16.
HILL	James Edward, *b* Manchester, *e* Manchester, 12871, Pte., d. of w., Home, 22-6-18.
HILL	Thomas, *b* Old Trafford, Manchester, *e* Manchester, 8652, Pte., k. in a., F. & F., 10-7-16.
HILLIER	James, *b* Manchester, *e* Manchester, 59583, Pte., k. in a., F. & F., 22-3-18.
HILLEBRAND	Louis Francis, *b* Amsterdam, Holland, *e* Cricklewood, Middlesex (Golder's Green, London), 51183, Pte., d. of w., Home, 22-5-18.
HILLS	Ernest Edward, *e* Margate, Kent, 41631, Pte., k. in a., F. & F., 23-4-17, formerly G/17284 R. W. Kent R.
HILTON	John H., *b* Liverpool, *e* Liverpool, 54731, Pte., d., F. & F., 17-10-18.
HILTON	Walter, *b* Hulme, Manchester, *e* Manchester, 8654, Pte., k. in a., F. & F., 1-7-16.

HOBSON	William, *b* Buerton, Cheshire, *e* Crewe (Frodsham, Cheshire), 26433, Pte., k. in a., F. & F., 1-7-16.
HOBSON	John Thomas, *b* Chesterton, Staffs., *e* Manchester, 9250, Sgt., k. in a., F. & F., 1-7-16, M.M.
HODGSON	Percy, *b* Buttercrombe, Yorks., *e* York (Sheriff Hutton, Yorks.), 42148, Pte., k. in a., F. & F., 31-7-17, formerly T4/15959 R.A.S.C.
HOLBROOK	Albert, *b* Newton Heath, Manchester, *e* Ashton-u-Lyne, Lancs. (Failsworth, Lancs.), 45284, Pte., k. in a., F. & F., 31-7-17.
HOLLINGWORTH	Harry, *b* St. John's, Leeds, *e* Manchester (Bradford, Lancs.), 8609, Pte., d. of w., F. & F., 11-2-16.
HOLMES	John, *b* Miles Platting, Manchester, *e* Manchester (Bradford, Lancs.), 8656, Pte., k. in a., F. & F., 1-7-16.
HOLT	James, *b* Heywood, Lancs., *e* Manchester, 8637, L/Cpl., k. in a., F. & F., 1-7-16.
HOLT	John Pownall, *b* Heywood, Lancs., *e* Manchester, 8638, Pte., k. in a., F. & F., 11-1-16.
HOOLEY	Alfred, *b* Cheadle Hulme, Cheshire, *e* Manchester, 8180, Pte., d. of w., F. & F., 1-7-16.
HOPE	Albert, *b* Pendleton, Lancs., *e* Manchester (Blackley, Manchester), 33608, Pte., k. in a., F. & F., 12-10-16.
HORN	Arthur, *b* Ivenhoe, Bucks., *e* Harrow, Middlesex, 43420, Pte., k. in a., F. & F., 23-4-17, formerly 5270 Middlesex R.
HOUGH	Arthur, *b* Ardwick, Manchester, *e* Manchester, 8173, L/Cpl., d., F. & F., 6-5-18.
HOUSEMAN	William, *b* Abbey Hey, Manchester, *e* Manchester, 8182, Pte., k. in a., F. & F., 1-7-16.
HOWARD	Frederick, *b* Easthampstead, Berks., *e* Wokingham, Berks., 43300, Pte., k. in a., F. & F., 7-4-17, formerly 20959 R. Berks. R.
HOWARD	James, *b* Salford, Lancs., *e* Manchester, 20790, Pte., k. in a., F. & F., 27-3-17.
HOWARD	Joseph, *b* Moston, Manchester, *e* Manchester (Moston), 8657, Pte., k. in a., F. & F., 1-7-16.
HOWARTH	Herbert, St. Mark's, Bury, Lancs., *e* Manchester (Bury), 8658, Pte., k. in a., F. & F., 1-7-16.
HUBBARD	Thomas, *b* St. Paul's, Bury., Lancs., *e* Manchester (Bury), 8189, Pte., d. of w., F. & F., 11-7-16.
HUDSON	Benjamin, *b* Prestwich, Lancs., *e* Manchester (Ashton-on-Mersey, Lancs.), 9299, Pte., k. in a., F. & F., 15-10-16.
HUDSON	William, *b* Abingdon, Berks., *e* Abingdon, 42145, Pte., k. in a., F. & F., 31-7-17, formerly T4/059891 R.A.S.C.
HUDSPITH	James, *b* Leigh, Lancs., *e* Leigh, 39531, Pte., k. in a., F. & F., 23-4-17.
HUGHES	Harold, *b* Greenheys, Manchester, *e* Manchester, 8183, Pte., k. in a., F. & F., 30-7-16.
HUGILL	James, *b* Houghton-le-Spring, Durham, *e* Manchester, 304168, Pte., k. in a., F. & F., 30-4-18.
HULME	Thomas, *b* Failsworth, Lancs., *e* Manchester (Gorton, Manchester), 18907, Pte., k. in a., F. & F., 22-3-18.
HUMPHREYS	William Edward, *b* St. Mark's, Bolton, Lancs., *e* Bolton, 43123, Pte., k. in a., F. & F., 26-9-17, formerly 15027 N. Lancashire R.
HUNT	Daniel, *b* Poplar, Middlesex, *e* Poplar (Bromley-by-Bow, Middlesex), 377961, Pte., k. in a., F. & F., 22-3-18.
HURST	Charles, *b* Ardwick, Manchester, *e* Manchester (Failsworth, Lancs.), 8158, Pte., k. in a., F. & F., 1-7-16.

HUNTBACK Charles, *b* Market Drayton, Shrops., *e* Manchester (Blackley, Manchester), 9193, Pte., k. in a., F. & F., 1-7-16.

HUTCHINSON Alfred, *b* Ashton-u-Lyne, Lancs., *e* Oldham, Lancs., 54724, Pte., k. in a., F. & F., 22-3-18.

HYNCH William, *b* Hulme, Manchester, *e* Manchester (Lymm, Cheshire), 8174, L/Cpl., d. of w., F. & F., 13-8-16.

ILLINGWORTH Alma, *b* Leeds, Yorks., *e* Manchester, 48987, Pte., k. in a., F. & F., 22-3-18.

JACKSON Frank Andrew, *b* Norbury, Hazel Grove, Cheshire, *e* Manchester (Hazel Grove), 8679, L/Cpl., k. in a., F. & F., 1-7-16.

JACKSON Mark, *b* Salford, Lancs., *e* Manchester, 8197, Sgt., k. in a., F. & F., 1-7-16.

JACKSON Robert, *b* Flixton, Lancs., *e* Manchester (Urmston, near Manchester), 8683, Pte., k. in a., F. & F., 11-10-16.

JACKSON William Lewis, *b* Royton, Lancs., *e* Ashton-u-Lyne, Lancs. (Oldham, Lancs.), 48647, Pte., k. in a., F. & F., 14-9-17.

JACKSON William, *b* Hulme, Manchester, *e* Manchester, 8666, Pte., k. in a., F. & F., 10-7-16.

JAMES John Frederick Arthur, *b* Stowell's, Salford, Lancs., *e* Manchester (Pendleton, Lancs.), 8195, L/Cpl., k. in a., F. & F., 2-7-16.

JAMIESON George, *b* Manchester, *e* Manchester (Harpurhey, Manchester), 9330, Pte., k. in a., F. & F., 10-7-16.

JENNER John Richmond, *b* Ashton-u-Lyne, Lancs., *e* Ashton-u-Lyne, 32842, Pte., k. in a., F. & F., 15-10-16.

JENNINGS Robert, *b* Stanford-in-the-Vale, Faringdon, Berks., *e* Faringdon (Stanford-in-the-Vale), 43307, Pte., k. in a., F. & F., 12-10-16, formerly 20955 R. Berks. R.

JESSOP Fred, *b* Middleton, Lancs., *e* Manchester (Middleton), 12641, Pte., d., F. & F., 12-10-18.

JOHN Frank, *b* Patricroft, Lancs., *e* Eccles, Lancs. (Patricroft), 26495, Pte., k. in a., F. & F., 10-7-16.

JOHNSON Arthur, *b* Hulme, Manchester, *e* Manchester, 8198, Pte., k. in a., F. & F., 1-7-16.

JOHNSON Frederick William, *b* Manchester, *e* Manchester (West Gorton, Manchester), 9406, Pte., d., F. & F., 1-12-18.

JOHNSTONE Alexander, *b* Hulme, Manchester, *e* Manchester, 8685, Cpl., k. in a., F. & F., 1-7-16.

JONES Ernest, *b* Ardwick, Manchester, *e* Manchester, 8681, Pte., d. of w., F. & F., 15-5-16.

JONES John Edward, *b* Liverpool, *e* Shrewsbury, Shrops., 54741, Pte., k. in a., F. & F., 22-3-18.

JONES John Simon, *b* Lampeter, Cardigan., *e* Aberystwyth, Cardigan. (Lampeter), 51113, Pte., k. in a., F. & F., 30-4-18, formerly S4/128115 R.A.S.C.

JONES Lewis Edward, *b* Manchester, *e* Manchester (Middleton, Lancs.), 9375, Pte., k. in a., F. & F., 1-7-16.

JONES Frederick, *b* Gorton, Manchester, *e* Manchester, 9438, A/C.Q.M.S., k. in a., F. & F., 30-7-16.

JONES Lloyd, *b* Strangeways, Manchester, *e* Manchester, 8682, Pte., k. in a., F. & F., 13-10-16.

JONES Owen, *b* Harpurhey, Manchester, *e* Manchester, 8201, Cpl., k. in a., F. & F., 23-4-17.

JONES Percy, *b* Glascote, Warwick., *e* Nuneaton, Warwick. (Stockingford, Nuneaton), 43237, Pte., k. in a., F. & F., 12-10-16, formerly 18821 S. Lancashire R.

JONES — Percy Howard, *b* Didsbury, Manchester, *e* Manchester (Cheadle, Manchester), 8673, C.S.M., k. in a., F. & F., 11-10-16.

JUNIPER — Thomas Charles, *b* Clapham, Surrey, *e* Guildford, Surrey (Henley, Surrey), 43398, Pte., d., F. & F., 23-2-18, formerly G/4252 R. W. Surrey R.

KANE — Edmund, *b* Manchester, *e* Manchester, 9470, Cpl., k. in a., F. & F., 31-7-17.

KAY — Albert, *b* Eccles, Lancs., *e* Manchester (Ulverston, Lancs.), 8686, Pte., k. in a., F. & F., 12-6-17.

KAY — Anthony, *b* Widnes, Lancs., *e* Widnes, 54744, Pte., d., F. & F., 19-10-18.

KELSALL — Charles, *b* St. John's, Longsight, Manchester, *e* Manchester, 8690, Pte., d. of w., F. & F., 10-7-16.

KELLY — Henry, *b* Ancoats, Manchester, *e* Manchester, 5293, Pte., k. in a., F. & F., 23-4-17.

KELLY — Philip, *b* Newton, Manchester, *e* Manchester, 54982, Pte., k. in a., F. & F., 22-3-18, formerly 255949 R.E.

KEMP — Matthew, *b* Manchester, *e* Manchester, 9257, Pte., d. of w., F. & F., 7-7-16.

KENNY — William, *b* St. Bernard's, Leicester, *e* Loughborough, Leicester (Leicester), 41076, Pte., d., F. & F., 30-6-18, formerly 4612 Leicester R.

KENYON — Levi, *b* Manchester, *e* Manchester, 9515, Pte., k. in a., F. & F., 1-7-16.

KENYON — William, *b* Hulme, Manchester, *e* Manchester, 8025, Pte., d. of w., F. & F., 11-4-18.

KERR — Charles, *b* Stretford, Manchester, *e* Manchester, 8209, Pte., d., F. & F., 12-3-16.

KERRUISH — George John, *b* Birkenhead, Cheshire, *e* Birkenhead, 54743, Pte., k. in a., F. & F., 25-4-18.

KIMBER — Bernard, *b* Manchester, *e* Manchester, 9333, Pte., k. in a., F. & F., 1-7-16.

KING — George Henry, *b* Elmfield, Ryde, I. of Wight, *e* Ealing, Middlesex, 43348, L/Cpl., k. in a., F. & F., 12-10-16, formerly 8701 R. Fus.

KIRKHAM — Percy, *b* Stockport, Cheshire, *e* Ashton-u-Lyne, Lancs., 32448, Pte., k. in a., F. & F., 23-4-17.

KIRKPATRICK — Richard, *b* Heyside, Royton, Lancs., *e* Shaw, Lancs., 38755, Pte., k. in a., F. & F., 30-6-17.

KIRWAN — Joseph, *b* Dublin, *e* Manchester (Dublin), 9122, Pte., k. in a., F. & F., 3-3-16.

KNAPPER — Joe, *b* Hollinwood, Lancs., *e* Hollinwood 28464, Pte., k. in a., F. & F., 12-10-16.

KNIGHT — Herbert Edward, *b* Paddington, Middlesex, *e* Kilburn, Middlesex (Kensal Rise, Middlesex), 43422, Pte., k. in a., F. & F., 23-4-17, formerly 5051 Middlesex R.

KNOWLSON — Harold, *b* Ancoats, Manchester, *e* Manchester, 8207, Pte., d. of w., F. & F., 1-7-16.

KOCHY — Fritz, *e* Manchester, 33859, Pte., k. in a., F. & F., 30-7-16.

LAMB — Oscar, *b* Morecambe, Lancs., *e* Morecambe, 245157, Pte., k. in a., F. & F., 31-7-17, formerly 3149 R. Lancs. R.

LANGSHAW — William, *b* Hulme, Manchester, *e* Manchester, 8715, Pte., k. in a., F. & F., 1-7-16.

LAVILLE — James, *b* Longsight, Manchester, *e* Manchester (Clayton, Manchester), 34852, Pte., d., F. & F., 30-1-17

LAW John, *b* St. James, Salford, Lancs., *e* Manchester, 8703, Pte., k. in a., F. & F., 10-7-16.

LEAR Frank East, *b* Pendleton, Lancs., *e* Manchester (Pendleton), 8211, Pte., k. in a., F. & F., 10-7-16.

LEDGER Louis, *b* Harpurhey, Manchester, *e* Manchester (Blackley, Manchester), 8712, Pte., k. in a., F. & F., 23-4-17.

LEE Charles Herbert, *b* Redbourne, Herts., *e* St. Alban's, Herts. (E. Common, Redbourne), 41688, Pte., k. in a. F. & F., 31-7-17, formerly G/16505 R. W. Kent R.

LEE Thomas, *b* High Wycombe, Bucks., *e* High Wycombe, 41622, Pte., k. in a., F. & F., 19-10-17, formerly G/16885 R. W. Kent R.

LEES Joseph, *b* Oldham, Lancs., *e* Oldham, 54751, Pte., k. in a., F. & F., 22-3-18.

LEWIS John William, *b* Pendleton, Lancs., *e* Manchester (Pendleton), 8223, Pte., k. in a., F. & F., 30-7-16.

LINDSAY George Douglas, *b* Manchester, *e* Manchester, 9041, Pte., k. in a., F. & F., 1-7-16.

LINFOOT Herbert, *b* Hulme, Manchester, *e* Manchester, 8213, Sgt., k. in a., F. & F., 30-7-17.

LINNEY Louis, *b* Failsworth, Lancs., *e* Manchester (Clayton Bridge, Manchester), 8705, Sgt., k. in a., F. & F., 10-7-16.

LINTERN Charley Edward, *b* Blagdon, Somerset., *e* Axbridge, Somerset., 47620, Pte., k. in a., F. & F., 2-7-17, formerly R/4/140556 R.A.S.C.

LISTER John, *b* Royton, Lancs., *e* Royton, 33097, Pte., k. in a., F. & F., 22-3-18.

LLEWELLYN Hugh, *b* Godalming, Surrey, *e* Manchester (Moss Side, Lancs.), 12391, Pte., k. in a., F. & F., 22-3-18.

LOFTUS Thomas, *b* Manchester, *e* Manchester, 36937, Pte., k. in a., F. & F., 23-4-17.

LOMAX John, *b* Darwen, Lancs., *e* Ashton-u-Lyne, Lancs. (Hollinwood, Lancs.), 39979, Pte., k. in a., F. & F., 23-4-17.

LOMAX Richard, *b* Moston, Manchester, *e* Manchester (Warrington, Lancs.), 8708, Pte., k. in a., F. & F., 21-4-17.

LOVEGROVE Abraham, *b* Tilehurst, Berks., *e* Wokingham, Berks. (Tilehurst), 43312, Pte., k. in a., F. & F., 15-10-16, formerly 21010 R. Berks. R.

LOWE Henry Reginald, *b* Preston, Lancs., *e* Warrington, Lancs., 42158, Pte., d., F. & F., 3-5-18, formerly T4/124172 R.A.S.C.

LOWE Robert Hayhurst, *b* Latchford, Warrington, Lancs., *e* Warrington, 43240, Sgt., k. in a., F. & F., 23-4-17, formerly 16701 S. Lancashire R.

LUCAS Frank, *b* Ardwick, Manchester, *e* Manchester (Chorlton-on-Medlock, Manchester), 8219, Cpl., k. in a., F. & F., 30-7-16.

LUNDY Thomas, *b* Middleton-on-the-Wolds, Yorks., *e* Manchester, 9335, Pte., k. in a., F. & F., 15-10-16.

LUSHER Joseph, *b* Walkden, Lancs., *e* Heaton Park, Manchester (Wigan, Lancs.), 27135, Pte., k. in a., F. & F., 3-12-17.

MACKIE Alexander, *b* Salford, Lancs., *e* Manchester, 8230, Pte., k. in a., F. & F., 11-10-16.

MADDERS Alfred Walter, *b* Manchester, *e* Manchester, 34677, Pte., d., F. & F., 24-1-17.

MARSDEN James, *b* Oldham, Lancs., *e* Oldham, 54753, Pte., k. in a., F. & F., 22-3-18.

MARSDEN Stanley, *b* Longsight, Manchester, *e* Manchester, 8727, Pte., d. of w., F. & F., 1-7-16.

MARSH Thomas Henry, *b* Patricroft, Lancs., *e* Manchester (Winton, Manchester), 8744, Pte., k. in a., F. & F., 3-5-16.

MARSHALL Percy Robert, *b* Stockport, Cheshire, *e* Manchester (Withington, Manchester), 34855, Pte., k. in a., F. & F., 12-10-16.

MASON William, *b* Mossley, Lancs., *e* Mossley, 33040, Pte., k. in a., F. & F., 30-7-16.

MATHER Horatio, *b* Manchester, *e* Manchester (Heaton Park, Manchester), 33760, Pte., k. in a., F. & F., 12-10-16.

MAUDE Gibson, *e* Oldham, Lancs. (Chadderton, Lancs.), 48523, Pte., k. in a., F. & F., 22-3-18.

MAUND Charles, *b* Worcester, *e* Coventry, Warwick (Birmingham), 9263, Pte., k. in a., F. & F., 30-4-18.

MAY Walter, *b* Stockport, Cheshire, 352512, Pte., k. in a., F. & F., 27-3-18.

McCANN William, *b* Lr. Crumpsall, Manchester, *e* Manchester (Urmston, Lancs.), 32493, Pte., d. of w., F. & F., 31-8-17.

McCORMACK Edmund, *b* Chelsea, Middlesex, *e* Hounslow, Middlesex (Chelsea), 43360, L/Cpl., k. in a., F. & F., 25-3-17, formerly L/5/10377 R. Fus.

McDERMOTT Daniel, *b* Co. Galway, *e* Manchester (Co. Galway), 34270, Pte., k. in a., F. & F., 30-7-16.

McDONALD George Burns, *b* Govan, Lanark., *e* Manchester, 47198 Pte., k. in a., F. & F., 22-3-18.

McEWEN William, *b* Ardwick, Manchester, *e* Manchester, 9034, Pte., k. in a., F. & F., 30-7-16.

McGRATH David, *b* Oldham, Lancs., *e* Oldham, 376303, L/Cpl., k. in a., F. & F., 22-3-18.

McGUIRE Patrick, *b* Manchester, *e* Manchester, 24744, Pte., k. in a., F. & F., 12-10-16.

McKENNA John, *b* Longsight, Manchester, *e* Manchester, 8228, Pte., d. of w., F. & F., 3-2-16.

McKENZIE John Dickson, *b* Kelso, Roxbro', *e* Altrincham, Cheshire, 44563, L/Cpl., k. in a., F. & F., 22-3-18, formerly G/18790 R. Fus.

McLINDEN Harry, *b* Walton, Liverpool, *e* Manchester (Great Lever, Bolton, Lancs.), 8738, Pte., k. in a., F. & F., 23-4-17.

McMENEMY Joseph, *b* Beswick, Manchester, *e* Manchester, 8730, A/C.S.M., k. in a., F. & F., 30-7-16.

McNABOE Thomas Arthur, *b* Manchester, *e* Manchester, 31178, Pte., d. of w., F. & F., 30-7-16.

McNEE George, *b* Temple Patrick, Co. Antrim, *e* Manchester (Stockport, Cheshire), 9234, Pte., d. of w., F. & F., 25-4-17.

McNEISH Henry, *b* Denton, Lancs., *e* Denton (Hooley Hill), Manchester), 29036, Pte., k. in a., F. & F., 22-3-18.

MENDES Norman Ernest, *b* Northwich, Cheshire, *e* Manchester (Chorlton-on-Medlock, Manchester), 8240, Pte., k. in a., F. & F., 1-7-16.

MERCER Herbert, *b* Pendleton, Lancs., *e* Manchester (Pendleton), 8236, Pte., k. in a., F. & F., 13-5-16.

MILLS Willoughby, *b* Kennington, Surrey, *e* Manchester, 8747, Pte., k. in a., F. & F., 1-7-16.

MILLYARD Henry Samuel, *b* Lymm, Cheshire, *e* Ashton-u-Lyne Lancs. (Fallowfield, Manchester), 34494, L/Cpl., d. of w., F. & F., 26-3-17.

MILVERTON Ernest George, *b* Chard, Somerset., *e* Weymouth, Dorset. (Crewkerne, Somerset), 51121, Pte., k. in a., F. & F., 29-10-17, formerly S4/125770 R.A.S.C.

MITCHELL Alec, *b* St. Bride's, Manchester, *e* Manchester (Sale, Cheshire), 8241, Pte., d. of w., F. & F., 12-10-16.

MITTON Charles, *b* Hulme, Manchester, *e* Manchester, 8763, L/Cpl., k. in a., F. & F., 1-7-16.

MOLLOY Joseph, *b* Manchester, *e* Manchester, 34546, Pte., k. in a., F. & F., 30-7-16.

MOORES Ernest, *b* St. Luke's, Manchester, *e* Manchester, 8237, L/Cpl., k. in a., F. & F., 30-7-16.

MOORES Herbert, *b* Ashton u-Lyne, Lancs., *e* Manchester (Seedley, Manchester), 8359, Pte., k. in a., F. & F., 1-7-16.

MORAN William, *b* St. Helens, Lancs., *e* Manchester, 34516, Pte., k. in a., F. & F., 12-10-16.

MORRIS David, *b* St. Helens, Lancs., *e* St. Helens, 43248, L/Cpl., k. in a., F. & F., 23-4-17, formerly 16741 S. Lancashire R.

MORRIS Robert Dickinson, *e* Lancaster (Bowerham, Lancaster), 245164, Pte., k. in a., F. & F., 30-4-18, formerly 3444 R. Lancs. R.

MORRISSEY John, *b* St. Philip's, Salford, Lancs., *e* Manchester (Salford), 8734, Pte., d. of w., F. & F., 2-11-16.

MORT John, *b* Hulme, Manchester, *e* Manchester, 32390, Pte., k. in a., F. & F., 12-10-16.

MUIR Leonard Alfred, *b* Manchester, *e* Manchester (Port Slade, Sussex), 12158, Pte., k. in a., F. & F., 22-3-18.

MULDOON John, *b* Grossboyn, Co. Mayo, *e* Normanton, Yorks. (Ballyhankin, Co. Mayo), 43247, Pte., k. in a., F. & F., 30-12-16, formerly 19173 S. Lancashire R.

MULLIGAN James, *b* Liverpool, *e* Liverpool (Cheriton, Kent), 43246, Pte., d. of w., F. & F., 18-10-16, formerly 1633 S. Lancashire R.

MURPHY George, *b* St. John's, Stalybridge, Cheshire, *e* Ashton-u-Lyne, Lancs. (Dukinfield, Cheshire), 47353, Cpl., k. in a., F. & F., 25-12-17.

MURRAY Thomas, *b* Manchester, *e* Manchester (Beswick, Manchester), 27501, Pte., k. in a., F. & F., 30-7-16.

MUSGROVE William, *b* Lumb, Lancs., *e* Rawtenstall, Lancs. (Piercey, Waterfoot, Lancs.), 43171, Pte., d. of w., F. & F., 13-10-16, formerly 26463 E. Lancashire R.

NEEDHAM Thomas, *b* Manchester, *e* Manchester, 8771, Pte., d. of w., F. & F., 21-10-16.

NEEDLEY Charles, *b* Moston, Manchester, *e* Manchester, 39884, Pte., k. in a., F. & F., 22-3-18.

NELSON Arthur William, *b* Osmotherley, Lancs., *e* Ulverston, Lancs., 61183, Pte., k. in a., F. & F., 22-3-18.

NELSON John, *e* Manchester (Chorlton-on-Medlock, Manchester), 47306, Pte., d., F. & F., 23-11-18.

NEWLAND William, *b* Hulme, Manchester, *e* Manchester (Stretford, Manchester), 8766, Pte., d. of w., F. & F., 12-10-16.

NIXON James Henry, *b* Ancoats, Manchester, *e* Manchester (Collyhurst, Manchester), 8253, Cpl., k. in a., F. & F., 8-5-18.

NOLAN William, *b* Dublin, *e* Ashton-u-Lyne, Lancs. (Southport), Lancs.), 34824, L/Cpl.. k. in a., F. & F., 12-10-16.

NORBURY Bernard, *b* Manchester, *e* Manchester (Chorlton-cum-Hardy, Manchester), 8251, Cpl., k. in a., F. & F., 30-7-16.

NORCROSS William Henry, *b* St. Helens, Lancs., *e* St. Helens, 61118, Pte., k. in a., F. & F., 22-3-18.

NORMAN George Alfred, *b* St. John's, Manchester, *e* Manchester (Chorlton-on-Medlock, Manchester), 8250, Sgt., k. in a., F. & F., 25-12-17.

NORTON Leonard, *b* St. Neots, Huntingdon, *e* Manchester, 8770, L/Cpl., k. in a., F. & F., 1-7-16.

NESTOR Joseph, *e* Failsworth, Lancs. (Moston, Manchester), 47330. Pte., k. in a., F. & F., 22-3-18.

OAKENFULL Frederick, *e* Canterbury, Kent, 41689, Pte., k. in a., F. & F., 23-4-17, formerly G/16222 R. W. Kent R.

O'CONNOR Francis, *b* Long Banton, Durham, *e* Consett, Durham, 43198, Pte., k. in a., F. & F., 23-4-17, formerly 30/272 Northumberland Fus.

OGDEN Thomas, *b* Salford, Lancs., *e* Manchester (Seedley, Manchester), 9496, Pte., d. of w., F. & F., 19-2-16.

ORMISHER James, *b* Wigan, Lancs., *e* Wigan, 35215, Pte., k. in a., F. & F., 12-10-16.

OVENS Walter, *b* Moss Side, Manchester, *e* Manchester, 8785, L/Cpl., d. of w., F. & F., 3-8-16.

OWENS Richard, *b* Holyhead, Anglesea, *e* Manchester (Tyldesley. Lancs.), 9314, Pte., k. in a., F. & F., 1-7-16.

PAGE Sidney, *b* St. John's, Pendlebury, Lancs., *e* Manchester (Irlams-o'th'-Height, Lancs.), 8800, Pte., k. in a., F. & F., 12-10-16.

PALMER Harold, *b* Greenheys, Manchester, *e* Manchester, 8265, Sgt., k. in a., F. & F., 12-10-16.

PALMER Robert, *e* Manchester, 47452, Pte., d. of w., F. & F., 1-5-17.

PARKER Charles Frederick, *b* Ashton-on-Mersey, Cheshire, *e* Manchester, 34307, Pte., k. in a., F. & F., 23-4-17.

PARKINSON John Harold, *b* Oldham, Lancs., *e* Oldham, 32281, Pte., k. in a., F. & F., 30-7-16.

PARROTT Richard Frederick, *b* Bradford, Manchester, *e* Manchester (Bradford), 8267, Pte., d. of w., Home, 27-7-16.

PARSONS Stephen, *b* Crawley, Sussex, *e* Horsham, Sussex (Crawley). 43409, Pte., k. in a., F. & F., 12-10-16, formerly G/8057 R. Sussex R.

PAYNE Montague Sinclair, *b* Edmonton, Middlesex, *e* Tottenham (Edmonton), 43362, Pte., k. in a., F. & F., 12-10-16, formerly 15734 Royal Fus.

PEARCEY James, *b* St. Mary's, Ashton-u-Lyne, Lancs., *e* Ashton-u-Lyne (Dukinfield, Cheshire), 3438, Pte., k. in a., F. & F., 22-3-18.

PEARSON Allen, *b* Altrincham, Cheshire, *e* Altrincham (Barnton, Cheshire), 43214, Pte., k. in a., F. & F., 27-3-18, formerly 33160 Cheshire R.

PEARSON Reginald, *b* Newport, Mon., *e* Newport, 302464, Pte., k. in a., F. & F., 30-4-18.

PEAT Joseph, *b* Manchester, *e* Manchester, 26269, Pte., k. in a., F. & F., 1-7-16.

PEDLEY Thomas, *e* Manchester, 47434, L/Cpl., k. in a., F. & F., 23-4-17.

PENDLEBURY Thomas, *b* Astley, Lancs., *e* Manchester (Astley), 9358, Pte., k. in a., F. & F., 1-7-16.

PEPWORTH Edwin Arthur, *b* Stowell's Memorial, Salford, Lancs., *e* Salford, 54921, Pte., k. in a., F. & F., 27-12-17, formerly 18551 Lancashire Fus.

PHILLIPS Herbert, *e* Manchester, 22891, Pte., k. in a., F. & F., 30-4-18.

PHILPOTT Arthur Millington, *b* Ludlow, Shrops., *e* Eccles, Lancs. (Urmston, Lancs.), 34829, Pte., k. in a., F. & F., 30-7-16.

PICKTHALL Harry, *b* Kendal, Westmorland, *e* Manchester (Kendal), 8804, Pte., k. in a., F. & F., 1-7-16.

PORTER John Schofield, *b* Haulgh, Bolton, Lancs., *e* Manchester (Bolton), 8269, Sgt., d. of w., F. & F., 1-8-16.

POTKIN James, *b* Manchester, *e* Ashton-u-Lyne, Lancs. (Hulme, Manchester), 45006, Pte., k. in a., F. & F., 23-4-17.

POWELL Tom, *b* Faringdon, Berks., *e* Faringdon (Letcombe Regis, Wantage, Berks.), 43326, Pte., k. in a., F. & F., 22-3-18.

POWER James Edward, *b* Manchester, *e* Manchester, 9399, Pte., k. in a., F. & F., 30-7-16.

PRENDERGAST John, *b* St. Paul's, Oldham, Lancs., *e* Oldham, 15482, L/Cpl., k. in a., F. & F., 23-4-17.

PRESCOTT Thomas Cyril, *b* Moss Side, Manchester, *e* Manchester, 9523, Pte., k. in a., F. & F., 10-7-16.

PRESCOTT William, *b* Oldham, Lancs., *e* Chadderton, Lancs. (Oldham), 49745, Pte., k. in a., F. & F., 22-3-18.

PRESTON William Moon, *b* Southampton, *e* Manchester (West Newport, Fifeshire), 8811, Pte., d. of w., F. & F., 5-7-16.

PRICE George, *b* Crewe, *e* Crewe, 61133, Pte., k. in a., F. & F., 22-3-18.

QUINN John George, *b* Douglas, I. of M., *e* Manchester, 8815, Cpl., k. in a., F. & F., 1-7-16.

QUIRK Edward, *b* Leeds, *e* Manchester, 39908, Pte., k. in a., F. & F., 31-7-17.

RAIN Ralph, *b* Collyhurst, Manchester, *e* Manchester, 8816, Pte., k. in a., F. & F., 1-7-16.

RAMSDEN Norman Wood, *b* Prestwich, Lancs., *e* Manchester (Prestwich), 9521, Pte., k. in a., F. & F., 1-7-16, formerly 15568 R. Lancs. R.

RAMSDEN Percy Gordon, *b* Prestwich, Lancs., *e* Manchester (Whitefield, Manchester), 8834, Cpl., k. in a., F. & F., 23-4-17.

RAMSEY Robert, *e* Romford, Essex, 43365, Pte., d. of w., Home, 18-4-17, formerly 10379 R. Fus.

RATCLIFF Douglas, *b* Manchester, *e* Manchester (Timperley, Cheshire), 8844, Cpl., k. in a., F. & F., 23-4-17.

RAWLINSON Clifford, *b* Lytham, Lancs., *e* Manchester (Cheadle Hulme, Manchester), 8831, L/Cpl., k. in a., F. & F., 10-7-16.

READ Clifford, *b* Moston, Manchester, *e* Ashton-u-Lyne, Lancs. (Failsworth, Lancs.), 39986, Pte., d. of w., F. & F., 28-5-17.

REDFERN Ida, *b* Droylsden, Manchester, *e* Ashton-u-Lyne, Lancs., 45264, Pte., k. in a., F. & F., 22-3-18.

REMMOS Albert Alfred Oscar, *b* Finchley, Middlesex, *e* Manchester, 8273, L/Cpl., k. in a., F. & F., 1-7-16.

REYNOLDS John, *b* Horwich, Lancs., *e* Manchester, 9243, Sgt., d. of w., F. & F., 3-7-16.

RHODES Albert, *b* Heaton Norris, Manchester, *e* Manchester, 8835, C.S.M., k. in a., F. & F., 22-3-18.

RHODES Thomas Frederick, *b* Birmingham, *e* Birmingham, 49367, Pte., k. in a., F. & F., 22-3-18.

RICHARDSON Robert, *b* Shoreditch, Middlesex, *e* Hounslow, Middlesex (Barnsbury, Middlesex), 43363, Pte., k. in a., F. & F., 23-4-17, formerly G/18530 R. Fus.

RICHARDSON William, *b* Bury, Lancs., *e* Manchester (Bury), 203181. Pte., k. in a., F. & F., 9-9-17.

RIGBY Henry, *b* Croston, Preston, Lancs., *e* Salford, Lancs., 29409, Pte., k. in a., F. & F., 31-7-17.

RIGBY Philip, *b* Manchester, *e* Manchester, 7552, Pte., k. in a., F. & F., 8-9-17.

RILEY Edward Henry, *b* Chorlton-on-Medlock, Manchester, *e* Manchester (Gorton, Manchester), 8838, Pte., k. in a., F. & F., 2-7-16.

RILEY James Alfred, *b* Ancoats, Manchester, *e* Manchester, 17738, Pte., k. in a., F. & F., 12-10-16.

RITCHIE James B., *e* Manchester (Chorlton-on-Medlock, Manchester), 47433, L/Cpl., k. in a., F. & F., 23-4-17.

ROBERTS Alfred Sheldon, *b* Manchester, *e* Manchester (Salford, Lancs.), 27733, Pte., d. of w., Home, 10-8-16.

ROBERTS Harry, *b* Sale, Cheshire, *e* Salford, Lancs. (Irlams-o'th'-Height, Lancs.), 303149, Pte., d. of w., F. & F., 4-12-17.

ROBERTS James, *b* Manchester, *e* Manchester (Pendleton, Lancs.), 8840, L/Cpl., k. in a., F. & F., 12-10-16.

ROBERTS Maurice, *b* Ancoats, Manchester, *e* Manchester, 9218, L/Cpl., k. in a., F. & F., 1-7-16.

ROBERTS Vincent Hamer, *b* Liverpool, *e* Liverpool (Litherland, Lancs.), 30218, Pte., k. in a., F. & F., 23-4-17.

ROBINSON Frank Griffin, *b* Harpurhey, Manchester, *e* Manchester, 8821, L/Cpl., k. in a., F. & F., 30-7-16.

ROBINSON Richard, *b* Ancoats, Manchester, *e* Manchester, 9186, Pte., k. in a., F. & F., 2-7-16.

RODGER George William, *b* Manchester, *e* Manchester, 9511, Pte., d. of w., F. & F., 1-7-16.

ROGAN John, *b* Newcastle-on-Tyne, *e* Manchester, 34422, Pte., k. in a., F. & F., 30-7-16.

ROGERS Arthur, *b* New Moston, Manchester, *e* Manchester, 8826, Pte., k. in a., F. & F., 12-10-16.

RONALD Fergus, *b* Hulme, Manchester, *e* Manchester, 8850, L/Cpl., k. in a., F. & F., 23-4-17.

ROSE George, *b* Manchester, *e* Salford, Lancs. (Hulme, Manchester), 34685, Pte., k. in a., F. & F., 30-7-16.

ROSTRON Ernest, *b* Manchester, *e* Manchester, 34692, L/Cpl., k. in a., F. & F., 23-4-17.

ROTHWELL Albert, *b* St. Stephen's, Longsight, Manchester, *e* Manchester, 9078, Pte., k. in a., F. & F., 2-7-16.

ROTHWELL Joseph Wallace, *b* Manchester, *e* Manchester (Bradford, Manchester), 27335, Pte., k. in a., F. & F., 1-7-16.

ROUNDING Hugh, *b* Leeds, *e* Harrogate, Yorks. (Knaresborough, Yorks.), 42182, Pte., k. in a., F. & F., 31-7-17, formerly T4/161216 R.A.S.C.

ROWLAND George Henry, *b* Newton, Cheshire, *e* Manchester (Newton), 17211, Sgt., k. in a., F. & F., 22-3-18.

ROWLAND John, *b* Lees, Oldham, Lancs., *e* Oldham (Lees), 33381, L/Cpl., k. in a., F. & F., 12-10-16.

RULE Frank Rennie, *b* Bishop Auckland, Durham, *e* Manchester (Accrington, Lancs.), 8853, Pte., k. in a., F. & F., 10-7-16.

RUMSBY Albert George, *b* Somerleyton, Suffolk, *e* Epping (Woodford Green), 41681, Pte., k. in a., F. & F. 31-7-17.

RUSHTON Fred, *b* Baxenden, Lancs., *e* Accrington, Lancs. (Baxenden), 43173, Pte., k. in a., F. & F., 17-10-16, formerly 26150 E. Lancashire R.

SALT Fred, *b* Swinton, Lancs., *e* Manchester (Swinton), 9129, Pte., k. in a., F. & F., 15-3-16.

SALTER Wilfred William, *b* Culmstock, Devon., *e* Culmstock, 51133, Pte., d. of w., F. & F., 26-4-18, formerly S4/125392 R.A.S.C.

SCHOFIELD Arthur, *b* Manchester, *e* Manchester, 39959, Pte., k. in a., F. & F., 23-4-17.

SCHOFIELD Henry, *b* Royton, Lancs., *e* Royton, 27251, Pte., k. in a., F. & F., 22-3-18.

SCHOFIELD Reuben, *b* St. Matthias', Manchester, *e* Salford, Lancs., 9519, Pte., k. in a., F. & F., 1-7-16, formerly 10611 Lancashire Fus.

SCHOFIELD Leonard, *b* Prestwich, Lancs., *e* Manchester (Prestwich), 8863, Pte., k. in a., F. & F., 10-7-16.

SCHOLES Thomas, *b* St. John's, Bolton, Lancs., *e* Bolton, 43131, Sgt., d. of w., F. & F., 12-10-16, formerly 16467 N. Lancashire R.

SCHOLEY Cornelius, *b* St. Andrew's, Salford, Lancs., *e* Manchester, 8875, L/Cpl., k. in a., F. & F., 27-4-18.

SCOTT Walter, *b* Manchester, *e* Manchester, 8856, Pte., k. in a., F. & F., 1-7-16.

SCOTT William Henry, *b* Manchester, *e* Manchester, 9417, Pte., k. in a., F. & F., 1-7-16.

SEABORN Edward, *b* Openshaw, Manchester, *e* Ashton-u-Lyne, Lancs. (Droylsden, Manchester), 27606, L/Cpl., k. in a., F. & F., 23-4-17.

SELBY Charles Henry, *b* Ardwick, Manchester, *e* Manchester (Moston, Manchester), 12696, Pte., k. in a., F. & F., 22-3-18.

SETTLE Fred, *b* Withington, Manchester, *e* Manchester, 12451, Pte., k. in a., F. & F., 22-3-18.

SETTLE Robert Jackson, *b* Farnworth, Lancs., *e* Manchester (Farnworth), 18421, L/Cpl., k. in a., F. & F., 12-10-16.

SEYMOUR Frederick William, *b* Tilehurst, Berks., *e* Reading, Berks. (Tilehurst), 43336, Pte., k. in a., F. & F., 12-10-16, formerly 20171 R. Berks. R.

SHARPLES Tom, *b* St. John's, Cheetham, Manchester, *e* Manchester, 9048, L/Cpl., k. in a., F. & F., 1-7-16.

SHAW Charles, *b* Harpurhey, Manchester, *e* Manchester (Mellor, Stockport, Cheshire), 8895, Pte., k. in a., F. & F., 1-7-16.

SHAW Harry, *e* Oldham, Lancs., 47314, Cpl., k. in a., F. & F., 26-4-17.

SHAW Robert Edward, *b* Chesterton, Newcastle, Staffs., *e* Manchester (Newcastle), 8857, Pte., d., F. & F., 18-8-16.

SHEEN David, *b* Wigan, Lancs., *e* Manchester (Swinton, Lancs.), 9180, Pte., k. in a., F. & F., 30-7-16.

SHELDON Arthur Leonard, *b* Aston, Birmingham, *e* Manchester (Newton, Manchester), 9258, Pte., k. in a., F. & F., 30-7-16.

SIDDALL Arthur, *b* Crumpsall, Manchester, *e* Manchester, 26546, Pte., k. in a., F. & F., 22-3-18.

SIDWELL Frederick Henry, *b* Manchester, *e* Manchester, 9253, Sgt., k. in a., F. & F., 1-7-16.

SILLEY Richard, *b* Ilminster, Somerset, *e* Aldershot (Chippenham, Wilts.), 51132, Pte., k. in a., F. & F., 26-12-17, formerly S4/143449 R.A.S.C.

SIMMS Frederick, *b* Sparsholt, Berks., *e* Wantage, Berks., 43333, Pte., k. in a., F. & F., 7-4-17.

SIMISTER Douglas, *b* Hollinwood, Lancs., *e* Ashton-u-Lyne, Lancs. (Stalybridge, Cheshire), 47351, Pte., k. in a., F. & F., 23-4-17.

SIMMONDS Tom Alfred, *b* Winkfield Row, Berks., *e* Wokington, Berks. (Bracknell, Berks.), 43329, Pte., k. in a., F. & F., 22-4-17.

SIMPSON Harry, *b* Collyhurst, Manchester, *e* Manchester, 26378, Pte., d. of w., F. & F., 6-7-16.

SKELLAND John James, *b* Liverpool, *e* Liverpool, 59587, Pte., k. in a., F. & F., 22-3-18.

SLATER James Harold, *b* Oldham, Lancs., *e* Oldham, 48515, Pte., k. in a., F. & F., 22-3-18.

SMALLEY Herbert George, *b* Nuneaton, Warwick., *e* Ashton-u-Lyne, Lancs. (Hollinwood, Lancs.), 33305, d. of w., F. & F., 18-6-17.

SMITH Albert, *b* Stalybridge, Lancs., *e* Manchester, 8301, Pte., k. in a., F. & F., 10-2-16.

SMITH Bertram, *b* Penketh, Lancs., *e* Warrington, Lancs. (Penketh), 61153, Pte., k. in a., F. & F., 22-3-18.

SMITH Frank Clarke, *b* Miles Platting, Manchester, *e* Manchester, 9505, Pte., k. in a., F. & F., 10-7-16.

SMITH George William, *b* St. Andrew's, Salford, Lancs., *e* Manchester (Lr. Broughton, Salford, Lancs.), 8866, L/Cpl., k. in a., F. & F., 1-7-16.

SMITH Gordon, *b* Didsbury, Lancs., *e* Manchester, 32381, L/Cpl., d. of w., F. & F., 4-12-17.

SMITH Hubert Francis, *b* Manchester, *e* Manchester, 15722, Sgt., d. of w., F. & F., 29-4-17.

SMITH John, *b* Salford, Lancs., *e* Manchester (Salford), 203118, Pte., k. in a., F. & F., 25-9-17.

SMITH John Gordon, *b* Pendlebury, Lancs., *e* Manchester (Pendlebury), 8867, Pte., d. of w., F. & F., 1-7-16.

SMITH Stanley, *b* Hulme, Manchester, *e* Manchester (Gorton, Manchester), 8859, Pte., d. of w., F. & F., 13-7-16.

SMITH William, *b* Accrington, Lancs., *e* Manchester, 8898, Sgt., k. in a., F. & F., 30-7-16.

SMITH Wilfred Ernest Branwell, *b* Lr. Broughton, Salford, Lancs., *e* Manchester, 8884, Pte., k. in a., F. & F., 11-7-16.

SMITHSON Harold Geoffrey, *b* Newmarket, Suffolk, *e* London (Newmarket), 42178, L/Cpl., k. in a., F. & F., 31-7-17, formerly T4/159833, R.A.S.C.

SNELSON George, *b* Lostock Gralam, Cheshire, *e* Manchester (Lostock Gralam), 12449, Pte., k. in a., F. & F., 22-3-18.

SOUTHERN John, *b* High Legh, Cheshire, *e* Knutsford, Cheshire (High Legh), 43210, Pte., k. in a., F. & F., 31-7-17, formerly 33126 Cheshire R.

SPENCER Herbert, *e* Colne, Lancs. (Wirewall, Lancs.), 43177, Pte., d. of w., F. & F., 22-4-17, formerly 26157 E. Lancashire R.

SPRIGGS Sidney, *b* Leicester, *e* Leicester, 41015, L/Cpl., k. in a., F. & F., 22-3-18, formerly 1672 Leicester R.

SPURR Harry, *b* Hartford, Oldham, Lancs., *e* Oldham (Chadderton, Lancs.), 375269, Sgt., k. in a., F. & F., 31-7-17.

STABLEFORD	Donald Scotson, *b* Fallowfield, Manchester, *e* Manchester, 8282, Sgt., k. in a., F. & F., 1-7-16.
STAFFORD	Fred, *b* St. Mary's, Oldham, Lancs., *e* Oldham, 2702, Cpl., k. in a., F. & F., 30-4-18, M.M.
STAFFORD	Harry, *b* Hooley Hill, Guide Bridge, Lancs., *e* Ashton-u-Lyne, Lancs. (Hooley Hill), 48817, Pte., k. in a., F. & F., 22-3-18.
STAFFORD	William Ives, *b* Manchester, *e* Manchester, 45005, Pte., k. in a., F. & F., 23-4-17.
STALEY	John, *b* Collyhurst, Manchester, *e* Manchester, 8873, Pte., k. in a., F. & F., 10-7-16.
STANSFIELD	James Abner, *b* Royton, Lancs., *e* Royton, 35158, Pte., k. in a., F. & F., 23-4-17.
STARKIE	Louis, *b* Oswaldtwistle, Lancs., *e* Accrington, Lancs. (Oswaldtwistle), 31155, Pte., k. in a., F. & F., 11-10-16.
STARKIE	Richard, *b* Manchester, *e* Manchester, 26441, Pte., k. in a., F. & F., 1-7-16.
STEVENS	James Alfred, *b* Oldham, *e* Oldham, 47327, Pte., k. in a., F. & F., 23-4-17.
STEWART	Robert, *b* Whalley, Manchester, *e* Manchester (Waddington, Clitheroe), 8899, Sgt., d. of w., F. & F., 8-1-18.
STOCKS	Ralph, *b* Salford, Lancs., *e* Manchester (Salford), 26303, Pte., k. in a., F. & F., 1-7-16.
STODDART	Arthur, *b* Southport, Lancs., *e* Manchester (Chorlton-on-Medlock, Manchester), 9379, Pte., k. in a., F. & F., 10-7-16.
STORER	Ernest, *b* Droylsden, Lancs., *e* Manchester (Droylsden), 9167, Pte., k. in a., F. & F., 10-7-16.
STOREY	Harry, *b* Ware, Herts., *e* Ware, 51134, Pte., d. of w., F. & F., 3-9-17, formerly S4/184645 R.A.S.C.
STOTT	George Willie, *b* Oldham, Lancs., *e* Ashton-u-Lyne, Lancs., (Oldham), 36934, Pte., d., F. & F., 25-11-16.
STRATFORD	Harold, *b* Radnage, Bucks., *e* High Wycombe, Bucks., 41637, Pte., k. in a., F. & F., 31-7-17.
STUART	George William, *b* Leith, *e* Hounslow, Middlesex (Twickenham, Middlesex), 43366, Pte., k. in a., F. & F., 20-4-17, formerly G/25600 R. Fus.
STURGEON	Robert Victor, *b* Wilmslow, Manchester, *e* Manchester (Colwyn Bay, Denbigh.), 8298, Cpl., k. in a., F. & F., 10-3-16.
STURGIS	Erris Victor, *b* Swallanfield, Berks., *e* Stratford, Essex (Canning Town, Essex), 400154, Pte., d. of w., Home, 26-5-18, formerly 4877 Lancs. Yeo.
STYLES	Ernest, *b* Manchester, *e* Manchester, 32499, Pte., k. in a., F. & F., 15-10-16.
SUGARMAN	Maurice, *b* Manchester, *e* Manchester, 27829, Pte., k. in a., F. & F., 30-7-16.
SUTTON	Alfred, *e* Manchester (Marple, Cheshire), 47215, Pte., k. in a., F. & F., 23-4-17.
SWALES	Alfred, *b* Oldham, Lancs., *e* Oldham, 30494, L/Cpl., k. in a., F. & F., 23-4-17.
SYKES	Walter, *b* Manchester, *e* Manchester, 33851, Pte., k. in a., F. & F., 30-7-16.
TABBRON	Albert, *b* Urmston, Lancs., *e* Manchester, 8904, Pte., d. of w., F. & F., 1-7-16.
TAYLOR	Albert, *e* Manchester (Bollington, Cheshire), 9132, Pte., k. in a., F. & F., 10-7-16.
TAYLOR	Charles Francis, *b* Manchester, *e* Rugby (Harpurhey, Manchester), 33853, L/Sgt., k. in a., F. & F., 12-10-16.

TAYLOR Francis James, *b* Johnstown, Denbigh., *e* Manchester, 49416, Pte., k. in a., F. & F., 22-3-18.

TAYLOR Joseph, *b* Golborne, Warrington, Lancs., *e* Wigan (Warrington), 44565, Pte., k. in a., F. & F., 23-4-17.

TAYLOR Peter, *b* Pendleton, Lancs., *e* Manchester, 8908, Pte., d. of w., F. & F., 2-7-16.

TAYLOR Samuel Ernest, *b* Oldham, Lancs., *e* Oldham, 38500, Pte., k. in a., F. & F., 3-12-17.

TAYLOR Thomas, *b* Pendleton, Lancs., *e* Manchester (Pendleton), 203100, Pte., k. in a., F. & F., 25-9-17.

TAYLOR William, *b* Manchester, *e* Manchester (Blackpool), 31214, Pte., k. in a., F. & F., 22-3-18.

THOMAS Arthur James, *b* Penzance, Cornwall, *e* Reading, Berks. (Penzance), 43339, Pte., k. in a., F. & F., 12-10-16.

THOMAS George Humphrey Gordon, *b* Moss Side, Manchester, *e* Manchester, 8309, Pte., k. in a., F. & F., 1-7-16.

THOMPSON George Henry, *b* Salford, Lancs., *e* Manchester (Chorlton on-Medlock, Manchester), 47442, Pte., k. in a., F. & F., 23-4-17.

THOMPSON Wilfred, *e* Manchester, (Gorton, Manchester) 47453, Pte., k. in a., F. & F., 23-4-17.

THOMSON James, *b* Chorlton-on-Medlock, Manchester, *e* Manchester, 8901, L/Cpl., k. in a., F. & F., 1-7-16.

THOMSON Reginald, *b* Southwark, Surrey, *e* Southwark (Camberwell, Surrey), 43263, Pte. k. in a., F. & F., 23-4-17, formerly 22957 Suffolk R.

TIERNAN John Edward, *b* Manchester, *e* Manchester, 33761, L/Cpl., k. in a., F. & F., 12-10-16.

TIGHE John, *b* Beswick, Manchester, *e* Manchester, 8906, Pte., k. in a., F. & F., 9-7-16.

TIMMS William Henry, *b* Islington, Liverpool, *e* Liverpool, 43261, Pte., k. in a., F. & F., 31-7-17, formerly 1917 South Lancs. R.

TOOLE William, *b* Salford, Lancs., *e* Manchester, 8312, Pte., k. in a., F. & F., 1-7-16.

TOPHILL George Savigny, *b* Manchester, *e* Manchester, 9345, Pte., k. in a., F. & F., 23-4-17.

TRAVIS Phillip, *b* Newton Heath, Manchester, *e* Manchester, 47446, Cpl., d. of w., F. & F.., 13-8-17

TRUEMAN Cyril, *b* Longsight, Manchester, *e* Manchester, 8306, Pte., k. in a., F. & F., 1-7-16.

TURBEFIELD Benjamin, *b* Oldham, Lancs., *e* Ashton-u-Lyne, Lancs. (Oldham), 45065, Pte., d., F. & F., 25-10-18.

TUPMAN Edward, *e* Oldham, Lancs. (Royton, Lancs.), 47328, Pte., k. in a., F. & F., 3-12-17.

TURNER James, *b* Manchester, *e* Manchester, 8903, Sgt., k. in a., F. & F., 1-7-16.

TURNER Leonard, *b* Hyde, Cheshire, *e* Manchester (Stockport, Cheshire), 8919, Pte., k. in a., F. & F., 1-7-16.

TURNER Percy, *b* Salford, Lancs., *e* Manchester (Salford), 11010, Pte., k. in a., F. & F., 23-4-17.

TURPIN Fred, *b* Manchester, *e* Manchester, 26268, Pte., k. in a., F. & F., 12-10-16.

TWEDDLE Charles, *b* Ancoats, Manchester, *e* Manchester, 8313, Pte., k. in a., F. & F., 1-7-16.

TWEEDALE Arthur, *b* Oldham, Lancs., *e* Oldham, 47067, Pte., k. in a., F. & F., 30-4-18.

TWINN Cyril Arthur, *b* Glemsford, Suffolk, *e* Wokingham, Berks. (Glemsford), 41614, Pte., d. of w., Home, 4-10-17, formerly G/15128 R. W. Kent R.

TWYNHAM Joseph, *b* Manchester, *e* Manchester (Chorlton-on-Medlock, Manchester), 26294, Pte., k. in a., F. & F., 30-7-16.

TYE Walter Edward, *b* Paddington, Middlesex, *e* Gosport, Hants. (Kensington, Middlesex), 43346, Sgt., k. in a., F. & F., 23-4-17, formerly S/2552 R. Fus.

TYLDESLEY William Gladstone, *e* Manchester (Tyldesley, Lancs.), 46598, Pte., k. in a., F. & F., 23-4-17.

UPTON Joseph Scott, *b* Salford, Lancs., *e* Manchester (Salford), 10998, L/Sgt., k. in a., F. & F., 30-7-16.

UPTON Henry, *b* Salford, Lancs., *e* Manchester, 27586, Pte., k. in a., F. & F., 23-4-17.

UTTING George, *b* Liverpool, *e* Manchester, 39950, Pte., k. in a., F. & F., 23-4-17.

VALANTINE Moses, *b* Standish, Lancs., *e* Wigan, Lancs. (Standish), 35375, Pte., k. in a., F. & F., 12-10-16.

VARAH George Edward, *b* Salford, Lancs., *e* Manchester (Hale, Cheshire), 20336, Cpl., k. in a., F. & F., 22-3-18.

VICKER Ernest, *b* South Petherton, Somerset, *e* Manchester (Rochdale, Lancs.), 35102, Pte., k. in a., F. & F., 23-4-17.

VICKERS Richard, *b* St. John's, Normanton, Derby., *e* Witley Camp, Surrey (Normanton), 43434, Pte., k. in a., F. & F., 19-4-17, formerly 4647 Middlesex R.

VIGGERS Richard William, *b* Audlem, Cheshire, *e* Crewe (Audlem), 26435, Pte., k. in a., F. & F., 1-7-16.

WADE Percy, *b* Middleton, Lancs., *e* Manchester (Middleton Junction), 8317, Pte., k. in a., F. & F., 1-7-16.

WAKELIN John, *b* Ealing, Middlesex, *e* Ealing, Middlesex (West Ealing), 43372, Pte., k. in a., F. & F., 12-10-16, formerly G/26267 R. Fus.

WALDRON Harry, *b* Withington, Lancs., *e* Manchester (Withington), 8949, Pte., d. of w., F. & F., 1-7-16.

WALKER George Ernest, *b* Manchester, *e* Manchester (Bradford, Manchester), 46710, Pte., d. of w., F. & F., 6-8-17.

WALKER Peter Swan, *e* Manchester (Newton Heath, Manchester), 33876, Cpl., k. in a., F. & F., 12-10-16.

WALKER Wilfred W., *b* Brierfield, Lancs., *e* Nelson, Lancs. (Brierfield), 43179, Pte., k. in a., F. & F., 12-10-16, formerly 26308 E. Lancashire R.

WALLEN Stanley, *b* Harlesden, Middlesex, *e* London (Harlesden), 42190, Pte., k. in a., F. & F., 30-4-18, formerly T4/161173 R.A.S.C.

WALLWORK Gilbert, *b* St. Jude's, Manchester, *e* Manchester (Clayton, Manchester), 8968, Cpl., k. in a., F. & F., 1-7-16.

WALSH Patrick, *b* Oldbury, Staffs., *e* Northampton (Stoke-on-Trent), 43438,, Pte., d. of w., F. & F., 30-10-16, formerly 5168 Middlesex R.

WALTON Frederick, *b* Chorlton-on-Medlock, Manchester, *e* Manchester, 10744, Pte., k. in a., F. & F., 10-7-16.

WALTON William Ernest, *b* Harpurhey, Manchester, *e* Manchester, 8958, Pte., k. in a., F. & F., 1-7-16.

WARBURTON Harry, *b* Shaw, Lancs., *e* Oldham, Lancs., 52059, Pte., k. in a., F. & F., 22-3-18.

WARD Arthur William, *b* Camberwell, Surrey, *e* Sunbury, Middlesex (Clapham, Surrey), 43343, Pte., k. in a., F. & F., 23-4-17, formerly 19640 R. Berks. R.

WATERSON Alan, *b* Waterfoot, Lancs., *e* Preston, Lancs. (Whitewell Bottom, Manchester), 42156, Pte., k. in a., F. & F., 30-4-18.

WEILDING James Henry, *b* Tyldesley, Lancs., *e* Atherton, Lancs. (Astley, Lancs.), 9503, Pte., k. in a., F. & F., 1-7-16.

WELCH James, *b* Bridport, Dorset., *e* Brentford, Middlesex, 51221, Pte., k. in a., F. & F., 22-3-18, formerly 5904 R. W. Surr. R.

WELSH William, *b* Crumpsall, Manchester, *e* Manchester, 26385, Pte., k. in a., F. & F., 30-7-16.

WELTON William, *b* Rawtenstall, Lancs., *e* Manchester, (Gorton, Manchester), 9488, Pte., d., F. & F., 20-10-18.

WEST John Hill, *b* Salford, Lancs., *e* Manchester, 33836, Pte., k. in a., F. & F., 23-4-17.

WHALLEY Walter, *b* Burnley, Lancs., *e* Burnley, 43185, Pte., k. in a., F. & F., 23-4-17, formerly 24151 E. Lancashire R.

WHARMBY Samuel Mottram, *b* Hyde, Cheshire, *e* Manchester (Clayton, Manchester), 25575, L/Cpl., k. in a., F. & F., 31-7-17.

WHATMOUGH Tom, *b* Hollingworth, Manchester, *e* Manchester, Hollingworth), 8928, Sgt., k. in a., F. & F., 1-7-16.

WHATMOUGH Frederick, *b* Adswood, Stockport, Cheshire, *e* Manchester (Heaviley, Stockport), 8959, Pte., d., F. & F., 2-6-16.

WHELAN William, *b* Hulme, Manchester, *e* Manchester, 8974, Pte., k. in a., F. & F., 1-7-16.

WHITEHEAD George, *b* Cheetham, Manchester, *e* Manchester, 8327, Pte., k. in a., F. & F., 1-7-16.

WHITTAKER John, *b* Accrington, Lancs., *e* Manchester, 8960, Pte., d. of w., Home, 19-7-16.

WHITTALL William Norbury, *b* Manchester, *e* Manchester (Chorlton-on-Medlock, Manchester), 24152, Cpl., k. in a., F. & F., 31-7-17.

WHITTINGHAM George, *e* Manchester, 47346, Pte., k in a., F. & F., 23-4-17.

WHITTLE Albert, *b* Manchester, *e* Manchester, 46911, Pte., k. in a., F. & F., 2-4-17.

WHITTLE William, *b* St. Helens, Lancs., *e* Manchester (Moston, Manchester), 8975, L/Cpl., d., F. & F., 26-10-18.

WHITWORTH Joseph, *b* Manchester, *e* Manchester (Beswick, Manchester), 31309, Pte., k. in a., F. & F., 1-7-16.

WIBDEN Harry, *b* Cloughfold, Lancs., *e* Bacup, Lancs. (Rawtenstall, Lancs.), 43181, Pte., k. in a., F. & F., 12-10-16, formerly 22145 E. Lancashire R.

WILCOX Joseph, *b* Walkden, Manchester, *e* Manchester (Walkden), 8930, Pte., d., F. & F., 18-8-16.

WILDS James, *b* Manchester, *e* Manchester, 36121, Pte., k. in a., F. & F., 31-7-17.

WILKINSON Arthur, *b* Salford, Lancs., *e* Manchester (Salford), 8976, L/Cpl., d. of w., F. & F., 25-4-17.

WILKINSON Charles, *b* Middleton, Lancs., *e* Failsworth, Lancs., 47365, L/Cpl., k. in a., F. & F., 23-4-17.

WILKINSON Edward, *b* Winlaton, Durham, *e* Consett, Durham, 43201, Pte., k. in a., F. & F., 3-12-17, formerly 267 Northumberland Fus.

WILKINSON Frederick Arthur, *b* Wilmslow, Cheshire, *e* Manchester (Wilmslow), 8336, Sgt., k. in a., F. & F., 1-7-16.

WILKINSON Harry, *b* Weaste, Lancs., *e* Manchester (Moston, Manchester), 35639, Pte., k. in a., F. & F., 30-7-16.

WILKINSON John, *b* Orrell, Lancs., *e* Wigan, Lancs., 47158, Pte., k. in a., F. & F., 23-4-17.

WILLETT William Edward, *b* Hurdsfield, Cheshire, *e* Manchester (West Gorton, Manchester), 34483, Pte., k. in a., F. & F., 22-3-18.

WILLIAM Alfred, *b* Salford, Lancs., *e* Salford, 61169, Pte., k. in a., F. & F., 21-3-18.

WILLIAMS Arthur, *b* Tottenham, Middlesex, *e* Ealing, Middlesex, 43373, L/Cpl., k. in a., F. & F., 22-4-17, formerly 10783 E. Kent R.

WILLIAMS Frank, *b* Chorlton-on-Medlock, Manchester, *e* Manchester, 8320, Pte., d. of w., F. & F., 4-9-16.

WILLIAMS George Henry, *b* St. John's, Worcester, *e* Carmarthen (Tenby, Pembroke.), 42171, Pte., d. of w., F. & F., 6-2-18, formerly T4/159554 R.A.S.C.

WILLIAMS Howell, *b* Salford, Lancs., *e* Manchester, 39963, Pte., k. in a., F. & F., 23-4-17.

WILLIAMS John James, *b* Bangor, Carnarvon, *e* Northwich, Cheshire (Penchwintan, Bangor), 302431, L/Cpl., d., F. & F., 2-10-18.

WILLIAMS Rowland Gould, *b* Bury, Lancs., *e* Manchester (Burnley, Lancs.), 45001, Pte., d, of w., Home, 26-4-18.

WILLIAMSON Frederick, *e* Leicester, 40988, Cpl., k. in a., F. & F., 22-3-18, formerly 3075 Leicester R.

WILLIS Thomas Edward, *b* Banham, Kent, *e* Canterbury, Kent, 51142, Pte., k. in a., F. & F., 31-7-17, formerly S4/242046 R.A.S.C.

WILLOTT Charlie, *b* Manchester, *e* Manchester, 9309, Pte., d. of w., F. & F., 10-7-16.

WILSON Alfred, *b* Manchester, *e* Manchester (Bradford, Manchester), 32494, Pte., d. of w., F. & F., 31-7-17.

WILSON Frank, *b* Belmont, Bolton, Lancs., *e* Manchester, 19787, Pte., d. of w., F. & F., 21-3-18.

WILSON Patrick Joseph, *b* Bagelstown, Co. Carlow, *e* Manchester (Collyhurst, Manchester), 28875, Pte., k. in a., F. & F., 30-7-16.

WILSON Sidney Douglas, *b* Dunston, Lincoln, *e* Manchester (Dunston), 8945, Pte., k. in a., F. & F., 11-7-16.

WILSON William, *b* Wigan, Lancs, *e* Wigan, 35238, Pte., k. in a., F. & F., 22-3-18.

WINTERBOTTOM Robert, *b* Nelson, Lancs., *e* Nelson, 54931, Pte., d. of w., F. & F., 26-4-18.

WITHEY John William, *b* Manchester, *e* Manchester (Oldham, Lancs.), 36200, Pte., k. in a., F. & F., 23-4-17.

WOLSTENCROFT Donald, *b* Levenshulme, Manchester, *e* Manchester, 8355, L/Cpl., d. of w., F. & F., 3-2-16.

WOOD Arnold, *b* Royton, Lancs., *e* Royton, 23092, Pte., k. in a., F. & F., 2-4-17.

WOOD Stanley, *b* Manchester, *e* Manchester, 8992, k. in a., F. & F., 1-7-16.

WOOLFORD Robert, *b* Hulme, Manchester, *e* Manchester, 8352, Pte., k. in a., F. & F., 1-7-16.

WOOLRICH George Thomas, *b* Hankelow, Cheshire, *e* Crewe (Nantwich, Cheshire), 26434, Pte., k. in a., F. & F., 1-7-16.

WORRALL Arthur, *b* Whitefield, Manchester, *e* Manchester (Whitefield), 8993, Cpl., k. in a., F. & F., 1-7-16.

WRAY Wilfred, *b* York, *e* Manchester (Stretford, Manchester), 8354, Pte., k. in a., F. & F., 10-7-16.

WRIGHT James, *b* Manchester, *e* Manchester, 34544, Pte., k. in a., F. & F., 23-4-17.

WRIGHT Robert Charles, *b* Meal House Lane, Bolton, Lancs., *e* Ashton-u-Lyne, Lancs., 27555, Pte., k. in a., F. & F., 30-4-18.

WRIGHT William Joseph, *b* Salford, Lancs., *e* Manchester, 9116, Sgt., k. in a., F. & F., 21-10-17.

YOUD Robert, *b* Ramsbottom, Lancs., *e* Darwen, Lancs. (Hoddlesden, Darwen), 61179, Pte., k. in a., F. & F., 22-3-18.

YOUNG Thomas, *b* Salford, Lancs., *e* Salford (Pendleton, Lancs.), 61177, Pte., k. in a., F. & F., 22-3-18.

18TH

CONTENTS

APPENDIX

CHAPTER I.

TRAINING

ON September 4th, 1914, the first enlistment for the 18th Battalion of the Manchester Regiment was made, and on September 9th the numbers were completed—this was the third of the City Battalions. Lieut.-Colonel W. A. Fraser took over command from the outset, and it was under him that the preliminaries of drill and organisation took place and by him that the officers were appointed.

From the formation until February 7th, 1915, we were stationed for training at the White City, Manchester, but until accommodation was ready parades were held daily in the City Hall, varied by marches to Alexandra Park.

The original members of the Battalion will not readily forget those early days when about a thousand men paraded and there were no N.C.O.'s, while the officers (few in number) were groping their way through a fog of doubt and uncertainty by dint of a careful study of "Infantry Training 1914" during the small hours. One officer recalls how he and perhaps five others were standing doubtfully before the Colonel in the little kennel which did duty for an orderly room. "Let's see," said the C.O., "which of you is Mr. Brown?" "Here, Sir." "You have been accustomed, I believe, to command a Company," said the Colonel, and with the courage born of ignorance, Brown, who had led his school bugle band six years before, answered without hesitation, "Yes, Sir." Thus were Company Commanders appointed in those days, and who shall say it was a bad way?

This officer's first duty on becoming a Company Commander so unexpectedly was to pay each of his 250 men a £1 note (Bradburys had just appeared and regarded with disfavour). He approached a long straggling double line of men, cloth-capped and mostly smoking cigarettes, and, drawing a bow at a venture, cried "About turn," which, to his undying astonishment, had an electrical effect. Much encouraged he tried "Quick March" and "Halt," with the same surprising and admirable results. After that the distribution of the Bradburys was easy.

But these were very early days and after a week or two of barrack life at the White City things began to look like "shaping." Our quarters were not in every way desirable, but there was one advantage which in the long run made up for the draughty and jerry-built erections in which we slept, and that was that we had good hard asphalt or wood on which to drill. This made all the difference in the days when drill was of paramount importance and was rightly given most of the time in our weekly programme.

It was a long day from 7-0 in the morning till 7-0 at night, with night operations once a week. It started with "physical jerks" carried out by Companies after an unsuccessful effort with the whole Battalion in the skating rink (another great boon in a Manchester winter), and ended with a lecture during which many a weary man enjoyed a well-earned sleep.

Christmas leave was given to everyone with the exception of the few who were required to carry on the work of the barracks, and so 1914 came to an end, and we began to think of 1915 and what it had in store for us. There was only one shadow—"Would the war be over before we were ready?"

At the beginning of February we started on the next stage and moved into huts in Heaton Park, where the other three battalions were already quartered, and it was one of the benefits of the change to be part of a Brigade, where not only was there the wholesome spirit of rivalry but also training on a larger scale was possible. We certainly disliked the seas of mud from which the huts emerged like islands, but the sleeping quarters were altogether superior to what we had been accustomed to at Old Trafford.

Khaki uniforms were still to come—we dressed in blue in those days, and became quite indifferent to remarks about tram-guards—and, of course, rifles were a far-distant dream, so that intensive training, without these aids to reality, began to produce signs of staleness among the men. So the Colonel decided to make Wednesday afternoon a holiday as well as Saturday afternoon, which was a most welcome and valuable arrangement, but it earned us the name of "the Shopkeepers" among the members of the other less fortunate battalions. These Wednesday afternoons enabled us to organise more and better football and sports of all kinds, which improved the physique of the men besides building up *esprit de corps*. Another nickname which we had, came to us after we had carried off most of the honours in the Brigade Steeplechase—it was "Scarlet Runners."

A great social function was the Brigade Sports which were held in April: this was a most successful afternoon and was largely attended by friends of the Brigade. The weather was fine though chilly, and the occasion served as an opportunity for people to see the last of the City Battalions before they left Manchester.

Our next move was made to Belton Park, Grantham, on April 24th. The camp was about three miles from Grantham, and with the glorious spring weather and the attractive surroundings the men began to feel a new zest in their work. Here the Brigade found itself part of the 30th Division, and the identification with a larger unit had the same good effects as our move to a brigade had made in January.

The four months spent in Belton Park remain a pleasant memory; true, as a centre of life and gaiety, Grantham compares but ill with Manchester, but there were compensations, and many a letter addressed to Grantham came to the officers for censoring after we had gone out to France. The words "Harlaxton Park" still mean to most of the Eighteenth long weary marches under a scorching sun, but the "Angel" and the "George" speak of refreshing draughts after the day's toil.

Several successful concerts were held while we were here: we had a good hut for the purpose and the Battalion was peculiarly rich in talent, and when, later on in France, the Divisional Troupe was formed, the Eighteenth provided about half its members. Games, of course, continued to play their part, and we achieved many successes at football, cricket, running, and so forth.

On September 7th the final move took place and we proceeded to Larkhill Camp, Salisbury Plain—a place, which is, perhaps less attractive to look back upon.

The weather did not favour us as it had done at Grantham, and a love for the wild, bleak, openness of the Plain does not lurk in every heart, and seldom if ever, in the heart of a Mancunian. This was a place of stern preparation for overseas, and the possession of rifles, the issue of all manner of kit for active service, Divisional training on a large scale, trench-digging, night operations, and last but not least, rumours made our departure seem imminent.

When the day came (November 8th) there was a hot autumn sun and the march to Amesbury Station with the mass of kit with which we started nearly exhausted us at the outset.

One of the most vivid memories of the old boys of the Eighteenth is the first two or three days of their campaign in France; the crossing—none too smooth—the toil up the hill to Ostrahove—the gloomy night in moist tents—the next day of rain and boredom—the march into Boulogne, officially supposed to cement in some mysterious way the "entente cordiale"—the tedious remainder of of the day till midnight—the move off in the dark—the train journey to Pont Remy, which was the first experience for most of us of the discomforts of a French train—the hopeless dawn—the interminable march to Coulonvillers, weighed down with hundredweights of kit and ammunition, soaking greatcoats that seemed to absorb tons of water, typewriters and all sorts of furniture, and to crown all—no breakfast, as the transport had gone via Havre, and was awaiting us at our destination.

It was a difficult start and a great test of the Battalion's good temper, but all's well that ends well, and food, which we eventually got some 23 hours after tea at Ostrahove, worked a rapid cure.

This march taught us many valuable lessons, and we must have greatly enriched the wretched villagers of Coulonvillers, who became the possessors of scores of shirts, socks, comforters and other surplus articles which we had no further inclination to carry all over France.

THE FOLLOWING IS A LIST OF OFFICERS WHO LEFT FOLKESTONE WITH THE BATTALION :—

O.C.: Lieut.-Col. W. A. Fraser. *Second-in-Command:* Major G. Lupton. *Adjutant:* Capt. G. E. Hoare.

"A" Company: Capt. D. Berry, Capt. L. Renshaw, Lieut. H. B. Harrison, Lieut. A. E. Townsend, Lieut. M. Brunton.

"B" Company: Capt. G. S. Lynde, Lieut. W. P. Knowles, Lieut. J. L. Nelson, Lieut. T. J. Kelly, Lieut. H. A. Powell, Lieut. J. S. Beaumont.

"C" Company: Capt. C. Henshall, Capt. S. E. Woollam, Lieut. P. A. Blythe, Lieut. A. J. Statham, Lieut. R. S. England, Lieut. J. G. Cunliffe, Lieut. H. H. Crawshaw.

"D" Company: Capt. P. Godlee, Capt. R. Hopkirk, Lieut. P. G. D. Haworth, Lieut. H. G. Watson, Lieut. D. Blenkiron.

Transport Officer: Lieut. H. G. S. Bower. *Quartermaster:* Lieut. T. C. Pierce. *Chaplain:* Capt. Rev. H. A. Thomson. *Medical Officer:* Capt. W. H. Butler, R.A.M.C.

The week that we spent at Coulonvillers was occupied with marches, bayonet-fighting, gas-drill and general training, and we left the place on November 17th without regret; billets were very poor, and the weather bad and cold, and it was with hopes of better things that we marched to Cardonette, spending a night at Vignacourt *en route*.

On November 25th a fatal accident took place during bombing practice. A sergeant threw a Hales No. 1 grenade—a bomb that exploded on percussion—which struck the top of the parapet and burst among the occupants of the trench. Sergt. Perkins and Pte. Bagnall were both hit, and Lieut. A. E. Townsend, the

Battalion bombing officer, was so seriously wounded that he died the next day. This sad accident occurring so soon after arrival in France cast a feeling of gloom over the Battalion.

A further move was made on the 28th to Canaples, where training and wood-cutting fatigues filled in the time.

On December 6th we had a ten-mile march to Puchevillers, which was the half-way house to the line, and moved on again next day, H.Q., " A " Company and "C" Company proceeding to Englebelmer, and " B " and " D " Companies to Mesnil, and here we had our first experiences of trench warfare and mud. We learnt a little about the former, but almost everything about the latter, which was as glutinous and abundant as anything that we had to cope with afterwards. This was a part of the line that became famous later on : Thiepval lay the other side of the Ancre valley and at the end of 1915 appeared to be a fairly passable village, though its Château was almost demolished even then, and Mesnil Château on our side was very superior and much more useful, in fact, it provided accommodation for the whole of the Company which was not undergoing instruction actually in the trenches. It was hardly luxurious and the officers' billet was called, with good reason, " Rat Cottage " : but luxury either in billets or in the line was hardly to be expected as we were only visitors and " supernumerary " to the establishment. We spent a very quiet time in this sector, though there were occasional outbreaks of machine-gun fire, and at least one whiz-bang as two of the officers can testify. They were paying a preliminary visit to the H.Q. of the Battalion, to whom they were taking their Company for instruction that afternoon, and they had to proceed down the weary length of a trench known as "Jacob's Ladder." It was a very wet trench : one of these officers was tall, and only got his legs wet, but the other was not, and he got extraordinarily wet, but that is beside the point. At any rate they got to the bottom of Jacob's Ladder at last and fell in with the working party of R.E.'s, who told them to get out of the trench and cut across the open to the sand-bagged house, which was Battalion H.Q. A whiz-bang or two were falling round the spot where this party was working and some very good sniping was put in as these two emerged, but they reached the friendly shelter of H.Q. alright, and had been there about half a minute when the wall was hit and the nose-cap of a shell came into the room and knocked a pot off the stove. As a first experience of shell-fire this apparent pursuit of the individual by shells was particularly alarming.

By December 16th the Battalion was back in Canaples, having halted again for a night at Puchevillers. It was at this village that rather an enterprising couple lived. They owned a large, and at one time, fine farmhouse, which was our chief quarters there. After we had left them we received a claim for a stuffed fox and a marble clock, stolen by our men, to which the Colonel replied that he " had not observed any man in his unit carrying either a stuffed fox or a marble clock on the march." It was afterwards discovered that this claim was made to every battalion that lodged there, and it seems a curious flight of fancy to suggest that anything so improbable and so very useless had been stolen, and the good people's income from this source must have been slender in the extreme.

Christmas 1915 was spent at Canaples: efforts were made to make it seem a little like the festive season by the provision of Christmas fare and abstinence from all except necessary work, and again we looked ahead into the coming year. We remained in this village till January 6th and on that date the Battalion—bereft temporarily of Capt. S. E. Woollam, who had been invalided home for an operation—marched eastwards to take up its first position in the line.

CHAPTER II

THE SOMME MARSHES, FARGNY MILL AND THE PERONNE ROAD SECTOR

THE Manchesters took over A1 subsector of the line from the 9th Royal Scots and North Hants Yeomanry. The distribution of the Battalion was as follows : " A " Company on the right in Dragon's Wood ; " B " Company in Vaux village ; " C " Company in Vaux Wood ; and " D " Company in Battle Dug-outs. Each Company, however, was ordered to send a platoon to the trenches at Moulin de Fargny, which was on the extreme left, under the command of O.C. " D " Company in A2 subsector.

In many ways the Vaux sector was unique. It was the right flank sector of the British front, and besides the pleasant intimacy with our Allies, which the work of liaison afforded to officers and men, the sector was attractive. It was extensive—covering nearly two miles of front—and its defence gave an interest which strongly contrasted with the monotony of trench warfare. In itself the battalion occupying this sector was complete. There was not the arduous change over to reserve or support every four or six days, the long march through muddy communication trenches loaded like Christmas trees with the means of life and death ; and for about 70 days the Eighteenth lived laborious but not unhappy days amid the marshes and the woods of the Somme.

On the right " A" Company, in actual touch with the French infantry at Eclusier, spent their leisure in bartering bully beef for wine and trying the difficult and mental gymnastics of learning French. They did not do this, but they became experts in the mysterious soldier language, the tongue of " Napoo," and when changes were made and the French peasant troops were relieved by Senegalese, whose knowledge of French was as scanty as that of our own men in the liaison continued to be perfect. " A " Company's lot was cast in pleasant places among the willows of Dragon's Wood " ; " B " holding Vaux village, had a more unpleasant time. Their outposts were placed in the marshes of the Somme. The chief post was situated on the end of a causeway which led across the marshes.

North of Vaux village was a little redoubt known as Fargny Mill—scene of a fierce struggle in the Franco-German War of 1870—where a composite company, formed from every Company in the Battalion, under the command of O.C. "D" Company, lived the ordinary life of British soldiers in the trenches. Above Vaux village, on a height crowned by a thick wood, "C" Company lived in rustic simplicity, disturbed at times by heavy bursts of shell-fire. It was a war within a war, as it were, for the Battalion was quite cut off from its neighbours. The nature of the country called for improvised methods of defence and brought out considerable originality among officers and men. The scouts became most versatile, and when the streams became too deep even for "gum-boots, thigh," they mobilised a water patrol in the duck-punts left behind by the sportsmen of happier days.

The task allotted to "B" Company was to guard Vaux village by occupying a series of posts on the edge of a maze of tributaries of the river Somme, which separated Vaux village from a large piece of land shaped like the tongue of a boot. This land was afterwards named by the Battalion Trafford Park. The foremost post was called Duck Post (owing, one supposes, to the prevalence of a quantity of wild fowl), in front of which was a swampy piece of land of some 60 yards in width, dividing the causeway on which the post stood from the dry land known as Trafford Park. It was decided after the Battalion had taken over this area to place an outpost on the edge of a small wood to protect Duck Post from surprise, and further to form a base for the scouts, whose duty it was to patrol the whole of Trafford Park, which was covered at the northern edge by thick woods and was some 800 yards in length, and in the widest part some 400 yards across. This post was known as Knowles Point, and was subsequently strengthened and made into a fortified post. The work of patrolling the innumerable tributaries of the river which surrounded Trafford Park was both hazardous and interesting, for which purpose the scouts used several of the duck-shooting punts to paddle quietly up the various streams to examine the duck-shooting huts, which huts would have made an excellent place for the enemy from which to observe the movements of our troops. It was the duty of the scouts to patrol as far south as the defences of Frise, which were held by the French, who kept a battalion of infantry there.

On the 11th the Battalion suffered its first battle casualty, No. 11005 Pte. Brown, of "D" Company, shot through the head by a sniper, and two other men wounded. On the 12th the Battalion lost two more men—one at Moulin de Fargny and one at Dragon's Wood. There was a heavy enemy bombardment of the subsector on the 28th, presumably to celebrate the Kaiser's birthday, and the Eighteenth had one man killed and eight wounded. It was estimated that the enemy had sent over about 4,500 shells during the day. One of the men of the Battalion in a letter home, with reference to this bombardment wrote, " Nothing inspires confidence more than the deeds of others, and we witnessed a fine spectacle a day or two ago, during a heavy bombardment, when the erect form of our Colonel was seen continually passing along the open road carrying stimulants to those who had been seriously wounded. Actions speak louder than words especially at the front."

In the evening the Germans attacked Fargny Mill and attempted to cut the wire but were driven back by bombs and rapid rifle fire.

Fargny Mill was an interesting place and incidentally the most eastern point in the British line at this time. The redoubt consisted of the actual Mill buildings, which afforded shelter for H.Q., from which ran a series of communication trenches in star formation, to three or four T-headed saps, each manned by a garrison. In addition to these sap-heads there was the " crow's nest," a listening post within 35 yards of the Germans, cut into the face of the cliff known as the Chapeau de Gendarme, and also a post in the marsh.

The Mill was practically isolated by day, the only approaches being a road along by the river from Vaux, to which it was wiser not to draw attention when it was under observation, as it was in constant use at night, and a trench which ran down the hill from Vaux Wood and was in full view of the German line for half its length, and in consequence visits from the Staff were rare, to the not inconsiderable relief of the Commander of the garrison. But the possession of a shot-gun and the fishing rights in the river enabled the mess on occasions to entertain those that braved the dangers of the journey to an unexpected meal of trout and wild duck, though, in contrast to this hospitality, it must be admitted that a certain very important personage, whose visit happened to coincide with a spy-scare, was brought to H.Q. at the point of a conscientious sentry's bayonet. But this is a digression ; to return to the night in question, this attack was evidently undertaken in order to obtain prisoners for intelligence purposes, but in this the enemy was completely foiled and met with a rude surprise, for the preliminary bombardment had given the defenders some intimation of what was coming and the Germans were greeted with a very heavy rifle fire—such men as were unable to find room to shoot from the trench contenting themselves with loading for their more fortunate comrades on the fire-step.

It reminded one of loaders in a grouse-butt.

The fact was that a relief was in progress at the time of the attack and the O.C. Mill, detained the out-going troops to assist in beating off the raiders, who it was afterwards learnt, numbered about 60—special troops sent up from the rear to carry out this operation.

Very few of them reached our line and of those who did several were killed, including their sergeant-major, and one was taken prisoner—the first prisoner captured by the Battalion. In recognition of the gallant and enterprising part played by Sergt. Hill, of "D" Company, in this engagement he was awarded the Military Medal.

Heavy shelling continued on the following day, and the Battalion had one man killed and seven wounded. The trenches had been badly knocked about, but as soon as any attempt at repair was started the whiz-bangs began to come over. During the attack by the enemy on the 28th they captured Frise village, together with some 600 French infantry, thus exposing the flank of the scouting area to attack. Prior to this information being conveyed to the 90th Brigade H.Q. at Suzanne, orders were received at the request of the French Commander on the right to send an officer and some scouts to try and get in touch with the French at Frise. Sec-Lieut. Blenkiron, with Cpl. Squibbs and several scouts, were accordingly despatched on this errand. When the scouts approached the wire entanglements at Frise, Sec.-Lieut. Blenkiron selected Cpl. Squibbs and Pte. Whitworth to accompany him and leaving the remainder before the wire he essayed to attract the attention of the supposedly French sentries, and on receiving an answer in French to his call at once pressed forward, only to find that the village was in the hands of the enemy and all three were taken prisoners.

On February 1st the Battalion received a draft of 25 N.C.O.'s and men from the 25th (Reserve) Battalion Manchester Regiment. On this date Lieut.-Col. W. A. Fraser, Lieuts. Knowles and Powell and 18 other ranks proceeded from Vaux to the N.W. end of Frise, a distance of one mile over the marshes, where the party split up into three sections of six each, under an officer. Three strands of wire had been cut when a sentry challenged. The sentry was promptly shot and thereupon fire was opened on the party from about thirty rifles. After throwing 25 grenades and pouring a heavy burst of fire the Manchesters party withdrew without casualty. A private soldier's account of this "incident" is of interest.

"A party of twenty men, scouts and bombers, were chosen to undertake the task of bombing the Huns at Frise, a distance of one mile over the marshes from our village. Fortunately for the success of the scheme the night was of the darkest, not even the flickering light of a star interspersing the blackness. This to those not acquainted with the intricate windings of the marshes, made the journey an unenviable one, for the slightest slip resulted in a ducking in mud and water. Apparently the Huns considered themselves immune from attack at this particular point for they did not resort to the use of flares. Marching, or rather moving in Indian file, we succeeded in reaching the German barbed wire, but unfortunately this obstruction had not been destroyed by artillery fire as we had anticipated, otherwise we should have made a big coup. As it was, after the leading men had cut through several strands of wire, our approach was observed by the Hun sentries, who after challenging opened with rapid fire. Our men withdrew from the wire and we replied with a terrific " rapid " and a score of bombs, inflicting severe casualties on the enemy, whilst we were able to withdraw without a casualty."

On the 3rd, Lieut.-Col. W. A. Fraser, Lieuts. W. P. Knowles and J. G. Cunliffe and seven other ranks, whilst making a reconnaissance on the enemy side of Trafford Park, were fired upon by a strong body of the enemy. They retaliated by throwing bombs and subsequently retired with the loss of one scout missing. The following day " B " Company suffered severe casualties in Vaux by shell-fire, having six men killed and fifteen wounded. On the 16th Lieut. H. A. Powell and four other ranks penetrated the northern end of Frise, then occupied by the enemy, and after making observations entered a building used as a guardroom, and came away with fifteen German hand grenades. For this smart action Lieut.-Gen. W. N. Congreve, commanding the XIIIth Corps, sent the following message :—

" Will you please convey my appreciation of this good work to Lieut. Powell, his N.C.O.'s and men."

The Brigade Major (Major H. F. Montgomery) also wrote :—

" G.O.C. 90th Infantry Brigade wishes to take this opportunity of congratulating Lieuts. Knowles and Powell and the scouts of the 18th Manchester Regiment on their excellent work during the last few weeks."

The 25th February was a day of heavy snow, which did not add to the comforts of trench life. On the following day a strong patrol of the enemy appeared on the Manchesters wire in front of Knowles Point, where " B " Company had a listening patrol of two N.C.O.'s and eight men. The Manchesters patrol sent in several bursts of rapid fire and threw bombs, and then withdrew to Duck Post without casualties. Sergt. Shirley and Ptes. R. Done and S. Forster were mentioned in despatches for their parts in this engagement. On the evening of the next day a party of Germans, estimated at sixty strong, attacked Knowles Point. Warning of the coming attack was given by scouts who had been sent out in front to protect a working-party, and as a consequence, the enemy were met by hand grenades and heavy rifle fire. Sec.-Lieut. Nelson, who was in command, sent back for reinforcements, holding his posts with great coolness by the rapid fire of his garrison of three N.C.O.'s and ten men until these were brought up by Lieut. T. J. Kelly and

Sec.-Lieut. Salmon, the former of whom assumed command of the party. A Lewis gun was also sent up. The enemy then retired, leaving two men dead on our wire, and were seen to carry off a number of wounded.

Our casualties were three men killed and nine wounded.

Cpl. Brooke, a scout, fell into the hands of the enemy and was taken towards Frise in charge of one man. He managed to secrete a Mills grenade in the lining of his tunic, and as the pair approached a group of Germans the Corporal stunned his escort with a blow from the bomb, and then drawing the pin, threw it amongst the group and made his escape.

Mr. Percival Phillips, the War Correspondent, gives the following account of Cpl. Brooke's adventure :—

" 'You English pretend to be stupid, but you are full of the devil's own tricks,' said an angry German officer after his capture the other day. There is something to be said for the German point of view. Thomas Atkins has shown himself to be resourceful and quick-witted, particularly in adversity. Not only is he capable of fooling the Boches when they are playing the trench game of hide-and-seek, but frequently he is able to extricate himself from a tight place when the game has gone against him. The latest instance of his adroitness occurred last week at a portion of the British front where the monotony of trench warfare is refreshingly varied by scrimmages between patrols.

" While a British detachment was reconnoitering in the direction of the German line it suddenly encountered a German patrol. One German was killed in the ensuing fight, but his companions carried away a British prisoner when they retired. The lone captive did not despair. They took away his rifle and cartridges, but the search of his person did not disclose a grenade hidden in a pocket of his tunic, although its presence seemed appallingly obvious to the owner, who imagined that it had suddenly attained the size of a football. He was hurried towards the German lines by his exultant captors, who agreed that their expedition had not been in vain.

" British prisoners are difficult birds to catch, and the German Staff is glad to get them. So confident were the Germans, that only one of them was told off to watch the prisoner, while the others made a temporary detour to investigate some suspicious movements on the other side of a field. Thomas Atkins thrust his hand in his bulging pocket without exciting suspicion. For a moment he fingered the grenade, debating whether to risk flight without using it, then with a sudden inspiration he clutched it as he might have seized a stone in a street riot, and hit his guard a terrific blow on the head. The safety pin was not withdrawn so that the bomb did not explode.

The unsuspecting German dropped as though bludgeoned. His prisoner darted back towards the British trenches; unluckily his path was not clear—for another German patrol loomed up and gave chase, firing at him. Clearly a case of retaliation—he stopped, pulled out the pin, took careful aim and hurled the bomb squarely at the advancing enemy. They scattered just as it exploded and he saw them no more."

At 12-25 a.m. on March 1st Knowles Point, still held by Lieut. T. J. Kelly with a garrison of sixteen men and a Lewis gun, was attacked by the enemy. The Germans reached the wire and threw several bombs, afterwards falling back and opening rapid fire at a distance of sixty yards. The Manchesters replied effectively with bombs, rifle and machine-gun fire, and the enemy were compelled to retire before the arrival of reinforcements. For his share in the defence of Knowles Point Lieut. Kelly was mentioned in despatches.

Military Crosses were awarded to Lieut. W. P. Knowles and Sec.-Lieut. H. A. Powell, and the D.C.M. to Cpl. (later Sergt.) A. J. B. Brooke. The *London Gazette* reading is as follows:—

" Lieut. W. P. Knowles guided raiding party with great skill and courage. He cut through three lines of barbed wire and when challenged shot the enemy sentry. When further progress was impossible he threw three bombs into the enemy, withdrew his men safely and opened rapid fire. His previous reconnaissance of the position was made with great skill and daring."

Sec.-Lieut. H. A. Powell, " for conspicuous gallantry—when in charge of the left group of grenadiers in a raid he cut through three lines of barbed wire. When the enemy opened fire at about twenty yards he threw about twenty-five grenades and stopped their fire. His prompt action enabled him to withdraw his men safely and to open rapid fire on the enemy."

Cpl. A. J. B. Brooke, " for conspicuous gallantry on several occasions, notably when he cut through three lines of barbed wire and after being discovered by the enemy opened rapid fire and withdrew his party. Also when he undertook and successfully carried out a most daring reconnaissance." The Brigadier-General also took the opportunity of warmly congratulating the three on " their well-earned rewards and on the skill, courage and initiative shown." These were the first honours to be bestowed on the Manchester " Pals," whose work in France and particularly that of the 18th Manchesters had been specially praised by the General Commanding Officer from time to time.

On March 5th a heavy burst of fire from Frise led the garrison at Knowles Point to suppose that an attack was imminent and an S.O.S.

signal was sent up; a reconnaissance, however, showed that all was clear.

Two serious accidents occurred during the early days of this month. On the 7th Lieut. Powell was seriously wounded by the accidental discharge of a revolver by a brother officer in "B" Company mess; and on the 8th Sec.-Lieut. J. L. Nelson was killed at Duck Post by the accidental discharge of a rifle.

Heavy shelling of the little outpost (one sergeant and six men) holding Knowles Point, at 7-0 p.m. on March 11th, heralded a most determined attempt on the part of the enemy to establish posts in Lodge Wood, an attempt which if successful would have given to him absolute control of the marshes and penned the Battalion to the village of Vaux, besides threatening the redoubt at Fargny Mill and making the holding of Duck Post well-nigh impossible. The outpost withdrew safely to the Duck Post, on which the enemy two hours later made a half-hearted attack with bombs, machine-gun and rifle fire. This attack was driven off and our men then withdrew to the wood. To force them to retire from Lodge Wood was a more difficult proposition. Between the Wood and the Duck Post lay nearly 200 yards of marsh, where if a man strayed from the track he sank up to the armpits and had to be rescued by his companions. In addition, two channels of the Somme, deep and swift flowing, lay between, and these had to be crossed on plank bridges. Our first counter attack at 1-30 a.m. on March 12th, led by Lieuts. Knowles, Kelly and Statham, failed owing to the impossibility of crossing these streams. The bridges had been destroyed by shell-fire, and, as there was no material of any kind, the attack was postponed a few hours until the Battalion pioneers had made rough planks in Vaux and man-handled them along the narrow causeway to the Duck Post. Scouts, who had never lost touch with the enemy, reported that he held Lodge Wood in force and had already made considerable progress in defensive works in preparation for the counter attack.

Orders were therefore issued from Brigade Headquarters for artillery support, and the thanks of the Battalion are due to D151 Battery, commanded by Major Fraser-Tytler, D.S.O., who co-operated in the counter attack. The range for their howitzers was very short, about 1,800 yards, and so excellent was the shooting that every shot fell about the enemy's position in Lodge Wood. At noon of the 12th Lieut. Knowles and Sec.-Lieut. Kavanagh led their men across the marsh. They had an easy task, for after a show of resistance the enemy retreated in haste, and our supports under Lieuts. Cunliffe and Kelly never got into action. Three dead Germans of the 63rd Infantry Regiment were found in the Wood and an immense quantity of stores of all kinds, rifles, bombs, equipment, blankets, snipers' shields, &c. In fact, of the fragments that remained there were eleven limber loads. Evidently " Jerry " had come to stay. The Duck Post, insignificant in itself—it consisted of two sand-bag huts and a barricade at the end of a causeway—was of some strategic importance and figured in several other sharp fights after we had left the sector. The attack on March 11th was the greatest of these attacks however and happily our casualties were nil.

These marsh fights were among the few incidents that occurred on the British front during the first three months of 1916 when the enemy was concentrating all his efforts on Verdun. They gave the Battalion a taste of war and earned it a mention in Sir Douglas Haig's despatch of June 1916. The price for this distinction was heavy—103 casualties, killed, wounded and missing in two months—and Lieut. Col. W. A. Fraser, who had been in command of the Eighteenth from its beginning had been forced by a return of an old malady, accentuated by the active part which he took in all the operations described above, to return home. Major W. A. Smith, 20th K.L.R., assumed command of the Battalion on this date and was gazetted Lieut.-Col. on April 20th.

The Battalion was relieved on March 19th by the 8th East Surreys and marched by half companies to the Bois de Tailles, near Etinehem. From now on to the 29th March the Battalion was engaged upon drill, route marching and general training. On the 23rd Lieut. P. A. Blythe was awarded the M.C., and No. 10355 Pte. A. Bancroft, " C " Company, the D.C.M., for gallantry on March 8th, when they along with three other men worked under heavy fire in an attempt to rescue five men from a dug-out in Vaux Wood which had been smashed in by a shell. The party was under heavy fire for twenty minutes but succeeded in rescuing all the men.

On the 29th the 19th King's Liverpools relieved and the Manchester's left Bois de Tailles for billets at Freshencourt. The stay here lasted until April 10th, during which time the Battalion was engaged under direction of the R.E. in constructing a new line of railway to link up the principal villages held by British troops in this part of the Somme area, and on the date named it marched to Poulainville, a matter of seven miles, and on the following day to Picquigny, a further seven miles, where platoon and company training was carried out.

Early in the month, " D " Company for a time lost the services of Capt. Hobkirk, who had been invalided to England with pneumonia; and at about this time, Capt. S. E. Woollam rejoined for duty, and Capt. F. Wolfenden was added to the strength. On the last day of the month the Battalion marched to Corbie, and May 1st found it at Bray in reserve to the 54th Brigade; and on the following day it was in billets at Suzanne, in reserve to the 90th Brigade. Here for some days the Battalion supplied working parties both day and night.

On the night of the 8th the Battalion took over from the 16th Manchesters in Y3 subsector. Major J. J. Whitehead, 17th Manchesters, took temporary command about this date, during the absence on leave of Lieut.-Col. W. A. Smith. It may also be noted that Capt. P. Godlee, who had been second-in-command since Major Lupton's return to England on March 18th, was gazetted Major on May 16th.

The sector taken over by the Eighteenth consisted of the front line trenches S.E. of Maricourt and just south of the Peronne Road. Maricourt at that time was the apex of a pronounced salient, being almost the extreme south of the British line which linked up with the French on the Somme. Preparations for the projected offensive were at once begun, and it was of course of vital importance that the enemy should obtain no knowledge of what was preparing. The Germans, however, were very much on the alert, and during the three days (May 10th—12th) the Manchester's trenches were heavily bombarded from time to time.

On the 10th, "C" Company (Capt. C. Henshall) and "D" Company (Capt. S. E. Woollam) held the front line trenches, having "A" Company in reserve and "B" Company in support. The "sector," writes one of the company officers, "had been very quiet for some two or three months, but about 5-30 p.m. on May 12th the Bosche commenced active sniping and sending over numerous rifle grenades on to our sentry posts. In the light of coming events this was obviously an attempt to prevent a careful look-out being kept."

At 1-0 a.m. on May 13th the enemy commenced a strong artillery bombardment of the 30th Divisional front and all telephonic communication was cut. After an hour's fierce bombardment the enemy left his trenches and attacked along the whole line. "C" and "D" Companies had received orders to stand-to prior to the assault, and in spite of the enemy's attacks being thrice renewed he was at length completely repulsed by steady rifle and Lewis gun fire, with artillery co-operation.

In the extreme south the attack in part succeeded and the line of a neighbouring battalion was pierced, and parties of Germans proceeded to work their way northwards against the two Eighteenth Manchester Companies. Here, however, their progress was arrested, and the attack was finally and completely repulsed. It was during this latter part of the attack that Pte. C. E. Brooke, of "D" Company, showed such gallantry as caused him to be recommended for and later to receive the D.C.M. Pte. Brooke was one of a Lewis gun section attacked by a bombing party, and four of the seven men of the section were wounded and the gun put out of action. The gun was withdrawn by two of the survivors and they immediately set to work to get it in order again. Meanwhile Pte. Brooke made his way in the direction of the enemy bombers and in the face of much opposition succeeded in carrying his four wounded comrades to cover, and in addition removed the ammunition and bomb supply of the section. At the same time he managed to disperse the enemy and captured one of their number.

"During the engagement," says the Battalion diary, "Pte. A. Marsden, 'D' Company, at the time of the fiercest bombardment volunteered to go to Company H.Q. for further supply of bombs and ammunition and afterwards distributed these supplies amongst the men of his platoon. For his coolness and courage Pte. Marsden was awarded the Military Medal."

From prisoners captured it was ascertained that the enemy attack was made for the purpose of obtaining information regarding preparations for the coming offensive, and to interfere as much as possible with these preparations. The enemy, however, achieved no success whatever and was repulsed with heavy casualties.

The success of the Eighteenth Manchesters was commended the following day by a special message of appreciation from the G.O.C. IVth Army, General Sir Henry (now Lord) Rawlinson, "C" and "D" Companies being especially complimented and later received a "mention" in one of the C.-in-C.'s despatches.

The Battalion diary also notes that Capt. C. Henshall, "C" Company, and Capt. S. E. Woollam, "D" Company, behaved with great courage and coolness throughout.

During this engagement Capt. L. Renshaw was killed, Capt. D. Berry wounded, five other ranks killed and a considerable number wounded and missing. During the engagement a mine shaft which was being pushed out towards the enemy trenches was pierced by a trench mortar, burying some fifteen men who were sheltering in the entrance to the mine shaft. Sec.-Lieut. Salmon with consummate coolness and courage climbed over the parados, and in spite of a heavy fire maintained by the enemy rescued three men by carrying them into the trench. He himself had a narrow escape, as another trench mortar shell exploded quite close to him. He then proceeded to help those working at the entrance to the mine shaft, but unfortunately only one man could be dug out owing to the soil falling in at every attempt made to move it. In consequence of this the remainder were lost in the shaft. Sec.-Lieut. Salmon received the Military Cross in recognition of his action, and Pte. Greatbanks the Military Medal.

The Battalion was relieved on the 14th by the 16th Manchesters and returned to billets in Suzanne, in reserve to the 90th Brigade, where day and night working parties under R.E's were supplied. From the 19th to 25th the Battalion was again in the trenches, but during this tour the enemy remained quiet for the most part, and on the 25th it was back in billets at Suzanne supplying working-parties under R.E's : there was also some bayonet fighting and gas helmet drill.

On June 1st the Eighteenth marched to camp at Billon Wood, remaining there until the 12th, when it was relieved by the 20th King's Liverpools, and moved to billets at Etinehem in reserve to the 30th Division.

Here working-parties under R.E. and fatigues filled up the time. A further move was made by the Battalion (less " D " Company) on the 18th to Saisseval, by train from Heilly to Ailly-sur-Somme. Meanwhile several drafts of men had been received and the following officers joined for duty :—Capt. W. F. Routley, Sec.-Lieut. S. J. Brown, Sec.-Lieut. H. C. Crichton, Sec.-Lieut. S. Fernyhough, Sec.-Lieut. J. S. Partington.

At Saisseval the Battalion was fully occupied with special training for the coming Somme battle until the 26th, when it was back at Etinehem, where " D " Company rejoined, and it was here that an unfortunate occurrence took place on June 29th, when twenty-three men were wounded by the explosion of a bomb.

While the Battalion was at Saisseval training for its part in the approaching Somme offensive, " D " Company remained with headquarters at Bray, engaged in other preparations for July 1st : the Company was made responsible for the placing in position of ammunition, stores, &c., to be used by the 90th Brigade when the time came.

For this purpose store-pits and shelters had to be dug in the forward trenches in front of Maricourt and immense quantities of stores placed in position.

An idea of the amount of labour involved and the preparations made will be seen when it is stated that the following is a list of supplies dealt with : —10,000 Mills' bombs, 4,300 rifle grenades, 480,000 rounds S.A.A., 6,000 rounds revolver ammunition, 2,000 Verey lights, 1,120 flares, 300 rockets, 4,000 Stokes mortar bombs, 600 petrol tins (for water), 400 trench ladders, 400 trench bridges, 700 iron pickets and 150 sundry wiring tools, 95 coils barbed wire.

In addition to being placed in position all bombs had to be detonated. " D " Company thus had a strenuous six days, but set about their task in a most willing fashion and accomplished it well within the prescribed time and without incurring any casualties. The G.O.C. 90th Brigade complimented the Company on the performance of its arduous labours.

July 1st and the Somme offensive was now fast approaching and it was evident from the preparations being made on the British and French side that the enemy was to have a warm time and that no effort was to be spared to make the attack a success. The valleys between Bray and Maricourt literally bristled with batteries of artillery and the bombardment of the Hun lines which preceeded the attack for three days was terrific in its intensity. Night-time enabled one to witness an awe-inspiring spectacle—vivid flashes of fire, spouts of flame and sudden upheavals of earth in the enemy lines all bearing witness to the whole-hearted efforts the artillery was making to prepare the way for the infantry attack. One was particularly thankful in those days that one's duty did not lie on the Bosche side of " No Man's Land."

CHAPTER III

THE BATTLE OF THE SOMME

MONTAUBAN : TRONES WOOD : GUILLEMONT

C.S.M. GEO. EVANS AWARDED THE VICTORIA CROSS

IN the attack upon the important village of Montauban on July 1st the 90th Brigade of the 30th Division had a very prominent share. The main brunt of the attack fell to the 16th and 17th Manchesters and the 2nd Royal Scots Fusiliers, while the 18th Manchesters served as carrying battalion to the Brigade.

During the late afternoon and evening of June 30th the Battalion moved up to the trenches, halting just behind their position to await the cover of darkness, to enable them to move quickly over the intervening ground and into their places previously allotted, thus saving an arduous journey through the long communication trenches. For once nature favoured the operation of our troops, since the attack was launched under cover of a thick morning mist, the sun breaking through just as everyone was under way. The Eighteenth being half in reserve and half acting as Brigade carrying party, was greatly elated to see bunches of doleful Hun prisoners as they came streaming back. These indeed were the first fruits of the great Somme offensive. The mist cleared quickly and the battle was fought in glorious sunshine, whilst the singing of a lark, heard after the first barrage ceased, seemed strangely incompatible with the scene being enacted below.

The operation order for the day provided that the 55th Brigade of the 18th Division would assault the west end of the village on the left of the 90th Brigade. The 21st Brigade was detailed to capture the enemy's first and second line trenches from the point where the road running north to Montauban cuts the Glatz Redoubt to the road running from Talus Boise to the west end of Montauban. The 89th Brigade was to attack and hold the line from the right of the 21st Brigade to the east end of Dublin trench.

The order proceeded that the 90th Brigade was to advance from the position of assembly (south of Cambridge Copse) at sixty minutes after zero, pass through the 21st Brigade and assault Montauban. The 17th Manchesters led the right of the attack, the 16th Manchesters the left. The 2nd Royal Scots Fusiliers were meantime in support and the 18th Manchesters in reserve. Details of the brilliant work accomplished by the attacking battalions has been recorded in another place. It remains to be said that an order for the day in reference to the carrying parties of the Eighteenth Battalion ran :—

" After the first bombardment has been completed they will come and go to Montauban by the communication trenches, moving on top of and beside the trench. In the event of coming under fire they will get into the trench and continue to move as fast as possible. As far as possible the loads of casualties will be picked up and taken on.

" Carrying parties must not halt on account of hostile fire."

Though other battalions won the glory that was achieved in the attack, the Eighteenth suffered a considerable mauling in performing its work.

Capt. S. E. Woollam, Lieut. H. B. Harrison, and Sec.-Lieuts. F. A. Esse and G. H. Doughty were wounded, while Sec.-Lieut. A. Cooper died a week later from wounds received. The Battalion also suffered one hundred and seventy casualties of other ranks. Of these about one hundred belonged to " C " Company, which was caught by enfilading machine-gun fire. Although the exultancy of this attack did not fall to the share of the Eighteenth, yet everyone experienced a feeling of pride in knowing that the help to which the supporting battalion had been pledged had been well and truly given. An officer describing the general work of the Brigade in this engagement said :—

" It was truly magnificent. The men advanced like veterans, and one could hardly believe they were entering upon a life and death struggle for they had the appearance of carrying out a practice manœuvre."

Lieut.-Col. Bedall, commanding the 16th Bavarian Infantry Regiment, who was taken prisoner by the British on the Somme,was found to have written in his diary : " The 6th Bavarian Reserve Regiment, which on the morning of July 1st was thrown into Montauban has been completely destroyed. Of 3,500 men only 500 remained and these are for the most part men who had not taken part in the battle, plus two regimental officers and a few stragglers who turned up on the following day. All the rest are dead, wounded or missing. The regimental staff and battalion staff have all been captured in their dug-outs."

During the following day the Eighteenth were in Train Alley—an old German support line—still in reserve to the 90th Brigade. On the 3rd. they were relieved and proceeded to Happy Valley, about two miles from Bray. Throughout the four days (4th—7th July) burying parties were provided from all Companies for clearing the battlefield.

On July 7th the first attack upon the German position in Trones Wood was carried out by the 21st Brigade. Accordingly, in the early morning the Battalion prepared to move up by Companies to the old British front line trenches north of Maricourt, and near to Talus Boise. There was no suspicion at the time of the first attack of the strength of the German position, and the 21st Brigade's attack was repulsed within two hours. The French on the right of the line, who were attacking Maltzhorn Farm had more success, and with the help of a Company of the 2nd Wilts, managed to gain a lodgment in the German trenches which connected Maltzhorn Farm with the southern end of Trones Wood. Further, with the assistance of a party of 19th Manchesters, this position was extended and permanently held.

At 1 p.m. the 21st Brigade made a second attack from the side of Bernafay Wood. A brilliant advance was made, though the casualties were considerable. Then about 3 o'clock the Eighteenth and 19th Manchesters went forward in support. German bombers were driving in from the north and the fighting was very severe. The Eighteenth Battalion was under orders to push into Trones Wood, and consequently it came in for its full share of the fighting. The experiences of Capt. Hobkirk—who had just returned from sick leave—in command of "D" Company, will give some idea of what the men of the Eighteenth had to endure. Word came to this officer early in the afternoon to move up to Train Alley. He had a short conversation with Lieut.-Col. Smith at Brigade H.Q., when he was ordered to push forward his Company into Trones Wood, where he would find "A" and "B" Companies holding a line across the Wood. He was to advance through them, drive the enemy out of the Wood, and then hold the farther side. Capt. Hobkirk advanced with the first platoon as far as the Briqueterie, where he awaited the approach of the remaining platoons. All this took a considerable time, as the advance proved very difficult. Meanwhile, the forward platoons were sheltering in shell holes. Finally, just as the Company was about to proceed, Lieut. M. Brunton, the Adjutant, brought word that Lieut.-Col. Smith had been wounded—he died of wounds in hospital on the following day—and Capt. C. Henshall had been killed by the same shell. At the same time Regt.-Sergt.-Major Murnaghan (popularly known as "Micky," who was the life and soul of regimental concerts and whose "bons mots" had spread throughout the Brigade) was knocked out by a fragment of a shell, and after carrying on for some time, was at length obliged to relinquish his duties and was admitted to Field Ambulance on the following day. Lieut. Brunton further stated that Major P. Godlee, who was in reserve, had been sent for to take over the command. In the meantime Capt. Hobkirk had to assume temporary command,being relieved later by Capt.Wolfenden. Forming his Battalion H.Q. in an old cellar in the Briqueterie Capt. Hobkirk put himself in communication with Brigade H.Q. and with the two advanced Companies in Trones Wood. Subsequently, on Capt. Wolfenden assuming temporary command, he caught up with his Company at Bernafay Wood ; and later by making short dashes from one shell hole to another the party gained the shelter of Trones Wood, but the advances had been very difficult owing to heavy shrapnel and machine-gun fire, and there were many casualties. Capt. Hobkirk then set about finding the rest of his Company, but only succeeded in collecting about thirty men of the 19th Manchesters and 2nd Wilts, whom he instructed to attach themselves to the Eighteenth and to consolidate the position so far as they were able, and to hang on until morning pending orders. There was an enemy bombing attack during the night, but it was eventually driven off. Major Godlee arrived in the early hours of Sunday July 9th with orders to support an attack which would be made by the 17th Manchesters at 2-30 a.m. The Battalion was then in the south end of the Wood, and also in the trench leading from Bernafay to Trones. The intended attack, however, did not materialise until 7 a.m., when the sun was up and visibility admirable.

An officer of "B" Company who took part in this attack writes :–

"'B' Company reached Trones Wood by way of Bernafay Wood and Trones Alley about 4-0 p.m. on the afternoon of the 8th July. At that time the damage by shell-fire was not extensive. The leaves were green and there was thick undergrowth, but already there were signs of the carnage to come. Dead and wounded of the 21st Brigade and the enemy lay about everywhere, and as it was not safe to show even a hand above the trench the work of trying to make some sort of a firestep in Trones Alley (which had been built by the enemy as a communication trench) was rendered extremely difficult. Shelling with '5.9's' and 'Whizzbangs' continued without interruption, varied now and again by an intensive burst which blew the trench and its wounded and unwounded occupants to the winds. Three times during the night of the 8th and 9th the enemy tried to attack from the northern edge of Trones Wood, his intention being to break in midway between Trones and Bernafay Woods, cut off the small British garrison in Trones, and roll up the French flank in Maltzhorn Farm. Each attack was defeated by the vigilance of the Lewis gunners and riflemen.

When word was received that the Eighteenth were to follow the 17th through Trones to the eastern fringe of the Wood the small body of survivors, mostly 'B' Company and a few men of 'A' and 'C' were rather surprised, to put it mildly. They had exhausted their ammunition (and themselves incidentally) in their efforts during the night, but by collecting from the dead and wounded they were able to replenish their pouches, and when the bayonets of the 17th Manchesters were seen flashing in the sun as they advanced across the open from the Briqueterie our men raised a cheer. It was splendid, but in view of the clear light and the vigilance of the German gunners one felt it was fatal. The 17th passed and, 100 yards behind, the remains of the Eighteenth followed. Our difficulties began as soon as we entered the Wood. Our advance had been clearly seen by the Germans who made preparations accordingly. A deluge of shells, such as can rarely have been equalled, even during the hurricane bombardments of 1918 fell upon the part of the Wood we had entered. Trees crashed down on every side, men lost touch in the undergrowth, wounded lay where they fell for no help could be given them, and within less than half an hour the attack of two battalions had been dissipated and small bodies of men wandered about the Wood, almost blind by shell fumes, struggling through undergrowth, dodging falling trees, having lost touch with their companions, having in fact, no sense of direction at all. And all the time the shells fell without ceasing.

I myself was fortunate. Chance guided my steps to the eastern fringe of the Wood, where I found myself alone with one officer and ten men, half of them wounded. Creeping cautiously to the edge of the trees we saw the Germans in the village of Guillemont and realised that we were surrounded. There was nothing to do but retreat. How we found our way back I don't know, but after nearly two hours wandering—during which two of the wounded died when being carried pick-a-back, for we had no stretchers—we reached the remnants of the Battalion still holding the southern fringe of the Wood.

Others were not so fortunate and wandered to the clearing in the Wood where they were shot by German machine-gunners who had established strong points there.

The Battalion's casualties were exceedingly heavy, especially in 'missing' most of whom fell in the advance through the Wood described above."

About mid-day the C.O. of the 2nd Royal Scots Fusiliers asked for assistance, and "A" Company was accordingly lent to that battalion and took up a position near Maltzhorn Farm. Between 3 and 4 p.m. the 17th Manchesters received orders to withdraw and the Eighteenth Battalion conformed, retiring past the Briqueterie to Glatz Redoubt. The reason for the withdrawal was that owing to the intense shelling the Battalion was being gradually wiped out to no purpose. Capt. Hobkirk, commanding "D" Company, was still holding on to the S.E. edge of the Wood, and the message to withdraw did not reach him. In consequence of which he remained with his small Company alone and isolated in the Wood and it was not until evening that they rejoined the Battalion.

Immediately after this gallant exploit Capt. Hobkirk was wounded by a shell splinter which served to put him out of action for the time being.

At about 10 p.m., with rather less than one hundred men ("A" Company still being temporarily attached to the Royal Scots Fusiliers), the Battalion moved up to Chimney Trench, a very wide communication trench, which afforded rather poor shelter. This was reached by midnight, and after an hour or two of uneasy rest, disturbed by frequent salvoes of shells entering the trench, the Battalion moved into Sunken Road, which was close at hand. The next twenty-eight hours were spent here as a reserve force, from which parties were sent to various points as required. This Sunken Road was subjected to a "strafe" every twenty minutes, and as the shelter given by the little ditch along the road was very inadequate, the result was that the casualty list was heavy. Trones Wood, it may here be noted, was the last point to which the Germans clung in their second general line. Before the attack on the Guillemont—Longueval—Bazentin line could be launched it was essential that Trones Wood should be taken. Consequently, the struggle for it was very bitter, and though it does not figure in the great advances, it was an operation of extreme importance. Before it was finally taken it changed hands many times, and each change meant a concentration of artillery fire and an infantry action of a more or less costly nature.

The Battalion was relieved at 4 a.m. on the morning of July 11th and proceeded to the old British trenches at Maricourt, where breakfast was provided and a halt for rest was made until 3 p.m. The Battalion then proceeded by Bray and the Bray-Corbie road to Bois-des-Celestins. The 12th was spent re-organising and on fatigues in camp. On the 13th the Battalion was addressed by the G.O.C. XIII Corps and by the Divisional Commander, who thanked them for their fine work in recent attacks. The Battalion was also promised a fortnight for training and re-organisation. It afterwards marched to billets at Daours. On the following day a lamentably composed draft of 440 men arrived, in which no less than twenty-seven different regiments were represented. This body consisted almost entirely of private soldiers, as most of the N.C.O.'s had been drafted to regiments actually in action on the Somme. As the Battalion was already short of officers and N.C.O.'s the training presented a very serious problem, which, however, was partially solved by a sudden order to move up to the line again—after only four days had been spent in an attempt to instil order and discipline into the new unit. Meantime, Lieut. T. J. Kelly had assumed the duties of Adjutant from the 9th in place of Lt. M. Brunton, who was one of the Trones Wood casualties, as was also Capt. W. P. Knowles, M.C. Major H. B. O. Williams (3rd Dragoon Guards) assumed command of the Battalion on the 17th. On the 18th the Battalion marched from Daours to Bois-des-Celestins, and on the following day to Happy Valley. The result of two days' marching on the new Battalion boded no good. It became all too clear that the absence of *esprit de corps* and the lack of officers and N.C.O.'s would make discipline in action almost impossible, and so it turned out.

Preparations were now approaching completion for the attack on Guillemont. On the 22nd the Battalion moved to Mansel Copse, the old British front line near Mametz, with H.Q. at the Citadel. The following day found it in the old British trenches at Gilson Street (Maricourt) and on the 24th it moved into Brick Lane, the old German front line opposite Talus Boise.

Sec.-Lieut. Hutchinson was killed on the 26th. On this date the Battalion moved back to Mansel Copse, remaining there until the 29th, when it changed to its former position in Brick Lane, in preparation for the attack on Guillemont. It had thus been in the trenches for eight days subjected to frequent shelling. The constant casualties, lack of accommodation, combined with all the disadvantages of living in the open under shell fire, had the worst possible effect on the troops and were a poor preparation for the coming attack.

At 11 p.m. on July 29th the Battalion left the assembly trenches at Brick Lane for a three-mile march through Trones Wood to Guillemont. It was a march which those who took part in it will never forget. Fearing that there was to be an infantry attack on Guillemont the enemy searched the whole area from Montauban to our front line with shells of all kinds. On passing the Briqueterie, orders were issued by Major Williams to put on gas helmets, and the rest of the march was made with the maximum of discomfort, for there are few things more unpleasant than to cross an old battlefield still littered with the wreckage of war in the blackness of the night while wearing a gas helmet. Many men after a time took the risk of being gassed rather than endure the pain of constant falls into deep shell-holes; many were completely lost and never took part in the battle. Fortunately, the enemy ceased gas-shelling and after a nightmare march in single file through Trones Wood with the unburied horrors—the Wood had been captured a day or two before at the 19th attempt and contained thousands of dead—the Battalion emerged on the eastern side at 4-30 a.m. There was little time to reach the assembly trenches before 5 a.m., which had been fixed as zero hour, but the men were in fine spirit despite their arduous march and punctually to the minute they moved off eastwards where the shadowy outline of Guillemont stood out dimly in the morning mist.

The attack on Guillemont was carried out despite the fact that during the earlier hours there was a heavy ground mist which made the keeping of direction difficult. This was responsible for "D" Company on the left losing direction and getting too near the Station which lay to the north of the village. But a much more serious feature was that the barrage did not materialise, and when the attack was launched the only artillery support was from 18-pounders. How this mistake occurred is not known, but some hours after zero there were batteries of "heavies" who were not even aware that a battle was in progress. The 89th Brigade advanced on the right and the 90th on the left, the latter Brigade directing its efforts straight for the village. The two leading battalions, the 2nd Royal Scots Fusiliers and the Eighteenth Manchesters, gained their objective and established themselves in the western suburbs of the village. The German barrage, however, fell so quickly behind them that neither help nor munitions could reach them. Between them the two battalions captured some one hundred and fifty prisoners; two companies of the 17th Manchesters contrived to make their way with heavy losses, through the fatal barrage, but their gallant endeavour failed to alleviate the situation. The Scots Fusiliers were surrounded and, it is to be presumed, fought to their last cartridge for none of the men ever returned. The Eighteenth Manchesters and the two companies of the 17th Battalion fared little better. The village was entered, but those that got in were taken prisoner, and the majority of the casualties were the missing who fell in the advance and lay in "No Man's Land" till September 15th—six weeks or so later.

The operations continued, however, until 3-30 a.m. on the morning of July 31st, when the relief of the 90th Brigade was effected. The depleted Battalion of the Eighteenth Manchesters then marched back to the "Citadel," where in the afternoon, the Divisional Commander (Major-General, now Sir, J. S. M. Shea, K.C.M.G.) addressed the troops and spoke of the attack as a success. He explained that though the objective had not been gained, a great German concentration had been broken up, and a heavy counter-attack nipped in the bud. He concluded by congratulating the remnant of officers and men on the gallant fight against odds they had made, and assured them that the attack, costly though it had been, had been of the greatest importance.

The casualties in the Guillemont attack amounted to four hundred and seventy men killed, wounded or missing, and of sixteen Company officers who took part in the attack only one returned. The Battalion's total casualties for the month of July numbered about thirty-two officers and 1,300 men. Amongst those captured in the Guillemont attack was C.S.M. George Evans, of "B" Company, an old Scots Guardsman, who had served in the South African War, and who went out to France with the Eighteenth Manchesters. For his gallant conduct at Guillemont, before being taken prisoner, he was recommended for, and subsequently received the coveted decoration of the Victoria Cross. The official record states that the award was made :—

"For most conspicuous bravery and devotion to duty during the attack at Guillemont on July 30th 1916, when under heavy rifle and machine-gun fire, he volunteered to take back an important message after five runners had been killed in attempting to do so. He had to cover about 700 yards, the whole of which was under observation from the enemy. Co.-Sergt.-Major Evans, however, succeeded in delivering the message, and although wounded, rejoined his Company although advised to go to the dressing-station. The return journey to the Company again meant a journey of 700 yards under severe rifle and machine-gun fire, but by dodging from shell hole to shell hole he was able to do so. He was taken prisoner some hours later."

On previous occasions at Montauban and Trones Wood this gallant warrant officer displayed great bravery and devotion to duty and had always been a splendid example to his men.

A staff officer interviewed in hospital said :—

"The 30th Division had done well in the fighting early in July, had taken Montauban and distinguished itself. It was withdrawn and made up to strength with new and inexperienced drafts, and sent in again to try its fortune against a very difficult position–Guillemont. With the original Division we believe we should have done it, but with new troops, new officers, N.C.O.'s and men, many untried and who had not been trained to work together, everything went wrong. Supports did not come up, orders miscarried or were countermanded, and the whole attack fell to pieces. The Germans were very strong, and were preparing a counter-attack with ten battalions against Trones Wood—which was indeed stopped, but at the price of the loss of two of the best battalions of the 90th Brigade—the 2nd Royal Scots Fusiliers and the Eighteenth Manchesters.

After the bombardment, about 4-30 a.m. on the morning of July 30th, the advance against Guillemont was continued, but on account of miscarriage of directions and the frightful fire which the men met from the German machine guns, only the 2nd R.S.F. and the Eighteenth Manchesters were able to advance. They actually entered the village but were again met by awful machine gun fire and intact barbed wire defences, and practically all who survived were taken prisoners by an overwhelming number of foes.

The attack was thus a failure, relieved only by the heroism of the Eighteenth Manchesters and the 2nd Royal Scots Fusiliers."

Among the casualties at Guillemont were the following officers killed :—

Capt. P. A. Blythe, M.C., Lieut. P. G. D. Haworth, Sec.-Lieut. F. C. O. Twist, Sec.-Lieut. J. F. Motler, Sec.-Lieut. E. Kavanagh, Sec.-Lieut. P. R. King.

Sir Arthur Conan Doyle in his history of the War describes this attack on Guillemont as " one of the tragic episodes of the great Somme battle."

CHAPTER IV

AT LIGNY-THILLOY AND BELLACOURT

AUGUST 1st was spent resting at Mansel Copse. The following day the Battalion marched to Dernancourt and entrained for Airaines. On the 4th the Manchesters entrained at Longpré for Berguette, and marched thence to Busnes. Here a draft of 507 men joined from the base. On the 10th the Battalion marched to new billets at Le Hamel and Essars, where the entire month of August was spent training and providing working-parties.

Major H. B. O. Williams, 3rd Dragoon Guards, who had recently been in temporary command, was appointed Lieut.-Colonel in command of the Battalion, with effect from July 15th. Lieut. T.J. Kelly was promoted Captain, vice Capt. P. A. Blythe (missing). Capt. Penn-Gaskell and Lieut. and Adjutant M. Brunton rejoined from base. The following officers al o joined the strength :—

Capt. F. J. Earles, Lieut. H. Peters, Sec.-Lieuts. H. Duncan, C. Homewood, G. Rissik, S. R. Rumney, T. E. Trimmer, B. A. Westphal.

September 1st and 2nd still found the Battalion at Le Hamel and Essars, but on the 3rd it relieved the 11th West Yorks in the trenches of the Festubert sector—" B " and " D " Companies taking the front line, " A " the support, and " C " the reserve. This tour lasted until the night of the 8th, when the Battalion was relieved and went into Brigade reserve billets at Le Touret. Whilst here Capt. T. J. Kelly was awarded the Military Cross for gallant service and devotion to duty during the Somme battle. On the 13th a move was made to billets at Hingette, and on the following day the Eighteenth were back in the line at Festubert. They were again at Hingette on the 16th; in billets at Rue Bellervive, Gonnehem, on the 17th; and on the following day marched to Chocques, where they entrained for Candas (Somme). Flesselles was reached on the 21st and here the Battalion remained training for the rest of the month.

On October 4th the Battalion moved by motor-omnibuses to Buire-sur-Ancre, and on the 6th marched to Fricourt Camp, some three-quarters of a mile north of King George's Hill. Here a serious mishap occurred. As the last Company was entering the camp in the darkness someone trod on a bomb which was lying on the ground, and which exploded. One man was killed outright, Major P. Godlee and Sec.-Lieut. H. C. Crichton were both very seriously wounded, besides nine other ranks. Sec.-Lieut. Crichton succombed to his wounds on the following day, and was buried at Dartmoor Cemetery, Becordel. Major Godlee, being disabled, was replaced by Capt. (T/Major) C. E. Lembcke, Northumberland Fusiliers, as Second-in-Command. The Battalion marched to Marlborough Wood on the 10th, where it rested until dark, and then moved on to the support trenches in front of Ligny-Thilloy, relieving a unit of the 41st Division. The next day the Battalion moved from Grove Alley support trench to Factory trench, H.Q. being in the sugar factory in the road from Flers to Le Barque.

From the 1st July onwards by a series of sledge-hammer blows the Germans had been slowly pressed back from their position on the Somme, but their resistance was stiffening daily, and if the important position of Bapaume was to fall, it was essential that the villages on the hills west of it, Ligny-Thilloy, Thilloy and Le Barque should be captured by the British. Despite the most heroic efforts of our best divisions, however, the enemy held these villages intact until the voluntary withdrawal to the Hindenburg line in the following year. The 30th Division were among the first to try to capture this stronghold and on the 12th October the Eighteenth Manchesters, in company with the 2nd Royal Scots Fusiliers and the 89th Brigade, attacked the enemy position south of Ligny-Thilloy.

On this occasion our enemy consisted of German marines, comparatively fresh troops, whose discipline and morale were as yet unshaken by the inferno of the Somme. The attack was heralded by a barrage which according to some accounts fell in "No Man's Land" and gave the marines full warning of what was coming. At any rate on this occasion the Bosche knew what was going to happen and was quite ready to meet the attack. Zero hour was 2 p.m. and as our men were waiting to go over the parapet they saw the Germans run from their trenches and lie in the open fifty or one hundred yards behind. Then the barrage lifted two hundred yards to the next line of trenches and the Bosche dashed back to their front line and manned their machine guns. Our men had about three hundred yards to go. It was an impossible task. They were mown down by the machine gunners and the counter barrage, which curiously enough opened at exactly the same hour as the barrage, an instance of unpleasantly accurate synchronisation. Only a small number of the attackers, led by Sec.-Lieut. Trimmer, succeeded in finding their way into the German front line. When last seen Trimmer was endeavouring to consolidate a section of trench. A few prisoners were captured, but the counter barrage was so fierce that it was impossible to push home the attack, and the survivors were imprisoned in shell holes in " No Man's Land " until just before dawn next morning, when following a not unusual habit, the German gunners broke off their work for the morning coffee. Nothing exceeded the gallantry shown by the Battalion stretcher bearers in their work on this occasion. Though constantly under fire they never desisted until a thorough search had shown that all the wounded had been recovered. Our casualties were very heavy, for out of an actual rifle strength of three hundred and fifty who went " over the top," we had two hundred and fifty killed, wounded and missing. Capt. Penn-Gaskell, an officer who had joined the Battalion at Heaton Park, was among those who fell. " He was struck by a shell while leading ' D ' Company," writes a brother officer, " and his orderly (Pte. J. Wright) remained with him after the attack had been beaten back and paid the price of his devotion with his life, for he was shot dead while trying to bandage ' Penn.' Though well over age and without previous military experience of any kind ' Penn ' had come from South America to join up. He had a presentiment of death and told me so a few minutes before going ' over the top,' but he was as cheery and happy as he climbed out of the trench as if he had been going on an ordinary parade and not on his last."

Among those killed were Lieut. H. Peters and Sec.-Lieut. Taylor. Sec.-Lieut. Trimmer was posted wounded and missing, and Lieuts. Brown, Evans and Rumney were wounded.

After the attack the Battalion withdrew, and on the night of the 16th was relieved by the 21st Brigade and marched back to bivouac in Marlborough Wood. Here for some days it provided working-parties on the roads to Longueval. The 22nd found the Battalion in billets at Ribemont; and on the 25th it entrained for Doullens, arriving there in the early hours of the next morning. After four hours' rest the march was begun, via Lucheux, to Sus St. Leger. On the 30th the Battalion left Sus St. Leger and marched, via Warluzel, Saulty, Labrett and Bailleulval, to Bellacourt, relieving the 7th Notts and Derby Regiment in support to the 90th Brigade, which was now holding the sector opposite Blairville and Ransart. During the month drafts of one hundred and eighty-four men were received. The following officers also joined from base :—

Sec.-Lieuts. W. H. B. Burkitt, L. F. Elliott, G. G. Miller, W. F. Ogden, H. Sedgwick, J. E. M. Taylor, J. F. Waring.

The Battalion remained in support at Bellacourt until the 6th November, when it relieved the 16th Manchesters in the line in sub-sector D2, east of Brétencourt. This tour lasted until the 12th when it marched back to Divisional reserve billets at Bailleulval. It was back in the trenches, however, on the 18th, and the rest of the month was spent alternately in the two places. The winter lull in the fighting had now set in and consequently there was little worthy of note to record. The whole of the month of December was spent either in the trenches opposite Blairville, or in divisional reserve billets at Bailleulval and Basseux.

Lieut.-Col. Williams, whose health had never been good, suffered continually during the severe weather in November and December, and a few days before the end of the year he was compelled, under medical advice, to accept a less arduous post on the Army Staff. Major C. E. Lembcke succeeded him in command. The post of second-in-command was subsequently filled by the promotion of Capt. T. J. Kelly, M.C., who had been acting as Adjutant since the end of July. Thus the year 1916 came to an end, a year which opened with the Battalion untried in war, taking its place for the first time in the line, and closed with it tested and proved but sadly changed. Of the old Eighteenth that left England in 1915 very few remained, but traditions go on and 1917 did not find the Battalion wanting.

CHAPTER V

THE BATTLE OF ARRAS

HÉNINEL AND NEUVILLE-VITASSE

JANUARY 1st, 1917, still found the Eighteenth in Brigade reserve at Bailleulval, and on the 3rd the Earl of Derby, Secretary of State for War, inspected the Battalion, and a congratulatory message from the Divisional Commander was received.

The Battalion marched to Sus. St. Leger on the 5th, and remained there training and providing working-parties until the end of the month.

No. 10772, Sergt. A. Haworth, and No. 9917, Sergt. W. Reeves, were awarded the Military Medal during the month; and the following officers were "mentioned in despatches" for distinguished and gallant service and devotion to duty:—

Lieut.-Col. W. A. Smith (died of wounds); Capt. P. A. Blythe (missing); Lieut. J. S. Beaumont; Sec.-Lieut. F. C. O. Twist (killed).

The undermentioned officers joined for duty from base:—

Lieut. R. S. England, Sec.-Lieuts. D. Adshead, J. H. Hague, W. Lindsay, G. S. Martin, R. Maybury, J. S. Shanahan, J. T. Smart, S. J. L. Wyatt.

February was a quiet month and the Battalion, still providing working-parties, moved from Sus. St. Leger to Doullens, Halloy and Beaurepaire Farm on the Arras-Doullens Road.

On March 12th the Battalion moved to Pommern, and on the 19th marched to Monchiet, where it relieved the 18th King's Liverpools in Brigade reserve. Monchiet was left on the 21st, the Battalion moving via Beaumetz, Bac Dunord and Wailly to Agny, where it rested in the old British line until 11 p.m., when it moved into the outpost line in front of Neuville-Vitasse, relieving the 20th King's Liverpools. On the following day the outpost line was advanced about five hundred yards. This tour of duty lasted until the 29th and was particularly trying on account of the very severe weather—frost, snow and heavy rain—to which the men were exposed without cover of any sort. In the front line they had to depend on dry rations and water, without hot food of any kind. Though the shelling during this period was not severe, the conditions of semi-open warfare which the Battalion for the first time experienced provided a test of soldierly steadiness and efficiency and the ability to cope with a new situation. All ranks came through the test very satisfactorily, and the G.O.C. 30th Division, calling on the Commanding Officer, expressed his high appreciation of the splendid work done by the Battalion.

The 18th King's Liverpools relieved on the 29th and the Manchesters marched, via Ficheux, Blairville Brétencourt, to Basseux, where the next few days were spent in rest billets.

On April 3rd part of the Battalion relieved the 2nd Royal Scots Fusiliers in Brigade reserve, Madeleine Redoubt, west of Mercatel, while the remainder moved to Boisleux-au-Mont, providing working and carrying parties. The Battalion moved to the trenches east of Ficheux on the 8th, but on the following day at 2 p.m. orders were received to occupy the old outpost line south of Mercatel.

"A" and "C" Companies were sent forward on the 10th to reinforce the 19th Manchesters in the line. On the morning of the 11th the Battalion was ordered to cross the Cojeul river and move forward to the Hindenburg line. The details of this operation are as follows :—

At 9 a.m. two platoons of "A" Company were ordered to proceed to the triangle where Magpur trench crossed the Hindenburg line and join a Company of the 16th Manchesters, who were to bomb their way along the line. It was found, however, that the situation was not what it had been supposed on the preceding day. Accordingly at 10 a.m. preparations were made for the Battalion to move forward to the Hindenburg line in the vicinity of Panther Lane. The Eighteenth had now come under orders of the 89th Brigade. By 4-30 p.m. the manœuvre was complete, headquarters were established, and companies were disposed in Panther Lane, Buff Lane, Neuville-Vitasse trench, The Cot, Héninel trench and Héninel support, the right flank sentry groups being in position just N.E. of the St. Martur-sur-Cojeul-Héninel road.

A minor bombing operation was undertaken by two platoons of "D" Company, under Sec.-Lieuts. W. D. Truswell and W. Lindsay. Their object was to bomb along an unmarked trench, and thence if possible to Nepal trench. The party moved off at 5-15 p.m. and made some progress, finally carrying a block after throwing a few bombs. The road, however, was found to be strongly held, and as the operations were hampered by driving snowstorms and darkness the Company Commander decided to withdraw, considering that the gain would hardly have been worth the possible loss of life. Acting on the suggestion of the G.O.C. 90th Brigade, the Commanding-Officer, Lieut.-Col. Lembcke, issued orders at 8-30 p.m. for companies to be ready to move off at dawn and bomb down the Hindenburg line. At 9 p.m. the G.O.C. 90th Brigade ordered that this attack should be carried out forthwith, and instructions were given out accordingly. A preliminary reconnaissance, however, showed that the operation was likely to be a difficult one, for apart from the severe fighting that might have to be undertaken, the trenches were in a very bad state as a result of the snow, and the men themselves had suffered greatly from the cold and wet.

The actual operation was carried out on the 12th by " A " and " C " Companies, later reinforced by " D " Company. " A " Company's task was to work its way down the support line, whilst " C " moved along the fire trench. Before starting, Sec.-Lieut. Martin, who was in command of " A " Company, crossed the river with Sec.-Lieut. S. M. Shirley and one man to endeavour to find out how strong the enemy were on the other side. The three were met with rifle fire, but made good the crossing, and finding a group of four Germans at the junction of the trench returned without mishap.

Sec.-Lieut. N. B. Gill and a sergeant who attempted to make a similar reconnaissance further north, to find a crossing for "C " Company, were held up by wire, but, after sending back for wire-cutters, they were able to make a crossing. Owing to this delay " A " Company was away first, and its bombing section, led by Sec.-Lieut. Shirley, crossed the river under a barrage provided by rifle-grenadiers and Lewis gunners about 3 a.m. and advancing across the open reached the front line at Héninel trench. On nearing the sentry group the officer who was on the parapet, called upon the enemy to surrender, but as they hesitated he emptied his revolver into them and threw a bomb. One man ran away; the others were killed. About one hundred yards further down the trench the Manchesters party saw a number of the enemy emerging from a dug-out, and immediately attacked them with bombs. The enemy, who had been reinforced by others in the trench, gave way slowly, replying to our bombs and rifle-grenades with their own bombs and small aerial torpedoes, but were gradually forced back. On reaching a certain point the officer of the Manchesters, who was leading, found that his supply of grenades and bombs was very low, and forming a block at the junction of the trench he sent back for further supplies and also asked for reinforcements. As he and his men were waiting here a party of the enemy, about thirty strong, were seen coming towards the post from the direction of Héninel support. The Lewis gun sections under the command of Sec.-Lieut. Lawrence, who had followed the bombing party, were then brought into action, inflicting a number of casualties on the enemy and wholly breaking up the counter attack. Those of the enemy who were not hit immediately fled in the direction of Héninel support trench.

Meanwhile " C " Company had been overcoming difficult obstacles in the vicinity of the river. They had to cut the wire, not only in the river, but on the marshy banks as well, and they did not succeed in making the crossing until " A " Company was hotly engaged. Sec.-Lieut. Westphal, who was in command, judged by the firing and bomb explosions that " A " Company had got into the front instead of the support line, so he judged it advisable to push down the support line and establish touch with them by means of one of the communication trenches. Finding, moreover, that he was being sniped from the direction of Héninel he sent a platoon under Sec.-Lieut. Smart to deal with this danger. This officer made a wide detour and succeeded in dislodging several snipers who were enfilading Héninel support from the road. He then made his way back and joined his Company.

Meanwhile Sec.-Lieut. Westphal met with a strenuous opposition, but gradually made progress, the enemy weakening as the flanking platoon came forward from the north. Taking one platoon across the open to the fire-trench the Commander of " C " Company established touch with " A " Company and was able to supply it with bombs and rifle-grenades. Reinforcements of two platoons of " D " Company for " A " and two platoons for " C " also arrived, bringing with them fresh supplies of ammunition. The two Company-Commanders thereupon decided to proceed with the attack simultaneously: but it was broad daylight before arrangements could be completed.

The enemy continued his former tactics of using aerial torpedoes and rifle-grenades and then retiring down the trench. Progress was slow for a time. The opposition appeared to grow weaker as the attackers neared the ridge, and just before the objective was gained it was observed that the enemy was evacuating his own trenches further south and making off to the north. These movements offered a target such as rarely occurred, and the Lewis guns of " C " Company in Héninel support were promptly brought to bear. The guns were placed on the parapet, and taking the fleeing enemy in the rear, inflicted, as far as could be judged, about one hundred casualties.

The objective having been gained, posts were at once established. About 10 a.m. an officer patrol searched Héninel and reported it clear of the enemy, and a little later the advanced scouts of the Queen Victoria Rifles (56th Division) established touch with the Manchesters' left flank, and a battalion of the 21st Division came forward into Héninel support, thus supplying communication with the right. Altogether over 1,700 yards of trench were captured by bombing, and very heavy casualties were inflicted on the enemy. The attack is thus recorded in Doyle's "British Campaign, 1917":—

"The clearing of the front of the 21st Division was done by the 18th Manchesters, who, unsupported, bombed their way down 1,700 yards of Hindenburg line, a very notable achievement."

It was found impossible to carry the line further forward, for though the enemy was so obviously disorganised our own men were extremely fatigued, and the work of consolidating and holding what had been taken, and clearing out dug-outs, had stretched their physical powers to the extreme limit.

Though the Hindenburg line, both firing and support trenches, was found unfinished for defence—no firesteps having been made and M.G. emplacements were only half constructed—there were many deep dug-outs in the support and communication trenches. They were connected up by a continuous passage parallel with the front line, which fact enabled many of the enemy to escape. In two dug-outs were found twelve wounded men of the 21st Division, who had been captured the previous day; they had been bandaged and given food and drink by their captors. The Manchesters' haul of prisoners numbered ten, four of whom were wounded, and one was accidentally killed by a bomb. Many more prisoners would have been taken had the attacking force been fresh enough to gather the full fruits of victory. Also owing to the thick mud, many rifles became choked and it was impossible to bring them to bear upon the enemy as they fled across the open. One trench gun and two machine guns were captured, besides a number of aerial-torpedo-throwers, many rifles and hand-grenades, and a considerable quantity of ammunition. It was estimated that the enemy casualties were over one hundred killed in the open, while thirty bodies were found in the fire-trench alone, and the support trench was thickly strewn with dead. The Manchesters' own casualties were six men killed and twenty-seven wounded.

The following message of congratulation was received from the Divisional Commander:—

"Please convey to all ranks of the Battalion my very hearty thanks and admiration for the magnificent conduct they displayed during the recent operations, and the splendid manner in which they attacked and routed the enemy, thereby rendering substantial assistance to another Division."

The Battalion was relieved at 6 p.m. on the 12th by the 20th Royal Fusiliers, and marched to billets in Basseux. The following day it moved to Bienvillers-au-Bois, and remained there in rest billets until the 18th, when it relieved the 3rd London Regiment in the trenches N.W. of Neuville-Vitasse. From the 19th to the 22nd the Battalion was in Brigade reserve in the area S.E. of Neuville-Vitasse, relieving the 1/14th London Scottish, its work being to hold Nepal trench. But another attack was now pending. Leaving the trenches S.E. of Neuville-Vitasse at 11 p.m. on April 22nd the Battalion reached the assembly positions in the vicinity of Héninel at 3 a.m. on the 23rd, being in reserve to the 90th Brigade. At 9-30 a.m. an order was received to reinforce the 16th Manchesters with one Company, and "C" Company was accordingly sent forward. The remaining three Companies then moved up to the old British front line. At 11 a.m. "A" and "D" were called up to reinforce, and the three Companies thus came under the orders of the O.C., 16th Manchesters, and so remained until 3 p.m. when an order was issued to re-establish the old front line. Thereupon, the other three battalions of the Brigade withdrew, and the 18th Manchesters took over that section of the line. During these operations there were few casualties, though the three Companies which had been attached to the 16th Battalion had borne an active share in the attack.

An order to attack the Blue line in conjunction with the 19th Manchesters was received at 4-40 p.m., and, though from the disposition of the Battalion at that time it was not easy to get into fighting formation, the necessary manœuvres were carried out speedily, and at 6 p.m. (zero) the advance towards the distant objective was begun. The formation followed was that laid down in Brigade Orders: four waves, each of two lines, on a four-platoon frontage. "D" Company was on the right, supported by "A," and "C" Company was on the left, supported by "B." The leading wave kept fairly close to the barrage as they advanced, and had hardly left the line when the enemy machine guns opened from the front and both flanks. Despite casualties the advance continued unchecked up to a particular point. But here the whole line was temporarily held up, not only on account of the heavy machine-gun fire, but also because there had been a number of officer casualties, and some little re-organisation was necessary. Nevertheless it was found possible to push forward very soon, though by this time the supporting Companies, had merged into the firing-line. Moving steadily on, the Battalion led by Lieut. Watson and Sec.-Lieut. Lawrence—the only officers remaining, reached the objective about 8 p.m. Almost immediately afterwards both these officers were wounded, and the Companies, by this time reduced to less than one hundred strong, were left to the direction of N.C.O.'s. The trench itself was not yet clear of the enemy, and sharp hand-to-hand fights took place, a number of Germans being killed. Finally, for about twenty minutes the Manchesters were left in undisturbed occupation, but the enemy then launched a counter-attack, first opening fire from the front and right flank with rifle grenades. Under such a barrage strong bombing parties advanced towards the trench and though the Manchesters put up a gallant fight, using all their Mills bombs and rifle-grenades with good effect, they were subsequentiy overwhelmed by weight of numbers and forced to withdraw. As they fell back the enemy followed, showing great daring in bringing forward his machine guns. About fifty-three men of all companies reached the old front line between 9-30 p.m. and midnight, and with these and details of the 17th Manchesters and some King's Liverpools the line was made secure. Later the 2nd Wilts took over. Though every Company officer who took part in the attack became a casualty a few succeeded in making their way back. Had any officers remained unwounded to organise the defence of the position, and had supports arrived in time, it is probable that the objective might have been held. Unfortunately the battalion in support suffered in the advance, and lost direction and consequently were unable to render any assistance.

"This battle, unlike those of the Somme in 1916, which had been chiefly trench-to-trench attacks, was a curious mixture of open warfare and trench warfare. The enemy, driven out of his so-called impregnable Hindenburg line at this point, had not been able to dig a continuous line of trenches and so had resorted to that system of defended areas—outposts and machine-gun nests, échelonedin tactical positions affording mutual support to each other and enabling a post always to bring flanking fire on troops attacking neighbouring posts. There was perhaps nothing very new in the idea, which was simply a clever adaptation of tactics to the use of modern weapons and the conditions of the moment, but it was comparatively new at the time and our men had not acquired the skill in out-flanking and smashing machine-gun nests with Stokes guns which they developed later. As a consequence of the situation the artillery barrage when the Eighteenth attacked at 6 p.m. in the evening of the 23rd was practically of no help owing to the enemy's dispositions. The objective, it may be stated, was over half-a-mile away and during the long attack (as stated above) every officer became a casualty, so that the chances of coping with an unusual situation were small. Conditions in modern war are such that once his troops are launched to the attack the Colonel of a battalion is practically unable to control them, and no better proof of this could be shown than this attack. The troops surviving the attack were brought back by corporals and lance-corporals, and upon them fell the work of defending the old front line until relief came. The casualties were fifteen officers and three hundred and forty-six other ranks killed, wounded and missing. The names of the officers killed in the these operations are :—

Sec.-Lieuts. S. D. Adshead, N. B. Gill, F. A. Eminton, B. A. Westphal, S. J. L. Wyatt, H. Duncan, J. E. M. Taylor, G. H. Doughty, S. M. Shirley.

It should be noted that the following were mentioned in Earl Haig's despatch, dated April 9th, for "Gallant and Distinguished

Conduct" in the field :—

No. 10838, Sergt. C. Sedgwick (since killed) ; No. 9921, Sergt. H. J. Ravenscroft ; No. 10119, Cpl. A. B. Fergie ; No. 10826, P. J. Kennedy.

After the 2nd Wilts had taken over the line on the night of the 23rd April the Manchesters left for the trenches S.E. of Neuville-Vitasse which they had previously occupied. On the 27th the Battalion marched to Arras, entrained for St. Pol, and marched thence on the 28th to billets in Croisette, where it remained training, reorganising and refitting.

CHAPTER VI

THE YPRES SALIENT AND END OF THE BATTALION

THE Battalion remained at Croisette until May 3rd where it received a draft of one hundred and forty-eight men. The following officers were also added to the strength during the month :—

Major J. K. Aitken, Capt. J. M. Greer, Lieuts. N. Kohnstamm, J. F. Lewis, J. O. McElroy, H. G. Watson, Sec.-Lieuts. T. W. Cowan, E. Holland, J. E. Love, H. Whincup, O. Wilcox.

On May 3rd the Battalion marched to billets at Le Quesnoy, remaining there training until the 20th, when the 30th Division moved to the Hazebrouck area, the Manchesters marching from Le Quesnoy to Croisette. The 21st found the Battalion at Pressy-les-Pernes, the next day at Auchy-au-Bois, and on the 25th at a camp north of Hazebrouck, where it remained until the 31st, when it moved to billets at Lumbres, travelling by train to St. Omer and thence by 'bus.

The Battalion remained at Lumbres until June 6th, when it was moved by 'bus to an area west of Poperinghe, and billeted in the vicinity of Hipshok. Drafts numbering one hundred and eleven men were received and the following officers joined the strength :—

Sec.-Lieuts. R. F. Brenton, J. E. Cross, A. V. Dyson, E. J. Griffith, W. E. Harding, H. Maden, H. G. S. Reynolds, H. Simmonds.

On June 9th the Battalion marched to Toronto Camp (Brandhoek area), remaining until the 14th, when it left the camp at 8-45 p.m. to relieve the 17th Manchesters in the left Hooge sector, moving by Companies via Zillebeke and Vince Street to allotted positions. By 2 a.m. on the 15th the relief was complete, and the Companies disposed as follows :—

" A " Company in front line, " C " Company in Maple trench, " B " Company in Wellington crescent, " D " Company in Ritz street, Headquarters in Maple trench.

On the night of June the 16th a patrol of ten men led by Sec.-Lieut. J. E. Smart reconnoitered " No Man's Land " with a view to the construction of a forward trench. Work was commenced in this trench on the following night, but progress was slow owing to the difficult nature of the ground and the thick undergrowth. By the third night, however, a considerable amount had been dug to a depth varying from two to four feet. About 4 a.m. on the morning of the 20th a hostile patrol of one N.C.O. and eleven men attempted to enter the front line. Rapid fire was opened on them by the troops, after which the O.C. " A " Company, Capt. J. G. Cunliffe, led a party of men over the parapet and succeeded in taking four prisoners, including the N.C.O. in charge of the patrol.

The relief of the Battalion by the 2nd Wilts commenced about 10-30 p.m. on the 21st, and on completion the Battalion marched by Companies to Micmac Camp. The following day the Manchesters left this camp, marched to Reninghelst, entrained at 10 a.m. for Watten, and marched thence to billets at Nordansques. There most of the remainder of the month was spent resting, training and providing working-parties.

The casualties for the period 13th—22nd June were: Sec.-Lieut. J. E. Shanahan (wounded) and six men killed, three died of gas poisoning, and twenty-two wounded. A draft of one hundred and forty-one men joined on the 28th, on which date the Battalion returned to Micmac Camp by train from Watten to Abeele, and thence by route-march, via Reninghelst and Ouderdom, and on the 29th moved on to Dickebusch huts.

The following N.C.O. and men were awarded the Military Medal during the month :—

No. 9946, L/Cpl. W. G. Webb ; No. 28752, Pte. W. Brooks ; No. 47856, Pte. S. Glinternick.

During the first few days of July the Battalion was engaged on working and carrying parties in the forward area or took its share with the remainder of the Brigade in digging assembly trenches, and on July 6th it marched from Dickebusch to Reninghelst, thence by train to Watten, and from here by march to billets at Ruminghem. Next day it left Ruminghem and marched to billets at Louches. Here Capt. J. G. Cunliffe was awarded the Military Cross for his gallant services in the engagement of June 20th, and C.S.M. G. Ryan the D.C.M. for gallantry in action. Lieut. M. Brunton rejoined on July 8th from sick leave, and Sec.-Lieut. J. Walsh was added to the strength.

On July 15th was held the Divisional Horse Show and Band Display as Nordansques. The Battalion was at Ottawa Camp (Wippenhoek area) on the 22nd, and left for Château Segard on the night of the 23rd, arriving in position by 1-30 on the morning of the

24th. From this date to the 27th the Battalion provided working and carrying parties in the forward area. On the 26th the Manchesters carried out a daylight raid on the enemy trenches and obtained information as to the German dispositions. The casualties sustained were: Sec.-Lieut. W. Phythian (wounded); three other ranks killed and nine wounded.

At 9 p.m. on the 28th the Battalion left Château Segard to relieve the 19th King's Liverpools in the line, the relief being complete by 3-0 the following morning. During the whole of the 29th and 30th the Companies remained in the front line and support trenches and at 10 p.m. on the night of the 30th assembled in "No Man's Land" in readiness for the attack next morning.

At 3-50 a.m. (zero) on the 31st the Eighteenth Manchesters advanced across Sanctuary Wood, and by 5-30 a.m. succeeded in capturing its final objective, the Blue line east of Stirling Castle.

The casualties were:—

Sec.-Lieut. H. Maden (killed); Sec.-Lieut. H. Simmonds (killed); Capt. J. G. Cunliffe, M.C. (died of wounds 1-8-17); and other ranks three hundred and twenty-seven killed, wounded and missing.

A short general description of this operation is given in Doyle's "1917 Campaign":—

"The 30th Division, which consisted, as will be remembered, to a large extent of 'Pal' Battalions from Liverpool and Manchester, advanced to the south of the Eighth. Sanctuary Wood and other strong points lay in front of the 90th and 21st Brigades, which provided the first line of stormers. The resistance was strong, the fire was heavy, and the losses were considerable, so that the assailants were unable to do more than carry the front trenches, whence they repulsed repeated counter attacks during the rest of the day. In the initial advance the 2nd Scots Fusiliers, that phœnix of a battalion, so often destroyed and so often renewed, wandered in the dusk of the morning away from its allotted path and got as far north as Château Wood in the path of the 24th Brigade. This caused some dislocation of the front line, but the Manchester men on the right of the Scots pushed on and struck the Menin road as far forward as Clapham Junction.

The 21st Brigade, in the meantime, had to pass a great deal of difficult woody ground and met so much opposition that they lost the barrage, that best friend of the stormer. Bodmin Copse was reached, but few penetrated to the eastern side of it. The strong point of Stirling Castle was, however, taken by the Manchesters of the 90th."

Only those who have actually experienced the conditions of the Ypres battlefield in 1917, when three years of intensive war had blotted out every landmark, can realise the difficulties which the Battalion encountered in this attack on Stirling Castle. Maps were of no avail, for the simple reason that the whole landscape was one vast barren tract of shell-holes. No single landmark showed to relieve the monotony—roads, woods, farms, lakes—everything was swallowed up. Only the compass and that inborn genius of orientation which some men possess enabled companies to keep anything like true direction. Small wonder that once the attack was launched to the accompaniment of a barrage and counter barrage as awe inspiring and destructive as any that had been seen in modern war until that date, not only platoons and companies, but sometimes battalions and brigades lost direction. Soon the battle resolved itself into a series of small attacks delivered by independent bodies of men, twenty or thirty at most, led perhaps by a junior subaltern or a sergeant or corporal. This kind of fighting depends for its success on good discipline and individual courage and initiative, and it is a tribute to the Battalion that in such conditions they pressed steadily forward and won. The final objective, Stirling Castle, a strongly fortified mound which bristled with machine guns and trench mortars was taken and with it a large number of prisoners.

Like ourselves, the Germans suffered from losing direction and losing touch with battalion commanders, and when their orders to retire were given they did not reach everybody. In consequence "mopping up" parties reaped a rich harvest, but none was more successful than that led and constituted solely by Pte. Piggott (batman to Lieut. W. E. Ogden, the Adjutant), who was acting as Battalion runner. Towards evening on the 21st Piggott was sent to Brigade headquarters with a message. He had half-a mile to go and lost his way in the gloom. Stumbling across the shell-holes he was astonished to find three Germans sitting outside a dug-out. They were armed. A Mons and South African veteran, Piggott had all the resource of the British soldier and promptly shouted "hands up," lowered his bayonet, and began beckoning to imaginary companions to come to him. The ruse succeeded and the Bosches put up their hands. Piggott thereupon ordered them to march in front. Two did so but one began to get excited and pointed down the dug-out steps. Then to the utter astonishment of Piggott sixteen more Bosches solemnly filed out with their hands above their heads. The Englishman did not hesitate. He stood with his rifle at the ready and pointed out the direction in which he believed the British line to be, and slowly the odd procession wound its way across the shell-holes in the heavy rain. Within twenty minutes or so the party reached the British front line. Piggott did not stop to explain to his delighted colleagues, but continued his triumphal progress to the prisoners of war cage, where he handed over his charges and obtained a receipt for two N.C.O.'s and seventeen O.R. Then he delivered his message at Brigade headquarters and returned to the Adjutant (who thought he had been killed) and presented his receipt. Piggott was awarded the

D.C.M. Several other feats were recorded in this battle, for which three M.C.'s and six M.M.'s were given to the Battalion.

It was a costly battle, however, and among the officers who fell was one, Capt. Cunliffe, M.C., who had done splendid work with the Eighteenth since its formation. A clever engineer, Cunliffe had been pressed many times to transfer to the R.E., but he steadfastly refused because he felt that to do so would not be playing the game. He was mourned by officers and men as a very dear friend and gallant comrade.

The worst feature of the Ypres attack was undoubtedly the suffering of the wounded. Heavy rain began to fall at mid-day on July 31st and continued for over twenty-four hours. The marshy ground became more difficult than ever, the shell-holes filled with water adding the peril of drowning to the anguish of those unfortunate wounded who were helpless, and under such conditions the Battalion stretcher-bearers worked manfully without rest in the pouring rain and under incessant shell-fire clearing the battlefield. Capt. Stansfield had only been able to find a poor shelter for his aid-post and many of his patients lay outside when an artillery major more enterprising than thoughtful, took up his position with four guns outside and made ready to open fire. There are some things no one can stand, even in a battle, and the " doc." earned gratitude from the wounded and unstinted admiration from his small staff by the short but forceful address he gave to that officer. The battery sought another position immediately.

August was a quiet month so far as the Eighteenth Manchesters were concerned. On August 1st the Battalion was holding the positions east of Sanctuary Wood, captured on the previous day. Relief commenced at 11 a.m. by Companies, the last Company reaching Château Segard at 6 p.m. The following day a move was made to Dickebusch New Camp and on the 3rd by lorry to the area east of Steenvoorde.

On the 4th the Battalion proceeded by lorry and route-march to a camp near Terdeghem. The 6th found it in billets in Strazeele—resting and training. On August 10th it moved to the frontier camp, east of Berthen, where the 90th Brigade was inspected on the 15th by General Sir Herbert Plumer, commanding the Second Army. During the month Major J. K. Aitken transferred to the Fourth Army and the following officers were added to the strength :—

Sec.-Lieuts. J. Arnold, J. B. Barker, L. S. Burgess, E. Burgis, T .W. Green, J. Houghton, L. Illingwarth, F. Pickering, F. Schofield.

The following awards were made during the month :—

Lieut. W. E. Ogden, Military Cross ; Sec.-Lieut. W. E. Harding, Military Cross ; Sec.-Lieut. E. Holland, Military Cross ; No. 37552, Pte. Piggott, D.C.M. ; Sergt. S. Forster, Military Medal ; Sergt.

A. C. Dean, Military Medal; L/Cpl. E. Deale, Military Medal; L/Sergt. F. G. Shuttleworth, Military Medal; No. 21337, Pte. W. Hodgert (Military Medal).

The Battalion left the Berthen district on August 22nd and moved to Parrain Farm Camp in Divisional reserve. On the 29th it pro ceeded to the Messines area, and relieved the 16th Manchesters in Brigade support. The 9th King's Royal Rifles relieved on September 2nd, and the Eighteenth Manchesters marched to camp near Dranoutre, remaining there until the 9th, and supplying working-parties in the forward area. On the 9th the battalion relieved the 19th Manchesters in support, being disposed in the vicinity of Lumm Farm and Wytschaete. The following day it moved into the line, relieving the 2nd Wilts. This tour of duty lasted until the 22nd. Wiring-parties and patrols went out each night along the whole Battalion sector, but no enemy patrols were encountered. During the night 15-16th September a patrol, consisting of Cpl. Leach and four men of " D " Company, supported by a Lewis gun, attempted to rush an enemy M.G. post, after subjecting it to a severe bombardment with rifle-grenades. The effort however, was unsuccessful, owing to the marshy nature of the ground and the thickness of the enemy wire, but the patrol was enabled to gain much useful information, and to establish the location of an enemy trench mortar and two machine guns.

On the 22nd the Battalion was relieved by the 19th Manchesters, and moved back in Brigade reserve in Chinese Wall, and supplied working-parties.

Sec.-Lieuts. L. H. Burrows and A. E. Wakefield were added to the strength.

The Battalion left Chinese Wall on October 1st, and moved to Kemmel Château area, and within the next day or two the following officers joined for duty :—

Sec-Lieuts. J. H. Platt, F. Potts, J. D. Preston, A. H. Smith.

The entire Battalion was engaged on hut building under R.E.'s. On the 5th a move was made to camp at Daylight Corner, and on the 10th the Battalion relieved the 2nd Wilts in support. Next day it went into the line (right subsector) relieving the 19th Manchesters.

Major T. J. Kelly, M.C. now assumed temporary command, *vice* Lieut.-Col. C. E. Lembcke admitted to hospital. On the 12th a thorough reconnaissance of the wire in the Battalion sector was made with a view to improving and strengthening it during this tour of duty. Patrols were also out on the whole front, reconnoitering " No Man's Land " and establishing touch with the battalions on the left and right. Working and wiring parties were employed for some days and patrols went out nightly. The Battalion was relieved on October

17th by the 2nd Royal Scots Fusiliers and marched to camp at Vroilandhoek. Here it rested for a day or two and was subsequently employed refitting, training and building hutments.

Lieut.-Col. C. E. Lembcke rejoined on the 18th and resumed command. It was only for a short period, however, for he left the Battalion again on the 27th to take over the command of th 30th Divisional Reinforcement Camp, and was succeeded by Major H. C. W. Theobald, D.S.O.

At 5 p.m. on the 29th the Battalion left Vroilandhoek to relieve the 19th Manchesters in the front line, Kilo Farm, in the right subsector. On October 10th Sec-Lieut. F. Pickering was killed in the Kemmel Château area, and on the 16th Sec.-Lieut. E. Burgis. The following officers were added to the strength :—

Sec.-Lieuts. E. L. Capper, T. Hartley, R. F. James, A. V. Michaelis.

The Battalion remained holding the right subsector of the line—from the Wambeek on the north to the Blauwepoortbeek on the south—until the night of November 4th, when it was relieved by the 2nd Royal Scots Fusiliers and went into support. On the 6th the Battalion moved to camp at Daylight Corner, where the following day was spent resting and refitting, prior to going north. On November 8th the Battalion moved by 'bus to Ypres, and marched thence to camp at St. Jean, Battalion H.Q. being at English Farm. Here it remained until the 24th, supplying working-parties in the forward area, under orders of the Canadian (and subsequently VIII) Corps Heavy Artillery. The work the Battalion was called upon to undertake during this period proved to be of an exceedingly difficult and arduous nature, consisting as it did, to a great extent, in carrying up ammunition to the forward battery positions on the Passchendaele Ridge under heavy shell-fire. That the high standard of work maintained throughout was fully appreciated by the Higher Command is shown in the following letter from Lieut.-General Sir G. W. Currie, commanding Canadian Corps :—

" *To the Officer Commanding*

18th Battalion Manchester Regiment

On handing over command of the Passchendaele Front I wish to express to you and to the officers, non-commissioned officers and men under your command my warm appreciation of the excellent work which they have done for the Canadian Corps, while under my command. Their work has had to be carried out under very arduous and trying circumstances without the stimulus of actually taking part in the offensive themselves, although exposed to heavy shell-fire which has, I am sorry to say, at times resulted in considerable casualties.

The work that they have done has contributed to the success of the operations in the most direct degree, and it is no exaggeration to say that without such work no offensive could be successfully undertaken.

G. W. CURRIE, Lieut.-General
Commanding Canadian Corps."

On the 25th November the Battalion was relieved by the 17th Sherwood Foresters, and marched to camp at Swan Château. During the preceding tour of duty the Battalion had the following casualties :

Capt. T. Stansfield, R.A.M.C., wounded; two other ranks killed, and nineteen other ranks wounded. Whilst at Swan Château the Battalion was engaged in training and supplying working-parties under the 200th Field Co. R.E. in the forward area. The following officers joined for duty during the month :—

Capt. E. A. Walker, M.C., R.A.M.C., Lieut. H. P. Sawyer (U.S.A.), Sec.-Lieuts. J. Chapman, S. G. Heyhoe.

The Battalion remained at Swan Château until December 11th, when it relieved the 2nd Bedfordshires in the Polderhoek sector of the left front line, and came under orders of the 21st Brigade. The 12th and 13th passed fairly quietly, the enemy's activity being mainly confined to trench mortar bombardments. At 2 a.m. on the morning of the 14th, however, a message was received from Brigade H.Q. that the enemy was suspected to be preparing for an attack on the sector held by the Battalion. This warning was at once conveyed to the troops in the front line, who stood-to in readiness. The enemy's attack was delivered at 6 a.m. and was preceded by a very heavy trench mortar bombardment of the front and support lines, accompanied by vigorous shelling of the back areas and Battalion H.Q.

The disposition of the Battalion at the beginning of the attacks was as follows :—

"A" on the right, "B" in the centre, "C" on the left, with "D" in support. The front line was a continuous trench, deep and narrow, fire-stepped by sand-bag steps capable of accommodating three men. The enemy was roughly thirty to fifty yards away, in small trenches and posts, and appeared to have no connected line. There was good wire in front of our left Company, but very little in the centre or on the right. The attack began simultaneously along the whole front at 6 a.m. A body of the enemy, estimated at fifty in number, appeared in front of the shell-hole, which was held by posts of the centre Company, and crossing our trench began to move left and right along the parados. They threw bombs as they went. The enemy also effected an entrance on the right Company front, following the same tactics. On the left front, thanks to the wire which had been strengthened during the night—forty coils having been put out—the enemy was checked, and a heavy fire brought to bear on him. He failed to enter the left Company's trench at any point and a strong party of Germans who attempted to rush the left flank post was beaten off.

The enemy pushed home his attack until the whole of the centre and right Company fronts were in his possession, and then sought to drive out the remaining troops by simultaneous attacks on their right flank and front with bombs. He was again repulsed and the officer commanding the left Company, Capt. J. N. Smart, then organised a counter-attack in the hope of regaining the front line. He made good progress for a time, but was eventually forced back through failure of his bomb supply, and he finally established a block seventy yards to the right of his original right flank.

The Company commander of the right Company was in his headquarters (the pill-box Jericho) when the attack began and only had with him the Company sergeant-major and about ten other ranks. He attempted to reach the front line over the open but was taken in enfilade by a party of the enemy to the S.W. of Jericho, who opened a heavy fire with light machine guns. Concluding that his flank was in danger, this officer took up a position in the communication trench, and formed a defensive flank. The support Company sent up a platoon to the left Company as soon as the attack commenced, and also gave support on the right, but they were too few in number to give sufficient weight for a counter-attack.

Between 10 a.m. and noon two companies of the 17th Manchesters about seventy in number—reinforced the front line, and between 4 p.m. and 5 p.m. two companies of the 2nd Royal Scots Fusiliers also reinforced. A counter-attack was then organised. The plan was to attack simultaneously on both flanks, and also to move across the open and retake the pill-box Jericho. Harassing and protective fire from the field guns had been kept up throughout the day, and a barrage was put down from 6-30 to 7-25 p.m., with an interval of ten minutes, on that portion of the front line held by the enemy, and also upon his original position in front of the left Company. The attack took place at 8 p.m. and though the enemy offered stout resistance, he was driven back by both attacks until the supply of bombs gave out.

"C" Company attacking from their right flank met with strong opposition, but Sec.-Lieut. W. E. Harding, who led the bombing attack on the right, made very good progress, and at one time was within sixty yards of "C" Company. His stock of bombs then failed completely, and strong reinforcements of the enemy appearing from his rear endeavoured to cut him off, but he brought back his party safely after suffering casualties. In this operation we regained one of the Lewis guns lost during the early morning operation.

The assault across the open to regain Jericho was made successfully and with few casualties. The enemy had apparently decided not to occupy this strong point at such a stage of the operations, for everything was found just as it was felt earlier in the day.

Whilst concentrating his attention on Sec.-Lieut. Harding's party the enemy weakened his position against " C " Company, who were able to push their attack home until practically the whole of the line formerly held by " B " and " A " had been occupied. Unfortunately Sec.-Lieut. Harding had by this time been forced back and found himself utterly unable to co-operate. The enemy again brought up fresh supplies of bombs, and pursuing his tactics of the morning, got in shell-holes in " No Man's Land," and began to throw grenades in order to cut off " C " Company. This Company's supply, diminished by the fighting they had done, was soon exhausted by this fresh attack, and they were compelled to fall back to their original position, They again established a block where they made had it previously, and as the trench at this point was fairly straight for about thirty yards they were able to keep the enemy out of bombing range.

In the early hours of the 15th the men of the Eighteenth Manchesters, greatly exhausted, were replaced at the bombing block in the original front line by a party of the Royal Scots Fusiliers. At 8 a.m. the enemy, who had by this time ceased to occupy our old front line, established himself in shell-holes some twenty yards in front, attempting to get behind the block and take the garrison in the rear. No difficulty was experienced in keeping him back so long as the supply of bombs lasted, but when it failed the garrison was compelled to evacuate the front line and take up a position in the support trench. This trench was then held continuously throughout its whole length, as a front line, and no further change took place in the situation.

There appeared to be little doubt that the enemy attacked a battalion strong—probably about four hundred rifles. His men had all been carefully rehearsed in their parts and were thoroughly trained in the tactics of trench warfare. They were all experienced in the use of our bombs, rifles, Vickers and Lewis guns, and all the weapons and bombs which had been captured in the morning were used by the enemy in the subsequent fighting. His men had also been taught several English words of command, and frequent shouts of " Retire." " Withdraw !" and " Surrender !" were uttered. Throughout the fighting the enemy showed a most determined front, and the many separate parties composing his attacking force collaborated by the use of coloured lights.

Later information received from prisoners shows that this attack was delivered by the battalion of Sturmtruppen, supported by the troops holding the line. The enemy's casualties were exceedingly heavy, and though he occupied our front line for a time he failed in his objective. It should be added that two companies in the front line consisted largely of nineteen year old boys who had not been a week in France and had had no sort of trench training whatever. Later the Army Commander decided that the position—it was a hastily consolidated position left by Dominion troops after an unsuccessful attack on Polderhoek Château—should be evacuated, and our line was formed in a stronger position a hundred yards in rear.

The following officer was killed in this engagement :— Sec.-Lieut. J. Houghton, and of other ranks there were one hundred and nineteen killed, wounded and missing.

At 8 p.m. on the 18th December the 2nd Royal Scots Fusiliers took over the whole of the left subsector and the Eighteenth Manchesters moved back to Forrester Camp, where they remained until the afternoon of the 16th, when they entrained for Alberta Camp, Reninghelst. The following day was spent reorganising and refitting. During the earlier part of the month a draft of eighty-five men had been been received.

Lieut. D. Davies (U.S.A.) had replaced Lieut. H. Sawyer (U.S.A.) as M.O., and the following officers had also joined the strength :—

Sec.-Lieuts. H. Byron, W. Downie, A. G. Harman, A.W. Richards.

December 18th to 21st were spent training and supplying working-parties. Christmas services were held on the 22nd in the Y.M.C.A. at Reninghelst, and the rest of the day was treated as a holiday. Special Christmas dinners were provided for the men, followed by an entertainment in the evening by " The Blue Birds."

The 2nd Royal Scots Fusiliers generously consented to relieve the Battalion of all working-parties for the day, a kindly act which was greatly appreciated by all ranks.

The 23rd was spent training. On the 24th the Battalion relieved the 2nd Royal Scots Fusiliers in Brigade reserve (Torr Top tunnels), moving by rail from Fuzeville to Manor Halt, a tour of duty which lasted until the 27th, during which time it supplied working-parties in the forward area. On the date named the Battalion relieved the 17th Manchesters in the centre subsector—astride the Menin road. Here it remained until the 30th. This tour passed quite uneventfully and though during the first twenty-four hours the enemy was inclined to be aggressive, the Manchesters' Lewis guns and snipers very soon obtained the mastery, and for the remainder of the time he showed much less activity.

Patrols went out nightly, and gained useful information, but no hostile patrols were encountered. Extremely bright nights, with snow on the ground, rendered the work of patrols and carrying-parties extremely difficult, but in spite of these conditions, every party accomplished its allotted task. Wire was put out along the whole sector, and trenches improved in many places. On the night of the 30th the Battalion was relieved by the 17th King's Liverpools, and marched back to Forrester Camp. The casualties for the three days were one man killed and four wounded. Lieut.-Col. H. C. W. Theobald, D.S.O., was admitted sick to field ambulance on the 29th, and Major T. J. Kelly, M.C., assumed command. December 31st was devoted to resting and clearing up. The following were mentioned in despatches (Sir D. Haig) for gallantry in the field :—

Capt. H. G. S. Bower, Capt. T. Stansfied, R.A.M.C., No. 10826, Pte. P. J. Kennedy (" D " Company).

Thus ended the year 1917.

January 1st—4th, 1918, found the Battalion still training at Forrester Camp. On the morning of the 5th it entrained at Dickebusch and moved to billets at Ebblinghem. This place was left at 7-30 p.m. on the 7th for Steenbecque. At midnight it entrained for Longueau, which place was reached at 8 a.m. on the 8th. The Manchesters now marched to billets at Vaire-sous-Corbie, where they remained training until the 13th. In the New Year's List of Honours Capt. J. E. Smart was awarded the Military Cross for distinguished and valuable services in the field. Lieut.-Col. H. C. W. Theobald, D.S.O., who had returned to the Battalion on the 6th was again compelled to retire on the 11th, and Major F. Walton, M.C. (6th Durham Light Infantry), assumed command.

There were now some rapid movements. On January 13th the Manchesters marched via Hamel, Warfusse, Abancourt, and Barjonvillars to Harbonnieres, and the following day via Lihons, Chaulnes and Puzeaux to Nesle. Whilst training here a draft of ninety-eight men joined from the Divisional Reinforcement Camp. On the 19th the Battalion marched to billets at Libermont. Here it remained training until the 26th, on which date it marched to billets at Behericourt; and on the 27th to Chauny Sud, remaining until the 29th. On the latter date the Eighteenth left Chauny Sud and proceeded to the trenches to relieve the 15th French Cavalry Regiment. This sector, the Foret d'Epinois, remained very quiet during the tour of duty which lasted until February 9th. On this date the 6th London Regiment relieved the Manchesters and they marched back to billets at Chauny, continuing next day via Neuffleux and Guivry to Guiscard. On the 11th they were in billets at Golancourt. A working-party of fifty men under Sec.-Lieut. A. E. Wakefield was detached to Ham, and on the 15th the detachment moved to Roye. The 17th found the Battalion in billets at Lanquevoisin.

And now the end of the Eighteenth as a separate unit was at hand. The tremendous casualty list in the 1917 fighting had made some reorganisation of the Army necessary, and it had been decided to adopt the German formation of three battalions to a brigade and nine to a division. This decision affected the Eighteenth, the junior of the 90th Brigade, and it fell to their lot to be disbanded.

On February 19th 1918, amalgamation with the 17th Entrenching Battalion took place at Haut Allaines in the VIIth Corps area, where they had arrived the previous day.

The Eighteenth Battalion Manchester Regiment is no more ; it is probable that it will never be re-formed, but the memory of the men and of the part they played will not die, and their colours, which hang in the Cathedral in Manchester, bear silent witness for all time to the sacrifices which they made in adding a page of history to the glorious annals of the Manchester Regiment.

APPENDIX I
HONOURS

Photo *Carl Cloud*

SERGEANT-MAJOR GEORGE EVANS, V.C.
18TH BATTALION MANCHESTER REGIMENT

Victoria Cross

10947. EVANS, GEORGE, *Co.-Sgt.-Major, 18th Batt., 30th January* 1920

For most conspicuous bravery and devotion to duty during the attack at Guillemont on the 30th July 1916, when under heavy rifle and machine-gun fire he volunteered to take back an important message after five runners had been killed in attempting to do so. He had to cover about 700 yards, the whole of which was under observation from the enemy.

Company-Sergeant-Major Evans, however, succeeding in delivering the message and although wounded rejoined his Company, although advised to go to the dressing-station.

The return journey to the Company again meant a journey of 700 yards under severe rifle and machine-gun fire, but by dodging from shell-hole to shell-hole he was able to do so, and was taken prisoner some hours later.

On previous occasions at Montauban and Trones Wood this gallant warrant officer displayed great bravery and devotion to duty and has always been a splendid example to his men.

DISTINGUISHED SERVICE ORDER

Name		*Rank*	*Place and date of deed*	*Gazetted*
FOULKES, John Simpson	..	T/Major		26-9-17
(R.F.C.) *attached*				19-1-18
KELLY, Thomas Joseph	..	T/Major	Trescault, 27-9-18	18-2-19
(*Attached 6th*)				30-7-19

MILITARY CROSS

Rank	*Name*	*Gazetted*	*Remarks*
T/Lieut.	BLYTHE, Percy Alfred ..	29-3-16	K. in a., 30-7-16
T/Capt.	CUNCLIFFE, James Grimshaw	25-8-17	D. of w., 1-8-17
T/Lieut.	KNOWLES, William Penderleith	30-3-16	
Q. & Hn.-Cpt.	PIERCE, Thomas Courtney ..	3-6-18	
T/Sec-Lt.	POWELL, Harry Alderson ..	30-3-16	
T/Capt.	WATSON, Henry Gilbert ..	30-1-20	To date 5-5-19
T/Sec.-Lt.	HAYHOE, Stanley George .. (*Attached 1/6th*)	2-12-18	
T/Sec.-Lt.	HARDING, William Eric ..	26-9-17 9-1-18	
T/Lieut.	HARRISON, Frank Valentine	30-1-20	To date 5-5-19
T/Sec.-Lt.	HILL, Cecil	16-9-18	
T/Sec.-Lt.	HOLLAND, Edwin	26-9-17 9-1-18	
T/Sec.-Lt.	SELIGMANN, Leopold Benjamin	26-7-18	
T/Lieut.	KELLY, Thomas Joseph, D.S.O. (4th B. Man. R.) *attached*	26-9-16	
T/Sec.-Lt.	SALMON, Bernard Bryant .. (25th B. Man. R.) *attached*	24-6-16	K. in a., 9-7-16
Sec.-Lieut. (T/Lieut.)	OGDEN, William Edward .. (5th B. Man. R.) *attached*	26-9-17 9-1-18	

DISTINGUISHED CONDUCT MEDAL

No.	*Name*		*Rank*	*Place and date of deed*	*Gazetted*
10355.	BANCROFT, A.	..	Pte.		15-4-16
10872.	BROOKE, A. J. B.	..	Cpl.		30-3-16
10612.	BROOKE, C. E.	..	Pte.		24-6-16
10235.	BUTTERWORTH, A. M.M.	..	L/Cpl.		26-9-16
10835.	POTTS, F. W. ..	..	Sgt.		3-6-16 21-6-16
10207.	RYAN, G. ..	..	A/C.S.M.		25-8-17
10569.	SMITH, G. H. ..	..	Sgt.		26-9-16
10721.	TOMLINSON, F.	..	Sgt.		
9952.	WOODWARD, C. G.	..	L/Cpl.		4-6-17 9-7-17
43658.	DEAN, A. C., M.M.	..	Cpl.		4-6-17 9-7-17
10426.	McNAMARA, J.	..	Sgt.		22-9-16

MILITARY MEDAL

No.	*Name*	*Rank*	*Place and date of deed*	*Gazetted*
28752.	BROOKS, W.	Pte.		16-8-17
10235.	BUTTERWORTH, A. .. D.C.M.	Pte.		10-8-16
10239.	CLEGG, S.	L/Sgt.		3-6-16
43658.	DEAN, A. C., D.C.M. ..	Sgt.		28-9-17
10390.	FORSTER, S. ..	Sgt.		28-9-17
47856.	GLINTERNICK, S. ..	Pte.		16-8-17
11215.	GREATBANKS, G. H...	Pte.		10-8-16
10777.	HAWORTH, H. ..	Sgt.		22-1-17
10818.	HILL, E. C.	Sgt.		11-11-16
21337.	HODGERT, W.	Pte.		28-9-17
9869.	HOLLAND, W. T. ..	Pte.		16-11-16
34141.	HOPE, R. B.	Cpl.		9-7-17
50960.	KEITH, D.	Cpl.		12-6-18
10423.	LAW, A.	Pte.		11-11-16
10305.	LEES, J. C.	Cpl.		11-11-16
41770.	LINDSELL, R.	Pte.		12-6-18
10683.	MARSDEN, E.	Pte.		10-8-16
7881.	NEALE, E.	Pte. (L/Cpl.)		28-9-17
9906.	NICHOLL, G. T. ..	L/Cpl.		23-8-16
10951.	PYGOTT, T.	Sgt.		28-9-17
9917.	REEVES, F.	Sgt.		22-1-17
43957.	SHUTTLEWORTH, F. G.	L/Sgt.		28-9-17
10464.	TINKER, G. H. ..	Cpl.		26-5-17
10047.	TONGE, F.	Pte.		21-10-16
12484.	WARD, E. G.	Pte.		11-11-16
18764.	WILLIAMSON, E. ..	Sgt.		26-5-17

MERITORIOUS SERVICE MEDAL

No.	*Rank*	*Name*	*Gazetted*
10069.	Sgt. ..	ALLAN, P. R.	17-6-18
43665.	C.S.M. ..	HAYTER, J.	17-6-18

FOREIGN DECORATIONS

BELGIUM—CROIX DE GUERRE

No.	*Rank*	*Name*	*Gazetted*
10088.	Sgt.	BANKS, Norman	12-7-18

APPENDIX II
OFFICERS KILLED
(IN ORDER OF DATE)

OFFICERS KILLED (in order of date)

Rank	*Name*	*Date*	*Place*
T/Sec.-Lt.	TOWNSEND, Arthur Evans .. (d. of w.)	26-11-15	Cardonette
T/Sec.-Lt.	NELSON, Joseph Lawrie (accidentally)	8-3-16	DuckPost(Somme)
T/Capt.	RENSHAW, Leonard	13-5-16	Maricourt
T/Capt.	HENSHALL, Charles	8-7-16	Trones Wood
T/Sec.-Lt.	SALMON, Bernard Bryant .. (25th B. Man. R.) *attached*	9-7-16	Trones Wood
T/Lt.-Col.	SMITH, William Alfred (d. of w.)	9-7-16	Trones Wood
T/Sec.-Lt.	COOPER, Arthur .. (d. of w.) (14th B. Man. R.) *attached*	10-7-16	Montauban
T/Sec.-Lt.	HUTCHINSON, James .. .. (27th B.Man. R.) *attached*	26-7-16	Guillemont
Capt.	BLYTHE, Percy Alfred	30-7-16	Guillemont
T/Lieut.	HAWORTH, Percy Geoffrey du Val	30-7-16	Guillemont
Sec.-Lieut.	KAVANAGH, Edward	30-7-16	Guillemont
Sec.-Lieut.	KING, Percy Reginald	30-7-16	Guillemont
Sec.-Lieut.	TWIST, Francis Cecil Orr.. ..	30-7-16	Guillemont
Sec.-Lieut.	MOTLER, John Frederick ..	30-7-16	Guillemont
T/Sec.-Lt.	TAYLOR, Harry	12-10-16	Ligny-Thilloy
T/Lieut.	PETERS, Henry .. .. .. (26th B. Man. R.) *attached*	12-10-16	Ligny-Thilloy
T/Capt.	PENN-GASKELL, William .. (25th B. Man. R.) *attached*	12-10-16	Ligny-Thilloy
T/Sec.-Lt.	CRICHTON, Herbert Clowe (d.of w.)	7-10-16	Fricourt
T/Sec.-Lt.	ADSHEAD, Sydney Douglas ..	23-4-17	Héninel
T/Sec.-Lt.	DUNCAN, Harry	23-4-17	Héninel
Sec.-Lieut.	EMINTON, Frederick Arthur ..	23-4-17	Héninel
Sec.-Lieut.	GILL, Noel Brendan	23-4-17	Héninel
Sec.-Lieut.	WESTPHAL, Benjamin Augustus	23-4-17	Héninel
Sec.-Lieut.	WYATT, Samuel John Livesley ..	23-4-17	Héninel
T/Sec.-Lt.	TAYLOR, John Edward Middleton (d. of w.)	24-4-17	Héninel
Sec.-Lieut.	DOUGHTY, George Harry ..	25-4-17	Héninel
T/Sec.-Lt.	SHIRLEY, Samuel Myatt (d. of w.)	1-5-17	Héninel
T/Sec.-Lt.	MADEN, Harold .. (*attached*)	29-7-17	Ypres
Sec.-Lieut.	SIMMONDS, Harold (*attached*)	31-7-17	Ypres
T/Capt.	CUNLIFFE, James Grimshaw, M.C. (d. of w.)	1-8-17	
Sec.-Lieut.	PICKERING, Freeman (d. of w.)	10-10-17	Kemmel Château
Sec.-Lieut.	BURGIS, Edward	16-10-17	Kemmel Château
T/Sec.-Lt.	HOUGHTON, John	14-12-17	Polderhoak
T/Sec.-Lt.	SMITH, Arthur Harold	27-3-18	
T/Sec.-Lt.	ARNOLD, Joseph .. .. .. (1/5th B.Man. R.) *attached*	2-9-18	
T/Sec.-Lt.	JAMES, Roy Francis	2-9-18	
T/Sec.-Lt.	LOVE, James Ellis..	2-9-18	

APPENDIX II
continued
W.O.'s, N.C.O.'s
AND MEN
KILLED

AKEHURST John Robert, *b* Brighton, Sussex, *e* Brighton, 41692, Pte., k. in a., F. & F., 12-4-17, formerly 12783 R. Sussex R.

ALDRED Samuel, *b* Hulme, Manchester, *e* Manchester, 10070, Pte., k. in a., F. & F., 4-2-16.

ALGER William, *b* Oldham, *e* Oldham, 203407, Pte., k. in a., F. & F., 31-7-17.

ALLEN Charles, *b* Chadderton, Lancs., *e* Oldham, 32099, Pte., d. of w., F. & F., 19-6-17.

ALLEN Hugh, *b* Widnes, Lancs., *e* Manchester (Widnes), 31307, Pte., k. in a., F. & F., 11-5-16.

ALLEN Robert Hounsome, *b* St. Peter's, Manchester, *e* Manchester, 10589, Pte., d. of w., F. & F., 2-7-16.

ALLISON John, *b* Glasgow, *e* Manchester, 10271, Pte., d. of w., F. & F., 22-5-16.

ALLPORT George, *b* Chorlton-cum-Hardy, Lancs., *e* Manchester (Chorlton-cum-Hardy), 10296, Pte., k. in a., F. & F., 23-4-17.

ALMOND William, *b* Orton, Northampton, *e* Manchester (Kingsthorpe, Northampton), 15599, Sgt., k. in a. F. & F., 12-10-16.

ANDERSON Leslie Scott, *b* Barrow-in-Furness, Lancs., *e* Manchester (Urmston, Lancs.), 9963, A/Cpl., k. in a., F. & F., 30-7-16.

ANDERSON William MacDougall, *b* Glasgow, *e* Manchester (Blackpool, 23292, L/Cpl., k. in a., F. & F., 23-4-17.

ARMSTRONG Thomas, *b* Wigan, Lancs., *e* Wigan, 47839, Pte., k. in a., F. & F., 23-4-17.

ASHCROFT James Henry, *b* Manchester, *e* Manchester, 10074, Pte., k. in a., F. & F., 30-7-16.

ASHCROFT Richard, *b* Christ Church, Chadderton, Lancs., *e* Manchester (Chadderton), 43997, Pte., k. in a., F. & F., 12-10-16.

ASHTON Samuel, *b* Ashton-u-Lyne, Lancs., *e* Stalybridge, Cheshire (Ashton-u-Lyne), 203345, Pte., d. of w., F. & F., 11-11-17.

ASHWORTH Bristow, *b* Ashton-u-Lyne, Lancs., *e* Manchester (Ashton-u-Lyne), 10906, Pte., k. in a., F. & F., 12-10-16.

AUSTIN Harry, *b* Hove, Sussex, *e* Burnham, Sussex (Yapton, Sussex), 41741, Pte., k. in a., F. & F., 23-4-17, formerly G/12055 R. Sussex R.

AUSTIN Thomas William Edward, *b* Salford, Lancs., *e* Manchester (Salford), 10603, Pte., k. in a., F. & F., 12-10-16.

AYLWARD William Percy, *b* Croydon, Surrey, *e* Croydon, 50930, Pte., k. in a., F. & F., 31-7-17, formerly G/19002 Middlesex R.

BAGSHAW James, *b* Manchester, *e* Manchester (Ardwick, Lancs.), 44168, Pte., k. in a., F. & F., 12-10-16.

BAILEY Arthur, *b* Wilmslow, Cheshire, *e* Manchester (Reddish, Cheshire), 11058, Pte., k. in a., F. & F., 22-3-18.

BAILEY Ernest, *b* Salford, Lancs., *e* Manchester (Salford), 9812, Pte., k. in a., F. & F., 30-7-16.

BAINES Joseph, *b* Salford, Lancs., *e* Manchester (Eccles, Lancs.), 11004, Pte., k. in a., F. & F., 11-7-16.

BALDWIN Mark, *e* Wigan, Lancs. (Orrell, Lancs.), 43824, Pte., k. in a., F. & F., 23-4-17.

BALL Harold, *b* Macclesfield, Cheshire, *e* Shaw, Lancs. (Moorside, Lancs.), 33459, Pte., k. in a., F. & F, 30-7-16.

BANKS Robert, *b* Newtown, Wigan, Lancs., *e* Wigan, 27305, Pte., k. in a., F. & F., 30-7-16.

BANNISTER Harold Parkinson, *b* Barrow-in-Furness, Lancs., *e* Manchester (Eccles, Lancs.), 9823, Pte., k. in a., F. & F., 1-7-16.

BARDSLEY Alfred, *b* Royton, Lancs., *e* Royton, Lancs. (Royton), 27249, Pte., k. in a., F. & F., 30-7-16.

BARKER Harold, *b* Ancoats, Manchester, *e* Manchester, 43936, Pte., k. in a., F. & F., 23-4-17.

BARKER John, *b* Manchester, *e* Ardwick, Manchester, 301738, Pte., k. in a., F. & F., 23-4-17.

BARLOW James, *b* Hulme, Manchester, *e* Manchester, 10086, Pte., k. in a., F. & F., 9-7-16.

BARTON Henry, *e* Wigan, Lancs. (Ashton-in-Makerfield, Lancs.), 43898, Pte., k. in a., F. & F., 30-10-16.

BATCHELOR Harry, *b* Reigate, Surrey, *e* Red Hill (Reigate), 50993, Pte., k. in a., F. & F., 31-7-17.

BATESON Herbert, *b* Chadderton, Lancs., *e* Oldham, Lancs, 61196, Pte., k. in a., F. & F., 14-12-17.

BEASLEY Walter, *b* Hulme, Manchester, *e* Manchester, 8434, L/Cpl., k. in a., F. & F., 30-7-16.

BEATTIE Arthur, *b* Manchester, *e* Manchester, 33705, Pte., k. in a., F. & F., 30-7-16.

BEATTIE Frank William, *b* Manchester, *e* Manchester, 31317, Pte., k. in a., F. & F., 9-7-16.

BECKETT Bernard Taylor, *b* Fallowfield, Manchester, *e* Manchester, 300319, Pte., k. in a., F. & F., 23-4-17.

BECKETT John William, *b* Manchester, *e* Ashton-u-Lyne, Lancs. (Manchester), 25363, Pte., k in a., F. & F., 13-6-17.

BEECROFT Albert Henry, *b* Manchester, *e* Manchester, 31312, A/Cpl., k. in a., F. & F., 30-7-16.

BEILBY John, *b* DroysIden, Lancs., *e* Manchester (Droylsden), 31367, Pte., k. in a., F. & F., 9-7-16.

BELL Charles Alexander, *b* Salford, Lancs., *e* Manchester, 10338, Pte., k. in a., F. & F., 1-7-16.

BELL George, *b* Manchester, *e* Manchester, 202884, Pte., k. in a., F. & F., 31-7-17.

BELL Herbert, *b* Carlisle, *e* Manchester, 33702, Pte., k. in a., F. & F., 30-7-16.

BELL William, *b* Newton Heath, Manchester, *e* Manchester 10958, Pte., d. of w., F. & F., 9-7-16.

BELLIS Harry, *b* Manchester, *e* Manchester, 33684, Pte., k. in a., F. & F., 30-7-16.

BICK George Victor, *b* St. Pancras, Middlesex, *e* Camberwell, Surrey (Alnwick Castle, Northumberland), 43693, Pte., F. & F., 12-10-16, formerly G/21620 Middlesex R.

BILLINGTON George Edwin, *b* Oldham, Lancs., *e* Oldham, 36864, Cpl., d., F. & F., 4-11-18.

BILLINGTON Henry, *b* West Gorton, Manchester, *e* Manchester, 9811, Pte., d. of w., F. & F., 13-7-16.

BILSBURY George Edward, *b* Dukinfield, Cheshire, *e* Denton, Lancs., 203346, Pte., k. in a., F. & F., 1-8-17.

BIRCH Thomas Edward, *b* Salford, Lancs., *e* Manchester (Salford), 48004, Pte., k. in a., F. & F., 23-4-17.

BIRD Reginald Robert James, *b* Wrentham, Suffolk, *e* Lowestoft, Suffolk (Wrentham), 50935, Pte., k. in a., F. & F., 31-7-17, formerly G/86504 Middlesex R.

BIRDSALL Ernest, *b* Lr. Broughton, Manchester, *e* Manchester, 10345, Pte., k. in a., F. & F., 1-7-16.

BISHOP William, *b* Manchester, *e* Manchester, 36005, Pte., k. in a., F. & F., 23-4-17.

BLAIR John Robert, *b* Manchester, *e* Manchester (C.-on-M., Manchester), 26338, Pte., d. of w., F. & F., 14-11-16.

BLEASE John Douglas, *b* Stockport, Cheshire, *e* Manchester (Stockport), 10081, Sgt., k. in a., F. & F., 9-7-16.

BLISS Frederick John, *b* Mardford, near Towcester, Northants., *e* Eastbourne, Sussex, 41735, Pte., k. in a., F. & F., 12-4-17, formerly 12480 R. Sussex R.

BOLDSTRIDGE Henry, *b* Liverpool, *e* Manchester, 7591, Pte., k. in a., F. & F., 23-4-17.

BOOKER James, *b* Salford, Lancs., *e* Manchester, 44129, Pte., k. in a., F. & F., 12-10-16.

BOOTH Albert, *b* West Derby, Liverpool *e* Manchester, 11007, Pte., k. in a., F. & F., 30-7-16.

BOOTH Archie, *b* Derby, *e* Manchester, 10528, L/Cpl., k. in a., F. & F., 30-7-16.

BOOTH Samuel Dutton, *b* Hulme, Manchester, *e* Manchester, 10764, Pte., k. in a., F. & F., 30-7-16.

BOOTHAM Samuel, *b* Moss Side, Manchester, *e* Manchester, 9966, Pte., d. of w., F. & F., 13-6-17.

BORLAND Frederick John, *b* Manchester, *e* Manchester, 27851, L/Cpl., d. of w., F. & F., 27-3-17.

BOSTOCK Charles Thomas, *b* Birkenhead, Cheshire, *e* Birkenhead, 40495, Pte., k. in a., F. & F., 31-7-17, formerly 2015 Cheshire Yeo.

BOSWORTH Thomas, *b* Northampton, *e* Northampton, 50997, Pte., k. in a., F. & F., 26-7-17, formerly G/86549 Middlesex R.

BOWLES Harry, *b* Mildenhall, Suffolk, *e* Manchester (Salford, Lancs.), 10762, Pte., d., F. & F., 24-3-16.

BOYD Walter, *b* Harpurhey, Manchester, *e* Manchester, 27057, Pte., k. in a., F. & F., 1-7-16.

BRADSHAW Colin, *b* Withington, Manchester, *e* Manchester (Chorlton-cum-Hardy, Lancs.), 10527, Pte., d. of w., F. & F., 4-7-16.

BRANSTON Henry, *b* Bolton, Lancs., *e* Manchester, 10007, Sgt., k. in a., F. & F., 1-7-16.

BRANT Robinson, *b* Failsworth, Lancs., *e* Manchester (Skendleby, near Spilsby, Lincs.), 9824, A/Sgt., k. in a., F. & F., 30-7-16.

BRAY George Llewellyn, *b* Newtown, Montgomery, *e* Manchester (Newtown), 31311, A/Cpl., k. in a., F. & F., 23-4-17.

BREWER James, *b* Manchester, *e* Manchester, 7526, Pte., k. in a., F. & F., 9-7-16.

BRIDGE Herbert Walter, *b* Ardwick, Manchester, *e* Manchester, 11081, Pte., k. in a., F. & F., 27-2-16.

BRIERLEY Frederick, *b* Manchester, *e* Manchester (Chorlton-cum-Hardy, Lancs.), 31427, Pte., k. in a., F. & F., 13-5-16.

BRITTEN John Henry, *b* Salford, Lancs., *e* Manchester, 11758, L/Sgt., d. of w., F. & F., 15-12-17.

BROADHURST Harold, *b* Ardwick, Manchester, *e* Manchester (Ardwick), 1828, Pte., k. in a., F. & F., 14-12-17, formerly 30188 Linc. R.

BROCKBANK Thomas, *b* Salford, Lancs., *e* Manchester (Salford), 12577, Pte., k. in a., F. & F., 31-7-17, formerly 30330 Linc. R.

BROCKLEHURST Arthur James, *b* Salford, Lancs., *e* Manchester, 11295, Pte., k. in a., F. & F., 30-7-17.

BROMLEY Albert, *b* Oldham, Lancs., *e* Hollinwood, Lancs. (Oldham), 28465, Pte., k. in a., F. & F., 31-7-17.

BROOKE Arthur James Balfour, *b* St. Margaret's, Moss Side, Manchester, *e* Manchester, 10272, Sgt., k. in a., F. & F., 1-7-16, **D.C.M.**

BROOKE Conrad Ernest, *b* St. Peter's, Southport, Lancs., *e* Manchester (Birkdale, Lancs.), 10612, L/Cpl., k. in a., F. & F., 1-7-16, **D.C.M.**

BROWN Albert Edward, *b* Newton Heath, Manchester, *e* Manchester, 9809, Pte., k. in a., F. & F., 9-7-16.

BROWN Charles, *b* Manchester, *e* Manchester, 31271, L/Cpl., k. in a., F. & F., 9-7-16.

BROWN Claud Basil, *b* Hull, Yorks., *e* Manchester (Liverpool), 11142, Pte., k. in a., F. & F., 9-7-16.

BROWN Edward, *b* Birkenhead, Cheshire, *e* Birkenhead, 352381, Pte., d., F. & F., 6-1-18.

BROWN Frederick, *b* Longsight, Manchester, *e* Manchester, 9825, Pte., k. in a., F. & F., 9-7-16.

BROWN Henry Lewis, *b* Manchester, *e* Manchester, 11039, Pte., d. of w., F. & F., 10-7-16.

BROWN Robert Gordon, *b* Manchester, *e* Manchester, 27357, Pte., k. in a., F. & F., 1-7-16.

BROWNE Bernard, *b* Manchester, *e* Manchester (Salford, Lancs.), 11005, Pte., k. in a., F. & F., 11-1-16.

BULL Harold, *b* Willington, Derby, *e* Manchester, 48690, Pte. d. of w., F. & F., 29-7-17, formerly 51215 R. W. Fus.

BULLOCK Christopher, *b* Burnley, Lancs., 47842, Pte., k. in a., F. & F., 23-4-17.

BURNS Thomas, *b* Manchester, *e* Manchester, 44140, Pte., k. in a., F. & F., 23-4-17.

BURROWS Frank, *b* Stockport, Cheshire, *e* Manchester, 27139, Pte., k. in a., F. & F., 9-7-16.

BURTON Charles, *b* Ardwick, Manchester, *e* Manchester, 10323, Pte., k. in a., F. & F., 8-7-16.

BUTLER John Jenkinson, *b* Bradford, Lancs., *e* Manchester, 23432, Pte., k. in a., F. & F., 14-12-17.

BUTLER Walter, *b* Altrincham, Cheshire, *e* Manchester (Hale, Cheshire), 10342, Pte., d. of w., F. & F., 18-3-16.

BYE Alfred Charles, *b* Hornsey, Middlesex, *e* Wood Green, Middlesex (Hornsey), 51000, Pte., d. of w., F. & F. 4-8-17, formerly G/19265 Middlesex R.

BYRNE Andrew, *b* West Gorton, Manchester, *e* Manchester, 43962, Pte., k. in a., F. & F., 25-4-17.

CALLOWAY Henry Robert, *b* Cheetham, Manchester, *e* Manchester, 9222, L/Cpl., d. of w., F. & F., 14-12-16.

CALVERT Thomas Albert, *b* Ardwick, Manchester, *e* Manchester, 10372, Pte., k. in a., F. & F., 9-7-16.

CARDOE Thomas Harold, *b* Stourbridge, Staffs., *e* Warrington, 61216, Pte., k. in a., F. & F., 14-12-17.

CARESWELL George Wilfred, *b* Manchester, *e* Manchester, 31360, Pte., k. in a., F. & F., 9-7-16.

CARR Richard, *b* St. Paul's, Salford, Lancs., *e* Manchester, 9832, Pte., d. of w., F. & F., 6-3-16.

CARRUTHERS George Alfred, *b* St. John's, Salford, Lancs., *e* Manchester (Salford), 10591, L/Cpl., k. in a., F. & F., 9-7-16.

CARRUTHERS William, *b* Manchester, *e* Manchester, 32533, Pte., k. in a., F. & F., 30-7-16.

CARTER — Charles Edward, *b* Bethnal Green, Middlesex, *e* Stepney, Middlesex (Shadwell, Middlesex), 43702, Pte., k. in a., F. & F., 23-4-17, formerly G/21650 Middlesex R.

CARTER — Frank, *b* Ashton-u-Lyne, Lancs., *e* Manchester, 11131, Pte., k. in a., F. & F., 1-7-16.

CARTRIDGE — John Edgar, *b* Levenshulme, Manchester, *e* Manchester, 44078, Pte., k. in a., F. & F., 31-7-17.

CARTWRIGHT — John, *b* St. Helens, Lancs., *e* St. Helens, 61206, Pte., k. in a., F. & F., 14-12-17.

CATON — Thomas, *b* Ardwick, Manchester, *e* Manchester, 44013, L/Cpl., k. in a., F. & F., 14-10-16.

CATTERALL — George, *e* Wigan, Lancs., (Newtown, Wigan), 43865, L/Cpl., k. in a., F. & F., 23-4-17.

CHAMBERS — Charles, *e* Louth, Lincs. (Mablethorpe, Lincs.), 42223, Pte., k. in a., F. & F., 30-7-17, formerly T4/161056 R.A.S.C.

CHAPMAN — Samuel, *b* Seedley, Manchester, *e* Manchester (Salford, Lancs.), 9972, Pte., k. in a., F. & F., 30-7-16.

CHEASE — William Edward, *b* Plymouth, *e* Manchester (Mutley, Devon.), 10967, Pte., k. in a., F. & F., 30-7-16.

CHORLTON — Colin, *b* Stockport, *e* Manchester (Heaton Mersey, Lancs.), 10097, Pte., d., Home, 29-4-15.

CLIFFORD — Arthur, *b* Huddersfield, Yorks., *e* Salford, Lancs. (Huddersfield), 32526, Pte., k. in a., F. & F., 30-7-16.

COATS — Thomas, *b* Penicuik, Midlothian, *e* Ashton-u-Lyne, Lancs. (Oldham, Lancs.), 48009, Pte., d. of w., F. & F., 29-4-17.

COGHLAN — James Leo, *b* St. Mary's, Manchester, *e* Manchester (Eccles, Lancs.), 9829, Pte., k. in a., F. & F., 30-7-16.

COLDWELL — Frank, *e* Wigan, Lancs. (Manchester), 43805, Pte., k. in a., F. & F., 12-10-16.

COLES — Ernest Victor, *b* Finedon, Northants., *e* Northampton (Finedon), 41774, Pte., k. in a., F. & F., 23-4-17, formerly 11762 R. Sussex R.

COLLINS — Frederick George, *b* Liverpool, *e* Liverpool, 60670, C.S.M., d. of w., F. & F., 23-5-18, formerly 4042 N. Lancashire R.

COLLINS — Lewis Arthur, *b* Hastings, Sussex, *e* Hastings (Ore, Sussex), 41696, Pte., d. of w., F. & F., 13-4-17, formerly 12845 R. Sussex R.

CONNOLLY — William, *b* Liverpool, *e* Manchester, 10365, Pte., k. in a., F. & F., 1-7-16, formerly 9167 A. Cyclist Corps.

COOKSON — Henry, *b* Harpurhey, Manchester, *e* Manchester, 10096, L/Cpl., k. in a., F. & F., 9-7-16.

COOMBER — Arthur, *b* Cowden, Sussex, *e* Eastbourne (Withyham, Sussex), 50939, Pte., k. in a., F. & F., 29-7-17, formerly 86507 Middlesex R.

COOPER — Ernest, *b* Gorton, Manchester, *e* Manchester, 10240, Pte., k. in a., F. & F., 27-2-16.

COOPER — Thomas, *b* Bradford, Lancs., *e* Manchester, 26346, Pte. k. in a., F. & F., 30-7-16.

COPE — Charles William, *b* Pendleton, Manchester, *e* Manchester (Salford, Lancs.), 10374, Pte., k. in a., F. & F., 30-7-16.

CORKER — Frank, *b* Hulme, Manchester, *e* Manchester, 10920, Pte., k. in a., F. & F., 9-7-16.

CORNALL — William Coulborn, *b* Old Trafford, Manchester, *e* Manchester, 10628, Pte., d. of w., Home, 5-8-16.

COSGROVE — Thomas Joseph, *b* Collyhurst, Manchester, *e* Manchester, 10101, Pte., k. in a., F. & F., 12-10-16.

COULTHARD Frederick David, *b* Liverpool, *e* Liverpool, 61208, Pte., k. in a., F. & F., 14-12-17.

COURT William, *b* Manchester, *e* Manchester, 34491, A/Cpl., d. of w., F. & F., 27-4-17.

COWLEY Fred, *b* Rusholme, Manchester, *e* Manchester, 10805, Pte., k. in a., F. & F., 12-10-16.

CRANSHAW John, *b* Widnes, Lancs., *e* Manchester, 44061, Pte., k. in a., F. & F., 12-10-16.

CROKER Arthur, *b* St. George's, Pendleton, Lancs., *e* Manchester (Pendleton), 10650, Pte., k. in a., F. & F., 1-7-16.

CROOK George, *b* Radcliffe, Lancs., *e* Manchester (Radcliffe), 11177, Pte., k. in a., F. & F., 1-7-16.

CROOP Maurice, *b* Manchester, *e* Manchester, 34134, Pte., d. of w., F. & F., 30-7-17.

CROSSLEY James Leslie, *b* Rawtenstall, Lancs., *e* Rawtenstall, 61213, Pte., k. in a., F. & F., 14-12-17.

CUBITT Laurence, *b* Brandon, Suffolk, *e* Wisbeck, Norfolk (Walsoken, Wisbeck), 43680, Pte., k. in a., F. & F., 12-10-16, formerly 23276 Suffolk R.

CUMMINGS William Eric, *b* Droylsden, Lancs., *e* Manchester (Broadbottom, Cheshire), 26367, Pte., d. of w., Home, 13-7-16.

CUNNINGHAM Thomas, *b* Ennis, Co. Clare., *e* Manchester, 47847, Pte., k. in a., F. & F., 22-3-17.

CURRY Joseph, *b* Bradford, Lancs., *e* Manchester, 10102, L/Sgt., d. of w., Home, 20-5-16.

DALE James, *b* Manchester, *e* Manchester, 26448, Pte., d. of w., Home, 22-7-16.

DALEY Patrick, *b* West Ham, Middlesex, *e* Manchester, 10108, Pte., k. in a., F. & F., 30-7-16.

DALEY William, *b* Ancoats, Manchester, *e* Manchester, 26452, Pte., d. of w., F. & F., 1-8-17.

DANIEL Joseph, *b* Manchester, *e* Salford, Lancs., 11253, Pte., k. in a., F. & F., 12-5-16, formerly 10868 Lancashire F.

DARBYSHIRE Edward, *b* St. Paul's, Manchester, *e* Manchester, 10482, Sgt., k. in a., F. & F., 9-7-16.

DARWEN William, *b* Hindley Green, Lancs., *e* Ashton-u-Lyne (Hindley Green), Pte., 203409, k. in a., F. & F., 16-9-17.

DAUNCEY George, *b* Bristol, *e* Manchester, 10768, Pte., k. in a., F. & F., 1-7-16.

DAVIES Albert, *b* Harpurhey, Manchester, *e* Manchester, 9837, Pte., k. in a., F. & F., 14-1-16.

DAVIES Alfred, *b* Beswick, Manchester, *e* Manchester, 10533, Pte., k. in a., F. & F., 9-7-16.

DAVIES Arthur, *b* Salford, *e* Manchester, 10105, Pte., k. in a., F. & F., 4-2-16.

DAVIES Reginald, *b* Rhuddlan, Flint., *e* Manchester (Rhuddlan), 10486, Pte., k. in a., F. & F., 12-1-16.

DAVIES Thomas, *b* Manchester, *e* Manchester, 33467, Pte., k. in a., F. & F., 30-7-16.

DAVIES Walter, *b* Alderley Edge, Cheshire, *e* Wilmslow, Cheshire (Manchester), 24863, Pte., k. in a., F. & F., 14-12-17, formerly 30386 Linc. R.

DAVIES William Bourne, *b* Ladybarn, Manchester, *e* Manchester, 10377, Sgt., d. of w., F. & F., 20-8-16.

DAVIS Bert, *b* Newport, Mon., *e* Manchester (Newport), 31351, Pte., k. in a., F. & F., 9-7-16.

DAWES Allen, *b* Bardsley, Lancs., *e* Ashton-u-Lyne, Lancs., 47850, Pte., k. in a., F. & F., 23-4-17.

DAWSON John, *b* Millom, Cumberland, *e* Lancaster (Millom), 61219, Pte., k. in a., F. & F., 14-12-17.

DAWSON Joseph, *b* Heaton Park, Manchester, *e* Manchester (Prestwich, Lancs.), 10015, Pte., k. in a., F. & F., 1-7-16.

DAY Archie, *b* Manchester, *e* Manchester, 11277, Pte., k. in a., F. & F., 30-7-16.

DEAKIN Robert, *b* Pendleton, Lancs., *e* Manchester (Salford, Lancs.), 10376, L/Cpl., k. in a., F. & F., 12-5-16.

DEAKIN Vernon John, *b* Pendleton, Lancs., *e* Manchester (Worsley, Lancs.), 9838, A/Cpl., k. in a., F & F., 30-7-16.

DEAN James, *b* Ardwick, Manchester, *e* Manchester, 44021, Pte., d. of w., F. & F., 18-11-16.

DELAHOY George James, *b* Doncaster, Yorks., *e* Doncaster, 42231, Pte., k. in a., F. & F., 31-7-17, formerly T4/185147 R.A.S.C.

DELANEY Fred, *b* Oldham, Lancs., *e* Oldham, 27291, Pte., k. in a., F. & F., 30-7-16.

DELANEY Robert John, *b* St. Cullen, Dublin, *e* Manchester (Hulme, Manchester), 10858, L/Cpl., k. in a., F. & F., 6-9-16.

DENNETT James, *e* Wigan, Lancs., 43904, Pte., k. in a., F. & F., 12-10-16.

DENNISON Samuel, *b* St. Annes, Antrim, *e* Belfast, 42234, Pte., k. in a., F. & F. 14-12-17, formerly T4/174362 R.A.S.C.

DENTON Benjamin, *b* St. Helens, Lancs., *e* Manchester, 9844, Pte., k. in a., F. & F., 30-7-16.

DEVENPORT John, *e* Wigan, Lancs. (Patricroft, Lancs.), 43889, Pte., k. in a., F. & F., 23-4-17.

DEVLIN James, *b* Manchester, *e* Manchester, 48012, Pte., k. in a., F. & F., 23-4-17.

DICKENS George Charles, *e* Staines, Middlesex (Teddington, Middlesex), 50941, Pte., d. of w., F. & F., 31-7-17, formerly G/27135 Middlesex R.

DILEY Alexander, *b* Manchester, *e* Manchester, 26251, Pte., k. in a., F. & F., 12-10-16.

DOHERTY Thomas, *b* Wigan, Lancs., *e* Wigan, 203354, Pte., k. in a., F. & F., 31-7-17.

DOLAN William, *b* Manchester, *e* Manchester, 33460, Pte., k. in a., F. & F., 30-7-16.

DOMNEY William, *b* Hulme, Manchester, *e* Manchester, 9840, Pte., k. in a., F. & F., 30-7-16.

DONALDSON James, *b* Edinburgh, *e* Manchester (Altrincham, Cheshire), 11001, A/Sgt., k. in a., F. & F., 30-7-16.

DOOGUE Thomas, *b* St. Mary's, Failsworth, Lancs., *e* Oldham, Lancs. (Failsworth), 203371, Pte., k. in a., F. & F., 31-7-17.

DOOTSON Reginald, *b* St. John's, Cheetham, Manchester, *e* Manchester (Gorton, Manchester), 10106, C.S.M., k. in a., F. & F., 30-7-16.

DOYLE John, *b* Hulme, Manchester, *e* Manchester, 10110, L/Cpl., d. of w., F. & F., 10-7-16.

DRURY Hugh, *b* Pendleton, Lancs., *e* Bolton, Lancs. (Liverpool), 43663, Pte., k. in a., F. & F., 23-4-17, formerly 8769 Lancashire Fus.

DUCKWORTH Frank, *b* Warrington, Lancs., *e* Manchester, 25535, Sgt., k. in a., F. & F., 14-12-17.

DUNN Arthur Charles, *b* St. Peter's, Levenshulme, Manchester, *e* Manchester, 10103, Sgt., k. in a., F. & F., 30-7-16.

DUNN Richard, *b* Salford, Lancs., *e* Salford, 29342, Pte., k. in a., F. & F., 23-4-17.

DYAS Joseph, *b* Market Drayton, Shrop., *e* Manchester (Market Drayton), 44144, L/Cpl., d. of w., F. & F., 7-1-17.

DYSON John, *b* Colne, Lancs., *e* Manchester, 9973, Cpl., k. in a., F. & F., 30-7-16.

EASTWOOD William Patchett, *b* Manchester, *e* Manchester, 10955, Pte., k. in a., F. & F., 9-7-16.

EATON Harold, *b* Manchester, *e* Manchester, 34096, Pte., k. in a., F. & F., 30-7-16.

EATOUGH Gilbert, *b* Manchester, *e* Manchester, 31448, Pte., k. in a., F. & F., 30-7-16.

EDGE Edwin, *e* Atherton, Lancs., 43762, Pte., k. in a., F. & F., 23-4-17.

EDMONDSON Bruce Gladstone, *b* Collyhurst, Manchester, *e* Manchester, 9845, Pte., k. in a., F. & F., 30-7-16.

EDWARDS Edward, *b* Liverpool, *e* Manchester, 47853, Pte., d. of w., F. & F., 3-5-17.

EGAN Francis, *b* Salford, Lancs., *e* Manchester (Pendleton, Lancs.), 10016, Sgt., k. in a., F. & F., 30-7-16.

ELIFFE Harry, *b* St. James', Ashton-u-Lyne, Lancs., *e* Manchester (Heywood, Lancs.), 10862, L/Cpl., k. in a., F. & F., 30-7-16.

ELLET Charles, *b* West Hoathly, Sussex, *e* Brighton, 41739, Pte., k. in a., F. & F., 30-7-17, formerly 12465 R. Sussex R.

ELLIS Andrew Moir, *b* Leith, *e* Edinburgh, 42236, Pte., k. in a., F. & F., 14-12-17, formerly T4/174497 R.A.S.C.

ELLIS William, *e* Newcastle-on-Tyne (Hessle, Yorks.), 42084, Pte., k. in a., F. & F., 31-7-17, formerly 165294 R.F.A.

ELLISON Albert, *b* Bradford, Manchester, *e* Manchester, 10386, Pte., k. in a., F. & F., 1-7-16.

EMRICK Ernest, *b* All Saints', Blackpool, Lancs., *e* Manchester (Manchester), 43994, Pte., k. in a., F. & F., 23-4-17.

ENTWISTLE Gilbert, *b* Bolton, Lancs., *e* Manchester (Manchester), 49836, Pte., k. in a., F. & F., 30-7-17.

ENTWISTLE James Alfred, *b* Hulme, Manchester, *e* Manchester, 35522, Pte., k. in a., F. & F., 23-4-17.

FARLEY Frank Victor, *b* Enfield, Middlesex, *e* Edmonton, Middlesex (Ponders End, Middlesex), 50947, Pte., k. in a., F. & F., 31-7-17, formerly G/19282 Middlesex R.

FARNWORTH Fred, *e* Atherton, Lancs. (Hindsford, near Atherton), 43818, Pte., d. of w., F. & F., 20-10-16.

FARNWORTH Tom, *b* Manchester, *e* Manchester, 44158, Pte., d. of w., F. & F., 13-10-16.

FAULKNER Edward, *b* Manchester, *e* Manchester, 44186, Pte., k. in a., F. & F., 23-4-17.

FAUX Frederick, *b* Hulme, Manchester, *e* Manchester, 4248, Pte., k. in a., F. & F., 30-7-16.

FEARN Ethelbert, *b* Mexborough, Yorks., *e* Manchester, 44073, L/Cpl., d. of w., F. & F., 15-11-16.

FEHRS Henry Campbell, *b* Liverpool, *e* Bridgend, Glam. (Pontycymmer, Glam.), 61232, Pte., k. in a., F. & F., 14-12-17.

FIDDES Richard, *b* Ardwick, Manchester, *e* Manchester, 10487, Pte., k. in a., F. & F., 23-4-17, formerly 9166 A. Cyclist Corps.

FIRMAN — William, *e* Birmingham, 42237, Pte., k. in a., F. & F., 14-12-17, formerly T4/128597 R.A.S.C.

FITZPATRICK — Joseph, *b* Salford, Lancs., *e* Manchester (Salford), 10537 Sgt., k. in a., F. & F., 30-7-16.

FORD — Peter, *b* Manchester, *e* Manchester, 31281, Pte., k. in a., F. & F., 12-5-16.

FOSTER — Edgar, *b* Sale, Cheshire, *e* Manchester, 11028, Pte., k. in a., F. & F., 9-7-16.

FOWLER — Henry Chappell, *b* Salford, Lancs., *e* Manchester (Salford), 11082, Pte., k. in a., F. & F., 1-7-16.

FOX — Louis, *b* Northwich, Cheshire, *e* Manchester, 11129, Pte., k. in a., F. & F., 9-7-16.

FRANKISH — John Anderson, *b* Frodsham, Cheshire, *e* Manchester, 10115, L/Cpl., d. of w., F. & F., 2-7-16.

FRENCH — Alfred, *b* St. Helens, Lancs., *e* Manchester (St. Helens), 35116, Pte., k. in a., F. & F., 23-4-17.

FRITH — John, *b* St. Jerome's, Manchester, *e* Manchester, 6573, L/Cpl., k. in a., F. & F., 1-8-17.

FROST — William, *b* Ardwick, Manchester, *e* Manchester, 44026, Pte., k. in a., F. & F., 12-10-16.

GAMBLE — William Henry, *b* Newbridge, Kildare, *e* Manchester (Salford, Lancs.), 10489, Pte., d., F. & F., 13-7-18.

GARGAN — Francis Joseph, *b* Salford, Lancs., *e* Manchester (Salford), 10817, L/Cpl., k. in a., F. & F., 30-7-16.

GARNER — Archibald, *b* Pendleton, Lancs., *e* Manchester (Pendleton), 44103, Pte., k. in a., F. & F., 12-10-16.

GARRY — John, *b* Ancoats, Manchester, *e* Manchester, 44069, Pte., k. in a., F. & F., 12-10-16.

GASKELL — John, *e* Wigan, Lancs. (Newtown, Wigan), 43857, Pte., k. in a., F. & F., 12-10-16.

GATE — Charles, *b* Ardwick, Manchester, *e* Manchester, 44083, Pte., k. in a., F. & F., 31-7-17.

GEORGE — Dennis, *b* Collyhurst, Manchester, *e* Manchester, 10538, Pte., k. in a., F. & F., 13-2-16.

GERRARD — Edward, *b* Northwich, Cheshire, *e* Manchester (Northwich), 31384, Pte., k. in a., F. & F., 1-8-17.

GEST — Alfred, *e* Chatham, Kent, 42240, Pte., k. in a., F. & F., 31-7-17, formerly 276917 R.A.S.C.

GIDMAN — Joseph, *b* Knutsford, Cheshire, *e* Manchester, 31382, Pte., k. in a., F. & F., 30-7-16.

GILL — Clarence William, *b* Hightown, Manchester, *e* Manchester, 10122, Sgt., k. in a., F. & F., 7-3-16.

GODDARD — John, *b* Ardwick, Manchester, *e* Manchester, 10128, Pte., k. in a., F. & F., 7-3-16.

GOODWIN — Arthur, *b* Openshaw, Manchester, *e* Manchester, 44041, Pte., k. in a., F. & F., 23-4-17.

GORTON — John, *b* Heaton Mersey, Manchester, *e* Manchester, 10816, Pte., k. in a., F. & F., 9-7-16.

GOUGH — John, *b* Manchester, *e* Manchester, 10586, L/Cpl., k. in a., F. & F., 30-7-16.

GOULD — Fred Lewty, *b* Harpurhey, Manchester, *e* Manchester (Edgeley, Cheshire), 10396, Pte., d. of w., F. & F., 4-7-16.

GRANGE — Harold, *b* Miles Platting, Manchester, *e* Manchester (Irlams-o'th'-Height, Lancs.), 10985, Pte., k. in a., F. & F., 4-2-16.

GRATRIX — Frederick, *b* Davyhulme, Lancs., *e* Manchester (Flixton, Lancs), 9851, Pte., k. in a., F. & F., 13-5-16.

GREEN Edward, *b* Manchester, *e* Oswestry, Shrops. (Blackpool, Lancs.), 42239, Pte., k. in a., F. & F., 31-7-17, formerly T4/197557 R.A.S.C.

GREEN James, *b* Hulme, Manchester *e* Manchester, 47857, Pte., k. in a., F. & F., 23-4-17.

GREEN William, *b* Leigh, Lancs., *e* Manchester, (Hollinwood, Lancs.), 9850, Pte., k. in a., F. & F., 9-7-16.

GREENALL Edwin, *b* Manchester, *e* Manchester, 9849, L/Cpl., k. in a., F. & F., 1-7-16.

GREENHALGH John, *b* Oldham, Lancs., *e* Lees, Oldham, 27231, Pte., k. in a., F. & F., 30-7-16.

GREENHALGH William Arthur, *b* Prestwich, Lancs., *e* Manchester, 10022, Pte., k. in a., F. & F., 1-7-16.

GREENWOOD James, *b* Royton, Lancs., *e* Royton, 32941, Pte., d. of w., F. & F., 25-4-17.

GRICE John, *b* Manchester, *e* Manchester, 31273, Pte., k. in a., F. & F., 12-5-16.

GRICE Wilfred B., *b* Leeds, *e* Denton, Lancs., 352178, Pte., k. in a., F. & F., 23-4-17.

GRIFFIN Vincent, *b* Collyhurst, Manchester, *e* Manchester, 10813, Pte., k. in a., F. & F., 30-7-16.

GRIFFIS Alfred, *b* Ardwick, Manchester, *e* Manchester (Sale, Cheshire), 10646, A/Sgt., k. in a., F. & F., 30-7-16.

GROVER Francis Sidney, *b* Bermondsey, Surrey, *e* Manchester, 26478, Pte., k. in a., F. & F., 1-7-16.

GRUNDY Thomas, *e* Atherton, Lancs. (Tyldesley, Lancs.), 43814, Pte., d. of w., Home, 27-11-16.

HAFT Israel, *b* Liverpool, *e* Manchester, 47879, Pte., k. in a., F. & F., 23-4-17.

HALL Charles, *b* Hulme, Manchester, *e* Manchester, 10546, Pte., k. in a., F. & F., 12-5-16.

HALL Ralph, *e* Atherton, Lancs., 43778, Pte., k. in a., F. & F., 23-4-17.

HALL William, *b* Atherton, Lancs., *e* Wigan, Lancs. (Atherton), 47877, Pte., k. in a., F. & F., 27-7-17.

HAMMOND Arthur Frederick, *b* Ardwick, Manchester, *e* Manchester, 10779, L/Cpl., k. in a., F. & F., 1-7-16.

HAMNETT Arthur, *b* Manchester, *e* Manchester, 44145, Pte., k. in a., F. & F., 12-10-16.

HAMPSON Frederick, *b* Aden, Africa, *e* Manchester, 18597, Pte., k. in a., F. & F., 31-7-17.

HAMPSON John William, *e* Manchester, 47858, Pte., k. in a., F. & F., 23-4-17.

HAMPTON Harold, *b* Pendlebury, Lancs., *e* Manchester (Pendlebury), 9860, Pte., k. in a., F. & F., 13-5-16.

HANVEY David, *b* Collyhurst, Manchester, *e* Manchester, 11023, Pte., d. of w., F. & F., 12-2-16.

HARRINGTON James, *b* Bradford, Manchester, *e* Manchester, 10547, Pte., k. in a., F. & F., 12-1-16.

HARRISON Lewis, *b* Burnley, Lancs., *e* Burnley, 61241, Pte., k. in a., F. & F., 14-12-17.

HARRISON Cyril John Norman, *b* Countesthorpe, Leicester, *e* Leicester, 41591, Pte., d. of w., F. & F., 13-6-17, formerly, 26028, Lancashire Fus.

HART Charles William, *e* Newcastle-on-Tyne (Bilston, Staffs.), 42083, Pte., k. in a., F. & F., 31-7-17, formerly 165977 R.F.A.

HARWOOD Joseph William, *b* Odiham, Hants., *e* Manchester, 9861, A/Cpl., k. in a., F. & F., 30-7-16.

HASLAM Samuel, *b* Pendleton, Lancs., *e* Salford, Lancs. (Pendleton), 47867, Pte., k. in a., F. & F., 29-7-17.

HASSETT Peter, *b* Salford, Lancs., *e* Manchester, 9117, Pte., k. in a., F. & F., 23-4-17.

HATFIELD Thomas Arthur, *b* West Ham, Essex, *e* Manchester, 11128, Pte., d. of w., F. & F. 20-1-16.

HAYES George William, *b* Openshaw, Manchester, *e* Manchester, 10490, Cpl., k. in a., F. & F., 30-7-16.

HEANEY George William, *b* Ardwick, Manchester, *e* Manchester, 43924, Pte., k. in a., F. & F., 23-4-17.

HEATH George, *b* St. Simon's, Salford, Lancs., *e* Manchester, 10140, Pte., k. in a., F. & F., 9-7-16.

HEGGS George, *b* Gorton, Lancs., *e* Manchester, 203067, Pte., d. of w., F. & F., 13-8-17.

HENSTOCK Frank, *b* Hulme, Manchester, *e* Manchester, 48014, Pte., k. in a., F. & F., 23-4-17.

HEWITT William Henry, *b* St. Thomas', Hyde, Cheshire, *e* Manchester (Hyde), 9866, Pte., k. in a., F. & F., 30-7-16.

HEWLETT Cyril George, *b* Ballydunnagan, Co. Cork, *e* Oldham, Lancs., 29170, Pte., k. in a., F. & F., 23-4-17.

HEYWOOD Frank, *b* Oldham, Lancs., *e* Oldham, 35835, Pte., k. in a., F. & F., 23-4-17.

HICKES William Henry, *b* Salford, Lancs., *e* Manchester (Salford), 10136, Pte., d. of w., Home, 31-7-16.

HICKS Dennis Middleton, *b* Gatley, Cheshire, *e* Manchester (Chorlton-cum-Hardy, Lancs.), 10407, Pte., k. in a., F. & F., 31-7-17.

HICKS William, *b* St. Thomas', Pendleton, Lancs., *e* Manchester, 10775, Pte., d. of w., Home, 19-7-16.

HIGGINBOTTOM Robert Kirkby, *b* Manchester, *e* Manchester, 44149, L/Cpl., k. in a., F. & F., 12-10-16.

HIGGS George Henry, *b* Weaste, Manchester, *e* Manchester (Weaste), 10131, Pte., k. in a., F. & F., 9-7-16.

HIGSON William, *e* Wigan, Lancs. (Atherton, Lancs.), 43866, Pte., k. in a., F. & F., 12-10-16.

HILL John Richard, *b* Oldham, Lancs., *e* Oldham, 377063, Pte., k. in a., F. & F., 23-4-17.

HILTON Jack, *b* Manchester, *e* Manchester, 11013, L/Cpl., k. in a., F. & F., 30-7-16.

HILTON James, *b* Kirkham, Lancs., *e* Wigan, Lancs. (Daubhill, Bolton, Lancs.), 43836, Pte., k. in a., F. & F., 12-10-16.

HINCHLEY Harry, *b* Manchester, *e* Manchester, 27328, Pte., k. in a., F. & F., 30-7-16.

HINDLEY Robert, *b* Manchester, *e* Manchester, 31412, Pte., k. in a., F. & F., 9-7-16.

HOBBS Harry, *b* St. James', Oldham, Lancs., *e* Oldham, 28210, Pte., k. in a., F. & F., 23-4-17.

HODGKINSON Fred, *b* Leigh, Lancs., *e* Wigan, Lancs. (Leigh), 43879, L/Cpl., k. in a., F. & F., 1-8-17.

HODSON James, *b* Pennington, Leigh, Lancs., *e* Atherton, Lancs. (West Leigh, Lancs.), 43734, Pte., k. in a., F. & F., 12-10-16.

HOLLAND Harold, *b* Wigan, Lancs., *e* Wigan, 203379, Pte., k. in a., F. & F., 31-7-17.

HOLLINGSWORTH, Arthur, *b* Northwich, Cheshire, *e* Atherton, Lancs., 43731, Pte., k. in a., F. & F., 12-4-17.

HOLLINGWORTH Wilfred, *e* Oldham, Lancs., 41463, Pte., k. in a., F. & F., 31-7-17.

HOLMES Charles Edward, *b* Manchester, *e* Manchester (Dukinfield, Cheshire), 47866, Pte., k. in a., F. & F., 23-4-17.

HOLMES George William, *b* Longton, Staffs., *e* Manchester (Chorlton-cum-Hardy, Lancs.), 31435, Pte., k. in a., F. & F., 30-7-16.

HOLT George William, *b* St. John's, Altrincham, Cheshire, *e* Manchester (Hale, Cheshire), 10398, Sgt., d. of w., F. & F., 3-7-16.

HOLT Herbert, *b* Brantford, Ontario, Canada, *e* Manchester (Ashton-u-Lyne, Lancs.), 10402, Pte., k. in a., F. & F., 8-3-16.

HOLT James, *b* Carrington, Manchester, *e* Manchester, 10027, Pte., d., F. & F., 20-4-16.

HOLT John Percy, *b* Dunham Massey, Cheshire, *e* Manchester (Dunham Massey), 10650, Sgt., d. of w., F. & F., 3-7-16.

HOOSON Edward, *b* Flint, North Wales, *e* Manchester, 44161, Pte., k. in a., F. & F., 12-10-16.

HORNBY Fred, *b* Oldham, Lancs., *e* Hollinwood, Lancs. (Oldham), 27299, Pte., k. in a., F. & F., 1-7-16.

HORNER Harry, *b* St. Andrew's, Salford, Lancs., *e* Manchester, 9978, Pte., k. in a., F. & F., 13-5-16.

HORROCKS John William, *b* Leigh, Lancs., *e* Atherton, Lancs. (Leigh), 43842, Sgt., k. in a., F. & F., 12-10-16.

HOUGHTON James Henry, *b* Queenstown, Co. Cork., *e* Manchester, 40062, Pte., k. in a., F. & F., 12-10-16.

HOWARD Harry, *b* Ardwick, Manchester, *e* Manchester, 10409, Pte., k. in a., F. & F., 1-7-16.

HOWARD William, *b* Ashton-u-Lyne, Lancs., *e* Manchester, 11266, Pte., k. in a., F. & F., 9-7-16.

HOWARTH Arthur, *b* St. Michael's, Hulme, Manchester, *e* Manchester, 10492, L/Cpl., k. in a., F. & F., 12-5-16.

HOWARTH Edward, *b* Timperley, Cheshire, *e* Manchester (Sale, Cheshire), 10648, Pte., k. in a., F. & F., 9-7-16.

HOWARTH Ernest, *b* St. Mark's, Bury, Lancs., *e* Manchester (Bury), 10400, Pte., k. in a., F. & F., 30-7-16.

HOWARTH Ernest, *b* Manchester, *e* Manchester, 11178, Pte., k. in a., F. & F., 9-7-16.

HOWARTH John, *b* Wigan, Lancs., *e* Wigan, 43871, Pte., k. in a., F. & F., 23-4-17.

HOWARTH William Gladstone, *e* Atherton, Lancs. (Manchester), 43747, L/Cpl., k. in a., F. & F., 23-4-17.

HUDSON William Seekings, *b* St. Ives, Cornwall, *e* Spalding, Lincs., 41592, Pte., k. in a., F. & F., 23-3-17, formerly 140858 R.F.A.

HUGHES John Henry, *b* Collyhurst, Manchester, *e* Manchester (Pendleton, Lancs.), 10543, Pte., k. in a., F. & F., 9-7-16.

HUGHES Stephen Richard Fletcher, *b* Bilston, Staffs., *e* West Bromwich, Staffs. (Stafford), 42248, Pte., k. in a., F. & F., 31-7-17, formerly T4/174499 R.A.S.C.

HULTON Oswald, *b* Moston, Manchester, *e* Manchester, 9872, Cpl., k. in a., F. & F., 14-1-16.

HUMPHREYS Joe, *b* Oldham, Lancs., *e* Hollinwood, Lancs. (Oldham), 48023, L/Cpl., k. in a., F. & F., 23-4-17.

HUMPHREYS Walter, *b* Manchester, *e* Manchester, 11090, L/Cpl., d. of w., F. & F., 9-7-16.

HUNT Alfred, *b* St. Matthew's, Salford, Lancs., *e* Manchester (Salford), 9873, A/Cpl., k. in a., F. & F., 30-7-16.

HUNT George, *e* Manchester (Didsbury, Lancs.), 11278, Pte., k. in a., F. & F., 23-4-17.

HUNTER Walter, *b* Ardwick, Manchester, *e* Manchester, 10129, Pte., k. in a., F. & F., 23-4-17.

HURST William, *b* Hindley, Lancs., *e* Wigan, Lancs., 203378, Pte., d., F. & F., 22-7-18.

HUTCHINSON Robert Harold, *b* North Otterington, Yorks., *e* Manchester (Thornton-le-Moor, Yorks.), 10029, Sgt., k. in a., F. & F., 30-7-16.

HYDER Fred, *b* Withyham, Sussex, *e* Tunbridge Wells, Kent (Jarvis Brook, Sussex), 41703, Pte., k. in a., F. & F., 23-4-17, formerly G/12834 R. Sussex R.

INGHAM Sidney, *b* Heaton Mersey, Lancs., *e* Manchester, 10253, Pte., k. in a., F. & F., 9-7-16.

INGOE Herbert, *b* Miles Platting, Manchester, *e* Manchester, 10411, Pte., k. in a., F. & F., 1-7-16.

IRELAND Richard Matthew, *e* Lancaster, 245232, Pte., k. in a., F. & F., 31-7-17., formerly 201844 R. Lan. R.

IRELAND Samuel, *b* Ormskirk, Lancs., *e* Oswestry, Shropshire (Poulton, Lancs.), 42252, Pte., k. in a., F. & F., 31-7-17, formerly T4/197569 R.A.S.C.

JACKSON George, *b* Manchester, *e* Manchester, 61251, Pte., k. in a., F. & F., 14-12-17.

JACKSON John, *b* Oldham, Lancs., *e* Farnworth, Lancs. (Oldham), 36374, Pte., k. in a., F. & F., 23-4-17.

JACKSON John Alfred, *b* Manchester, *e* Manchester, 48017, Pte., k. in a., F. & F., 31-7-17.

JACOBS Hyman, *b* Manchester, *e* Manchester, 27325, Pte., k. in a., F. & F., 23-4-17.

JERMYN Harold, *b* Manchester, *e* Manchester, 9448, Pte., k. in a., F. & F., 13-5-16.

JEWERS Joseph Henry, *b* Derby, *e* Rochdale, Lancs., 61256, Pte., d. of w., F. & F., 17-12-17.

JOHNSON James Henry, *b* Manchester, *e* Manchester, 48018, Pte., d., F. & F., 8-11-18.

JONES Edwin, *b* Manchester, *e* Manchester, 10413, Pte., k. in a., F. & F., 12-5-16.

JONES Hubert Leslie, *b* Mold, Flint, *e* Manchester, (Southport, Lancs.), 10666, Pte., k. in a., F. & F., 30-7-16.

JONES William James, *b* Devonport, *e* Manchester, 61253, Pte., k. in a., F. & F., 14-12-17.

JORDAN John Leonard, *b* Manchester, *e* Manchester, 26453, Pte., k. in a., F. & F., 9-7-16.

JOYCE Patrick, *b* Glasgow, *e* Manchester (Somerville, Mass., U.S.A.), 10151, Cpl., k. in a., F. & F., 9-7-16.

KANE Maurice, *b* Manchester, *e* Manchester, 44173, Pte., k. in a., F. & F., 31-7-17.

KAY Carswell Groves, *b* Ramsbottom, Lancs., *e* Manchester (Ramsbottom), 33492, Pte., k. in a., F. & F., 30-7-16.

KAY Charles Percy, *b* St. Paul's, Withington, Lancs., *e* Manchester, 10418, L/Cpl., k. in a., F. & F., 8-3-16.

KAY Roy, *b* Northfleet, Kent, *e* Manchester, Lancs., 10975, Pte., d. of w., Home, 15-2-16.

KAY	Thomas, *b* Queensland, Australia, *e* Manchester, Lancs. (Higher Broughton, Manchester), 44085, Pte., k. in a., F. & F., 12-10-16.
KAY	William, *b* Wigan, Lancs., *e* Wigan, 203358, Pte., k. in a., F. & F., 31-7-17.
KELLEY	William Victor, *b* Brighton, Sussex, *e* Brighton, 41772, Pte., d. of w., F. & F., 25-4-17, formerly G/11523 R. Sussex R.
KELLY	Sydney Hartley, *b* Manchester, Lancs., *e* Manchester, 8687, Pte., d. of w., F. & F., 9-7-16.
KELLY	William, *b* St. Luke's, Manchester, *e* Manchester, 10671, L/Sgt., k. in a., F. & F., 23-4-17.
KELSALL	Wilfred, *b* Manchester, Lancs., *e* Manchester, 43940, Pte., k. in a., F. & F., 12-10-16.
KENNARD	Harry, *b* Eastbourne, Sussex, *e* Eastbourne, 41707 Pte., d. of w., F. & F., 6-7-17, formerly 12821, R. Sussex R.
KENNEDY	James, *b* Manchester, Lancs., *e* Ardwick, Lancs. (Beswick, Lancs.), 44099, Pte., k. in a., F. & F., 12-10-16.
KENNEDY	William, *b* Manchester, *e* Manchester, 10961, L/Cpl., k. in a., F. & F., 13-5-16.
KERSHAW	Tom, *e* Oldham, Lancs., 41482, Pte., d. of w., Home, 24-6-17.
KETTLE	Arnold, *b* Stockport, Cheshire, *e* Manchester (Chorlton-cum-Hardy, Lancs.), 10284, Pte., k. in a., F. & F., 30-7-16.
KILGOUR	Frederick George, *b* Salford, Lancs., *e* Salford, 35149, Pte., k. in a., F. & F., 31-7-17.
KINSEY	John James, *b* St. Helens, Lancs., *e* St. Helens, 61258, Pte., k. in a., F. & F., 14-12-17.
KIRKHAM	Samuel, *b* Barnton, Cheshire, *e* Manchester, 44056, Pte., k. in a., F. & F., 23-4-17.
KNAGG	James, *b* Manchester, *e* Manchester, 31349, Pte., d. of w., F. & F., 9-7-16.
KNIGHT	Talbot, *b* Worsley, Birmingham, *e* Manchester, 10153, Pte., k. in a., F. & F., 27-2-16.
KNOWLES	Henry, *b* Hindsford, Atherton, Lancs. *e* Atherton, (Hindsford), 43785, Pte., d. of w., F. & F., 25-4-17.
LADLEY	James, *b* Ancoats, Manchester, *e* Ardwick, Manchester, 44119, Sgt., k. in a., F. & F., 31-7-17.
LANCASTER	Richard, *b* Ancoats, Manchester, *e* Manchester, 10174, Pte., k. in a., F. & F., 7-3-16.
LANGAN	Anthony, *b* Ardwick, Manchester, *e* Ashton-u-Lyne, Lancs. (Manchester), 2771, L/Cpl., d. of w., F. & F., 30-7-17.
LANGTON	Joseph, *b* Wigan, Lancs., *e* Hollinwood, Lancs., 27294, Pte., k. in a., F. & F., 30-7-16.
LEIGH	Fred, *b* Grantham, Lincs., *e* Manchester, 10501, L/Cpl., d., F. & F., 3-1-19.
LEMMON	Bertram, *b* Leeds, *e* Manchester, 47918, Pte., k. in a., F. & F., 23-4-17.
LIPTROT	Herbert, *b* Wigan, Lancs., *e* Wigan (Hindley, Lancs.), 43782, Pte., k. in a., F. & F., 31-7-17.
LLEWELLYN	James Henry, *b* Lr. Openshaw, Manchester, *e* Manchester, 10165, Pte., k. in a., F. & F., 9-7-16.
LOCKWOOD	Richard, *b* Longsight, Manchester, *e* Manchester (Chorlton-cum-Hardy, Lancs.), 10160, L/Cpl., k. in a., F. & F., 9-7-16.
LOGAN	David, *b* Salford, Lancs., *e* Manchester, 10273, L/Cpl., k. in a., F. & F., 4-2-16.

LOMAS	Samuel, *b* Oldham, Lancs., *e* Ashton-u-Lyne, Lancs., 377213, Pte., k. in a., F. & F., 23-4-17.
LOMAX	Abraham, *b* Pendleton, Lancs., *e* Manchester (Pendleton), 10161, Pte., k. in a., F. & F., 9-7-16.
LONG	Leo, *b* Manchester, *e* Manchester, 34926, Pte., k. in a., F. & F., 23-4-17.
LONGLEY	John, *b* Horwich, Lancs., *e* Manchester, 47882, Pte., k. in a., F. & F., 23-4-17.
LORD	Reginald, *b* Rochdale, Lancs., *e* Rochdale, 43666, Pte., d. of w., F. & F., 13-12-17, formerly 29358, Lancashire Fus.
LORD	Stephen, *b* Manchester, *e* Manchester, 34115, Pte., k. in a., F. & F., 30-7-16.
LOUGHLER	Harry, *b* Fallowfield, Manchester, *e* Manchester, 10164, Pte., k. in a., F. & F., 29-1-16.
LUNT	James, *b* Stockport, Cheshire, *e* Manchester (Stockport), 10162, Pte., k. in a., F. & F., 30-7-16.
LUNT	William Eric, *b* Chorlton, Manchester, *e* Manchester, 43949, Pte., d. of w., F. & F., 14-10-16.
LYNCH	Ernest, *e* Atherton, Lancs., 43777, Pte., k. in a., F. & F., 23-4-17.
LYNCH	James, *b* Oldham, Lancs., *e* Ashton-u-Lyne, Lancs. (Stockport, Cheshire), 29037, Pte., k. in a., F. & F., 14-12-17.
LYNCH	Thomas, *b* Manchester, *e* Manchester, 26287, Pte., k. in a., F. & F., 12-10-16.
LYTHGOE	Thomas Bertram, *b* Stretford, Manchester, *e* Manchester (Chorlton-cum-Hardy, Lancs.), 18941, Pte., d. of w., F. & F., 1-7-17.
MABEY	Reginald Charles, *b* Freshwater, Isle of Wight, *e* Manchester, 11140, Pte., d., Home, 27-8-16.
MACAULEY	Francis, *b* Oldham, Lancs., *e* Oldham, 34028, Pte., k. in a., F. & F., 30-7-16.
MADDEN	Dennis, *e* Wigan, Lancs. (Peel Green, Lancs.), 43768, Pte., k. in a., F. & F., 12-10-16.
MADELEY	Leonard, *b* Hulme, Manchester, *e* Manchester, 9889, Pte., d. of w., F. & F., 13-5-16.
MAHER	James, *b* Salford, Lancs., *e* Manchester (Stockport), 10178, L/Sgt., k. in a., F. & F., 31-7-17.
MAIDEN	Arthur, *e* Wigan, Lancs., 43870, Pte., d. of w., F. & F., 16-10-16.
MAKINSON	Frederick, *b* Pendleton, Lancs., *e* Manchester (Pendleton), 11055, L/Cpl., k. in a., F. & F., 9-7-16.
MAKINSON	Robert, *b* Eccles, Lancs., *e* Manchester (Bowdon, Cheshire), 10432, Pte., d. of w., F. & F., 29-1-16.
MANNION	Patrick, *b* Ardkeel, Co. Roscommon, *e* Manchester (Ardkeel), 44127, Pte., k. in a., F. & F., 1-8-17.
MANUEL	Charles, *b* Irlams-o'th'-Height, Lancs., *e* Manchester (Pendlebury, Lancs.), 11016, Pte., k. in a., F. & F., 9-7-16.
MARLER	Harold, *b* Oldham, Lancs., *e* Ashton-u-Lyne, Lancs. (Oldham), 36754, Pte., k. in a., F. & F., 23-4-17.
MARR	William, *b* Ancoats, Manchester, *e* Manchester, 10994, Pte., k. in a., F. & F., 9-7-16.
MARSDEN	Wilfred, *b* Chadderton, Lancs., *e* Oldham, Lancs., 29365, Pte., k. in a., F. & F., 23-4-17.
MARSHALL	Albert Edward, *b* Longsight, Manchester, *e* Manchester, 11146, Pte., d., F. & F., 29-3-16.

MARTIN Reuben, *b* Ancoats, Manchester, *e* Manchester, 10427, L/Cpl., k. in a., F. & F., 30-7-16.

MARTIN Robert, *b* St. John's, Oldham, Lancs., *e* Oldham, 33343, L/Cpl., d. of w., F. & F., 9-5-17.

MASON Harry, *b* Shaw, Lancs., *e* Ashton-u-Lyne, Lancs. (Shaw), 48944, Pte., k. in a., F. & F., 31-7-17.

MASON Joseph Lawrence, *b* Oldham, Lancs., *e* Hollinwood, Lancs., 27265, Pte., d., F. & F., 9-7-18.

MASSEY Herbert, *b* Gorton, Manchester, *e* Manchester, 17163, Pte., k. in a., F. & F., 31-7-17.

MATTHEWS Isaac, *b* Irlams-o'th'-Height, Lancs., *e* Manchester, 11240, Pte., d. of w., F. & F., 4-2-16.

MAY Frank Harold, *b* Manchester, *e* Manchester, 11089, Pte., k. in a., F. & F., 30-7-16.

MAYER Amos, *b* Dukinfield, Cheshire, *e* Manchester, 21943, Pte., k. in a., F. & F., 23-4-17, formerly 9030 A. Cyclist Corps.

MAYOR Thomas, *b* Wigan, Lancs., *e* Wigan, 49930, Pte., k. in a., F. & F., 31-7-17.

McCANN William, *b* Dublin, *e* Manchester, 10036, A/Sgt., k. in a., F. & F., 30-7-16.

McCARTHY Austin, *e* Atherton, Lancs. (Boothstown, Manchester), 43736, Pte., k. in a., F. & F., 30-10-17.

McCARTHY John William, *b* Hulme, Manchester, *e* Manchester, 31380, L/Cpl., d. of w., F. & F., 3-8-16.

McCAULEY Alexander, *b* Greenheys, Manchester, *e* Manchester, 10187, Pte., d. of w., Home, 5-8-16.

McCORMACK James, *b* Knott Mill, Manchester, *e* Manchester, 10684, Pte., k. in a., F. & F., 9-7-16.

McCREERY William, *b* Manchester, *e* Manchester (Moston, Lancs.), 10256, L/Cpl., k. in a., F. & F., 30-7-16.

McELROY William Alexander, *b* Manchester, *e* Manchester, 27129, Pte., k. in a., F. & F., 30-7-16.

McGINTY John, *b* Manchester, *e* Manchester, 10921, Pte., d. of w., F. & F., 8-3-16.

McINTYRE Daniel, *b* Darlington, Durham, *e* Manchester, 11252, A/Cpl., k. in a., F. & F., 30-7-16.

McLAREN William, *b* Oldham, Lancs., *e* Manchester, 23514, Pte., k. in a., F. & F., 30-7-17, formerly 30446 Lincs. R.

McLOW Hubert Henry, *b* Ancoats, Manchester, *e* Manchester, 10557, L/Cpl., k. in a., F. & F., 1-7-16.

McMAHON John, *b* Manchester, *e* Manchester (Halifax, Yorks.), 4318, Pte., k. in a., F. & F., 19-6-17.

McNAMARA Ernest, *b* Greenheys, Manchester, *e* Manchester, 10555, Pte., k. in a., F. & F., 1-7-16.

McNAMARA John, *b* Hulme, Manchester, *e* Manchester, 2638, Pte., k. in a., F. & F., 30-7-17.

McNEISH Frank, *b* Denton, Lancs., *e* Ashton-u-Lyne, Lancs., 49281, Pte., k. in a., F. & F., 31-7-17.

MEADOWS Allan, *b* Eccles, Manchester, *e* Eccles, 31490, Pte., k. in a., F. & F., 9-7-16.

MELEM Ernest, *b* Ancoats, Manchester, *e* Manchester, 10503, Pte., k. in a., F. & F., 8-3-16.

MELLOR Sidney Gregson, *b* Moston, Lancs., *e* Manchester (Crumpsall, Lancs.), 10686, Sgt., k. in a., F. & F., 8-7-16.

MELLOR William, *b* Manchester, *e* Manchester, 31288, Pte., k. in a., F. & F., 30-7-16.

MIDDLETON George, *b* Manchester, *e* Manchester, 44162, Pte., k. in a., F. & F., 23-4-17.

MIDGLEY William Henry, *b* Castleford, Yorks., *e* Manchester, 11033, Pte., d. of w., F. & F., 20-4-17.

MILLARD Jesse, *e* Atherton, Lancs. (Boothstown, Manchester), 43738, Pte., k. in a., F. & F., 12-10-16.

MILLER Albert, *b* Acton, Middlesex, *e* London (Hanwell, Middlesex), 1836, L/Cpl., k. in a., F. & F., 23-4-17.

MILLER Frederick Charles, *b* Brighton, Sussex, *e* Brighton, 41709, Pte., k. in a., F. & F., 31-7-17, formerly G/12839 R. Sussex R.

MILLER James, *b* Old Trafford, Manchester, *e* Manchester (Stockport, Cheshire), 12147, L/Cpl., k. in a., F. & F., 23-4-17.

MINGHAM Walter, *b* Withington, Lancs., *e* Manchester, 11280, Pte., d. of w., F. & F., 12-7-16.

MITCHELL Daniel Smithies, *b* Oldham, Lancs., *e* Manchester (Oldham), 36279, Pte., k. in a., F. & F., 23-4-17.

MITCHELL John, *b* St. Patrick's, Harpurhey, Manchester, *e* Manchester, 9897, L/Cpl., k. in a., F. & F., 30-7-16.

MITCHINSON John, *e* Wigan, Lancs. (Patricroft, Lancs.), 43766, Pte., d. of w., F. & F., 13-6-17.

MOORES Bernard, *b* Stretford, Manchester, *e* Manchester (Stretford), 10425, Pte., k. in a., F. & F., 12-5-16.

MOORES Herbert, *b* Swinton, Lancs., *e* Manchester (Worsley, Lancs.), 9895, Sgt., d. of w., Home, 18-7-16.

MORRIS George, *e* Hamilton, Lanark, 42283, Pte., k. in a., F. & F., 31-7-17, formerly T4/043430 R.A.S.C.

MORRIS Harry, *b* Ancoats, Manchester, *e* Manchester, 10431, Pte., k. in a., F. & F., 28-1-16.

MORRISON John, *b* Belfast, *e* Manchester, 9894, Pte., k. in a., F. & F., 30-7-16.

MORRISON Thomas, *b* Miles Platting, Manchester, *e* Manchester, (Harpurhey, Manchester), 10682, Pte., d. of w., F. & F., 6-10-16.

MORSE Lionel Gordon, *b* Patricroft, Lancs., *e* Eccles, Lancs. (Barton, Lancs.), 31480, Pte., d., F. & F., 30-12-18.

MOSS Ernest Leonard, *b* Bredbury, Stockport, Cheshire, *e* Manchester (North Reddish, Cheshire), 10559, Pte., d. of w., F. & F., 30-1-16.

MOXON Fred, *b* Cawthorne, Barnsley, Yorks., *e* Manchester, 44030, Pte., k. in a., F. & F., 12-10-16.

MURPHY Joseph, *b* St. James', Pendleton, Lancs., *e* Manchester, 10783, Pte., k. in a., F. & F., 9-7-16.

MUSGROVE Arthur, *b* Newark, Notts., *e* Newark, 40822, Pte., k. in a., F. & F., 29-7-17. formerly 3011 Notts. & Derby. R.

NAYLOR William Thomas, *b* Lower Broughton, Manchester, *e* Manchester, 10691, Pte., k. in a., F. & F., 30-7-16.

NELSON Samuel Horace, *b* Liverpool, *e* Liverpool, 47645, L/Cpl., k. in a., F. & F., 31-10-17, formerly 47497 Liverpool R.

NEWTON Wilfred, *b* Manchester, *e* Manchester (Lancaster), 10689, Sgt., d. of w., F. & F., 9-7-16.

NICOLL Gilbert Thompson, *b* Halifax, Yorks., *e* Manchester, 9906, L/Cpl., d. of w., F. & F., 9-7-16.

NICHOLSON George Robert, *b* Tadcaster, Yorks., *e* Pocklington, Yorks. (Bramham, Yorks.), 42086, Pte., d. of w., F. & F., 1-8-17, formerly 165832 R.F.A.

NORBURY Thomas, *b* Manchester, *e* Manchester, 36194, Pte., k. in a., F. & F., 23-4-17.

NORMINGTON Edwin, *b* St. Paul's, Stalybridge, Cheshire, *e* Manchester (Stalybridge), 10038, Pte., k. in a., F. & F., 30-7-16.

NORRIS John, *b* Moss Side, Manchester, *e* Manchester, 44113, Pte., k. in a., F. & F., 12-10-16.

NUNN Frederick Charles, *b* Margate, Kent, *e* Margate, 50971, Pte., k. in a., F. & F., 18-11-17, formerly G/24772 Middlesex R.

NUTTALL William, *b* Ramsbottom, Lancs., *e* Manchester (Ramsbottom), 32563, Pte., d. of w., F. & F., 20-6-17.

NUTTER George, *b* Ramsbottom, Lancs., *e* Bury, Lancs. (Ramsbottom), 31293, Pte., k. in a., F. & F., 30-7-16.

OAKES William, *b* Manchester, *e* Manchester, 26850, Pte., k. in a., F. & F., 23-4-17.

OLIVER Frederick Samuel, *b* Broughton, Manchester, *e* Manchester, 10437, Pte., k. in a., F. & F., 30-7-16.

ORMAN George, *b* Collyhurst, Manchester, *e* Manchester, 10192, Pte., k. in a., F. & F., 30-7-16.

ORRELL Harry, *b* Bury, Lancs., *e* Manchester (Bury), 17719, Pte., d. of w., F. & F., 23-4-17.

OSBALDISTON Willie, *b* Oldham, Lancs., *e* Oldham, 36817, Pte., k. in a,. F. & F., 14-12-17.

OSWALD Charles Walter, *b* Longsight, Manchester, *e* Manchester, 10193, Pte., k. in a., F. & F., 9-7-16.

OWEN John, *b* Manchester, *e* Manchester, 11147, L/Cpl., k. in a., F. & F., 23-4-17.

PACKINGHAM John, *e* Wigan, Lancs., 43859, Pte., k. in a., F. & F., 12-10-16.

PALIN George Thomas, *b* Shavington, Cheshire, *e* Crewe (Shavington), 26477, Pte., k. in a., F. & F., 9-7-16.

PALMER Herbert, *b* Manchester, *e* Manchester, 2864, L/Cpl., k. in a., F. & F., 23-4-17.

PARKER Alfred Thomas, *e* Manchester (Middleton), Lancs., 47869, Pte., k. in a., F. & F., 23-4-17.

PARRY John Robert, *b* Bury, Lancs., *e* Manchester (Bury), 10439, Cpl., k. in a., F. & F., 30-7-16.

PARRY Stanley Herbert, *b* Urmston, Lancs., *e* Manchester (Urmston), 10195, Pte., k. in a., F. & F., 7-2-16.

PAYNE Fred Cecil, *b* Westminster, Middesex, *e* London (Stockwell, Surrey), 42266, Pte., k. in a., F. & F., 13-6-17, formerly T4/159609 R.A.S.C.

PAYNE Reginald Harry, *b* Southsea, Hants., *e* Manchester, 9912, Pte., k. in a., F. & F., 1-7-16.

PEARCE Herbert, *b* Poplar, Middlesex, *e* Tottenham, Middlesex, 50973, Pte., k. in a., F. & F., 26-7-17, formerly G/19287 Middlesex R.

PERCIVAL Harry, *b* Manchester, *e* Manchester, 10196, Pte., d. of w., F. & F., 8-3-16.

PETTIGREW Harold Wallace, *b* Manchester, *e* Manchester, 33476, Pte., k. in a., F. & F., 30-7-16.

PHILLIPS Clifford, *e* Manchester, 43986, Pte., k. in a., F. & F., 12-10-16.

PIMLOTT Percy Enoch, *b* Dorking, Surrey, *e* Hove, Sussex, 41747, Pte., d. of w., F. & F., 9-5-17, formerly G/12499 R. Sussex R.

POOLE Thomas, *b* West Gorton, Manchester, *e* Manchester, 44007, Pte., k. in a., F. & F., 12-4-17.

POTTS Clifford, *b* Rochdale, Lancs., *e* Oldham, Lancs. (Harpurhey, Manchester), 34024, Pte., k. in a., F. & F., 30-7-16.

PRICE John, *b* Knutsford, Cheshire, *e* Manchester, 10987, Pte., d. of w., F. & F., 24-4-17.

PYE William, *e* Wigan, Lancs. (Hindley, Lancs.), 43816, Pte., k. in a., F. & F., 10-4-17.

QUEEN David, *b* Tottington, Lancs., *e* Bury, Lancs. (Tottington), 26455, Pte., k. in a., F. & F., 9-7-16.

QUINN Norbert William, *b* Miles Platting, Manchester, *e* Manchester (Moston, Lancs.), 10261, Sgt., k. in a., F. & F., 23-4-17.

RAINSBURY Edmund, *b* Broughton, Manchester, *e* Manchester, 10204, Pte., k. in a., F. & F., 9-7-16.

REDFORD George, *b* Whitefield, Lancs., *e* Manchester (Whitefield), 10444, Pte., d. of w., F. & F., 9-7-16.

REDMAN Maurice, *b* Lydwick Comer, Sussex, *e* Horsham, Sussex (Slinfold, Sussex), 41731, Pte., k. in a., F. & F., 23-4-17, formerly G/11875 R. Sussex R.

REEVES Frederick William, *b* Salford, Lancs., *e* Manchester, 9923, Pte., d. of w., Home, 14-8-16.

RENSHAW William, *b* Oldham, Lancs., *e* Oldham, 35836, Pte., d. of w., Home, 12-5-17.

RICHARDSON Henry, *b* Hulme, Manchester, *e* Manchester, 10206, Pte., k. in a., F. & F., 9-7-16.

RIDDLE James, *b* Ware, Herts., *e* Hertford (Ware), 50981, Pte., k. in a., F. & F., 14-12-17.

RIDGE Alfred, *b* Holy Trinity, Manchester, *e* Ashton-u-Lyne, Lancs. (Hulme, Manchester), 1095, L/Cpl., k. in a., F. & F., 21-1-18.

RIGBY Henry, *e* Wigan, Lancs. (Platt Bridge, Lancs.), 43882, Pte., d. of w., F. & F., 23-10-16.

RIGBY John, *b* Hulme, Manchester, *e* Manchester, 44034, Pte., k. in a., F. & F., 23-4-17.

RIGBY William, *b* Hindley, Lancs., *e* Hindley, 203380, Pte., k. in a., F. & F., 31-7-17.

RILEY Frank, *b* Oldham, Lancs., *e* Oldham (Chadderton, Lancs.), 34025, Pte., k. in a., F. & F., 30-7-16.

ROBERTS Robert, *b* Farnworth, Lancs., *e* Leigh, Lancs., 43723, L/Cpl., k. in a., F. & F., 12-10-16.

ROBERTS William Oswald, *b* Timperley, Cheshire, *e* Manchester (Timperley), 43651, Pte., k. in a., F. & F., 31-7-17.

ROBINSON William, *b* Manchester, *e* Manchester, 31425, Pte., k. in a., F. & F., 9-7-16.

ROBINSON William, *e* Wigan, Lancs., 43821, Pte., k. in a., F. & F., 12-10-16.

ROEBUCK Albert, *b* Ancoats, Manchester, *e* Manchester, 44002, L/Cpl., k. in a., F. & F., 12-4-17.

ROSE Thomas Sellman, *b* Prescot, Lancs., *e* Widnes, Lancs. (Hough Green, Lancs.), 61142, Pte., k. in a., F. & F., 23-12-17.

ROWLAND William Ewart, *b* Haverigg, Cumberland, *e* Ulverston, Lancs. (Millom, Cumberland), 245196, Pte., k. in a., F. & F., 14-12-17.

ROYLE Ernest, *b* Lower Broughton, Manchester, *e* Manchester, 9994, Pte., k. in a., F. & F., 9-7-16.

RUDDLE George, *b* Hulme, Manchester, *e* Manchester, 4872, Pte., k. in a., F. & F., 31-7-17.

RUSHTON Alfred, *b* Salford, Lancs., *e* Manchester, 9919, Pte., d. of w., F. & F., 7-6-16.

RUSHTON Joseph Edward, *b* Ramsbottom, Lancs., *e* Bury, Lancs. (Ramsbottom), 31294, Pte., d., F. & F., 15-5-17.

RYAN John, *b* Salford, Lancs., *e* Manchester (Salford), 34016, Pte., k. in a., F. & F., 30-7-16.

RYDE Frank Edgar, *b* Belper, Derby, *e* Manchester (Belper), 10917, Pte., d. of w., F. & F., 12-7-16.

RYDER Wilfred, *b* Gorton, Lancs., *e* Manchester (Gorton), 43925, Pte., k. in a., F. & F., 23-4-17.

SALMON Thomas Cyril, *b* Leicester, *e* Manchester, 44146, Pte., d. of w., F. & F., 20-6-17.

SANDERSON Ernest, *b* Collyhurst, Manchester, *e* Manchester, 9217, Pte., k. in a., F. & F., 8-7-16.

SANDERSON Frederick Wilson, *b* Wavertree, Liverpool, *e* Manchester (Seacombe, Cheshire), 44037, Pte., k. in a., F. & F., 23-4-17.

SANT Frederick, *b* Ancoats, Manchester, *e* Manchester, 32068, Pte., k. in a., F. & F., 14-12-17.

SANT Harry, *b* Harpurhey, Manchester, 9997, L/Cpl., k. in a., F. & F., 1-7-16.

SAYERS James, *b* Manchester, 27036, Pte., k. in a., F. & F., 30-7-16.

SAYLE William Ernest, *b* Whitehaven, Cumberland, *e* Manchester, 47914, Pte., k. in a., F. & F., 23-4-17.

SCHOFIELD John Joseph, *b* Oldham, Lancs., *e* Oldham, 36856, Pte., d. of w., F. & F., 6-12-16.

SCOTT Albert Oliver, *b* Manchester, *e* Manchester, 10974, L/Cpl., d. of w., F. & F., 29-2-16.

SCOTT Herbert, *b* Hackney, Middlesex, *e* Hackney (Bow, Middlesex), 44738, Pte., k. in a., F. & F., 23-4-17, formerly G/21612 Middlesex R.

SEDGWICK Christopher, *b* Stalybridge, Cheshire, *e* Manchester (Moston, Lancs.), 10838, C.S.M., k. in a., F. & F., 23-4-17.

SEEL Ralph, *b* Clayton, Manchester, *e* Manchester, 44101, Pte., k. in a., F. & F., 3-12-16.

SELLERS Alfred Hardy, *b* Dukinfield, Cheshire, *e* Manchester (Dukinfield,) 11110, Pte., k. in a., F. & F., 1-7-16.

SHAW Thomas, *b* Heyside, Shaw, Lancs., *e* Royton, Lancs. (Heyside), 34890, Pte., d. of w., F. & F., 30-4-17.

SHEAL Robert, *b* Busby, Stirlingshire, *e* Mossley, Lancs., 203423, Pte., d. of w., F. & F., 27-7-17.

SHEPHERD Richard H., *b* Parbold, Wigan, Lancs., *e* Wigan, 43826, Pte., d. of w., F. & F., 25-4-17.

SHEPLEY George Baldwin, *b* Urmston, Lancs., *e* Manchester (Flixton, Lancs.), 9932, Cpl., k. in a., F. & F., 1-7-16.

SHERIDAN Ernest Stanley, *b* Salford, Lancs., *e* Manchester (Salford), 20722, L/Cpl., k. in a., F. & F., 8-2-16.

SHIELDS Charles, *b* Manchester, *e* Manchester, 32502, Pte., k. in a., F. & F., 30-7-16.

SIDEBOTHAM John Heap, *b* Eccles, Lancs., *e* Wigan, Lancs. (Eccles), 43810, Pte., k. in a., F. & F., 12-10-16.

SILCOCK Fred, *b* Longsight, Manchester, *e* Manchester, 10454, Pte., k. in a., F. & F., 11-3-16.

SILCOCK John William, *e* Wigan, Lancs., 43884, L/Cpl., k. in a., F. & F., 12-10-17.

SILVERSTEIN Samuel, *b* Manchester, *e* Manchester, 31302, Pte., k. in a., F. & F., 30-7-16.

SIMISTER William, *b* Hulme, Manchester, *e* Manchester, 203107, Pte., k. in a., F. & F., 31-7-17.

SIMPSON Harry, *b* Salford, Lancs., *e* Manchester (Salford), 10952, Sgt., d. of w., F. & F., 27-4-17.

SINKINSON William, *b* Manchester, *e* Manchester, 34105, Pte., d. of w., F. & F., 31-7-16.

SKAIFE Percy, *e* Ashton-u-Lyne, Lancs., 52079, Pte., k. in a., F. & F., 27-12-17.

SKEGGS John, *b* Tottenham, Middlesex, *e* Hove, Sussex, 41722, Pte., d. of w., Home, 8-5-17, formerly G/12797 R. Sussex R.

SLADIN James, *b* Oldham, Lancs., *e* Oldham, 48026, Pte., d. of w., F. & F., 30-3-18.

SLATER Thomas, *b* Ancoats, Manchester, *e* Manchester, 44014, Pte., k. in a., F. & F., 12-10-16.

SLOAN Irvine, *b* West Derby, Liverpool, *e* Liverpool, 2280, Pte., k. in a., F. & F., 25-4-17.

SMITH Alexander, *b* Blackburn, Lancs., *e* Manchester, 9929, Pte., k. in a., F. & F., 9-7-16.

SMITH Arthur, *b* Manchester, *e* Manchester, 44006, Sgt., k. in a., F. & F., 12-10-16.

SMITH John William, *b* Liverpool, *e* Manchester, 10876, Pte., k. in a., F. & F., 1-7-16.

SMITH Leonard, *b* Beswick, Manchester, *e* Manchester (Denton, Lancs.), 10265, Pte., k. in a., F. & F., 3-2-16.

SMITH Percy Robert, *b* Epsom, Surrey, *e* Epsom, 50984, Pte., k. in a., F. & F., 31-7-17, formerly G/19033 Middlesex R.

SMITH Samuel Thomas, *b* Tyldesley, Lancs., *e* Atherton, Lancs. (Tyldesley), 43831, Pte., k. in a., F. & F., 12-10-16.

SOWERY John James, *b* Beswick, Manchester, *e* Manchester, 44093, Pte., k. in a., F. & F., 26-7-17.

STALLARD Kenneth, *b* Ledbury, Herts., *e* Manchester, 10457, Sgt., k. in a., F. & F., 9-7-16.

STAMP Ralph William, *b* Manchester, *e* Manchester (Gorton, Lancs.), 44130, Pte., k. in a., F. & F., 23-4-17.

STANWAY William, *b* Macclesfield, Cheshire, *e* Manchester, 11204, Pte., k. in a., F. & F., 9-7-16.

STARKEY Harold, *b* St. Clement's, Broughton, Manchester, *e* Manchester, 7295, Pte., k. in a., F. & F., 1-7-16.

STEVENSON Bruce, *b* Dublin, *e* Manchester, 43964, L/Cpl., k. in a., F. & F., 29-7-17.

STEWART Alexander, *b* Pendleton, Lancs., *e* Manchester, 10954, L/Cpl., d. of w., F. & F., 9-7-16.

STOCK John, *b* Wigan, Lancs., *e* Ashton-u-Lyne, Lancs. (Wigan), 48028, Pte., k. in a., F. & F., 31-7-17.

STOTT Albert, *b* Middleton, Lancs., *e* Manchester (Flixton, Lancs.), 9995, Pte., k. in a., F. & F., 30-7-16.

STOTT James, *b* Royton, Lancs., *e* Royton, 36058, Pte., k. in a., F. & F., 12-4-17.

STUBBS Alfred Norman, *b* Manchester, *e* Manchester (Prestwich, Lancs.), 44184, Pte., k. in a., F. & F., 12-10-16.

SUMNER John Edward, *b* Dilworth, Preston, Lancs., *e* Manchester (Kendal, Westmorland), 9934, Pte. k. in a., F. & F., 28-1-16.

SUTTON James, *b* Ancoats, Manchester, *e* Manchester, 10217, Pte., k. in a., F. & F., 30-7-16.

SWIFT Thomas, *b* Southport, Lancs., *e* Preston, Lancs. (Crawshawbooth, Lancs.), 42101, Pte., k. in a., F. & F., 14-12-17.

SWINDELLS Frank, *b* Miles Platting, Manchester, *e* Manchester, 31375, Sgt., k. in a., F. & F., 30-7-16.

TAFT Fred, *b* Chorlton-on-Medlock, Manchester, *e* Manchester, 10723, Pte., d. of w., F. & F., 1-7-16.

TATHAM Benjamin James, *b* Ripponden, Yorks., *e* Todmorden, Yorks. (Cornholme, Yorks.), 302048 Pte., k. in a., F. & F., 23-3-18.

TAWS Albert Edward, *b* St. George's, Manchester, *e* Manchester, 10860, Sgt., d. of w., F. & F., 19-10-16.

TAYLOR Francis Thomas Albert, *b* Manchester, *e* Manchester, 31327, Pte., k. in a., F. & F., 9-7-16, formerly 21085 R. Scots.

TAYLOR Frederick, *b* Bury, Lancs., *e* Manchester, 10970, Pte., d. of w., F. & F., 30-7-16.

TAYLOR Frederick James, *b* Manchester, *e* Manchester, 35057, Pte., k. in a., F. & F., 30-7-16.

TAYLOR Harry, *b* Oldham, Lancs., *e* Ashton-u-Lyne, Lancs. (Oldham), 48027, Pte., d. of w., F. & F., 30-4-17.

TEDSTONE Claude Henry, *b* St. Bartholomew's, Salford, Lancs., *e* Manchester, 31373, L/Cpl., k. in a., F. & F., 9-7-16.

THEAKER Harry Procter, *b* Manchester, *e* Manchester, 44027, Pte., k. in a., F. & F., 12-10-16.

THOMAS Harold, *b* Oldham, Lancs., *e* Oldham, 47900, Pte., d., F. & F., 27-10-18.

THOMAS William, *b* Hulme, Manchester, *e* Manchester, 9998, Sgt., k. in a., F. & F., 23-4-17.

THOMPSON Frank, *b* Ardwick, Manchester, *e* Manchester, 10731, L/Cpl., d. of w., F. & F., 19-7-16.

THOMPSON John, *b* Urmston, Lancs., *e* Manchester, 10724, Pte., d. of w., F. & F., 16-7-16.

THOMPSON Louis, *b* Chorlton-on-Medlock, Manchester, *e* Manchester, 18738, L/Cpl., k. in a., F. & F., 31-7-17.

THOMPSON William, *b* Moston, Lancs., *e* Manchester, 10583, Pte., d. of w., F. & F., 30-7-17.

THORNE Wilfred, *b* Leigh, Lancs., *e* Shaw, Lancs. (Leigh), 27274, Pte., k. in a., F. & F., 8-7-16.

THORPE Richard, *b* Forest Hill, Surrey, *e* Manchester (Bloomsbury, Middlesex), 10895 Pte., k. in a., F. & F., 4-2-16.

TIDSWELL James, *b* Beswick, Manchester, *e* Manchester, 10984, Pte., k. in a., F. & F., 30-7-16.

TIMPERLEY Thomas, *b* Longsight, Manchester, *e* Manchester, 10722, A/Cpl., d. of w., F. & F., 27-4-17.

TINKER George Herbert, *b* St. George's, Altrincham, Cheshire, *e* Manchester (Altrincham), 10464, Cpl., d. of w., F. & F., 9-5-17, **M.M.**

TOOLE Edward, *b* Ancoats, Manchester, *e* Manchester, 10223, Sgt., k. in a., F. & F., 23-4-17.

TOWERS Thomas, *b* Hulme, Manchester, *e* Manchester, 10572, L/Cpl., d. of w., F. & F., 10-3-16.

TRUEMAN Harold, *b* Ardwick, Manchester, *e* Manchester, 10221, Pte., k. in a., F. & F., 9-7-16.

TUBBS Arthur Charles Brooke, *b* Cobham, Surrey, *e* Manchester (Cobham, Surrey), 245215, Pte., k. in a., F. & F., 1-8-17, formerly 5002 E. Lancashire R.

TUCKER James, *b* London, *e* Manchester, 31394, Pte., k. in a., F. & F., 30-7-16.

TUNSTALL Samuel Edward, *b* Cheadle Hulme, Stockport, Cheshire, *e* Manchester, 10573, L/Cpl., k. in a., F. & F., 30-7-16.

TURNER Percival, *b* Hastings, Sussex, *e* Manchester (Battle, Sussex), 11166, Pte., d., Home, 19-5-15.

TWENTYMAN Frederick, *b* Manchester, *e* Manchester, 202999, Pte., k. in a., F. & F., 31-7-17.

VALENTINE Richard, *b* Manchester, *e* Manchester (Gorton, Lancs.), 34227, Pte., k. in a., F. & F., 30-7-16.
VAUGHAN Frank, *b* Ashton-u-Lyne, Lancs., *e* Ashton-u-Lyne, 35411, Pte., d. of w., F. & F., 4-8-17.
VICKERS William, *b* Kearsley, Lancs., *e* Manchester (Kearsley), 11153, Pte., k. in a., F. & F., 23-4-17.

WAINWRIGHT John William, *e* Atherton, Lancs., 43084, Pte., k. in a., F. & F., 23-4-17.
WALDRON Thomas, *b* Hulme, Lancs., *e* Manchester, 43921, Pte., k. in a., F. & F., 12-10-16.
WALL George Herbert, *b* Wigan, Lancs., *e* Wigan, 43909, Pte., k. in a., F. & F., 11-10-16.
WALLER John Frederick, *b* Mottram, Cheshire, *e* Manchester (Alderley Edge, Cheshire), 11025, L/Cpl., k. in a., F. & F., 9-7-16.
WALSH John, *b* Hazel Grove, Cheshire, *e* Manchester, 44139, Pte., k. in a., F. & F., 23-4-17.
WALSH Thomas, *e* Stalybridge, Cheshire, 245221, Pte., k. in a., F. & F., 3-7-17, formerly 51119 R. Welch Fus.
WALTON Ernest, *b* Moss Side, Manchester, *e* Manchester, 10515, Pte., k. in a., F. & F., 12-5-16.
WALTON Henry, *b* Oldham, Lancs., *e* Oldham, 36828, Pte., k. in a., F. & F., 30-7-17.
WARD William, *b* Manchester, *e* Manchester, 44179, Pte., k. in a., F. & F., 12-10-16.
WARDLE Andrew, *b* Ashton-u-Lyne, Lancs., *e* Manchester (Ashton-u-Lyne), 22099, L/Cpl., k. in a., F. & F., 29-7-17.
WARHAM John Thomas, *b* Ardwick, Manchester, *e* Manchester (Salford, Lancs.,) 10227, Pte., d. of w., F. & F., 22-4-17.
WARREN James, *b* Manchester, *e* Manchester (Moston, Lancs.), 11070, Pte., d. of w., F. & F., 11-7-16.
WAUGH James, *b* Openshaw, Manchester, *e* Manchester (Gorton, Lancs.), 44106, Pte., k. in a., F. & F., 29-7-17.
WAUGH William, *b* Keighley, Yorks., *e* Morecambe, Lancs., 245246, Pte., k. in a., F. & F., 31-7-17, formerly 265397 R. Lancs. R.
WEARING Harry Douglas, *b* Islington, Middlesex, *e* Holloway, Middlesex, 50988, Pte., d. of w., F. & F., 31-7-17, formerly G/19284 Middlesex R.
WEBB Arthur, *b* Pendleton, Lancs., *e* Manchester, 9948, Pte., k. in a., F. & F., 30-7-16.
WEBSTER Alan, *b* Manchester, *e* Manchester, 31261, Pte., k. in a., F. & F., 13-5-16.
WEBSTER James, *b* St. John's, Deansgate, Manchester, *e* Manchester, 10517, Cpl., k. in a., F. & F., 10-2-16.
WEST Walter, *b* Salford, Lancs., *e* Manchester, 44052, Pte., k. in a., F. & F., 17-6-17.
WHALLEY James, *b* Atherton, Lancs., *e* Atherton, 43845, L/Cpl., d., F. & F., 19-4-17.
WHARTON Alfred, *e* Wigan, Lancs., 43822, Pte., k. in a., F. & F., 12-10-16.
WHARTON Francis, *b* Manchester, *e* Manchester, 44057, Pte., k. in a., F. & F., 12-10-16.
WHEALE Ernest, *b* Salford, Lancs., *e* Salford, 48030, Pte., k. in a., F. & F., 23-4-17.
WHITBY Alfred, *b* Salford, Lancs., *e* Manchester (Salford), 11085, Pte., k. in a., F. & F., 9-7-16.

WHITE Hugh Campbell, *b* Hooley Hill, Manchester, *e* Ashton-u-Lyne, Lancs., 41558, Pte., d. of w., F. & F., 29-1-17.

WHITEHEAD Alfred, *b* Manchester, *e* Manchester (Northenden, Cheshire), 35107, L/Cpl., k. in a., F. & F. 23-4-17.

WHITEHEAD Richard, *b* Edgeworth, Manchester, *e* Manchester (Radcliffe, Lancs.), 9960, Cpl., k. in a., F. & F., 1-7-16.

WHITELY Edward Arthur, *b* Bradford, Lancs., *e* Manchester, 10746, Pte., k. in a., F. & F., 1-7-16.

WHITTAKER Hugh, *b* Manchester, *e* Manchester, 10317, Pte., k. in a., F. & F., 9-7-16.

WHITTAKER William, *b* Salford, Lancs., *e* Manchester (Salford), 31355, Pte., k. in a., F. & F., 1-7-16.

WHITTLE Herbert, *b* Ancoats, Manchester, *e* Manchester, 8952, L/Cpl., d. of w., F. & F., 28-4-17.

WHITWORTH Walter, *b* St. Margaret's, Heywood, Lancs., *e* Manchester, 10742, L/Cpl., k. in a., F. & F., 30-7-16.

WICKMAN William, *b* Collyhurst, Manchester, *e* Manchester (Moston, Lancs.), 10232, L/Cpl., k. in a., F. & F., 4-2-16.

WILBER Frank, *b* Manchester, *e* Manchester, 31274, Pte., k. in a., F. & F., 30-7-16.

WILDE Jack, *b* Springhead, Yorks., *e* Lees, Lancs., 27228, Pte., k. in a., F.& F., 9-7-16.

WILFORD Robert Bertram, *b* Chorlton-on-Medlock, Manchester, *e* Manchester, 9959, A/C.S.M., k. in a., F. & F., 30-7-16.

WILKINSON David, *b* South Shields, Durham, *e* Manchester (Irlams-o'th'-Height, Lancs.), 9953, Pte., k. in a., F. & F., 29-1 16.

WILKINSON Percy, *b* Prestwich, Lancs., *e* Manchester, 9955, L/Cpl., k. in a., F. & F., 30-7-16.

WILLIAMS Laurence, *b* Tullamore, King's Co., *e* Manchester (Salford, Lancs.), 11043, Pte., k. in a., F. & F., 9-7-16.

WILLIAMS Ralph, *b* Hulme, Manchester, *e* Manchester (Stockport, Cheshire), 44019, Pte., k. in a., F. & F., 23-4-17.

WILLIAMS Richard Harding, *b* Harpurhey, Manchester, *e* Manchester (Chorlton-cum-Hardy, Lancs.), 10001, L/Cpl., k. in a., F. & F., 28-1-16.

WILLIAMS Samuel, *b* Tyldesley, Lancs., *e* Atherton, Lancs., 43827, Pte., k. in a., F. & F., 23-4-17.

WILLIAMSON Alfred Thomas, *b* West Hampstead, Middlesex, *e* Kilburn (West Hampstead), 43697, Pte., k. in a., F. & F., 23-4-17, formerly G/16951 Middlesex R.

WILLIAMSON Samuel, *b* Manchester, *e* Manchester, 47916, Pte., k. in a., F. & F., 23-4-17.

WILLS Abraham, *b* Manchester, *e* Manchester (Moston, Lancs.), 31326, Pte., k. in a., F. & F., 1-7-16.

WILSON Fred, *b* Millom, Cumberland, *e* Lancaster, 245234, Pte., k. in a., F. & F., 31-7-17, formerly 1676 K. O. R. Lancaster R.

WILSON James, *e* Ayr, 42274, Pte., k. in a., F. & F., 31-7-17, formerly T4/174494 R.A.S.C.

WILSON James Robert, *b* Failsworth, Lancs., *e* Failsworth, 33334, Pte., d. of w., F. & F., 5-5-17.

WILSON Nathan, *b* St. George's, Hulme, Manchester, *e* Manchester, 10519, Pte., k. in a., F & F., 9-7-16.

WINCHESTER William, *b* Brighton, Sussex, *e* Brighton, 41768, Pte., k. in a., F. & F., 31-7-17, formerly G/11519 R. Sussex R.

WINSBY Walter Ratcliffe, *b* Hulme, Manchester, *e* Manchester (Pendleton, Lancs.,) 10225, L/Cpl., d. of w., F. & F., 11-7-16.

WITHERS	Arthur, *b* Salford, Lancs., *e* Manchester (Salford), 10518, Pte., k. in a., F. & F., 1-7-16.
WITHINGTON	William, *e* Manchester (Salford, Lancs.), 43974, Pte., k. in a., F. & F., 23-4-17.
WOOD	Edmund Francis, *b* Wragby, Lincoln, *e* Manchester (Spilsby, Lincs)., 9951, Cpl., k. in a., F. & F., 23-4-17.
WOOD	Frank, *b* Salford, Lancs., *e* Manchester (Sale, Cheshire), 10226, Pte., d. of w., F. & F., 10-7-16.
WOOD	George, *b* Bury, Lancs., *e* Manchester, 20671, Pte., d. of w., F. & F., 23-3-17.
WOOD	John Leonard, *b* Manchester, *e* Manchester (Northenden, Cheshire), 11053, Pte., d. of w., Home, 24-7-16.
WOOD	Thomas, *b* Salford, Lancs., *e* Manchester, 10747, Pte., d. of w., F. & F., 2-2-16.
WOODALL	Frank, *b* St. Mark's, Cheetham Hill, Manchester, *e* Manchester, 10865, Pte., d. of w., F. & F., 14-5-16.
WOODCOCK	Abraham, *e* Wigan, Lancs., 43903, Pte., d., F. & F., 28-12-16.
WOODHOUSE	James, *b* Prestwich, Lancs., *e* Manchester (Prestwich), 34699, Pte., d., F. & F., 29-8-17.
WOODMAN	Reginald, *b* Seedley, Manchester, *e* Manchester (Salford, Lancs.,) 43713, Sgt., d. of w., F. & F., 27-7-17, formerly 4144 Lancashire Fus.
WOODWARD	Frank Newton, *b* Levenshulme, Manchester, *e* Manchester, 10735, Pte., k. in a., F. & F., 30-7-16.
WORSLEY	Richard, *b* Swinton, Lancs., *e* Manchester (Irlams-o'th'-Height, Lancs.), 44090, Pte., k. in a., F. & F., 12-4-17.
WORSWICK	Leo, *b* Manchester, *e* Manchester, 11199, A/Cpl., k. in a., F. & F., 30-7-16.
WRIGHT	Fred Stanley, *b* Moor Row, Cumberland, *e* Manchester, 44036, Sgt., d. of w., F. & F., 3-5-17.
WRIGHT	John, *b* Hulme, Manchester, *e* Manchester, 10857, Pte. k. in a., F. & F., 12-10-16.
WRIGHT	William, *b* New Mills, Derby., *e* Manchester (New Mills), 9956, Pte., k. in a., F. & F., 1-7-16.

19TH

NOTE

Since this volume went to press it has been found that Mr. Harry Lloyd, in addition to the four hundred pounds contributed to the 19th Battalion, made further generous donations, exceeding a total of one thousand pounds a year.

ERRATA

Page 288, para. 9, "C" Company: *for* A. W. Atkinson *read* K. H. Allen.

Page 229, para 3: Lieut. B. la T. Foster *afterwards reported killed.*

CONTENTS

APPENDIX

CHAPTER I

PRELIMINARY TRAINING AND EARLY DAYS IN FRANCE

ON the outbreak of the Great War the authorities of the City of Manchester approached the War Office for permission to raise local battalions of Infantry. The formation of the 1st, 2nd, 3rd, and 4th (City) Battalions began on August 28th, 1914, [Authority 20/ Infantry/ 756 (A.G. 1) d/ War Office 11-9-15]. The Battalions were recruited to establishment in rotation, the 4th Battalion commencing on September 2nd, 1914.

The first parade of the 4th (City) Battalion was held at the City Exhibition Hall, Manchester, on the 16th September, 1914.

As far as possible friends and men from the same offices and warehouses had been placed in the same Platoons and Companies. Ex-army and old Volunteer non-commissioned officers were temporarily promoted to the rank of Company Sergeant-Majors and Sergeants. Volunteers were called for to be trained as junior N.C.O.'s. With the exception of the old " volunteers " and ex-regulars, very few of the Officers and N.C.O.'s had had any military training at all, and even the old soldiers required to be brought up-to-date. These were mostly men of mature years and fixed ideas, each one trained under the particular regimental method which happened to prevail at the time of his discharge. They had to learn to conform to the current system of drill under the instruction of the newly-appointed Regimental Sergeant-Major, who had retired from the Lancashire Fusiliers only a few months before the War broke out.

Upon the Regimental Sergeant-Major largely devolved the responsibility of licking this medley of all sorts and sizes of young men into some semblance of soldiers, but his native Irish wit and energetic personality soon made an impression. He could be abusive, sarcastic, endearing, all in a breath. Although to be addressed in such terms as " you there, with the four-inch collar in the rear rank," or, " will the gentleman in the beautiful green waistcoat in the second row oblige," awakened no more alacrity according to the Sergeant-Major than would put an elephant to shame, the victims knew better.

For the first month the Battalion paraded at the City Exhibition Hall, and having learned to " form fours " and march off in column of route, alternated with the 3rd (City) Battalion between there and Hulme Barracks. Battalion orders were not as yet issued. Notices of parades were published in *The Manchester Evening News* as required. In the afternoons Lieut.-Col. W. E. Lloyd, the Second-in-Command, generally took a special parade for Officers and N.C.O.'s.

On the 15th October, thanks to the courtesy of the proprietors, Belle Vue Gardens were secured as a training ground, where the Battalion continued to parade daily from 9 a.m. until 4 p.m. for a further six weeks. The men were drawing their three shillings a day subsistence allowance, and came in daily from all round Manchester by tram and train.

It was suddenly realised that dinner would have to be provided on the spot to ensure a full day's training being carried out, and arrangements were accordingly made by the Quartermaster. Liberties had to be taken with the three shillings a day subsistence allowance, but no complaints were made, and the plan was carried through. Butchers and others were dragged unwillingly back to their own jobs. Dinner was served in the dining-room, and the sergeant-cook began to get into his stride. Orderly officers inspected the meat with a wise look and pronounced it good, but the sergeant-cook could not understand why his excellent roasts and stews did not find more favour with the men, who freely patronised the public refreshment room after a none too hearty meal. The " city " soldier missed the niceties of the table, and was not yet accustomed to the rough and ready methods of Army rationing.

Company and extended order drill were added to the programme of training, and officers began to take a more active part in the training of their own units. They were keen and interested in their work, and expressed it each in his own way. They had no established tradition to follow. Their constant endeavour was to increase the efficiency of their N.C.O.'s which required the most personal supervision. This personal contact made for some intimacy between officer and man, but it worked well in the circumstances, and was in no way prejudicial to discipline.

A spirit of rivalry began to appear between companies, route marching and running were practiced and a schoolmaster sergeant was discovered who could instruct in the regulation physical drill. Thenceforth physical drill was by companies. Hitherto, the R.S.M. had been the only instructor available, and he had had to instruct by half battalions.

Quite a number of men did not know how to run. They had to be taught the use of their toes. Alternate doubling and marching in short spurts by platoons soon found out the weak spots. The finish to a complete double round the lake, which was only about half a mile, resembled the finish to a cross-country run. That solid column of fours had degenerated into a straggling line extending half way round the lake. A commencement was made with trench digging. Even picks and shovels require to be handled rightly and used in some order. Lack of observance of the rules of procedure led to one " Pal " pickaxing another. This first casualty had to be removed to hospital. A limited number of old-fashioned rifles were issued for arms drill, which Companies had to utilise in turns.

An orderly-room and guard-room appeared. The first prisoner escaped. Rumour had it that the guards were spending their pay on the "figure eight" near by, while the N.C.O. in charge had gone for his pay. The R.S.M. was sure that the prisoner would be found at home, as indeed he was, comfortably ensconced in the bosom of his family. The police brought him back the next day. Another soldier on being brought up for absence without leave excused himself on the plea that he had been getting married, but was let off with a caution when he promised not to do it again!

Being on guard at night proved good training. The guard-room was near the sea lions, who used to make weird and disturbing noises in the silence of the night. Their barking seemed to provoke the whole Zoo to respond, so that the neighbourhood for miles around resounded with a raucous clangour. The soldier on duty always had it at the back of his mind that a lion or a man-eating tiger might have escaped, and was in consequence alert. Even the officers were not free from this effect of atmosphere. The orderly officer slept in an adjoining inn and visited the guard at intervals. One night the officer on duty returned breathless and pale convinced that he had been chased by a snake, only to discover that his puttee had come undone.

In wet weather Companies were detailed to different animal houses for instruction in arms drill and manual exercises. The astonished inmates gave expression to their feelings at this unusual intrusion on their privacy. One Company had so bad a reception in the monkey house that they petitioned for a change, but got scant sympathy from the R.S.M., who caustically suggested the alternative of throwing them to the lions. The rhinoceros was very offensive. Perhaps the solemn penguins were most kindly disposed towards their visitors ; and the elephant, too, was a sympathetic friend.

Another distraction was the presence of onlookers, many of them friends and relatives of the new soldiers. Their criticisms,which were sometimes overheard, were kindly meant, but were hard to bear. Visitors were most appreciated after parade hours, when the men lost no time in joining their friends, and found compensation for the routine of drill in the more fascinating pastimes of dancing and skating on the great floor to the music of the Gardens' band.

The Battalion lost its first Commanding Officer at Belle Vue, who died of pneumonia on the 28th October. Colonel G. C. P. Heywood, a retired Brigadier-General of Territorials, had seen service in South Africa in command of the Company of Volunteers, drawn from the Volunteer Battalions of the Manchester Regiment. He was an ideal Commander in every way and beloved by all who knew him. The Battalion paraded and marched to London Road Station, where they lined the approach as the funeral procession passed to the train.

Colonel E. A. Kettlewell, a retired Indian Army officer who was responsible for the raising of the Bikanin Camel Corps, took over command on the 19th November, and on the 30th marched the Battalion into hutments at Heaton Park. The police lent him the only horse used on the occasion. Lieut. J. A. Hislop, who had been appointed from the Battalion to succeed Colonel F. R. McConnel as Adjutant, marched alongside the C.O. The officers were in khaki, but only a few men had been provided with the blue uniform. Some wore their civilian overcoats, others carried them. The few old rifles scattered down the columns added to the picturesque effect. The Battalion marched well,however,and gave evidence of its preliminary training. It had begun to acquire *espirit de corps*, and was ready for the more strenuous training in Camp. Each platoon saluted Colonel McConnel as it passed him *en route*. The Battalion and its first Adjutant parted with mutual regret and respect.

By Authority 20/ Infantry 635/ (A.G. 1) D/ War Office 3rd December, 1914, the title of the Battalion was changed to the Nineteenth (Service) Battalion, Manchester Regiment. It was from this date that the War Office officially took over the City Battalion, of which the 16th, 17th, 18th and 19th Battalions formed the 90th Brigade, under the command of Brigadier-General H. C. E.Westropp.

Officers and men at once began to settle down to their new life. Office men and warehousemen, carters, etc., found themselves living together in the same huts. It took some little time for them to settle down together in harmony, but they gradually learned to leave each other to their own devices and so contributed to their mutual gain of a quieter life. They were comfortably housed and well provided for. Every man had his straw-stuffed palliasse and three good blankets. They kept their personal belongings in a variety of boxes on the shelf above their beds. In the absence of a dining-room the men fed in their own huts, one platoon to two huts. The feeding was lavish. A daily allowance of one shilling and ninepence a head per day gave ample provision for a generous and varied menu. Porridge was issued for breakfast every day, and was followed by bacon and as much bread and butter and jam as could be eaten. There was always a sweet to dinner and fresh fruit as well. Tea was at a quarter to five, when the remains of the bread and butter and jam were consumed. In fact, the issue of food was so generous that much waste occurred, and the supply had to be cut down to some extent. Sergt. S. Wilson, ex-Lancashire Fusiliers, was appointed Regimental Sergeant Cook at Heaton Park, from which time the Battalion never looked back on its feeding. Sergt. Wilson remained with the Battalion throughout its existence as a unit and proved himself a most devoted servant.

Each Platoon expressed its sentiments in the name of its hut, which were christened with such names as "Otazell," "Little Grey Home," "The Wattlers' Home" (What'll yer have), etc. Most of the huts hired pianos, and many artistes were discovered. The officers encouraged the musical proclivities of their men, and would not infrequently visit them in the evenings to lead them in music and song. No. 15 Platoon, which boasted a most musical officer, became famous for its singing on the march. Every Sunday after Church parade an almost unlimited number of passes were issued until midnight. The few who remained in camp entertained their numerous friends of both sexes to an afternoon tea, which included tinned fruit and cake. The sound of music and entertainment resounded in camp until well on into the evening.

On reveillé sounding enthusiastic young officers were with their Platoons to lead as many as would follow for an early morning double round the Park, but this was found to be rather too strenuous, and soon gave way to tea and biscuits before organised Company parades under the Company Sergeant-Majors. The huts were required to be clean and everything in uniform order for officers' inspection at the nine o'clock parade after breakfast.

The Battalion had a large area of training ground, unencumbered by flower beds and animal houses, which allowed of drilling to be carried on more efficiently than hitherto. Day after day section and platoon drill went on under the eagle eye of the Colonel—left-right, left-right, up and down the undulating ground. Extended order drill likewise improved under the more open conditions of Heaton Park. Visual training was begun, and musketry instruction advanced under Lieut. J. W. Myers, who with a N.C.O. had been sent to Altcar on a special course. He returned to instruct the other officers and N.C.O.'s in the grey hours of the early morning, while the rest of the Battalion paraded under the Company Sergeant-Majors. Lieut. B. de la T. Foster and a N.C.O. were similarly sent on a course of physical drill, and did the same service to the Battalion on their return. More route marching and scientific trench-digging were carried out, also night training—how to see and listen in the dark, &c. Wet days were rather a nightmare to Platoon officers, when they had to lecture their men on landscape targets, patrol, scouting, &c., but both officers and N.C.O.'s gradually grew in knowledge and efficiency, further aided by the more or less diligent study of the little red books and numerous lectures.

Saturday mornings were devoted to the cleaning of huts, and kit inspection by the Commanding Officer, tables and floors were scrubbed and stoves blackleaded. Boots were polished and each man's kit laid out to pattern. The lines had to be free from cigarette boxes, stray matches and bits of paper. The officers were in and out amongst their men all the time, and the men worked like slaves. As the C.O. appeared at each doorway, followed by the Adjutant, the Second-in-Command, the R.S.M., the Company Commander, and the C.S.M., the Platoon officer called his men to attention and with trepidation joined his Company Commander as the long line filed through his huts. It was a proud day for the Platoon which provoked no comment. It was so easy a thing to have overlooked one man's hair not being short enough, or perhaps a wrong arrangement of brushes. The whole Battalion felt that it had earned its Saturday afternoons' holiday after the ordeal.

The Battalion Signallers were formed under Lieut. A. T. Heywood. The signalling equipment was very primitive, but was enough to make a beginning with on the semaphore and morse alphabet. Sergt. Holborn, ex-Coldstream Guards, was invaluable as signalling-sergeant. The Battalion Scouts were formed under Lieut. G. R. Swaine. There was a rush of applicants for the Machine Gun Section, as indeed for all special sections, when it became known that they were excused all orderly work and fatigues, but Lieut. R. C. Mather, lately returned from a Vickers' gun course at Strensall, soon gave the machine gun section to understand that there was continuous hard work before them. Although there was no equipment, the machine gunners were never tired of their own parades owing to the varied programme their officer drew up. Their special instruction was all in theory, but before they left Heaton Park they had a fair idea of the mechanism of the machine gun and a working knowledge of semaphore. The special sections all paraded separately except on special occasions, and carried on with the ordinary infantry training as well as their special training.

The arrival of officers' mounts marked an epoch. Until then police horses had been freely drawn upon for route marches and ceremonial parades. Lieut. N. S. Ince was appointed Transport officer, but except for the necessary grooms the Transport Section was not formed until the Battalion reached Belton Park, Grantham.

At Christmas time about half the Battalion was allowed leave over the holidays. The other half had had theirs before. For those who remained in camp nothing was missing to the occasion. Geese, turkeys, Christmas pudding and a plentiful supply of fruit and drink were served for dinner. Much of it was given by Mr. Harry Lloyd, who was a most generous patron throughout. He contributed four hundred pounds a year to the Battalion throughout the period of its existence, and maintained the closest interest in its history through his cousin, Lieut.-Col. W. E. Lloyd, the Second-in-Command. About this time the whole Battalion was invited to the pantomime at the Theatre Royal, and attended by Companies under their officers.

All Manchester was intensely interested in her citizen soldiers.

With the issue of blue uniform and greatcoats, completed in January, 1915, the men began to take a pride in their appearance. One elegant private, thinking to improve on the regulation dress, started to walk out with the addition of spats, but the guard, with the Battalion's pride at heart, turned him back before the harm was done. The popularity of the blue uniform was short-lived however. It declined as the Battalion grew in efficiency and in a knowledge of its own value, and the teasing that the men got about their "tram-guards" uniform added to their chagrin. Khaki was issued in February, 1915, and was worn for the first time with the leather equipment on the 21st March, when Lord Kitchener inspected the Battalion. It was reserved for walking-out and ceremonial parades.

The whole Brigade paraded and marched into Manchester for Lord Kitchener's inspection, who took the salute on the steps of the Town Hall. The intervening month had effected a veritable transformation in the physique and general smartness of the troops. But they were still without service rifles. The few old-fashioned rifles were still being used for musketry instruction, and on the occasion of Lord Kitchener's inspection were supplemented by wooden dummies made by the Battalion pioneer.

At last the day arrived for the Battalion to leave Manchester. Clad in khaki and carrying full packs, with six months' of hard training behind them, they presented a very different appearance now to what they had done on the day that they marched to Heaton Park. The streets were lined with people who turned out to take farewell of the citizen soldiers, and were as moved by their departure as were the soldiers themselves. The move took place on the 24th April, 1915, when the Battalion proceeded to Belton Park, Grantham.

The 90th Brigade there formed part of the 30th Division, under the command of General Fry. Thanks to strenuous recruiting all four Battalions were over strength at Heaton Park, so that each was able to leave a double Company in reserve there.

The Divisional branch of the Army Service Corps came into existence at Belton Park, when the men found that they were not as well-rationed as they had been at Heaton Park. However, the sergeant-cook and Captain Hislop, with the aid of Mother Beeton, put their heads together and improved the feeding, but the troops always looked back with regret on their Heaton Park days, and always filled the cafés and restaurants at Grantham after parade hours.

Colonel Kettlewell relinquished his command on the 15th June, 1915, owing to ill-health, and was succeeded by Lieut.-Col. Sir H. B. Hill, Bart., retired Royal Irish Fusiliers. Colonel Hill had seen service in Egypt, had taken part in the battle of Khartoum in 1898, and had been Governor of Berber.

The new Commanding Officer was a great disciplinarian, and all ranks were in consequence braced up to a keener sense of their responsibilities. N.C.O.'s were interchanged between Companies in order to dissipate the too friendly feeling that perhaps existed between N.C.O. and man as a result of too much association together.

On September 7th, 1915, the Battalion moved to Larkhill Camp, Salisbury Plain.

LIST OF OFFICERS WHO PROCEEDED OVERSEAS

C.O.: Lieut.-Col. Sir H. B. Hill, Bart. *Second-in-command:* Lieut.-Col. W. E. Lloyd. *Q.M.:* Capt. J. F. O'Malley. *Adjutant:* Capt. J. W. Myers. *M.O.:* Capt. A. V. Stocks.

"A" Company: Major E. H. Howe, Capt. J. A. Hislop, Lieut. N. H. Craston, Lieut. L. A. Chadwick, Lieut. F. S. Boxall, Lieut. W. W. Smith.

"B" Company: Capt. H. K. Birley, Capt. R. C. Mather, Lieut. H. E. Turner, Lieut. N. S. Ince (*Transport Officer*), Lieut. H. S. Tidy, Lieut. E. W. Mawdsley, Lieut. P. de la T. Foster (*O.C. Machine Gun Section*).

"C" Company: Capt. W. S. Cunliffe, Capt. W. M. Clarke, Lieut.G. Leresche, Sec.-Lieut. F. Henshall, Sec.-Lieut. A. T. Heywood (*O.C. Battalion Signallers*), Sec.-Lieut. J. S. Higgins, Sec.-Lieut. A. W. Atkinson.

"D" Company: Capt. F. W. Royle, Capt. G. S. J. Owen, Lieut. B. de la T. Foster, Lieut. J. Caldwell (*O.C. Battalion Bombers*), Lieut. G. R. Swaine (*O.C. Battalion Scouts*), Sec.-Lieut. Ibbotson.

The Battalion left Larkhill Camp on the morning of November 7th, 1915, to entrain at Amesbury for Southampton. Embarking there Southampton was left at dusk—personnel aboard the S.S. "Queen Alexandra"; transport aboard the S.S. "Archimedes."

Havre was reached about midnight on the 8th. The Battalion disembarked at 7 a.m. and went to No. 5 Rest Camp. At night it entrained for Pont Remy. From the latter place the Battalion marched to Beaumetz, where it was billeted and remained there training until the 17th, when it moved to Flesselles. One day only was spent at Flesselles. On the 18th the Battalion moved to Coisy, where it remained training until the 28th. The next move was to Canaples and here the stay lasted until December 8th.

The Battalion next moved to Halloy, and on the 9th to Berles-au-Bois, where it was attached to the 110th Brigade.

Here the officers and N.C.O.'s went into the trenches for instruction under officers of the 6th Leicesters. Part of the Battalion also entered the trenches for instruction, whilst the remainder underwent instruction by R.E. in wiring, rivetting, digging, &c. This tour of instruction lasted until December 17th, when the Battalion left Berles-au-Bois and marched to La Herliere. Here it supplied working parties on a subsidiary line. La Herliere was left on December 24th for Halloy, and on Christmas Day the Battalion marched to Boisberques, where it remained training—with special training in bombing and sniping—until January 3rd, 1916. On this date it marched to Naours. The next day the Battalion was at Pont Noyelles, and on the following day it was at Sailly Laurette.

Sailly Laurette was left on January 6th and the Battalion marched to Bray. Here it was met by guides and taken to Bronfoy Farm—Battalion H.Q. and "A" Company being billeted; the remaining three Companies in Billon Wood about six hundred yards away. Here for a day or so the Battalion provided working parties for various purposes, but on the 8th it relieved the 14th Warwicks in the Carnoy trenches (B3 sector). This tour of duty lasted until the 12th. The situation was very quiet and the Battalion was able to carry on work in improving trenches.

The 19th King's Liverpool Regiment relieved on the 12th and the Manchesters marched to Bray, where they were billeted. But they were back in the trenches again on the 16th and found the enemy more active, a good deal of shrapnel dropping near the front line. From this date onwards to March 7th the Battalion alternated between billets at Bray and the Carnoy trenches. There was intermittent shelling during most of this period. Nevertheless the men were able to clean up and improve the trenches, which were in very bad condition, the mud being indescribable. On March 7th the Battalion marched to Bois des Tailles, remaining there until the 14th, when it moved to Corbie. The following day it was at Frechencourt, a tour which lasted till the 29th. Here the Battalion provided fatigue parties for work on the railway track. On the 29th it moved to Coisy, but one night only was spent here, the next move being to Breilly, where drill of various kinds was carried out. Brigadier-General C. J. Sackville-West inspected the Battalion on April 6th. Battalion sports were indulged in on the 9th. The next day the Manchesters were back at Coisy, and on the 12th at Frechencourt.

Here the Battalion supplied fatigue parties for work at Pont Noyelle. The stay at Frechencourt lasted until May 2nd and for the greater part of that month the Battalion alternated between Corbie, Bray, Bronfoy Farm and Billon Wood, and the Carnoy trenches. Training of various kinds was continued and the Battalion was also engaged on mining fatigues. There was occasional heavy shelling by both sides during the early part of the month of May. On May 24th the Battalion left the Carnoy sector and marched to Maricourt, the enemy keeping up a brisk M.G. and rifle fire while it was on the march. At Maricourt an advanced trench was being dug, in which work the Manchesters took their share along with the 2nd Wilts and 2nd Bedfords, and during this spell the enemy livened up the situation with his artillery. There were numerous casualties.

The first few days of June were uneventful. On the 5th the Battalion relieved the 2nd Wilts and took over the Maricourt defences. Mining and working parties were supplied by the Battalion.

The following officers joined the strength with effect from June 7th :—

Sec.-Lieuts. A. V. Cassall, A. J. Linnell, E. Outram.

The Battalion was relieved at midnight on the 11th by the 17th Manchesters, and halting for a time at Bray marched thence to Bois de Celestins. After a short rest it moved on to Heilly, where it entrained for Picquigny. From there it moved the same day to Briquemesnil. Here the Battalion commenced practising for an attack upon a large scale. In the mornings the officers went over the training ground, which had been arranged as a battlefield on a small scale ; in the afternoons the Battalion went over in attack formation. On the 15th the Manchesters moved on to Breilly, but owing to lack of billets the men had to be content with a bivouac on the Breilly-Picquigny roadside. The next day the Battalion moved on to Reincourt, where attack-training was continued. On the 21st it marched via Amiens to Corbie. The next day it was at Etinehem. On the 23rd the Battalion reached Bray. An attack was imminent.

The greater part of the Battalion moved up to the trenches of Z2 subsector on the 29th, leaving a reserve of officers and men in the transport lines off the Bray-Corbie road, just outside Bray. The same night Lieut. J. B. Higgins and Sec.-Lieut. Craston with thirty-seven other ranks undertook a raid on the German front line, with the object of securing a prisoner. The party left the trenches at 11-20 p.m. after fifteen minutes bombardment. They returned at 11-40 and regretted that no Germans were to be found and that the front line had been levelled by the bombardment. One man was wounded on the way up and one killed on the return journey. During the night of the 30th the Battalion took up battle positions :—

" A " Company on the left ; "C " on the right ; H.Q. in Cumberland Street ; " B " and "D " in Cumberland Street, Queen Victoria Street and Hill Street.

The 20th King's Liverpool Regiment was on the right of the Battalion and the 18th King's Liverpool Regiment on the left. Towards the end of the month the following officers had joined the strength :—

Sec.-Lieuts. Compton, E. D. Harrison, G. W. Hindle and W. Myers. Capt. W. M. Clarke also rejoined the Battalion from the 89th Brigade.

CHAPTER II

THE BATTLE OF THE SOMME

GLATZ REDOUBT AND GUILLEMONT

THE objective of the 90th Brigade (30th Division) on July 1st, 1916, was the capture of the important village of Montauban, which lay deep within the enemy's line. The special business of the Nineteenth Manchesters was to capture the Glatz Redoubt, which lay in the approach to Montauban. The breadth of the front to be attacked was from two hundred and fifty to three hundred yards. After an intense bombardment by guns of all calibres, and also from Stokes' mortars placed in Russian saps, the first wave went over the parapet at 7-30 a.m. and successive waves followed at about one hundred yards interval. There was no check to the advance, except such as was made necessary by our own artillery barrages, and these pauses were utilised for the reorganisation of the various waves. The final objective was carried to scheduled time at 8-35 a.m. precisely. At this time two sections of the support Company had been used as reinforcements. Meanwhile the remainder of the support Company addressed itself to consolidating a support trench position. The reserve Company took up its position and consolidated in a portion of Alt trench. The cleaners examined all trenches and dug-outs but found little opposition from German infantry left behind. During the advance the greater number of casualties were caused by an enemy machine gun situated well to the left of the Battalion. Two machine guns, three trench mortars and many prisoners were taken. Immediately the northern face of the Glatz Redoubt was reached smoke candles and red flares were lighted. This smoke barrage proved very effective in concealing the approach of the 90th Brigade, which passed through the Redoubt towards Montauban.

The following is a detailed narrative of the operations of each Company :—

" A " Company. No. 1 and 2 Platoons under Sec.-Lieuts. Boxall and Allen (*first wave*) ; No. 3 Platoon under Sec.-Lieut. Craston (*second wave*) ; No. 4 Platoon under Sec.-Lieut. Tidy, O.C. Company (*third wave*).

The first and second lines, Silesia trench and Silesia support trench, were carried without a halt and just after leaving the support line the first two waves merged into one, creeping close up to the barrage on Alt trench. When the barrage lifted on to the gorge of the Redoubt, the two waves continued separately until close up to this barrage and again halted for reorganisation. As soon as the barrage lifted on to the north-east face of the Redoubt the lines went forward, the left being a trifle in advance owing to the position of the barrage. Casualties were very slight up to this point. And the moment the barrage lifted the Redoubt was carried. Three platoons were put in the front line and one in support, facing N.E. Smoke candles and red flares were lighted and consolidation begun. Wire was put out; No. 2 strong point commenced; two T sap heads were dug and manned by Lewis guns, pending the arrival of Vickers guns; communication trenches were partially cleared; firesteps made; deep narrow trenches dug for protection; rifles cleaned; and water-bottles filled from supplies brought up by carriers. When the Briqueterie was taken at 12-45 p.m. the Company was reformed.

"C" Company. No. 11 and 10 Platoons under Sec.-Lieut. Atkinson and Lieut. Higgins (*first wave*); No. 12 Platoon under Lieut. Leresche (*second wave*); No. 9 Platoon under Capt. Cunliffe, O.C. (*third wave*).

Owing to the traversing effect of an enemy machine gun on the left this Company suffered about forty casualties before reaching the German front line. These casualties included Sec.-Lieut. Atkinson and several N.C.O.'s, but the men pushed on with great coolness and steadiness. The enemy threw hand-grenades at random from Silesia trench. In Silesia support trench the right platoon were bombed by about six Germans, but these were speedily accounted for. The left platoon met with no opposition. In Alt trench the enemy put up some show of fight with bombs, and then retreated along the trench towards the Glatz. From this point, however, the advance was not impeded and the Company reached Glatz Redoubt along with "A" Company. Consolidation was immediately begun and Nord Alley was blocked. Smoke candles and red flares were lighted at 8-38 a.m. When the 90th Brigade reported the capture of Montauban, a party was sent up Nord Alley to No. 5 strong post. Two Platoons of "D" (reserve Company) came up later and continued in the construction of this post. This party suffered from enfilade fire and intermittent shrapnel fire.

"B" Company.—No. 8, 7, 6 and 5 Platoons under Lieuts. Linnell and Pritchard (*fourth wave*); No. 8, 7, 6 and 5 Platoons under Lieut. Outram and Capt. Mather (*fifth wave*).

The waves were assembled in Queen Victoria Street and they went forward without a halt until Alt trench was reached, where the

Company was reorganised. The mouth of the gorge was reached with about fifteen casualties. Here the first waves were also halted and when they moved forward two sections of "B" Company were taken as reinforcements. An officer of the 6th R. Baverische Regiment was taken prisoner in the gorge. Sec.-Lieut. Linnell was sent forward to assist in work of consolidation, to replace Sec.-Lieut. Allen, who had been wounded. About mid-day he returned with seven men of "B" Company, as consolidation was then well advanced. Firesteps were made and trenches deepened. A couple of bombing parties were established at suitable points and Lewis guns were also provided at these places.

"D" Company.—No. 16, 15, 14 and 13 Platoons under Sec.-Lieut. Chadwick and Lieut. Sharpington (*sixth wave*).

The Company halted in Alt trench, with its left about fifty yards S.E. of No. 1 strong point, and touch was established with the 18th King's Liverpool Regiment on the left. Consolidation was commenced at once. About 10-30 a.m. two Platoons, under Sec.-Lieut. Keefe, were sent up to reinforce "C" Company in Nord Alley. This party suffered fairly heavy casualties whilst constructing No. 5 strong post. At 2-30 p.m. Capt. Owen, with one Platoon, moved into Train Alley (between No. 3 strong point and the railway) as support to the two Platoons in Nord Alley. Sec.-Lieut. Chadwick with one Platoon and a Lewis gun joined Capt. Owen on the morning of July 2nd. Train Alley was consolidated and at dawn No. 6 strong point was started where Train Alley forked fifty yards north of the railway. Three sides of No. 6 post were formed by Train Alley and on the fourth side a trench was dug.

Headquarters.—Before zero H.Q. was established in Cumberland Street, and about an hour after the battle began an advanced H.Q. was established in Alt trench, east of No. 1 strong point. To this point all messages from Companies were directed and were forwarded thence by runner or by disc to Cumberland Street, until telephonic communication was definitely established. Although lines had been laid early in the advance, communication by this means was long delayed owing to shell fire. The runners and scouts employed were very efficient and succeeded on every occasion in transmitting messages without delay. In addition they, with H.Q. bombers and others, consolidated about thirty yards of Alt trench, built firesteps and dug a deep protective trench. The C.O. and Sec.-Lieut. Swaine established this post. Later they were joined by the Adjutant, Capt. Myers.

Sec.-Lieut. Ibbotson was in charge of signallers and they laid a line to advanced H.Q. This wire was repeatedly broken and as often repaired. Wires were also run out to the Glatz Redoubt and to the support Company. Further, a lateral line was laid between advanced H.Q. and the H.Q. of the right battalion on the morning of July 2nd. The total casualties for this day were :—

Sec.-Lieut. A. W. A. Atkinson and forty men killed ; Sec.-Lieut. E. Outram and eleven men missing ; Sec.-Lieut. K. H. Allen and one hundred and thirty-six other ranks wounded.

The Battalion was relieved at 10 p.m. on July 2nd by the 20th King's Liverpool Regiment and withdrew to assembly trenches near Oxford Copse. During the evening, 4 p.m. to 8 p.m., the enemy heavily shelled the position, but no ground was lost. At 5-30 p.m. on the 3rd the South African Infantry relieved the Battalion, which proceeded to the Bois des Tailles for a few days rest.

At 10 p.m. on July 7th the Battalion returned to the trenches in reserve to the 2nd Yorks and 2nd Wilts, who were to attack Trones Wood and Maltzhorn trenches. The attack of the 2nd Yorks was held up on July 8th and it was decided to attack again at 12-30 p.m. Meanwhile orders were received by the Nineteenth Manchesters at 11 a.m. to move up in support to the 2nd Wilts, who were to take part in this second attack. Accordingly, " C " Company moved up to Briqueterie ; "A" to Glatz Redoubt, Train Alley and Nord Alley; " B " and " D " to Sunken Road, running S.E. from Briqueterie. At 2-30 p.m. " B " Company moved into Maltzhorn trench to reinforce " A " Company of the 2nd Wilts. This company was on the right, in touch with the French.

Sergt. Barnes and a bombing section covered a platoon of the Wilts while blocks were constructed in the left of the trench. This party discovered and brought in an enemy machine gun. Presently " B " Company was joined by twenty men of " D " Company, who had brought up ten boxes of S.A.A. to Maltzhorn trench. This Company sent out hourly patrols during the night. " D " Company remained in Sunken Road until 3-15 p.m. Here Capt. F. W. Royle was mortally wounded at 1-30 p.m. At 3-15 the Company moved up under Sec.-Lieut. Keefe to Trones Wood, in support to the 2nd Wilts. It took up a line in front of the Wilts, facing north across the south end of the Wood. Here the party proceeded to dig in. At 6 p.m. the left of the line was taken over by a detachment of the 18th Manchesters. All messages were sent via the 2nd Wilts, but none reached H.Q. at the Briqueterie. At 4 a.m. on the 9th a heavy bombardment began along the whole of the new line and this lasted until the Company was relieved by another party of 18th Manchesters. Runners and signallers kept up lateral communication very well. The Company was withdrawn about 1-30 p.m.

The Companies in Maltzhorn trench were relieved by the R.S.F.'s at 4-30 a.m. on the 9th. " B " and " C " Companies withdrew to assembly trenches. " A " remained until the R.S.F.'s had captured

Maltzhorn Farm, and then also withdrew. The whole Battalion remained resting until about 10 p.m. when it moved to Billon Valley, where a bivouac was established.

The casualties during these operations were :—

Killed, Capt. Royle and twelve men; wounded, Sec.-Lieut. Hindle and forty-three men ; missing, three men.

A draft of eighty-nine men was received before moving to Billon Valley. On the 11th the Battalion moved to Morlancourt, where it practised bayonet-fighting, physical drill, &c., together with classes in Lewis gun, signalling, scouting and bombing. The Battalion marched to Corbie on the 13th, and here a further draft of two hundred and twenty-four men arrived, being drawn from the Royal Fusiliers, East Surreys and Royal Sussex Regiments. On the 14th the transport left by road for Saisseval, and the Battalion marched from Corbie, at 6-30 a.m. entrained at Vacquemont, detrained at Ailly-sur-Somme, and marched to Saisseval. Here on the following day the Brigade was formed up in hollow square and addressed by G.O.C. 30th Division, who afterwards complimented each battalion separately on their work in recent actions. The next few days were spent in various kinds of training.

The Battalion left Saisseval on the 18th moving by Ailly and Mericourt to billets at Morlancourt. This place was left on the following day and the Battalion moved on to Wellington Redoubt, where training was continued for some days. Orders were received on the 21st that the Battalion was to attack Guillemont on the 23rd. Accordingly at 3-30 p.m. on the 22nd the Battalion moved from Wellington Redoubt to Silesia support trench. At 10 p.m. it moved in single file up the Montauban-Maricourt road until it reached the railway. At this point it swung eastwards along the railway until it reached Bernafay Wood. The Battalion now moved along the southern edge of the Wood, and then took a N.E. direction, crossing the communication trench between Bernafay and Trones Woods, and then following it on the north side until it reached a point about forty yards from Trones Wood. The Battalion then turned north, marching parallel to the Wood, and about forty yards west of it. At thirty yards from the railway the leading Platoon halted and turned to the right, the other Platoons of that Company forming in rear in single rank about twenty-five yards distance, the other Companies conforming as they came up. The Battalion was, in fact, in open mass in single rank, facing east on the western side of Trones Wood. There had been fourteen casualties on the way up. In the interval of waiting the Battalion bivouaced and the men dug themselves in in shell-holes. Trones Wood was continuously shelled during the night. At 2-30 a.m. on the 23rd "C" Company moved through the Wood by a path to the south of the railway and took up a position in four waves, with its centre on the Trones-Guillemont road. "A" Company moved along the railway and formed up to the north of "C" Company. "D" Company, moving by the south end of Trones Wood, took up a position to the south of "C" Company. Half of "B" Company followed "A" and one half of "D" formed two waves in their rear. The attack began at 3-40 a.m., and from the commencement, was subject to heavy shell, rifle and machine gun fire, but casualties were not very heavy until the German wire was reached, when the losses became very serious.

The following is a summary of each Company's operations :—

"A" Company.—The first two waves gained the German front trench without serious opposition and were about to leave for the second trench when the third wave joined them. Heavy fire was now encountered from six to eight machine guns on the flanks, besides a frontal fire from the ridge above the Sunken Road. The Company's Lewis gun No. 1, attached to the fourth wave, engaged and put out of action one of the enemy guns. A charge was then led by Sec.-Lieut. Tidy and the left half-Company, but it was held up by heavy fire and bombing. A second attempt was also stopped and the survivors to the number of about thirty fell back on the German front trench. Meanwhile, Sec.-Lieut. Craston and the right half-Company made good their way to the S.E. corner of the Redoubt, and held this position for some time.

No. 2 Lewis gun was then taken up to the Quarry by Sergt. Rothwell, where he occupied the southern position, supported by Sergt. Spencer and a party of bombers. The Germans were in strong force to the north of the Quarry and held higher ground. Subsequently, owing to pressure from north and east, the party was compelled to fall back and rejoin Sec.-Lieut. Craston. Sec.-Lieut. Tidy then sent forward ten men as reinforcements, and the Quarry was again partly occupied. Pte. Briggs, sent back for help, was unable to return until late in the day owing to the heavy fire. Sergt. Whitehead was also sent back to report the position. He left Sergt. Spencer in charge at the Quarry, supported by two other N.C.O.'s and fifteen men. Spencer had ordered his men to fight to the last, but to use bombs and ammunition sparingly. Sergt. Whitehead expressed the opinion that the men could not hold out much longer and would probably be overwhelmed. They had been practically surrounded three or four times, but had hitherto managed to drive the enemy back. Of this party it is believed that only the two messengers named above and one other survived.

Sec.-Lieut. Tidy was wounded in the German front trench, but was eventually helped back into the British lines. Sec.-Lieuts. Craston, Harrison and Walton were amongst the missing.

"*C*" *Company*.—This Company held the central position in the assault. The advance was carried out when visibility was bad, and the waves became uneven owing to the shell-holes and wire. The Company, however, went right through into the village, past the right of a small wood. The enemy's fire became intense when the men reached this copse, machine guns firing from both flanks. Both the Company's Lewis guns took up positions near the wood and opened fire on large bodies of Germans concentrated on the right. Subsequently, "C" Company appear to have been entirely cut off.

"*D*" *Company*.—This Company was on the extreme right and found the wire uncut at the first line. Here the Company was attacked by bomb, rifle and machine gun fire from the right. About thirty men faced this attack, but all were shot down. The remainder of the Company managed to get through the first line of wire in detached parties, when they formed up in line and attempted to force their way through the second wire defence, which was also uncut. This, however, proved an impossible task. Meanwhile, the Company lay down and opened fire on the enemy whilst waiting supports. The German trench was only a few yards away, and the Manchesters suffered so heavily from bombs and rifle fire that they were compelled to fall back. The Company withdrew by a trench running east and west to the Sunken Road running south-west. The Germans bombed up this road from the south. They were, however, held back by L/Corpl. Sharples and his Lewis gun until the withdrawal had been completed.

"*B*" *Company*.—This Company was in support, and the right half-Company followed in the rear of "D" Company. It was consequently forced to withdraw with "D" Company, after having lost many men. Part of the left half-Company, under Capt. Birley, managed to push its way forward to the first line of wire, but here it was held up and it was here that Capt. Birley was killed.

H.Q. moved at 2-30 a.m. from the west edge of Trones Wood to the trench on the S.E. edge of the Wood. This trench was heavily shelled and telephonic communication was constantly breaking down and pigeon messengers had to be relied on. Capt. Myers, Sergt. Spink and a party of bombers and Lewis gunners constructed a block in the Trones-Guillemont trench. They were, however, subjected to such heavy fire that they were eventually compelled to withdraw.

Sergt. Spink was killed by a sniper after doing very effective work.

Sir Arthur Conan Doyle in "The British Campaign, 1916," thus sums up the attack :—

"On July 23rd Guillemont was attacked by the 21st Brigade of the Thirtieth Division. The right of the attack, consisting of the 19th Manchesters, got into the village, but few got out again : and the left made no progress, the 3rd Yorkshires losing direction to the east and sweeping in upon the ground already held by the 2nd Royal Scots and other battalions of the 8th Brigade. The resistance shown by Guillemont proved that the siege of that village would be a serious operation and that it was not to be carried by the *coup-de-main* of a tired division, however valiantly urged."

The casualties suffered by the Battalion in this attack on Guillemont were as follows :—

Killed—Capt. H. K. Birley, Sec.-Lieuts. C. H. Walton, E. O. Harrison (3rd Royal West Kents) ; wounded—Lieut.-Col. Sir H. B. Hill, Bart., Capts. R. C. Mather, J. W. Myers, Sec.-Lieuts. H. H. Needham, W. E. Tidy ; missing—Capt. W. M. Clarke, Lieuts. J. A. Caldwell, B. la T. Foster, G. Leresche, Sec.-Lieuts. C. V. Cassal, N. H. Craston, C. H. Compton (3rd Royal West Kents) ; other ranks, killed—four ; wounded—fifty ; missing—four hundred and ninety-three.

At 3-30 p.m. on July 23rd the Battalion withdrew to Silesia support, and two hours later moved to Happy Valley. During the night Sec.-Lieut. Linnell, Sergts. Hart and Holding and about thirty men made their way back to the camp. The next day was spent resting. The following days to the end of the month were devoted chiefly to training. One hundred and eighty-two reinforcements joined on the 30th. Sports were held on the afternoon of the 31st.

CHAPTER III

AT LIGNY-THILLOY AND ELSEWHERE

THE Battalion now experienced a spell of comparative quietude, which lasted for a month or two. On August 1st Lieut.-Col. H. B. Hill, Bart., who had been slightly wounded in the attack on Guillemont, but remained at duty, went on leave to England, and Major White took over temporary command of the Battalion. The next day a move was made to Mericourt, where the Battalion entrained for Longpré, and proceeded thence to Citemes. On the 4th it was at Berguette and marched to Robecq. Here the Battalion remained training until the 10th, when it marched to Béthune *en route* for the trenches south of Givenchy. Next day it moved to Tuning Fork area at Gorre. The Battalion was now in Brigade reserve and was strengthened by the arrival of three officers from the 17th Manchesters and seven officers and one hundred and fifty men from other units. Bayonet fighting, physical drill and bombing practice was carried out, and Lewis gun, scouting and signalling classes were continued. On the afternoon of the 14th the Battalion relieved the 18th King's Liverpools in the Givenchy right subsector trenches. The next day there was a certain amount of activity on both sides and the Manchesters had two men killed and ten wounded. The Battalion was relieved on the 19th by the 2nd Wilts, and took over the defence of the village line, holding nine keeps. The work of improving these keeps occupied the men for the next day or two. The 23rd found the Battalion back in the front line. On the following day the British artillery bombarded the enemy mine-shafts behind Red Dragon crater, in which they were assisted by trench mortars and Stokes guns. The enemy reply was feeble. A raid was attempted on the night of the 26th by Sec.-Lieut. G. E. H. Parkes and thirty-two men. The object was to locate an enemy mine-shaft and drop incendiary bombs down it. The wire opposite the crater had already been cut by trench mortars. At 10-55 p.m. the raiding party left the trenches and divided into three bombing sections and a clearing party. Rain had been falling heavily, and the night was exceptionally dark. The raiders lost direction, and only Sec.-Lieut. Parkes and four men reached the objective. They found, however, the wire imperfectly cut and the Germans on the alert. The officer in charge and three of his men were wounded, and finding that his other sections had missed their way, he was compelled to withdraw.

The Battalion was relieved on the night of the 27th by the 19th King's Liverpools and marched to Hingette, where it was billeted, and training was continued. Lieut.-Col. Sir H. B. Hill, Bart., returned from leave on September 3rd and on that date the Battalion moved to La Hamel and Essars, and took over billets from the 18th Manchesters. Training was continued. On the 8th the Battalion was back in Givenchy right subsector trenches. During the following day the left Company was much troubled with Minenwerfer bombs, to which the trench mortars replied. Subsequently the 4·5 howitzers stopped the Minenwerfers for a time, and a code was arranged with the howitzers to retaliate immediately if they opened again. This code was found to be very effective. During the next day or two there was a fair amount of enemy trench mortar activity, which was replied to in kind. The Battalion was relieved in the front line on the 12th and took over the village line, where it was occupied in fatigues. It was back in the front line again on the 16th when there was a heavy bombardment of the enemy front at night, which failed to draw forth any retaliation. The next day the Battalion was relieved by the 16th West Yorks and marched to billets at Béthune. It was again on the move on the 18th. Entraining at Fonquereuil the Battalion arrived at Doullens, and marched thence to billets at Orville. On the 21st it was at Naours and remained there until October 4th carrying out intensive training of various kinds.

On the date named the Battalion left Naours, marched to Vignacourt and was conveyed thence in 'buses to Ribemont, where it bivouaced. The next day it moved to Pommern Redoubt. On the 9th there was an inspection by Major-General J. S. M. Shea. The Battalion paraded in lines in fatigue order. At 2 p.m. the N.C.O.'s paraded for demonstration when a German grenade exploded, from some unknown cause, and occasioned twenty-one casualties.

At 7 a.m. on October 10th the Battalion moved off and spent the day at work on a new road between High Wood and Longueval. The next day it proceeded by Montauban, Thistle Dump and Turk Lane to Crest Trench and spent the day at work on the trenches. During the afternoon the position was violently shelled by the enemy and the Battalion had six men killed and two wounded.

The ridge in front of Ligny-Thilloy was assaulted on the 12th by the 89th and 90th Brigades. The Manchesters had been in reserve, and from 4 a.m. on the 13th two hundred of the men were engaged for over twelve hours carrying the wounded from the front line to the dressing-station. Orders were received at night for the 21st Brigade to relieve the 89th Brigade, in consequence of which the Manchesters moved to Flers trench and Flers support. No sooner was the move completed than the enemy heavily shelled the front trenches and the line of trenches occupied by the Manchesters, evidently expecting a renewal of the previous day's attack. From 1 a.m. to 4-30 a.m. on the 14th, when the wind was blowing from the British towards the German lines, the enemy dropped gas-shells just behind the Manchesters' position. Gas-helmets, however, were quickly adjusted and only six men were slightly effected. The enemy also heavily shelled the New Zealand battery of eighteen guns, which was in position immediately behind the Battalion. On the 15th, from 7 a.m. to 5 p.m., the entire Battalion was at work on the road between High Wood and Longueval, but orders were received during the day for it to relieve the 2nd Wilts in the front line at night. The relief was completed by 10-30 p.m., two Companies being in the front line with two Companies in support, the latter being engaged throughout the night on a new assembly trench. For an hour during the afternoon of the 16th the British artillery bombarded the German front, and incidentally, badly damaged the Manchester line in the process. This naturally put a great strain on the men who had to work at high pressure in preparing the trenches for an intended assault. The shelling of the German lines was continued at intervals throughout the following day.

The attack was planned for the 19th. At zero hour, 3-40 a.m., there opened a terrific shelling by the British artillery. The 21st Brigade attacked Gird trench and Gird support—2nd Yorks, 18th King's Liverpools and 2nd Wilts. The 9th Division attacked on the left, while the 89th Brigade (30th Division) stood on the defensive on the Manchesters' right. At zero the two Companies in command of Capt. Keefe and Capt. Myers were already well up the communication trenches, which had been vacated by the assaulting battalions. As they passed Battalion H.Q., about five minutes after zero, they encountered an enemy barrage and suffered a few casualties. One of these was Sec.-Lieut. A. D. Walker, an officer of great merit, who was severely wounded and died during the day. By the time the Manchesters reached the front line it was apparent that the attack had failed, although a section of the 2nd Wilts had penetrated Gird trench in advance of the 9th Division. For a time it seemed possible that the rest of the Wiltshires had got into Gird trench further to the right. The 9th Division gained their objective and took some prisoners. One of these managed to stray down the trench occupied by the Manchesters and was stopped at H.Q. He stated that he belonged to the 3rd Battalion 104th (Saxon) Infantry Regiment. His age was eighteen and he had only been with the colours five weeks. Whilst waiting for an escort he was killed by a shell. At 10-30 a.m. a tank went over to the German line, cleared the trenches of the enemy, and coming back, reported no signs of the Wiltshires. For some unexplained cause the attack was not then followed up. At noon the Brigade-Major, Capt. Hobson (21st Brigade), came to Battalion H.Q. and said that the Brigadier wished the C.O. to attach a Company of 18th King's Liverpool Regiment for another attack. The C.O. suggested that two companies would be required, as the Battalion was not up to strength. Subsequently, the Brigadier ordered the whole of the Battalion to attack in conjunction with a tank.

The Battalion Diary records that :—

" At 12-35 p.m. operation orders were issued. The 18th King's Liverpools withdrew from our trenches. Remnants of the 2nd Wilts occupied one hundred and fifty yards on the left of our line.

The Nineteenth Manchesters assembled two Companies :—

No. 1, Lieut. Boxall, No. 2, Capt. Keefe, in the newly-dug forward trench. No. 3 and 4 Companies under Capt. Turner and Sec.-Lieut. Henshall occupied the whole front trench. The first two Companies were to form the first wave; the third and fourth the second wave. The four Companies were under the immediate command of Capt. Myers. There was to be no special artillery preparation. The signal for the simultaneous advance of both waves was to be the crossing of the forward trench by a tank. All was reported ready for the assault at 4-30 p.m., when the Brigadier cancelled the operation because the tank had broken down on its way to our assistance. We were then ordered to take over the whole front line from Goose Alley to Turk Lane, the remnants of the Wilts holding the line from Turk Lane to the Sunken Road, in touch with the 9th Division.

During the night (18th-19th) the front forward trench was continued and connected up to the German trench captured by the 9th Division on the previous day, and was occupied by us before day-break. During the night and early morning the enemy had made violent bombing attacks on the front of the 9th Division, using a flammenwerfer on the Sunken Road, but without any success. The 11th Black Watch, on our left, running short of hand-grenades, we were able to help them by sending along some ninety boxes of Mills bombs from the dumps which had been formed in our line. It had been raining heavily during the night and early morning and the trenches were, consequently, deep in mud. The transference of these boxes was, therefore, most difficult. In addition to the mud the men were under constant heavy shell fire, which made the labour very exhausting. There were a number of casualties, including Sec.-Lieut. R. Bagshaw and Sec.-Lieut. A. J. Linnell. Heavy rain continued throughout most of the day, and the shelling was especially severe towards midnight.

Early on the morning of the 20th the Brigadier rang up to enquire if the Battalion could hold on for another twenty-four hours. Although greatly exhausted the morale of the men had not been impaired and the C.O. replied that they could hold on.

At 9 a.m. the C.O. went round the trenches with the Brigade-Major (Capt. Hobson). The rain had now ceased, but the trenches were in a shockingly bad condition. There were many dead and wounded and several men had completely collapsed, but in spite of their hardships the remainder were cleaning their rifles, attempting to clear the mud from the trenches and were burying the dead.

Our casualties for the day were :—

Eight men killed ; thirty-one wounded and three missing.

During the afternoon Lieut.-Col. Scott, 56th Australian Regiment, reconnoitred our trenches preparatory to relieving us to-morrow."

There was a slight frost during the night and the morning of the 21st opened with fair weather. Relief commenced at 6 p.m. and was completed by 8-30 p.m. The Battalion marched back to Pommern Redoubt, via Thistle Dump and Montauban. Pack mules were provided at the ration dump near Flers village to carry the packs of some fifteen of the most exhausted men. At Thistle Dump, situated at the cross roads N.E. of Bazentin-le-Petit, ambulances picked up about twenty-five men who were in a state of collapse. The 23rd was spent resting and cleaning rifles, equipment and clothes.

The next day the Battalion marched to Dernancourt, where re-organisation was effected. The enemy shelled the village from 8-30 a.m. to 10-30 a.m., and again from 4-30 to 6-30 p.m. Several houses were demolished and a number of civilians killed. The Battalion had one man killed and seven wounded. On the 26th a move was made to Lucheux, where the Battalion was transferred from the Fourth to the Third Army. Here some days were spent in various kinds of training. The 30th found the Battalion at Bailleulmont, into which place the enemy dropped about thirty shells on the afternoon of the next day, but there were no casualties.

On November 4th the Battalion relieved the 2nd Yorks in the Berles trenches, and for some days the situation was quiet. The enemy shelled the position during the afternoon and evening of the 9th. At about 4-30 p.m. orders came that the Battalion should attempt to gas the Germans between the hours of 7 p.m. to 10 p.m. Unfortunately, however, the wind changed and the attempt had to be abandoned. The British artillery bombarded the enemy lines, dumps, etc., at various times during the night. The Battalion was relieved by the 2nd Yorks on the 11th, and for some days afterwards supplied working parties. But it was back in the front line on the 17th. The situation was fairly quiet. The weather cold and frosty, but fine.

On the 23rd the Battalion was relieved and proceeded to Bailleulmont. On this date it furnished one hundred men for work at Gastrineau, and a further hundred at Lanark Lane. The "Blue Birds" gave a performance in the recreation hut at night. The Battalion moved back into the front line on the 29th.

December 1st opened very misty, and during this and the following day the Battalion was occupied cleaning trenches. On the 4th the weather changed to a keen frost. Working was continued. On this date a bombing patrol went out and bombed a German sap in which six of the enemy were seen, causing casualties.

An exciting episode occurred when L/Cpl. Hobson was in the act of throwing a bomb, when he was hit in the wrist. The bomb fell from his hand. With great coolness, however, he picked it up again while it was hissing and threw it in the German trench, thereby probably saving the lives of his comrades. He was awarded the Military Medal. Later he was a second time wounded.

The Battalion was relieved on December 5th by the 2nd Yorks, and went into Brigade reserve at Bailleulval. Here training of various kinds was carried out. It was back in the line on the 11th. The situation at this time was quiet. The trenches in many places had fallen in and the men were principally occupied in repairing them. A draft of seventy-eight men joined on the 15th. On the 17th the Battalion moved to Bailleulmont. Here training was continued. The Manchesters went into the line again on the 23rd, and here Christmas was spent. There was considerable aerial activity on the 24th, but otherwise conditions were fairly quiet. Work on the trenches was continued. Boxing Day was enlivened by artillery activity on both sides. The weather was very wet. The 2nd Yorks relieved on the 29th and the Manchesters again went into Brigade reserve at Bailleulval. Working parties, however, were provided for the front for the next day or two. And so the year 1916 was brought to a close. Lieut.-Col. A. White was now in command.

CHAPTER IV

IN THE ARRAS SECTOR

JANUARY 1st, 1917, was a general holiday—a welcome change from working parties and fatigues. On the following day, however, the Battalion relieved the 2nd Yorks in the Berles line, when work was resumed in clearing out and rivetting the front line trenches. Also a further draft of sixty-seven men was received. There was an artillery duel on the 3rd, but otherwise little activity of a military character. Work was continued for some days, and the weather was very wet. The Battalion was relieved on the 6th and proceeded to La Cauchy, where it was billeted for the night, and moved the following day to Boquemaison. Here the Battalion remained training until the 15th. Sec.-Lieuts. G. E. Estill, H. M. Fort, C. P. Fripp and T. L. Swann joined the Battalion ; also forty-seven men.

On the 15th a move was made to Pommern, where training was continued and working parties provided. Here the Battalion remained until February 4th, when it proceeded to Humbercourt for the night, and next day moved to Beaumetz. On the 6th it made a further move to Achicourt, via Berneville, Warlus and Dainville. The following day the Battalion relieved the 2nd Yorks in the line. The situation was quiet and the weather very cold. On the 13th the Battalion proceeded to Arras in Brigade reserve. The situation remained quiet and working parties were provided. The Battalion left Arras on the 27th and moved to Beaumetz, marching the same day to Achicourt. This sudden move was occasioned by the 6th Sherwood Foresters being recalled to the 46th Division, they having recently been occupying Gommécourt.

March 1st opened with bright, fresh spring-time weather. The morning and afternoon were given up to cleaning and inspections. At 8 p.m. the Battalion furnished a working party of five officers and two hundred and fifty other ranks on a cable trench in the vicinity of Agny. The following day the work was continued. Those not engaged on fatigues carried on with rifle-grenade, bombing and Lewis gun classes. Part of the Battalion left Achicourt on the 3rd and proceeded to Beaumetz, being followed by the remainder on the 5th. During the night of the 3rd thirteen hostile shells were put into Beaumetz, but there were no casualties. From Beaumetz the Battalion proceeded to Saulty Divisional School for training purposes. There was a considerable fall of snow on the night of the 5th which did not add to the joys of soldiering. The Battalion remained in and about Beaumetz and Saulty until the 18th, when it moved to Arras.

The Battalion had received orders to proceed to Pommern on this date, and preparations had been made for so doing. Notice, however, was received cancelling this move, and it was directed to leave Beaumetz for Arras. Accordingly, whilst billeted in Arras on the 19th, an urgent order was received at 4-10 p.m. for the Battalion to move up in support, preparatory to moving forward at night. The move, however, did not develop. The Manchesters were relieved in the support line (Agny) by the R.S.F. on the following day, and returned to Beaumetz. On the 21st the Battalion moved to Pommern. The weather was now very cold and there was a slight fall of snow. On the 23rd a further move was made to Bavincourt. The weather had now turned very wet, and so continued for some days. Training was carried out. The Battalion received orders on the 28th to proceed to Madeleine Redoubt, which was reached at 8-30 p.m. The Manchesters provided working parties on the ammunition dump. The Redoubt was heavily shelled by the enemy during the three days following and there were a number of casualties. Lieut.-Col C. J. MacDonald, D.S.O. was now in command, succeeding Lieut.-Col. A. White, who had been appointed to the command of the Divisional Depôt. The great German retreat on the Arras-Soissons front was now in progress. From Arras to Roye the British were advancing, while the forward movement was carried to Soissons by the French. But at each end of the large curve—Arras in the north and Soissons in the south—the Germans held fast, though the intervening country, to a considerable depth, was being over-run by the Allies.

The operations of the Nineteenth Manchesters centred around Hénin-sur-Cojeul. At 8-30 p.m. on March 30th No. 3 Company moved off from Madeleine Redoubt and relieved "B" Company of the 2nd Yorks in the trenches, sending in two Platoons at a time. A few casualties were sustained during this operation, owing to heavy shelling. All necessary precautions were taken, and the Company got connection with the Wilts, but not with the Yorks. At dawn on the 31st the Company fell back to another line, leaving as garrison a bombing section at No. 1 outpost. Later it was learnt that both the Wilts and Yorks had had to leave their positions, but the Manchester Company had orders to hold on at all costs, which it did. At 2 a.m. on April 1st No. 1 post repulsed an attack from about fifty of the enemy, who were driven back to Nagpur trench.

No. 4 Company moved off from Madeleine Redoubt at 8-30 p.m. on March 30th and took over from " A " Company of 2nd Yorks three strong points which formed the support line. At 9-30 p.m. on April 1st No. 4 Company relieved No. 3 Company in outposts Nos. 1 and 2. A patrol from No. 1 post ascertained that the enemy was in occupation of Nagpur trench. A second patrol was sent out to discover whether the enemy had a bombing post in Nagpur trench. No such post was found, but movement was observed at the cross roads, and a machine gun was directed on the patrol from the west corner of the village. On April 2nd, during the attack on the village, the Lewis gun and machine gun of No. 1 outpost opened fire on an enemy strong point, which held up the advance for some time. On the night of April 2nd No. 4 Company dug a third outpost similar to No. 1 and 2 and about one hundred and fifty yards N.W. of No. 2. On the night of April 3rd the Company was relieved by the Royal Scots Fusiliers.

No. 1 Company moved off from Madeleine Redoubt at 10-30 p.m. on April 1st and reached assembly point at 4-40 a.m. At 4-50 a.m. it advanced to assault position, and at 5-15 a.m. advanced as moppers-up to " B " Company, 2nd Yorks. The Company was responsible for mopping-up the village up to and including the Central Road. When the village was entered the O.C. Company was wounded. On the right No. 3 Platoon was held up by snipers, and was afterwards forced back to the Red Wall. From here rifle-grenades were sent over on to snipers. Five prisoners were taken here and sent down. Sec.-Lieut. Estill, who was in charge behind the Red Wall, sent out a Lewis gun to play on snipers. In the centre No. 1 Platoon reached a point about one hundred yards to the left of the Red Wall, and took a prisoner there. Afterwards, part of this Platoon proceeded to No. 5 strong point, and thence to No. 3, both of which they helped to consolidate. On the left, No. 2 Platoon after clearing its sector, reported to No. 5 strong point and remained there until relieved by the 16th Manchesters on April 2nd. No. 4 Platoon carried up material for No. 4 and 5 strong points. The whole Company was relieved at 11-45 p.m. on April 2nd by the 16th Manchesters.

No. 2 Company moved off behind the 2nd Yorks, as moppers-up from left, but exclusive of Central Road. The right flank was held by No. 6 Platoon, under Sec.-Lieut. Fyfe, and worked all ground and buildings east of the river Cojeul. The river was crossed for this purpose and good direction kept. Enemy machine guns opened on the right of the village, but soon ceased fire. The village was a concentration of mines and debris, the latter affording good cover for snipers. No. 6 Platoon carefully explored the whole of the ground in its sector, captured several prisoners and suffered some slight casualties. It then crossed to the west side of the river and gave help elsewhere. Other Platoons rendered similar help. The Company was relieved by the 16th Manchesters at 11-45 p.m. on April 2nd.

The two Companies, which had acted as cleaners in Hénin-sur-Cojeul when relieved by the 16th Manchesters on April 2nd, moved to Blairville Quarry. The two remaining Companies remained in the outposts and front line N.W. of Hénin-sur-Cojeul. On April 3rd the four Companies moved to billets in Basseux. The 4th was given up to cleaning and inspections, and the reorganisation of Companies. There was an inspection by the C.O. on the morning of the 5th, and during the afternoon the Battalion proceeded to the training trenches, S.W. of Basseux, and practised for the pending assault on the Hindenburg line. Similar training took place on the following day, in conjunction with other battalions of the Brigade.

On the 7th the Battalion marched via Beaumetz, Brétencourt and Wailly to a point near the old British front line, where extra battle equipment, including tools and bombs, were drawn. After dusk the Battalion proceeded via Ficheux to the Schlangen Redoubt, where the night was spent. The following day a further move was made to Switch Lane. On the 11th, however, the Battalion was back at Basseux, and on the 12th it moved to billets at Berles-au-Bois. On the afternoon of the 13th notice was received by wire that the Battalion was to be prepared to move at short notice to Agny. Move orders were subsequently received, and at 6 p.m. the Battalion marched to Agny, where the night was spent in the old British trenches to the south of that place. On the 15th it moved back to Berles-au-Bois, remaining there training until the 19th, when it moved off by Companies to the Cojeul Switch in the Hindenburg line. Here S.A.A., grenades, bombs, Verey lights, etc., were issued to the Battalion in preparation for its acting as support in a projected attack on the 23rd.

On the morning of April 23rd the Battalion was in the trenches in the Hindenburg line, on the west side of the Cojeul river, in reserve to the 90th Brigade. At 9-15 a.m. it received orders to move across the river to the slopes S.E. of Héninel, and by 11-30 it was in position. At 12-40 p.m. the Battalion moved up to occupy the left of the old British front line, with the left resting on Wancourt Tower.

" D " Company moved off first, followed by " C," " B " and " A," in this order. On the way up to the trenches, however, the Battalion came under heavy artillery and machine gun fire, and upon its arrival in the trench the arrangement of Companies had become somewhat disorganised. On the left of the Battalion, and in touch with it, was the 150th Brigade.

At 5 p.m. the C.O. was sent for to Brigade H.Q. and informed that the attack would be renewed at 6 p.m. The objective was a line overlooking Cherisy and the attack was to be made by the Nineteenth Manchesters on the left and the 18th Manchesters on the right.

The C.O. found it a difficult operation to carry out at short notice. In order to have a depth of three waves, it was found necessary to attack on a frontage of three Platoons. The objective was eight hundred yards of trench still held by an active enemy. At the time the order to attack arrived the Battalion was being reorganised. The C.O. assembled his Company Commanders at H.Q. and explained the plan of attack. This was to attack on a three-company front—"C" on the right, "B" in the centre, "A" on the left—each Company consisting of two Platoons in depth. "D" Company, which consisted of but three Platoons, was to support each of the other Companies with one Platoon. Unfortunately, Sec.-Lieut. H. W. Purdy, in command of "D" Company, was killed on his way back from H.Q., and his Company having no orders and knowing nothing of the details of the intended attack, did not leave the assembly trenches. When the other officers reached their Companies they had only about five minutes in which to explain to their men the plan of attack, objective and rate of barrage.

At 6 p.m. the attack was launched. The frontage proved too wide for the Companies to keep effectively in touch, and the enemy trench was penetrated only in isolated points. During the advance, too, a good many casualties were suffered from our own barrage. When the men came under machine gun fire they doubled forward, and the officers and sergeants, owing to the noise and excitement, were unable to hold them back. "A" and "B" Companies were able to join up in the German front line. The trench on the left of "C" and on the right of "B" was still full of the enemy, and there was no sign of the Battalion which the C.O. had been informed, was to effect the clearing up. Meanwhile, heavy machine-gun fire was being poured in from the enemy second line trench. As "A" Company was by this time reduced to about nineteen men and "B" to about sixteen, it was impossible to advance further without leaving behind an unmopped-up trench full of the enemy. All the officers of both Companies had become casualties and the N.C.O.'s in charge decided to hang on to what they had gained. A similar state of affairs existed on the right where a sergeant of "C" Company, with thirteen men, had assaulted and was holding on to a portion of the German front line trench. But with this difference. Whereas "A" and "B" Companies held on all night the "C" Company party was ordered by an officer of another regiment to withdraw after dark. About midnight the tension was relieved by the arrival of the 2nd Yorks who moved up in support to the Manchesters.

At about 11 a.m. on the following morning when the 2nd Yorks moved forward to occupy the Blue line, Lieut.-Col. MacDonald advanced three Platoons of his Nineteenth Manchesters to occupy the German support line, making his H.Q. in the Quarry. Later he collected the various parties which had made the attack the night before and further garrisoned the German support line.

In the evening four strong points were constructed by a party of R.E. in the rear of the front line, and these were each garrisoned by one Platoon of Nineteenth Manchesters under Sec.-Lieuts. Cookson, Fyfe and Swann, and Sergt. Ford respectively. Two of the Platoons were relieved on the 25th by garrisons of the 89th Brigade; the remaining two being relieved on the 28th by parties from other units.

On the 29th the Battalion marched to Arras and entrained for Maisnil St. Pol, where on the following day physical training was commenced.

CHAPTER V

THE THIRD BATTLE OF YPRES AND DISBANDMENT

MAY 1st opened at Maisnil St. Pol with bright, warm, sunny weather. Now ensued a long period of training and many movements, and it was not until July 31st that the Battalion was again in action, when it took part in the attack on the German line east of Ypres.

On May 3rd the Battalion left Maisnil St. Pol and proceeded to Croisette, where various kinds of training were undertaken. A field practice was carried out on the 18th by the 21st Brigade, which was attended by General Lord Allenbury, K.C.B., who complimented the Divisional Commander, Major-General W. D. L. Williams, C.M.G., D.S.O., on the success of the operations. Unfortunately the day was very wet.

The Battalion had moved to Fillievres and Galametz on the 15th, and on the 20th proceeded to Beauvois. Rapid movements now took place. On the 21st the Battalion was at Fiefs, on the 22nd at Flechine. The 24th found it at Boeseghem, and on the following day it was at Hondeghem. Steenvoorde was reached on the 26th and on the 29th the Battalion moved to Toronto Camp in the Brandhoek area. Here it remained training and providing working parties on cable trenches until June 14th, where it moved to Dickebusch. This place was left on the 20th when a move was made to Château Segard, and on the following day the Battalion was in the trenches in the Ypres salient. Here the enemy artillery and aircraft kept things pretty lively and the Battalion suffered some casualties. A draft of ninety-eight men joined on the 25th. The 17th King's Liverpool Regiment relieved on the 29th and the Manchesters proceeded to Canal Reserve Camp, Dickebusch. The same day they marched to Busseboom, entrained for Watten, and so proceeded to Nordansques. Here training was continued. On July 18th the Battalion moved to the Abeele area. The 24th found it at Cornwall Camp. On the 28th the Battalion was at Château Segard; on the following day at Maple

Copse; and on the 30th it proceeded to Crab Crawl Tunnel in preparation for the attack on the German line east of Ypres on the 31st. The weather at this time was very wet.

The general characteristics and some details of the Third Battle of Ypres, on the 31st July and following days, have been described by Sir Arthur Conan Doyle :—

" At 4 o'clock in the morning, in the first grey light of a rainy morning, under a canopy of grey sweeping clouds, and in a fog-girt landscape of bedraggled fields and brown patches of wire, the French and British infantry sprang forward with splendid alacrity upon this dangerous venture which should culminate in taking the last dominant ridge upon the British front from those who had held them so long......

" The British line of battle was formed by five Corps, the XIVth (Cavan) to the north; the XVIIIth (Maxse) upon its right; the XIXth (Watts) upon the right of that; the IInd (Jacob) came next; and then upon the southern edge of the area, and hardly engaged in the main fighting, was the Xth (Morland). Each Corps had two Divisions in the line and two in reserve. It should be noted that the four first Corps made up Gough's Fifth Army, and that the Xth Corps was the only part of Plumer's Army to be engaged."

Further on, Doyle proceeds :—

" The Thirtieth Division, which consisted as will be remembered to a large extent of " Pal " Battalions from Liverpool and Manchester, advanced to the south of the Eighth. Sanctuary Wood, and other strong points lay in front of the 90th and 21st Brigades which provided the first line of stormers. The resistance was strong, the fire was heavy and the losses were considerable, so that the assailants were held up and were unable to do more than carry the front trenches, whence they repulsed repeated counter-attacks during the rest of the day."

The Thirtieth Division—to which the Nineteenth Manchesters were attached—in conjunction with other Divisions of the Fifth Army, were detailed to attack the enemy lines east of Ypres. The Twenty-fourth Division was on the right of the Thirtieth, the Eighth Division on its left, and the Eighteenth in support. Zero hour was 3-50 a.m. Heavy rain had fallen during the night and early hours and greatly impeded the movement of the troops.

The official record of the Nineteenth Manchesters thus describes the Battalion's share in the operations :—

At zero the Battalion was disposed as follows :—

Bn. H.Q. and " A " and " B " Companies in Crab Crawl Tunnel, " C " and " D " Companies in Maple Copse. At zero " A " and " B " Companies began to file out of the tunnel—" A " by Crab Crawl entrances and " B " by the Peter Street entrances. Almost immediately after zero these entrances became choked by wounded men and others trying to get into the tunnel. The out-going troops were very much hampered in their movements and were only able to get out by one's and two's at a time. This made assembly in the open very difficult, especially as it was still dark, and there was a heavy barrage on the British front line. Small parties pushed out into "No Man's Land" in order to get out of the enemy's barrage line with the result that these two Companies were unable to form up in their battle formations, and so cohesion was lost from the start. Half the officers of either Company became casualties before crossing the British front line. Consequently, the lack of leadership was felt both at this point and further on, when isolated groups arrived in the firing line.

"C" and "D" Companies began to move up from Maple Copse at zero. A reconnaisance of the day before had shown that the only practicable route by which these Companies would be likely to reach their position in time was via Observatory Ridge Road. Unfortunately the enemy put down a very heavy barrage on the ridge as these two Companies were going over and they suffered considerable casualties. "D" Company which was leading, was thrown into some confusion by the enemy barrage—two of its officers became casualties, and it is doubtful whether it ever regained its proper formation as a Company. On reaching the firing line it was not in sufficient strength to push the attack much further.

"C" Company, although suffering pretty heavily, remained under the control of the Company Commander, and on passing through the barrage shook out into lines of Platoons as originally intended. This Company arrived at the point where the 2nd Yorks were held up. The two leading Platoons kept too much to their left, and were a little to the left of the Battalion boundary. And they were not in touch with the 18th King's Liverpool Regiment, who should have been on their left.

During the advance over the German trenches there was a tendency on the part of all Platoons to veer to their left. This was due to two causes:—

(*a*) The troops of the Division on the right were edging strongly to their left and were pushing the Nineteenth Manchesters in that direction.

(*b*) The Battalion was not in touch with the troops whom it expected to find on its left flank.

On arrival at the point where the leading Battalions were held up an endeavour was made to continue the advance. This attempt was renewed two or three times. But the protective barrage was by this time too far forward to give any assistance. And, in the meantime, the enemy had remanned his strong points and machine gun positions, and was sweeping the ground between our front and the western edge of Dumbarton Wood. Moreover, the troops were not now in sufficient depth to give a further advance any great chance of success. Consequently, no further advance beyond a short rush of forty yards by one Platoon was achieved. Several tanks arrived on the scene between 6-30 a.m. and 7-30 a.m., but their arrival did not seriously alter the situation.

Finding a further advance impossible, consolidation of the position reached was at once proceeded with. The whole area was under machine gun fire, and it was necessary to take advantage of all existing cover and adapt that to the purpose of defence. Shortly after 8 a.m. a company of the 20th King's Liverpools reached the firing line and endeavoured to push forward. This attempt, however, was no more successful than previous attempts had been, and the Company remained as part of the garrison of this area until withdrawn to rejoin its unit on the evening of August 2nd. It may be noted, in conclusion, that the trenches became more and more difficult to hold owing to the rain. By the middle of the third day many of the men were standing up to their waists in water, and the whole area was too waterlogged to allow of any fresh trenches being dug. Heavy rain had fallen during the whole period.

The casualties during this action were :—

Capt. J. W. Myers (died of wounds) ; Sec.-Lieuts. A. H. W. Beatty S. G. Morton, B. Waldron (killed in action) ; Major R. C. Mather, Lieuts. W. Myers, H. F. Southon, Sec.-Lieuts. W. G. Brittlebank, J. Crompton, M. E. Humphrey Moore, O. M. Etherington, J. R. Powell, A. Shaw, P. C. Smyth, J. E. Taylor (wounded) ; other ranks, two hundred and eighty-three casualties.

The Battalion was relieved on the night of 2nd/3rd August and withdrew to Château Segard. Here it rested for a day, and the rain fell heavily. On the 4th the Battalion was moved by 'bus to the Eecke area. On the 7th it marched to the Merris area. Here it remained cleaning up and training until the 11th, when a further move was made to Stafford Camp in the IXth Corps reserve area. The next move was to the Kemmel Hill area on the 21st, and on the following day the Battalion moved to the right support subsector in the ridge defences south of Wytschaete, relieving the 2nd Wilts. Sec.-Lieuts. T. Gadsby, J. Leech, C. H. Spencer, F. G. Tomlinson and H. Twigg joined for duty.

The Battalion supplied working parties for some days. On the 30th it moved into the front line. The following officers joined for duty on the 31st :—

Sec.-Lieuts. A. S. Anderson, F. H. Clarke, C. Davies, G. Jackson. H. Kelly, F. P. Leybourn, O. W. Mitchell.

Wiring, rivetting and carrying parties were supplied by the Battalion until the 6th September, when the 2nd Wilts relieved, and the Manchesters moved back into the right support subsector in the ridge defences south of Wytschaete. Working parties were supplied for some days. On the 10th the Battalion moved to a camp south of Kemmel Hill. Here inspections, cleaning of equipment and training took place, and later the Battalion again supplied working parties. Lieut.-Col. C. L. MacDonald, D.S.O., went on leave on the 17th and Major W. S. Cunliffe took over the command. On the 22nd the Manchesters moved back into the Wytschaete ridge defences—wiring and strengthening breastwork in the picquet line for some days. On the 27th the Battalion was back in the ridge defences. The 30th September found it back in camp. During the early days of October the Battalion alternated between the camp and the ridge defences. A diversion was created on the 6th when an advanced Company H.Q. was raided by an enemy bombing party of twenty or so. They were not observed until they had reached the H.Q. dug-out when they threw several bombs and attempted to blow in the dug-out, wounding Sec.-Lieut. Twigg and four other ranks. Upon this officer rushing out and firing his revolver the party retreated and escaped. Working parties continued to be supplied for some time.

It was not until November 15th that any change took place, when the Battalion moved by 'bus to the Steenvoorde area. Whilst here Lieut.-Col. C. L. MacDonald, D.S.O., who had returned from leave on November 2nd, went into hospital on the 23rd, and Capt. G. F. E. Rapson (2nd Wilts) took over command of the Battalion. On the 26th the Manchesters relieved the 14th Hampshires in the Tower Hamlets ridge line, east of Zillebeke. There was an attempted enemy raid on the 30th, which proved ineffectual, and on this date the 2nd Wilts relieved, and the Manchesters moved back into support positions in and about Hedge Street Tunnel. Here the Battalion supplied tunnelling parties. Capt. Rapson went into hospital on December 7th and Capt. T. W. Baron, M.C. (2nd Yorks) took over the command. On the 17th the Battalion moved by rail to Chippawa Camp, where Company parades and training took place. The 23rd found it back in the Hedge Street Tunnel sector, and here Christmas Day was spent. On the 26th the Battalion relieved the 2nd Wilts in the line, where it was employed in digging and improving support trenches. This tour of duty lasted until the 29th when the Battalion was relieved by the 2nd Yorks, and moved by march-route to Scottish Wood Camp. Here on New Year's Eve the Battalion Christmas dinner was served to officers and men.

On January 4th, 1918, the Manchesters were back in the Tower Hamlets sector, east of Zillebeke. Lieut.-Col. C. L. MacDonald rejoined from hospital on the 6th. Some rapid moves now took place. On the 6th the Battalion moved to Alberta Camp. The following day it was in billets at Cercus. On the 10th it was at Longueau. The 13th found it at Quesnel. The next day the Battalion was at Margny and Cherisy. Next to Golancourt on the 20th. The Battalion was now in the St. Quentin area. At all these places training was continued. A move was made to Commenchon on the 27th, and to Camp Frieres on the following day.

The end of the Battalion as a separate unit was now at hand. On February 3rd it paraded in close column and was addressed by the C.O. He stated that it had been found necessary to reorganise the Army on a basis of three battalions to a brigade. To do this it had been decided to disband the Junior Battalion of each Brigade of the Division, and since the Nineteenth Battalion Manchester Regiment was the Junior Battalion of the Brigade, it would be disbanded at an early date. The right-half (" A " and " B " Companies) would be transferred to the 16th Manchesters ; the left-half (" C " and " D " Companies) to the 17th Manchesters. It was a hard necessity after the Battalion had been in existence since the outbreak of War. The C.O. read a letter from Field-Marshal Sir Douglas Haig expressing deep regret and sympathy at the necessity for measures so painful, but confident that they would be accepted in the best spirit. A letter was also read from Sir H. de la P. Gough, commanding the Fifth Army, expressing the like sentiments. The G.O.C. 21st Brigade then delivered a valedictory address.

On the 5th February the Battalion was addressed by the G.O.C. 30th Division with reference to its impending disbandment. He expressed his regret and sympathy, and referred to the part the Battalion had taken in the War, laying emphasis on the splendid work it had achieved in the taking of Glatz Redoubt. Although the Battalion would cease to exist as a separate unit, the officers and other ranks would remain in the Division. He referred to the prospect of an early enemy offensive and expressed his confidence that it would end in complete victory for the Allied Armies.

The disbandment took place on February 6th, when the officers and sections—less Battalion H.Q. and details— proceeded by march-route to join other units.

The following were posted to the 16th Battalion Manchester Regiment :—

Capts. O. T. Pritchard, T. Nicholson, Sec.-Lieuts. H. Kelley, G. A. Moss, F. J. Smith, W. H. J. Pennell, T. Gadsby, O. W. Mitchell, F. J. Durrant, W. G. Brittlebank, M. D. Pleasance, S. Findlay, J. H. Drine ; also two hundred and eighty other ranks.

The following were posted to the 17th Battalion Manchester Regiment :—

Capts. N. S. Ince, M.C., R. C. M. Keefe, M.C., Lieuts. J. Cookson, F. Henshall, Sec.-Lieuts. C. J. Backhouse, C. Davies, M.M., S. A. Jackson, A. S. Anderson, N. A. Arnold, G. Leech, M.M., F. P. Leybourn, M.M., F. Cartwright, S. W. Cannon, S. A. Halstead, F. Halliwell; also two hundred and eighty-two other ranks.

Unposted :—C.O., Second-in-Command, Adjutant and A.-Q.M., M.O., Chaplain, T.O., Lieuts. L. H. Ibbotson and J. O'Malley ; and seventy-eight other ranks.

On the 7th Battalion H.Q., details and transport moved by march to Caillouel and Crepigny. The next day they were at Buchoire and on the 9th at Berlancourt. There were Church parades on the 10th. The Rev. A. Roughley, C.F., left the Battalion on the 11th to report to 21st M.G.C. Parades continued for several days after disbandment. Battalion H.Q. and details moved to Golancourt on the 14th. Sec.-Lieut. F. C. Hemm and transport remaining at Berlancourt. At Golancourt Battalion H.Q. and details formed part of the 30th Division Surplus Reinforcements, under command of Lieut.-Col. J. W. H. T. Douglas, 20th King's Liverpool Regiment. Major W. S. Cunliffe rejoined from 30th Division Wing Corps Reinforcement Camp. From the 15th to 19th there were daily parades in signalling. On the 19th the section moved to Haut Allaines, when Lieut.-Col. C. L. MacDonald, D.S.O., took over command of Reinforcements from Lieut.-Col. J. W. H. T. Douglas on leave.

For the following days of the month there is nothing to record. Lieut.-Col. C. L. MacDonald, D.S.O., proceeded to England on leave on the 27th and on the following day the residue of the Battalion proceeded to the base.

APPENDIX I
HONOURS

DISTINGUISHED SERVICE ORDER

Name	Rank	Place and date of deed	Gazetted
MACDONALD, Charles Leslie	Capt. (T/Maj.)		1-1-17
" " (*Bar*)	T/Lieut.-Col.	Ypres, 1917 ..	26-9-17
(17th B. Man. R.) *attached*			9-1-18

MILITARY CROSS

Rank	Name	Gazetted	Remarks
T/Sec.-Lt.	HADDOCK, Eric Moselyn ..	26-7-17	
Lieut.	INCE, Norman Sedgwick ..	1-1-18	Zillebeke 1917
T/Capt.	KEEFE, Reginald Conrad Murray	1-1-17	Zillebeke 1917 K. in. a. 27-3-18
T/Sec.-Lt.	SMITH, Frank Julian ..	26-7-18	
T/Capt.	TIDY, Warwick Edward ..	1-1-17	
11576/C.S.M.	HOLDING, Harry	26-7-17	

DISTINGUISHED CONDUCT MEDAL

No.	Name	Rank	Place and date of deed	Gazetted
12337.	GREEN, C. B... ..	Sgt.		4-6-17 9-7-17
11978.	RILEY, H.	Sgt.		26-7-17
12235.	WAREHAM, W. ..	Pte.		14-11-16

MILITARY MEDAL

No.	Name	Rank	Place and date of deed	Gazetted
9417.	ARROWSMITH H. F.	L/Sgt.		26-5-17
6548.	BAILEY, E.	Pte.		28-9-17
1738.	BARNES, T.	Sgt.		9-12-16
8498.	BATTY, T.	Pte.		28-9-17
2010.	BIBBY, T.	Pte.		16-11-16
4694.	BRINDLEY, H. ..	Sgt.		9-7-17
2608.	COLLINS, F.	Pte.		18-6-17
8544.	CURRAN, J., D.C.M. ..	L/Cpl.		28-9-17
1789.	DERBYSHIRE, L. ..	L/Cpl.		21-9-16
5596.	DODD, N.	Cpl.		9-7-17
2642.	FERGUSON, C. D. ..	Pte.		20-9-17
2087.	GRAY, T. R.			20-2-17
0942.	HINTON, A.	Pte.		26-5-17
"	" (*Bar*) ..			28-9-17
45114.	HOBSON, H.	Pte. (L/Cpl.)		19-2-17
1844.	HOLMES, A. S.	Sgt.		28-9-17
18514.	HOWARTH, C. E. ..	Sgt.		28-9-17
1861.	JOHNSON, A.	Sgt.		28-9-17
12383.	KETTLEWELL, F. J. ..	Cpl.		21-9-16
44709.	KIRK, D.	Pte.		18-6-17
12146.	MILLER, D.	Pte.		23-8-16
1652.	ROTHWELL, H. ..	Sgt.		22-1-17
1928.	SMITH, A.	Pte.		16-11-16
1981.	WHEATCROFT, F. H.	Pte.		21-9-16
1975.	WYNNE, W. J. ..	Pte.		23-8-16

MERITORIOUS SERVICE MEDAL

No.	Rank	Name	Gazetted
9670.	Cpl. ..	DAGNALL, F.	29-8-18
11453.	R.Q.M.S. ..	MAGUIRE, J.	4-6-17
12236.	Pte. ..	WALSH, J.	18-1-19

FOREIGN DECORATIONS

BELGIUM—CROIX DE GUERRE

No.	Rank	Name	Gazetted
12057.	Sgt. ..	WILSON, Samuel..	12-7-18

FRANCE—CROIX DE GUERRE

No.	Rank	Name	Gazetted
119768.	L/Cpl. ..	RILEY, Harold, D.C.M.	14-7-17
12235.	Pte. ..	WAREHAM, W., D.C.M.	7-5-17

APPENDIX II
OFFICERS KILLED
(IN ORDER OF DATE)

OFFICERS KILLED (in order of date)

Rank	*Name*	*Date*	*Place*
T/Sec.-Lt.	ATKINSON, Arthur Wilfred ..	1-7-16	
T/Capt.	ROYLE, Frederick William (d. of w.)	8-7-16	
T/Capt.	HISLOP, John Arthur .. (died)	8-7-16	
T/Sec.-Lt.	SMITH, Willoughby Willard.. .. (T.M.B.) *attached*	9-7-16	
T/Capt.	BIRLEY, Hugh Kennedy	23-7-16	
T/Sec.-Lt.	WALTON, Charles Hindley	23-7-16	
Lieut.	FOSTER, Bernard La Trobe ..	24-7-16	
T/Sec.-Lt.	COPLEY, Alan	2-4-17	
T/Sec.-Lt.	MURPHY, Edward	2-4-17	
T/Sec.-Lt.	NICHOLSON, Arthur Harry (d. of w.)	9-4-17	
T/Sec.-Lt.	PURDY, Harry Wilfred	23-4-17	
Capt.	MYERS, James Wheatley (d. of w.)	14-8-17	
Sec.-Lieut.	CARTRIGHT, Frank..	22-3-18	
T/Capt.	KEEFE, Ronald Conray Murray ..	27-3-18	
T/Sec.-Lt.	FINDLAY, Scott .. .. .. (16th B. Man. R.) *attached*	8-5-18	Berrysheere
T/Sec.-Lt.	MOSS, Gerald Alex. .. .. .. (2nd B. Man. R.) *attached*	10-8-18	

APPENDIX II
continued
W.O.'s, N.C.O.'s
AND MEN
KILLED

ABBOTT Charles, *b* Mobberley, Cheshire, *e* Manchester (Northwich, Cheshire), 12548, Pte., d. of w., F. & F., 24-7-16.

ADDY Frederick, *e* Sheffield, 40995, Pte., d. of w., F. & F., 16-10-16, formerly 3736 York & Lancs. R.

ADSHEAD Alan Davenport, *b* Stockport, Cheshire, *e* Manchester (Heaton Chapel, Stockport), 11727, Pte., k. in a., F. & F., 23-7-16.

ADSHEAD William, *b* Manchester, *e* Manchester, 27863, Pte., k.in a., F. & F., 31-7-17.

AINSCOUGH Thomas Edward, *b* Parbold, Wigan, Lancs., *e* Preston, Lancs. (Parbold), 30307, Cpl., d. of w., F. & F., 27-9-17.

AINSWORTH Harry, *b* Leeds, Yorks., *e* Manchester, 202862, Pte., k. in a., F. & F., 31-7-17.

AKHURST Charles Ernest, *b* Islington, Middlesex, *e* Wood Green, Middlesex, 41806, Pte., k. in a., F. & F., 29-7-17, formerly G/12846 R. W. Surrey R.

ALLEN Harold, *b* Bonsall, Buxton, Derby, *e* Manchester, 2241, Pte., d. of w., F. & F., 2-4-17.

ALMOND Leo, *b* Manchester, *e* Manchester, 47366, Pte., k. in a., F. & F., 2-4-17.

ANDERSON Percy, *b* Broughton, Salford, Lancs., *e* Manchester, 11998, Pte., d. of w., F. & F., 9-7-16.

ANDREWS John Howard Parker, *b* Walsall, Staffs., *e* Manchester (Walsall), 12260, Sgt., d. of w., Home, 15-7-17.

ANGRAVE Gerald, *b* Thurmaston, Leicester, *e* Leicester, 40996, Pte., k. in a., F. & F., 14-10-16, formerly 5870 Leicester R.

APPLEYARD Albert Edward, *b* Ardwick, Manchester, *e* Manchester, 12512, Pte., k. in a., F. & F., 1-7-16.

ARMSBEY Ernest, *b* Chorlton-on-Medlock, Manchester, *e* Manchester, 12259, Pte., k. in a., F. & F., 31-5-16.

ARMSTRONG Joseph, *b* Manchester, *e* Manchester, 202982, Pte., k. in a., F. & F., 31-7-17.

ARMSTRONG William, *b* Manchester, *e* Manchester, 48749, Pte., k. in a., F. & F., 23-6-17.

ASHBY Bernard Harry, *b* Derby, *e* Manchester (Southport, Lancs.), 12811, L/Cpl., k. in a., F. & F., 23-7-16.

ASPELL Thomas Alfred Leather, *b* Deansgate, Manchester, *e* Manchester, 12262, Pte., d. of w., Home, 22-8-16.

ASPITAL Percy, *b* Leicester, *e* Leicester, 40950, Pte., k. in a., F. & F., 11-10-16, formerly 5071, Leicester R.

ATKINSON Wilfred, *b* Rusholme, Manchester, *e* Manchester, 12003, Pte., k. in a., F. & F., 23-4-17.

ATKINSON William Penrock, *b* Scarborough, *e* Manchester (Scarborough), 12002, Pte., k. in a., F. & F., 1-7-16.

BACKHOUSE Charles Frederick, *b* Oldham, Lancs., *e* Manchester (Oldham), 12279, Pte., k. in a., F. & F., 23-7-16.

BAILEY Frank, *e* Manchester, 47400, Pte., k. in a., F. & F., 23-4-17.

BAILEY Edward, *b* Manchester, *e* Manchester, 26548, Pte., k. in a., F. & F., 8-9-17. **M.M.**

BAILLIE William, *b* Openshaw, Manchester, *e* Manchester, 11735, Pte., d. of w., F. & F. 23-1-16.

BAINES Arthur, *b* Manchester, *e* Manchester, 27882, Pte., k. in a., F. & F., 2-4-17.

BAKER William Edward, *b* Manchester, *e* Manchester (Ripon, Yorks.), 31174, Pte., k. in a., F. & F., 23-7-16.

BALDWIN Arthur, *b* Reddish, Lancs., *e* Manchester, 12006, Cpl., k. in a., F. & F., 1-7-16.

BANNISTER Fred, *b* Farington, Preston, Lancs., *e* Manchester (Leyland, Lancs.), 12005, Pte., k. in a., F. & F., 1-7-16.

BARKER Walter, *b* Hollinwood, Lancs., *e* Oldham, Lancs., 14,073, Pte., k. in a., F. & F., 22-6-17.

BARRATT John Willie, *b* Oldham, Lancs., *e* Oldham, Lancs., 37810, Pte., d. of w., F. & F. 5-6-17.

BARTLETT Mack, *b* Christ Church, Hants., *e* Marylebone, Middlesex (Portsmouth), 47531, Pte., k. in a., F. & F., 9-4-17, formerly 28208 K.R. Rifle C.

BATE Charles Clifford, *b* Bury, Lancs., *e* Manchester (Ramsbottom, Lancs.), 11470, L/Cpl., k. in a., F. & F., 23-7-16.

BAYLEY William Andrew, *b* Manchester, *e* Manchester, 11471, L/Cpl., k. in a., F. & F., 23-7-16.

BAYTON Frederick James, *e* Kingston-on-Thames, 41914, Pte., k. in a., F. & F., 23-4-17, formerly 3258 E. Surrey R.

BEARDER Alfred, *b* Manchester, *e* Manchester, 49703, Pte., d. of w., F. & F., 20-12-17.

BEARDSLEY Harold, *b* Leicester, *e* Leicester, 41020, L/Cpl., k. in a., F. & F., 31-7-17, formerly 4142 Leicester R.

BEAVAN William, *b* Leominster, Hereford, *e* Hereford (Kingsland, Hereford), 41781, Pte., d., Home, 7-6-17, formerly 10338 E. Surrey R.

BECKETT John, *b* Manchester, *e* Manchester, 30481, Pte., k. in a., F. & F., 20-10-16.

BELL Arthur, *b* Oldham, Lancs., *e* Oldham, 36565, Pte., k. in a., F. & F., 2-4-17.

BELL Charles, *b* Norwich, Norfolk, *e* Thetford, Norfolk, 51158, Pte., d. of w., F. & F., 3-8-17.

BELL John Frost, *e* Manchester, 33887, Pte., k. in a., F. & F., 9-4-17.

BENNETT Frank, *b* Manchester, *e* Manchester, 12735, Pte., k. in a., F. & F., 1-7-16.

BENNETT Robert, *b* Davyhulme, Manchester, *e* Manchester (Flixton, Lancs.), 7199, Pte., k. in a., F. & F., 10-4-17.

BENNETT William, *b* Manchester, *e* Manchester, 10978, Pte., d. of w., F. & F., 16-4-17.

BENSON James Travis, *b* Manchester, *e* Manchester, 26535, Pte., d., F. & F., 7-11-18.

BERWICK George, *b* Rusholme, Manchester, *e* Manchester, 47181, Pte., k. in a., F. & F., 2-4-17.

BESWICK William, *e* Ramsbottom, Lancs., 47145, Pte., k. in a., F. & F., 31-7-17.

BILLSBOROUGH Harry, *b* Preston, Lancs., *e* Manchester (Burton-on-Trent, Staffs.), 6584, Pte., k. in a., F. & F., 31-7-17.

BIRCH Thomas Boys, *e* Mitcham, Surrey, 51160, Pte., k. in a., F. & F., 25-10-17.

BIRD Samuel, *b* Hulme, Manchester, *e* Manchester, 30371, Pte., k. in a., F. & F., 2-4-17.

BIRKENHOUT William Edward, *b* Miles Platting, Manchester, *e* Manchester, 26579, Pte., k. in a., F. & F., 23-7-16.

BLACKMAN Harry, *e* Middleton, Lancs. (Manchester), 48680, Pte., k. in a., F. & F., 31-7-17.

BLAIR William, *b* Ancoats, Manchester, *e* Manchester, 12273, Pte., k. in a., F. & F. 1-7-16.

BLAYDON Eric, *b* Earsfield, Middlesex, *e* Manchester (Winnipeg, Manitoba, Canada), 12014, Pte., k. in a., F. & F., 1-7-16.

BLEARS Fred, *b* Pendleton, Lancs., *e* Manchester, 12287, Pte., k. in a., F. & F., 23-7-16.

BLUNDELL Frank, *b* Hindley, Lancs., *e* Manchester (Hindley), 12283, Pte., d. of w., F. & F., 13-5-16.

BOLD Harry, *b* Disley, Stockport,Cheshire, *e* Manchester (Stockport), 11749, Pte., k. in a., F. & F., 23-7-16.

BOOTH Fred, *b* Oldham, Lancs., *e* Oldham, 50063, L/Cpl., k. in a., F. & F., 31-7-17.

BOOTHROYD Joseph, *b* Manchester, *e* Manchester, 18452, Pte., k. in a., F. & F., 26-12-17.

BOTT John Howard, *b* Ramsbottom, Lancs., *e* Manchester (Ramsbottom), 11480, Pte., k. in a., F. & F., 1-7-16.

BRADBURY Alfred, *b* Manchester, *e* Manchester, 31177, Pte., k. in a., F. & F., 23-7-16.

BRADY Arthur, *b* Barrow-in-Furness, Lancs., *e* Manchester (Barrow-in-Furness), 17833, Pte., k. in a., F. & F., 23-7-16.

BRANDRETH Albert, *b* Broughton, Salford, Lancs., *e* Manchester, 11752, Pte., d. of w., F. & F., 3-2-16.

BRATBY Albert Edward, *b* Congleton, Cheshire, *e* Congleton, 12897, Pte., k. in a., F. & F., 1-7-16.

BRAY Thomas, *b* Sapcote, Leicester, *e* Hinckley, Leicester (Sapcote), 40955, L/Cpl., k. in a., F. & F., 2-4-17, formerly 5838, Leicester R.

BREDBURY William, *b* Stalybridge, Cheshire, *e* Ashton-under-Lyne, Lancs., 351786, Pte., k. in a., F. & F., 31-7-17.

BRETT Harry, *b* Flixton, Lancs., *e* Manchester, 17564, Pte., k. in a., F. & F., 18-10-16.

BRIERLEY Charles, *b* Manchester, *e* Manchester, 26882, Pte., k. in a., F. & F., 23-7-16.

BRILL Cecil Ernest, *e* Manchester, 47182, Pte., k. in a., F. & F., 24-12-16.

BROOKES William, *b* Swinton, Lancs., *e* Manchester (Swinton), 11491, Sgt., k. in a., F. & F., 23-7-16.

BROWN James Lyndon, *b* Blackley, Manchester, *e* Manchester, 12537, Pte., k. in a., F. & F., 23-7-16.

BROWN Joseph, *b* Salford, Lancs., *e* Manchester, 11492, Pte., k. in a., F. & F., 23-7-16.

BROWN William, *b* Manchester, *e* Manchester, 49475, Pte., k. in a., F. & F., 31-7-17.

BROWNBILL Richard Henry, *b* Ainsdale, Southport, Lancs., *e* Manchester (Chorley, Lancs.), 11768, Pte., k. in a., F. & F., 23-7-16.

BRUCE William Small, *b* Hulme, Manchester, *e* Manchester, 11493, Pte., k. in a., F. & F., 23-7-16.

BRYAN Charles, *b* Deepcar, Yorks., *e* Manchester (Stockport. Cheshire), 11762, Pte., d. of w., Home, 16-9-16.

BRYANS William Wooton, *b* Manchester, *e* Manchester, 12840, Pte., k. in a., F. & F., 23-7-16.

BUCKLEY Robert Lamb, *b* Clayton, Manchester, *e* Manchester, 12272, Pte., d., F. & F., 1-6-16.

BURBRIDGE Joseph, *b* Failsworth, Lancs., *e* Failsworth (Newton Heath, Manchester), 203207, Pte., k. in a., F. & F., 31-7-17.

BURDETT Frank, *e* Leicester, 40916, Pte., k. in a., F. & F., 23-6-17, formerly 3299 Leicester R.

BURGESS John, *b* Marple, Cheshire, *e* Manchester, 34862, Pte., k. in a., F. & F., 23-4-17.

BURGESS Peter, *b* Gorton, Manchester, *e* Wigan, Lancs., 30154, A/Cpl., d. of w., F. & F., 20-4-17.

BURKE William, *e* Manchester, 38128, Pte., k. in a., F. & F., 26-10-17.

BURROWS Richard, *b* Ardwick, Manchester, *e* Manchester (Huddersfield), 47288, L/Cpl., k. in a., F. & F., 7-9-17.

BURTON Alfred Walter, *b* Manchester, *e* Manchester, 49714, Pte., k. in a., F. & F., 31-7-17.

BUTLER Albert, *b* Warfield, Berks., *e* Brentford, Middlesex (Bracknell, Berks.), 44673, Pte., k. in a., F. & F., 15-12-17, formerly G/26345 R. Fus.

BUTLER Walter, *b* Collyhurst, Manchester, *e* Manchester, 12793, L/Sgt., k. in a., F. & F., 23-7-16.

BUTTERWORTH Fred, *b* Newton Heath, Manchester, *e* Ardwick, Manchester, 48510, Cpl., k. in a., F. & F., 31-7-17.

CALLAN Arthur, *b* Manchester, *e* Manchester, 49692, Pte., d. of w., F. & F., 2-8-17.

CAMPBELL Harry, *b* Ashby, Lincoln, *e* Ashton-u-Lyne, Lancs. (Birmingham), 47078, Pte., d., F. & F., 10-3-17.

CARTER Harry, *b* Stepney, Middlesex, *e* London (Limehouse, London), 47577, Pte., k. in a., F. & F., 31-7-17, formerly 2392 R.A.S.C.

CARTER Stanley, *b* Manchester, *e* Manchester, 12033, Sgt., d. of w., F. & F., 25-2-16.

CASEWELL George, *b* Hollinwood, Lancs., *e* Manchester (Stockport, Cheshire), 11503, A/Cpl., k. in a., F. & F., 2-4-17.

CASS Albert, *b* Manchester, *e* Manchester, 26547, Pte., k. in a., F. & F., 1-7-16.

CHADAWAY George, *b* Collyhurst, Manchester, *e* Manchester, 12296, Pte., k. in a., F. & F., 1-7-16.

CHADWICK Cyril Stanley, *b* Salford, Lancs., *e* Manchester (Salford), 12297, Pte., k. in a., F. & F., 23-7-16.

CHADWICK Walter Ashworth, *b* Newton Heath, Manchester, *e* Manchester, 11506, Sgt., d. of w., F. & F., 1-7-16.

CHALMERS Cecil, *b* Bolton, Lancs., *e* Manchester (Chorlton-on-Medlock, Manchester), 12298, Pte., k. in a., F. & F., 23-7-16.

CHARNOCK Leonard, *b* Fairfield, Manchester, *e* Manchester (Reddish, Lancs.), 11507, Sgt., k. in a., F. & F., 1-7-16.

CHURCHOUSE Thomas William James, *e* Leicester, 40959, L/Cpl., k. in a., F. & F., 31-7-17, formerly 3000 Leicester R.

CLANCEY Owen Joseph, *b* Carrick-on-Shannon, Roscommon, *e* Manchester, 12650, Pte., d. of w., F. & F., 4-7-16.

CLARK Robert Douglas, *b* Kirkcudbright, Kirkcudbrightshire, *e* Manchester (Kirkcudbright, Scotland), 12039, Pte., d., Home, 18-10-14.

CLAYTON Albert, *b* Stockport, Cheshire, *e* Manchester (Stockport), 12760, A/Cpl., k. in a., F. & F., 2-4-17.

CLEGG Albert, *b* Miles Platting, Manchester, *e* Manchester (Warrington, Lancs.), 12040, Pte., k. in a., F. & F., 1-7-16.

CLOWES James, *b* Macclesfield, Cheshire, *e* Manchester, 11509, Pte., k. in a., F. & F., 23-7-16.

COBB Charles, *b* Winchester, Hants., *e* Gosport, Hants. (Fareham, Hants.), 29981, Pte., d., F. & F., 5-1-18.

COLLINGE Vernon, *b* Broughton, Manchester, *e* Manchester, 12042, Pte., k. in a., F. & F., 1-7-16.

COLLINGE William, *b* Hollinwood, Lancs., *e* Hollinwood, 25046, Pte., k. in a., F. & F., 23-7-16.

COLLINS Francis, *b* Dublin, *e* Curragh (Dublin), 2608, Pte., k. in a., F. & F., 23-4-17.

CONDLIFFE Samuel, *b* Sandbach, Cheshire, *e* Manchester (Stockport, Cheshire), 12043, L/Cpl., k. in a., F. & F., 13-2-16.

COOK Edward, *b* Manchester, *e* Manchester, 12300, Pte., k. in a., F. & F., 23-7-16.

COOKE Frederick Reginald, *b* Openshaw, Manchester, *e* Manchester, 12044, Pte., k. in a., F. & F., 6-2-16.

COOPE Fred, *b* Bury, Lancs., *e* Manchester, 12301, Pte., k. in a., F. & F., 11-5-16.

COOPER Thomas Sidney, *b* Chorlton-on-Medlock, Manchester, *e* Manchester, 11776, L/Cpl., k. in a., F. & F., 2-4-17.

CORNWELL Arthur, *b* Swaffham, Bulbeck, Cambs., *e* Newmarket, Suffolk (Bulbeck), 44679, Pte., k. in a., F. & F., 23-4-17, formerly 34641 R. Fus.

CORRIGAN Martin, *b* Bradford, Manchester, *e* Manchester, 25017, Pte., d., F. & F., 4-10-18.

COWBURN Alfred George, *b* Chorlton-on-Medlock, Manchester, *e* Manchester, 12304, Pte., k. in a., F. & F., 19-10-16.

CRAIG Henry Basil, *b* Manchester, *e* Manchester, 31076, Pte., k. in a., F. & F., 23-7-16.

CRAVEN Alfred Rudolph, *b* Manchester, *e* Manchester, 12295, Pte., k. in a., F. & F., 23-7-16.

CRAWFORD Granville, *b* Oldham, Lancs., *e* Chadderton, Lancs., 47519, Pte., d. of w., F. & F., 24-9-17.

CROSS Arthur Bertram, *b* Manchester, *e* Tooting, Surrey (Pendleton, Manchester), 41913, Cpl., k. in a., F. & F., 2-4-17, formerly 4533 Surrey R.

CROWDER Joseph, *b* Manchester, *e* Manchester, 49707, Pte., k. in a., F. & F., 31-7-17.

CROWE George Alexander, *b* Cheetham, Manchester, *e* Manchester, 12056, Cpl., k. in a., F. & F., 6-2-16.

CROWE William, *b* Harpurhey, Manchester, *e* Manchester, 12055, Pte., d. of w., F. & F., 11-7-16.

CRUMLEY Hugh James, *b* Manchester, *e* Manchester, 28699, Cpl., k. in a., F & F., 8-9-17.

CURRELL Norman, *b* Withington, Manchester, *e* Manchester, 26923, Pte., k. in a., F. & F., 23-7-16.

DAVIES George, *b* Miles Platting, Manchester, *e* Manchester, 12314, Pte., k. in a., F. & F., 1-7-16.

DAVIES Harold, *b* Manchester, *e* Manchester (Oldham, Lancs.), 25035, Pte., k. in a., F. & F., 1-7-16.

DAVIES John, *b* Manchester, *e* Manchester, 49706, Pte., k. in a., F. & F., 6-9-17.

DAVIS John James, *b* Islington, Middlesex, *e* Enfield, Middlesex, 51166, Pte., k. in a., F. & F., 31-7-17.

DAWBER John Vincent Standish, *b* Pendleton, Lancs., *e* Manchester, 12315, L/Cpl., k. in a., F. & F., 23-7-16.

DAWES Norman Labrow, *b* Rusholme, Manchester, *e* Manchester, 12063, Pte., k. in a., F. & F., 1-7-16.

DAWSON Ernest Jones, *b* Ardwick, Manchester, *e* Manchester 11106, Pte., k. in a., F. & F., 23-4-17.

DAWSON Wilfred, *b* Middleton, Lancs., *e* Manchester (Middleton), 12319, Cpl., k. in a., F. & F., 23-7-16.

DELL Albert John, *b* North Church, Herts., *e* Hinckley, Leicester (North Church), 41068, Pte., k. in a., F. & F., 23-4-17, formerly 4654 Leicester R.

DENTON John Leyland, *b* Ancoats, Manchester, *e* Manchester, 300449, Pte., k. in a., F. & F., 23-12-17.

DERBYSHIRE James Carson, *b* Sale, Cheshire, *e* Manchester (Stockport, Cheshire), 11788, Pte., d. of w., F. & F., 13-10-16.

DICKENSON Harold, *b* Prestwich, Lancs., *e* Manchester, 11790, Pte., d. of w., F. & F., 5-2-16.

DIGAN Henry, *e* Salford, Lancs. (Hightown, Manchester), 47371, Pte., k. in a., F. & F., 2-4-17.

DILLON James, *b* Chorlton-on-Medlock, Manchester, *e* Manchester, 7100, Pte., d. of w., F. & F., 10-8-17.

DIXON Hubert, *b* Oldham, Lancs., *e* Oldham, 25073, Pte., k. in a., F. & F., 1-7-16.

DODD Joseph, *b* Salford, Lancs., *e* Manchester, 31176, Pte., k. in a., F. & F., 23-7-16.

DODD William Albert, *b* Collyhurst, Manchester, *e* Manchester (Glasgow), 12066, Pte., k. in a., F. & F., 23-4-17.

DOONAN William John, *b* Carlisle, *e* Manchester, 12540, Pte., k. in a., F. & F., 2-4-17.

DOWNS John Thomas, *b* Manchester, *e* Manchester, 27368, Pte., k. in a., F. & F., 11-9-16.

DUCKWORTH Arthur, *b* Whitefield, Bury, Lancs., *e* Manchester, 11528, Pte., k. in a., F. & F., 1-7-16.

DUCKWORTH William, *b* Manchester, *e* Manchester, 11529, Pte., d. of w., F. & F., 10-8-16.

DUNN Francis James, *b* Buxton, Derby, *e* Manchester (Buxton), 31165, Pte., k. in a., F. & F., 23-7-16.

DUXBURY James, *b* Salford, Lancs., *e* Manchester, 12069, L/Cpl., k. in a., F. & F., 23-7-16.

DYE Arthur, *b* Lawshall, Suffolk, *e* Lakenheath, Suffolk (Bury St. Edmunds, Suffolk), 44680, Pte., d. of w., F. & F., 4-4-17, formerly 34663 R. Fus.

ECKERSLEY James Henry, *e* Manchester, 47190, Pte., k. in a., F. & F., 31-7-17.

EDWARDS George Edward, *b* Kingsthorpe, Northampton, *e* Manchester (West Grinstead, Sussex), 12071, Cpl., k. in a., F. & F., 23-7-16.

ELLIOTT Frank, *b* Denton, Manchester, *e* Ashton-u-Lyne, Lancs. (Denton), 48811, Pte., k. in a., F. & F., 31-7-17.

ELLIOTT George Edward, *b* Manchester, *e* Manchester (Sale, Cheshire), 31182, Pte., k. in a., F. & F., 30-7-16.

EVANS George Ernest, *b* Manchester, *e* Manchester, 12074, Pte., k. in a., F. & F., 1-7-16.

EVERY Ernest Charles, *b* Brighton, Sussex, *e* Clapham, Surrey (Shepherds' Bush, London), 41917, Pte., k. in a., F. & F., 2-4-17, formerly 32877 E. Surrey R.

EXLEY Alfred, *b* Rotherham, Yorks., *e* Manchester, 26927, Pte., k. in a., F. & F., 27-11-17.

FAIRCLOUGH Thomas, *b* Manchester, *e* Manchester, 12076, Cpl., k. in a., F. & F., 23-7-16.

FALLOWS Samuel, *b* Heywood, Lancs., *e* Manchester, 11537, Pte., k. in a., F. & F., 1-7-16.

FARNWORTH Fred, *b* Manchester, *e* Manchester (Pendlebury, Lancs.), 12729, Pte., k. in a., F. & F., 1-7-16.

FENTON Edwin Stanley, *b* Heywood, Lancs., *e* Manchester, 12328, Pte., k. in a., F. & F., 8-7-16.

FENTON Frank, *b* Salford, Lancs., *e* Manchester (Ansdell, Lytham, Lancs.), 11539, Cpl., k. in a., F. & F., 23-7-16.

FERNLEY Percy, *b* Denton, Manchester, *e* Ashton-u-Lyne, Lancs. (Denton), 352469, Pte., k. in a., F. & F., 31-7-17.

FINCH ThomasHenry, *b* Barrow-in-Furness, Lancs., *e* Manchester, 11806, Pte., k. in a., F. & F., 23-7-16.

FISH Arnold, *b* Bury, Lancs., *e* Manchester (Bury), 11540, Pte., k. in a., F. & F., 30-7-16.

FISH Norman, *b* Bury, Lancs., *e* Manchester (Bury), 11541, Pte., d., F. & F., 7-8-18.

FISHWICK James William, *b* Openshaw, Manchester, *e* Manchester, 11542, C.S.M., k. in a., F. & F., 26-12-17.

FITZPATRICK Edward, *b* Manchester, *e* Manchester, 31156, Pte., k. in a., F. & F., 23-7-16.

FLETCHER Frank, *b* High Lane, Cheshire, *e* Manchester, 26724, Pte., k. in a., F. & F., 23-7-16.

FOLEY Thomas Allan, *b* Gorton, Manchester, *e* Manchester, 12079, Pte., k. in a., F. & F., 23-7-16.

FORD Alfred, *b* Blackley, Manchester, *e* Middleton, Lancs. (Blackley), 48575, Pte., d., F. & F., 5-1-18.

FOSTER Albert Edward, *b* Barnet, Herts., *e* Bedford (Barnet), 51174, Pte., k. in a., F. & F., 2-9-17.

FOSTER Cecil William, *b* Leicester, *e* Leicester, 40917, Pte., d., Home, 10-4-17, formerly 5649 Leicester R.

FOSTER Percy John, *b* Clapham, Surrey, *e* Wandsworth, Surrey (Brixton, Surrey), 51238, Pte., k. in a., F. & F., 31-7-17.

FOSTER Robert, *b* Manchester, *e* Manchester, 26707, Pte., d., F. & F., 30-11-17.

FOY Fred Holding, *b* Bolton, Lancs., *e* Manchester (Gravesend, Kent), 11547, Pte., k. in a., F. & F., 19-7-16.

FREELAND George, *b* Walton, Surrey, *e* Kingston-on-Thames (Wallingford, Berks.), 51176, Pte., k. in a., F. & F., 31-7-17.

FREER Samuel, *b* Manchester, *e* Manchester, 12733, Pte., k. in a., F. & F., 1-7-16,

FRENCH Ernest, *b* Longsight, Manchester, *e* Manchester, 12327, L/Cpl., k. in a., F. & F., 9-7-16.

FRIDAY Robert Samuel, *b* Manchester, *e* Manchester, 31199, Pte., k. in a., F. & F., 23-7-16.

FURY John, *b* Rochdale, Lancs., *e* Manchester, 11810, Pte., k. in a., F. & F., 23-7-16.

GAINES Charles William, *e* Kensington-on-Thames (Plaistowe, Essex), 41918, L/Cpl., k. in a., F. & F., 5-1-18, formerly 32898 E. Surrey R.

GAME Alfred Bertie, *b* Ponders End, Middlesex, *e* Edmonton, Middlesex (Ponders End), 51178, Pte., k. in a., F. & F., 31-7-17.

GANNON James Thomas, *b* Leicester, *e* Leicester, 40964, Pte., k. in a., F. & F., 23-4-17, formerly 4002 Leicester R.

GARSIDE Edwin, *e* Ashton-u-Lyne, Lancs. (Droylsden, Manchester), 351809, Pte., k. in a., F. & F., 25-4-17.

GARSIDE Lees, *b* Hollinwood, Lancs., *e* Manchester (Failsworth, Lancs.), 11811, Cpl., k. in a., F. & F., 23-7-16.

GEORGE Thomas Henry, *b* Thupp Stroud, Glouc., *e* Manchester (Gloucester), 12347, Pte., k. in a., F. & F., 23-7-16.

GIBSON John, *b* Salford, Lancs., *e* Ashton-u-Lyne, Lancs. (Gorton, Manchester), 9126, A/Cpl., d., F. & F., 9-10-16.

GILMAN James, *b* Salford, Lancs., *e* Manchester, 11815, Pte., d. of w., F. & F., 3-7-16.

GLEADHILL Leonard Edward, *b* Beverley, Hull, Yorks., *e* Manchester (Beverley), 12342, Pte., k. in a., F. & F., 23-7-16.

GLOVER Percy Turner, *b* Birkenhead, Cheshire, *e* Manchester (Stockport, Cheshire), 12333, Pte., k. in a., F. & F., 23-7-16.

GLOVER Thomas, *b* Openshaw, Manchester, *e* Manchester, 11555, Pte., k. in a., F. & F., 23-7-16.

GLYNN John, *b* Oldham, Lancs., *e* Oldham, 25060, Pte., k. in a., F. & F., 9-4-17.

GODSALL Ernest, *b* Gorton, Manchester, *e* Manchester (Droylsden, Manchester), 11816, Cpl., d. of w., F. & F., 11-7-16.

GOSLING James, *b* Whaley Bridge, Derby., *e* Manchester (Macclesfield, Cheshire), 11558, Pte., d. of w., F. & F., 30-7-16.

GRANT Harold, *b* Salford, Lancs., *e* Manchester (Stretford, Manchester), 12342, Pte., k. in a., F. & F., 1-7-16.

GRAY Alexander, *b* Manchester, *e* Manchester, 47249, Pte., k. in a., F. & F., 26-4-17.

GRAY George Edmund Frank, *e* Wandsworth, Surrey, 41784, Pte., k. in a., F. & F., 23-4-17, formerly 19161 E. Surrey R.

GREEN Winston, *b* Oldham, Lancs., *e* Oldham, 45512, Pte., k. in a., F. & F., 21-6-17.

GREENWOOD John Ernest, *b* Gorton, Manchester, *e* Manchester, 11562, Pte., k. in a., F. & F., 11-9 16.

GREGORY George, *b* Manchester, *e* Manchester, 11563, Cpl., k. in a., F. & F., 23-7-16.

GREGORY Jesse, *b* Manchester, *e* Manchester, 28702, Pte., k. in a., F. & F., 31-7-17.

GRIMSHAW Raymond Hayes, *b* Wilmslow, Cheshire, *e* Manchester (Handforth, Cheshire), 11821, Cpl., k. in a., F. & F., 1-7-16.

GRIST Edwin, *b* Manchester, *e* Manchester, 12859, Pte., k. in a., F. & F., 9-7-16.

GRUNDY Fred, *e* Atherton, Lancs., 47237, L/Cpl., d. of w., F. & F., 27-12-17, formerly 31071 Lancashire Fus.

GRUNDY Henry, *b* Atherton, Lancs., *e* Atherton, 12863, Pte., k. in a., F. & F., 2-3-16.

GULVIN George, *b* Newington, Kent, *e* Sittingbourne, Kent (Newington), 51180, Pte., k. in a., F. & F., 31-7-17, formerly 9443 E. Kent R.

GUNNING John, *e* Manchester, 47252, Pte., d. of w., F. & F., 8-12-17.

GUY Adam, *b* Bury, Lancs., *e* Burnley, Lancs. (Padiham, Lancs.), 1273, A/Cpl., d. of w., F. & F., 10-10-16.

GWYTHER Joseph, *b* Manchester, *e* Manchester, 26531, Pte., k. in a., F. & F., 23-7-16.

HAGUE Arnold, *b* Hulme, Manchester, *e* Manchester, 12090, L/Sgt., k. in a., F. & F., 25-7-16.

HALLAM Tom Edward, *b* Leicester, *e* Leicester, 41037, Pte., k. in a., F. & F., 2-4-17, formerly 5339 Leicester R.

HAMILTON David Charles, *b* Richmond, Surrey, *e* Richmond (Woking, Surrey), 41921, Pte., k. in a., F. & F., 2-4-17, formerly 32881 E. Surrey R.

HANCOCK John, *b* Clayton, Manchester, *e* Manchester, 12361, Pte., k. in a., F. & F., 23-7-16.

HANNAY Ernest Brett, *b* Douglas, Isle of Man, *e* Manchester, 11567, Sgt., d. of w., F. & F., 14-8-16.

HANSON Arthur, *e* Manchester, 47253, L/Cpl., k. in a., F. & F., 23-4-17.

HARBUTT Albert, *b* Walthamstow, *e* Mitcham, Surrey (Billingshurst, Sussex), 51182, Pte., d. of w., Home, 2-10-17.

HARDING Frank, *b* Chadderton, Lancs., *e* Chadderton, 34049, Pte., k. in a., F. & F., 23-7-16.

HARPER William Percival, *b* Stockport, Cheshire, *e* Manchester (Stockport), 12368, L/Cpl., k. in a., F. & F., 1-7-16.

HARRISON Alfred, *b* Hulme, Manchester, *e* Manchester, 11828, Pte., d. of w., F. & F., 10-11-16.

HARRISON Alfred Samuel Robert, *b* Corpusty, Norfolk, *e* Norwich (Corpusty), 41033, Pte., k. in a., F. & F., 20-10-16, formerly 5949 Leicester R.

HARRISON John, *b* Preston, Lancs., *e* Oldham, Lancs., 48501, Pte., k. in a., F. & F., 27-4-17, formerly 376859 Manchester Regt.

HARRISON Robert, *b* Hulme, Manchester, *e* Manchester (Salford, Lancs.), 12095, Pte., k. in a., F. & F., 23-7-16.

HARROP Samuel, *b* Ashton-u-Lyne, Lancs., *e* Ashton-u-Lyne, 48518, Pte., k. in a., F. & F., 23-6-17.

HART Sidney, *b* Leicester, *e* Leicester (South Wigston, Leicester), 40968, Pte., k. in a., F. & F., 19-10-16, formerly 1955 Leicester R.

HEALEY Ross, *b* Swinton, Lancs., *e* Manchester (Eccles, Lancs.), 12098, Sgt., k. in a., F. & F., 9-7-16.

HEATON Alfred, *b* Manchester, *e* Manchester, 26725, Pte., k. in a., F. & F., 23-7-16.

HEATON Marshall, *b* Middleton, Lancs., *e* Manchester (Chester), 12099, Pte., k. in a., F. & F., 1-7-16.

HENDERSON Victor, *b* Manchester, *e* Manchester, 31071, Pte., d. of w., Home, 23-7-16.

HEROD James Thomas, *e* Ashton-u-Lyne, Lancs., 47378, Pte., k. in a., F. & F., 23-4-17.

HEWART William, *b* Manchester, *e* Manchester, 47254, Pte., k. in a., F. & F., 24-2-17.

HEWITT Walter, *e* Oldham, Lancs., 48517, L/Cpl., k. in a., F. & F., 31-7-17.

HEYWOOD John, *b* Parkfield, Manchester (Middleton, Lancs.), 12103, Sgt., d. of w,. F. & F., 29-1-16.

HIGGINBOTHAM Percy, *b* Altrincham, Cheshire, *e* Manchester (Didsbury, Lancs.), 31378, L/Cpl., k. in a., F. & F., 16-10-16.

HIGGINBOTTOM William Edwin, *b* Barrow-in-Furness, Lancs., *e* Manchester (Stockport, Cheshire), 17992, Pte., k. in a., F. & F., 23-7-16.

HILL Alfred Victor, *b* Richmond, Surrey, *e* Wandsworth, Surrey (Earlesfield, Surrey), 44713, Pte., k. in a., F. & F., 2-4-17, formerly 25053 R. Fus.

HILL Rowland, *b* Kibworth, Leicester, *e* Shepshed, Leicester (Leicester), 41083, Pte., k. in a., F. & F., 29-7-17, formerly 1927 Leicester R.

HILLEN James, *b* Bolton, Lancs., *e* Manchester (Bolton), 12845, Pte., d. of w., F. & F., 3-7-16.

HILTON Stanley, *b* Prestwich, Lancs., *e* Manchester, 12105, Pte., k. in a., F. & F., 14-5-16.

HINES Ernest Frederick, *b* Leicester, *e* Leicester, 41009, Pte., k. in a., F. & F., 31-7-17, formerly 1957 Leicester R.

HOBBS Henry Alexander, *b* Battersea, Surrey, *e* Wandsworth, Surrey, 51239, Pte., d. of w., F. & F., 4-8-17.

HODKINSON Harry, *b* Bradford, Manchester, *e* Manchester, 12659, Pte., d. of w., F. & F., 11-2-16.

HOLDSWORTH James, *b* Ardwick, Manchester, *e* Manchester, 12109, Pte., k. in a., F. & F., 23-7-16.

HOLGATE John, *b* Oldham, Lancs., *e* Oldham, 25062, Pte., d. of w., F. & F., 26-8-16.

HOLLINGWORTH William, *b* Hale, Cheshire, *e* Manchester (Altrincham, Cheshire), 33491, Pte., d., F. & F., 25-12-16.

HOLMES Philip Henry, *b* Manchester, *e* Manchester, 12710, Pte., k. in a., F. & F., 23-7-16.

HOLT George, *b* Longsight, Manchester, *e* Manchester, 12111, Cpl., k. in a., F. & F., 1-7-16.

HOOK Frederick George, *e* Croydon, Surrey (South Norwood, Surrey), 41811, Pte., k. in a., F. & F., 23-4-17, formerly 4207 R. W. Surrey R.

HOOPER Henry, *b* Longsight, Manchester, *e* Manchester, 12515, Pte., k. in a., F. & F., 20-10-16.

HOPE George William, *b* Little Drayton, Shrop., *e* Manchester, 12113, Pte., k. in a., F. & F., 6-2-16.

HOUGH John, *b* Manchester, *e* Manchester, 33633, Pte., k. in a., F. & F., 23-9-16.

HOVER Philip Frederick, *b* Patricroft, Lancs., *e* Manchester, 12114, Pte., k. in a., F. & F., 12-2-16.

HOWARTH William, *b* Hulme, Manchester, *e* Manchester, 12369, Pte., k. in a., F. & F., 1-7-16.

HOWES Frederick, *e* Manchester (Stockport, Cheshire), 46714, Pte., k. in a., F. & F., 31-7-17.

HULME George Henry, *b* Manchester, *e* Manchester (Urmston, Lancs.), 33864, Pte., k. in a., F. & F., 23-7-16.

HULSTON Albert, *b* Manchester, *e* Manchester, 47236, Pte., k. in a., F. & F., 31-7-17.

HURDLE George, *b* Moss Side, Manchester, *e* Manchester, 12355, Pte., k. in a., F. & F., 9-7-16.

HURLSTON George, *b* Heyside, Royton, Lancs., *e* Royton, 25053, Pte., k. in a., F. & F., 23-7-16.

HYNES James Joseph, *b* Dublin, *e* Manchester (Beswick, Manchester), 11858, Pte., k. in a., F. & F., 23-7-16.

ISHERWOOD John, *b* Newton Heath, Manchester, *e* Manchester (Failsworth, Lancs.), 26023, A/Sgt., k. in a., F. & F., 23-4-17.

JACKSON Harold, *b* Manchester, *e* Manchester, 12547, Pte., k. in a., F. & F., 23-7-16.

JARVIS Leonard Albert, *b* Forest Gate, Essex, *e* Manchester (Manor Park, Essex), 26121, Pte., d. of w., F. & F., 6-6-16.

JEFFREYS Frank, *b* Patricroft, Lancs., *e* Manchester, 12376, L/Cpl., k. in a., F. & F., 9-7-16.

JEFFRIES George, *b* Manchester, *e* Manchester, 33482, Pte., k. in a., F. & F., 20-10-16.

JEVONS Rupert, *b* Chorlton, Manchester, *e* Manchester, 12375, Pte., k. in a., F. & F., 23-7-16.

JOHNSON Alfred, *b* Manchester, *e* Manchester, 12533, Pte., k. in a., F. & F., 1 7-16.

JOHNSON Samuel William, *b* Salford, Lancs., *e* Manchester, 12816, Pte., k. in a., F. & F., 23-7-16.

JOLLEY Roy, *b* Swan Bank, Congleton, Cheshire, *e* Manchester (Congleton), 11863, L/Cpl., d., F. & F., 1-6-16.

JONES Albert, *b* Denbigh, *e* Manchester (Denbigh), 12374, Pte., k. in a., F. & F., 23-7-16.

JONES Benjamin, *b* Pendleton, Lancs., *e* Manchester (Swinton, Lancs.), 11864, L/Cpl., k. in a., F. & F., 11-10-16.

JONES Ernest, *e* Manchester, 47212, Sgt., d. of w., F. & F., 6-8-17.

JONES Ernest Eaton, *b* Ardwick, Manchester, *e* Manchester, 12124, Pte., k. in a., F. & F., 1-7-16.

JONES Frank, *b* Crewe, *e* Manchester (Crewe), 26928, Pte., k. in a., F. & F., 23-7-16.

JONES William Henry, *b* Salford, Lancs., *e* Manchester (Urmston, Lancs.), 11588, Pte., k. in a., F. & F., 23-7-16.

KAY Hubert, *b* Wigan, Lancs., *e* Darwen, Lancs., 202392, Pte., k. in a., F. & F., 31-7-17.

KAY William Harold, *b* Manchester, *e* Manchester, 26521, Pte., k. in a., F. & F., 23-7-16.

KELSEY Herbert, *b* Manchester, *e* Manchester (Salford, Lancs.), 27897, Pte., d. of w., F. & F., 9-8-17.

KETTLE Edward, *b* Manchester, *e* Manchester, 25022, Pte., k. in a., F. & F., 23-7-16.

KING Edward Peter, *e* Leicester, 40940, Pte., k. in a., F. & F., 11-10-16, formerly 2747 Leicester R.

KING Thomas, *b* Pendleton, Lancs., *e* Manchester (Rochdale, Lancs.), 16764, L/Cpl., k. in a., F. & F., 9-10-17.

KNIGHTON Albert Dennis, *b* Kentish Town, Middlesex *e* Manchester Coventry, Warwick.), 12129, Cpl., d. of w., F. & F., 4-7-16.

KNOWLES Geoffrey, *b* Birkdale, Southport, Lancs., *e* Manchester, 12382, Pte., d. of w., F. & F. 23-7-16.

LACEY Frederick, *b* St. Margarets, Leicester, *e* Leicester, 40923, A/Cpl., k. in a., F. & F., 23-4-17, formerly 4533 Leicester R.

LAMB James Hinchcliffe, *b* Manchester, *e* Manchester, 11871, L/Cpl., d. of w., F. & F., 1-11-16.

LAMBERT Lawrence Newstead, *b* Bowdon, Cheshire, *e* Manchester (Kersal, Manchester), 12395, Sgt., k. in a., F. & F., 23-7-16.

LANE Albert, *b* Northampton, *e* Northampton, 51246, Pte., k. in a., F. & F., 31-7-17.

LANE Joseph Thomas, *b* Liverpool, *e* Oldham, Lancs., 25066, Pte., d. of w., F. & F., 3-7-16.

LANGTON Basil, *b* Redvale, Bury, Lancs., *e* Manchester (Bury), 11592, Pte., d. of w., F. & F., 2-8-16.

LARMOUR Wilfred Thomas, *b* Levenshulme, Manchester, *e* Manchester (Reddish, Lancs.), 12130, Pte., k. in a., F. & F., 1-7-16.

LAWTON William, *b* Miles Platting, Manchester, *e* Manchester, 12656, Pte., d. of w., F. & F., 28-7-16.

LEE Joseph John, *b* Rotherham, Yorks., *e* Leicester, 41041, Pte., k. in a., F. & F., 2-4-17, formerly 4485 Leicester R.

LEE Robert, *b* Leicester, *e* Leicester, 40972, Pte., k. in a., F. & F., 19-10-16, formerly 4266, Leicester R.

LEECH William, *b* Hyde, Cheshire, *e* Manchester (Hyde), 18488, A/Cpl., k. in a., F. & F., 9-7-16.

LEEMING Harry, *b* Manchester, *e* Ashton-u-Lyne, Lancs., 34074, Pte., k. in a., F. & F., 23-7-16.

LEES John, *b* Salford, Lancs., *e* Manchester (Salford), 27189, Pte., k. in a., F. & F., 31-7-17.

LENIGAN Wilfred, *b* Middleton, Lancs., *e* Shaw, Lancs., 35744, Pte., k. in a., F. & F., 20-10-16.

LEVINGS Sydney Albert, *b* Collyhurst, *e* Manchester, 10551, L/Cpl., k. in a., F. & F., 16-10-16.

LEWIS Arnold, *e* Manchester, 33830, Pte., k. in a., F. & F., 23-7-16.

LINFORD George, *b* Harpurhey, Lancs., *e* Manchester (Harpurhey, Lancs.), 9985, Pte., d. of w., F. & F., 4-5-17.

LITHERLAND William, *b* Salford, Lancs., *e* Manchester (Salford), 12402, Pte., k. in a., F. & F., 9-7-16.

LLOYD Albert, *b* Stockport, Cheshire, *e* Cardiff (Stockport), 16697, Cpl., k. in a., F. & F., 31-7-17.

LLOYD John Thomas, *b* Salford, Lancs., *e* Manchester, 12714, Pte., k. in a., F. & F., 1-7-16.

LOGAN Edwin Broom, *b* Ardwick, Manchester, *e* Manchester, 12392, Pte., k. in a., F. & F., 9-7-16.

LOMAS William, *b* Weaste, Manchester, *e* Manchester, 12398, Pte., k. in a., F. & F., 23-7-16.

LORD Percy, *b* Urmston, Lancs., *e* Manchester, 19947, Pte., k. in a., F. & F., 2-4-17.

LORD Roland, *b* Goole, Yorks., *e* Birmingham (Rochdale, Lancs.), 30385, Pte., k. in a., F. & F., 18-10-16.

LOWE Sidney, *b* Ashton-u-Lyne, Lancs., *e* Ashton-u-Lyne, 48496, Pte., k. in a., F. & F., 8-4-17.

LOWRY William Edward, *b* Cheetham, Manchester, *e* Manchester, 12390, Pte., k. in a., F. & F., 1-7-16.

LUCAS Albert, *b* Old Trafford, Manchester, *e* Manchester, 11599, Cpl., k. in a., F. & F., 1-7-16.

LYNCH Martin, *b* Miltown Malbay, Co. Clare, *e* Manchester (Miltown Malbay), 26713, Pte., k. in a., F. & F., 23-7-16.

LYONS James, *b* Manchester, *e* Manchester, 11600, Pte., k. in a., F. & F., 23-7-16.

MACKERETH Frank, *b* Ambleside, Westmoreland, *e* Manchester(Ambleside), 12407, Pte., k. in a., F. & F., 23-7-16.

MADDEN James, *b* Whitefield, Lancs., *e* Manchester, 12831, Pte., k. in a., F. & F., 17-9-16.

MANFORD Joseph, *b* Manchester, *e* Manchester, 33898, Pte., k. in a., F. & F., 20-10-16.

MANN Walter, *b* Broughton, Manchester, *e* Manchester, 12588, Pte., k. in a., F. & F., 23-4-17.

MANNION John, *b* Kilmovee, Co. Mayo, *e* Manchester (Kilmovee), 12674, Pte., k. in a., F. & F., 23-7-16.

MAPLEY George Edmund, *b* Harpurhey, Manchester, *e* Manchester, 11886, Pte., k. in a., F. & F., 23-7-16.

MARKWICK Edwin, *b* Oldham, Lancs., *e* Chadderton, Lancs., 34793, Pte., k. in a., F. & F., 31-3-17.

MARRIOTT Frederick Thomas, *b* Bethnal Green, Middlesex, *e* Northampton, 41801, Pte., k. in a., F. & F., 2-4-17, formerly G/12564 R. W. Surrey R.

MARSDEN Robert, *b* Royton, Lancs., *e* Shaw, Lancs., 25089, Pte., k. in a., F. & F., 23-7-16.

MASON Arthur, *b* Manchester, *e* Manchester, 31157, Pte., k. in a., F. & F., 23-7-16.

MASON Herbert, *b* Denton, Manchester, *e* Denton, 352475, Pte., k. in a., F. & F., 31-7-17.

MASSEY Stephen, *b* Miles Platting, Manchester, *e* Manchester, 12410, Pte., k. in a., F. & F., 4-2-16.

MAYALL Herbert Charles, *b* Hollinwood, Lancs., *e* Oldham, Lancs., 27787, Pte., k. in a., F. & F., 20-10-16.

MAYNARD Herbert Arthur, *b* Richmond, Surrey, *e* Richmond, 41922, Pte., k. in a., F. & F., 2-4-17, formerly 3820 E. Surrey R.

McCLUSKEY William, *b* York, *e* Manchester, 12412, Pte., k. in a., F. & F., 23-7-16.

McDERMOTT Michael, *b* Boyle Roscommon, *e* Manchester, 12711, Pte., k. in a., F. & F., 11-10-16.

McDONALD Henry, *b* Moss Side, Manchester, *e* Manchester, 12139, Pte., k. in a., F. & F., 11-7-16.

McKIE William Alexander, *b* Tunstall, Staffs., *e* Manchester (Pulinkum, Drummore, Stranraer, Wigtown), 12143, Cpl., k. in a., F. & F., 23-7-16.

McNAMARA George, *b* Sale, Cheshire, *e* Manchester, 12144, Pte., k. in a., F. & F., 23-7-16.

MELLOR Edmund, *b* Oldham, Lancs., *e* Manchester (Oldham), 11612, Pte., k. in a., F. & F., 1-7-16.

MEREDITH Hugh, *b* Wrexham, Denbigh, *e* Manchester (Newton Heath, Manchester), 26627, Pte., k. in a., F. & F., 23-7-16.

MITCHELL Arthur, *b* Hemsworth, Yorks., *e* Manchester, 11614, Sgt., k. in a., F. & F., 1-7-16.

MOE Harold, *b* San Antonia, Texas, U.S.A., *e* Manchester, 11606, Pte., k. in a., F. & F., 23-7-16.

MOORHOUSE Edward, *b* Flixton, Lancs., *e* Manchester, 12414, Pte., k. in a., F. & F., 23-7-16.

MORGAN Eric Fennell Trevor, *b* Glamorgan, *e* Newport, Mon., 302466, Pte., d. of w., Home, 23-8-17.

MORRIS Nathan, *b* Manchester, *e* Ashton-u-Lyne, Lancs. (Hightown, Manchester), 34072, Pte., k. in a., F. & F., 18-8-16.

MORRIS Patrick, *b* Ancoats, Manchester, *e* Manchester, 2838, Pte., d. of w., F. & F., 27-1-18.

MORTON Harold Reginald, *b* Longsight, Manchester, *e* Manchester (Stockport, Cheshire), 11894, Pte., k. in a., F. & F., 29-11-16.

MORTON Tom Barker, *b* Moss Side, Manchester, *e* Manchester, 12663, Pte., k. in a., F. & F., 23-7-16.

MOSS Frederick James, *b* Glossop, Derby., *e* Manchester, 12155, Pte., d. of w., 5-7-16.

MOTTERSHEAD Stanley Saul, *b* Sale, Cheshire, *e* Manchester (Sale), 12594, Pte., k. in a., F. & F., 4-12-16.

MURPHY Joseph, *b* Hulme, Manchester, *e* Manchester, 26845, Pte., k. in a., F. & F., 2-4-17.

MYERSCOUGH Frank Dickinson, *b* Prestwich, Manchester, *e* Manchester (Beswick, Manchester), 26659, Pte., k. in a., F. & F., 23-7-16.

NELSON Oswald, *b* Salford, Lancs., *e* Manchester, 30210, Pte., k. in a., F. & F., 11-10-16.

NEWMAN Samuel, *b* Chorlton-on-Medlock, Manchester, *e* Manchester, 11892, Pte., d. of w., F. & F., 11-2-16.

NOLAN George, *b* Macclesfield, Cheshire, *e* Manchester (Macclesfield), 31389, Pte., k. in a., F. & F., 2-4-17.

NORRIS Thomas Ewart, *b* Congleton, Cheshire, *e* Manchester (Blackpool, Lancs.), 11898, L/Sgt., k. in a., F. & F., 23-7-16.

NORTH William Albert, *b* Sutton, Surrey, *e* Loughborough, Leicester., (Sutton), 41067, Pte., k. in a., F. & F., 31-7-17, formerly 5294 Leicester R.

NUNN Henry, *b* Aveley, Essex, *e* Grays, Essex (Aveley), 51199, Pte., k. in a., F. & F., 9-10-17.

NUTTALL Norman, *b* Newchurch, Waterfoot, Lancs., *e* Manchester (Rawtenstall, Lancs.), 11977, Pte., k. in a., F. & F., 2-4-17.

NUTTALL Robert, *b* Droylsden, Lancs., *e* Manchester, 26518, Pte., k. in a., F. & F., 23-7-16.

O'BRIEN	Michael John, *b* Manchester, *e* Manchester, 19992, Pte., d. of w., F. & F., 12-10-16.
O'CONNOR	Thomas Power, *b* Hyde, Cheshire, *e* Manchester, 12665, Pte., Home, 24-4-15.
OGDEN	Fred, *b* Oldham, Lancs., *e* Oldham, 31105, Pte., k. in a., F. & F., 23-7-16.
OGDEN	William, *b* Beswick, Manchester, *e* Manchester, 12601, Pte., k. in a., F. & F., 23-7-16.
OLDFIELD	Robert, *b* Salford, Lancs., *e* Manchester (Salford), 24722, Pte., k. in a., F. & F., 22-6-17.
OLDHAM	Percy Whitehurst, *b* Hyde, Cheshire, *e* Manchester, 34296, Pte., d. of w., F. & F., 22-8-16.
OLIVER	Samuel, Henry Richardson, *e* Manchester, 47260, L/Cpl., k. in a., F. & F., 31-7-17.
OLLERENSHAW	Charles Herbert, *b* Macclesfield, Cheshire, *e* Manchester, 26851, Pte., k. in a., F. & F., 1-7-16.
OPPENHEIM	Ernest Ellis, *b* Fulham, Middlesex, *e* Fulham, 51232, Pte., k. in a., F. & F., 31-7-17, formerly G/1348 Middlesex R.
ORME	Frederick Cecil, *b* Woolwich, Kent, *e* Manchester (Didsbury, Manchester), 12802, Pte., k. in a., F. & F., 23-7-16.
OSBORNE	Henry James, *b* Hampton Hill, Middlesex, *e* London (Hampton Hill), 41787, Pte., d. of w., F. & F., 24-4-17, formerly 20869 Surrey R.
OWEN	Cecil, *b* Chorlton-cum-Hardy, Manchester, *e* Manchester, 12419, Pte., k. in a., F. & F., 31-5-16.
OXLEY	George Arthur, *b* Stretford, Manchester, *e* Manchester, 12420, Pte., k. in a., F. & F., 1-7-16.
PACE	Frederick William, *b* Gold Hill, Staffs., *e* Manchester (Wednesbury, Staffs.), 34280, Pte., k. in a., F. & F., 20-10-16.
PAGE	George Henry, *b* Shutford, Oxon, *e* Banbury, Oxon, 41887, Pte., k. in a., F. & F., 31-7-17, formerly 4124 E. Surrey R.
PAIN	Herbert John, *b* Wimbledon, Surrey, *e* Merton, London, S.W. (Raynes Park, London), 41788, Pte., d., F. & F., 27-5-18.
PARKIN	Leonard, *b* Queen's Park, Manchester, *e* Manchester, 12172, L/Cpl., d. of w., F. & F., 27-7-16.
PARKINSON	James Robert, *b* Rusholme, Manchester, *e* Manchester, 11901, Pte., k. in a., F. & F., 16-10-16.
PARRY	Charles John, *b* Manchester, *e* Manchester, 12556, Pte., k. in a., F. & F., 1-7-16.
PARSONAGE	Frank, *b* Hulme, Manchester, *e* Manchester (Alderley Edge, Cheshire), 26745, L/Cpl., k. in a., F. & F., 30-11-17.
PATERSON	Frank, *b* Collyhurst, Manchester, *e* Manchester, 12429, Sgt., k. in a., F. & F., 23-7-16.
PATTINSON	George Ernest, *b* Northallerton, Yorks., *e* Manchester, 12171, Pte., d., F. & F., 4-5-16.
PATTMAN	Ernest Edmund, *b* Preston, Lancs., *e* Preston, 47220, Pte., d. of w., F. & F., 1-4-17, formerly 51206 R.W. Fus.
PAYNE	Horace, *b* Leicester, *e* Leicester, 40979, Pte., k. in a., F. & F., 23-4-17, formerly 4268 Leicester R.
PEARCE	Stanley, *b* Ardwick, Manchester, *e* Manchester, 12428, Pte., d. of w., F. & F., 3-7-16.
PEDLEY	John, *b* Chorlton-cum-Hardy, Manchester, *e* Manchester. (Wilmslow, Cheshire), 18098, Pte., k. in a, F. & F., 3-7-16.
PEDLEY	John Wilfred, *b* Howarth, Keighley, Yorks., *e* Manchester Harpurhey, Manchester), 11658, Pte., k. in a., F. & F., 9-10-17.

PENN Arthur Garnett, *b* West Bromwich, Staffs., *e* Manchester (Bootle, Liverpool), 12421, Pte., k. in a., F. & F., 26-2-16.

PERRY Thomas Henry, *b* Headless Cross, Redditch, Worcester, *e* Wimbleton, Surrey (Uxbridge, Middlesex), 41888, L/Cpl., k. in a., F. & F., 23-4-17, formerly 32840 E. Surrey R.

PERRY William, *b* Moston, Manchester, *e* Oldham, Lancs. (Failsworth, Lancs.), 48503, Pte., k. in a., F. & F., 2-4-17.

PETO Arthur, *e* Kingston-on-Thames, Surrey (Morden, Surrey), 41796, Pte., k. in a., F. & F., 2-4-17, formerly 24854 E. Surrey R.

PHŒNIX James William, *b* Glazebrook, Lancs., *e* Manchester (Cadishead, Lancs.), 32573, Pte., k. in a., F. & F., 23-4-17.

PHILLIPS Ralph, *b* Beswick, Lancs., *e* Manchester, 12177, Pte., d. of w., Home, 17-10-17.

PICKERING Edward, *b* Collyhurst, Manchester, *e* Manchester (Stalybridge, Cheshire), 11634, L/Cpl., k. in a., F. & F., 2-4-17.

PILKINGTON Louis, *b* Miles Platting, Manchester, *e* Manchester, 12432, Pte., k. in a., F. & F., 23-6-17.

PILLEY George, *e* Manchester, 26141, Pte., k. in a., F. & F., 23-7-16.

POIZER Sidney, *b* Broughton, Manchester, *e* Manchester (Pendleton, Lancs.), 12181, Sgt., k. in a., F. & F., 23-7-16.

POYNER Sydney, *b* Hartford, Cheshire, *e* Manchester, 12803, Pte., k. in a., F. & F., 23-7-16.

PRATT John Thomas, *e* Leicester, 41050, Pte., d. of w., F. & F., 17-10-16, formerly 11563 Leicester R.

PREECE Ernest James, *b* Ardwick, Manchester, *e* Manchester, 11636, Pte., k. in a., F. & F., 25-10-16.

PRESTAGE William Charles, *b* Kingsland, Middlesex, *e* Hackney, Middlesex, 41883, Pte., k. in a., F. & F., 23-4-17, formerly 4345 E. Surrey R.

PRICKETT Victor, John Edward, *b* London, *e* Manchester, 12552, Pte., k. in a., F. & F., 23-7-16.

PUGH Tom Atcherby, *b* Eccles, Lancs., *e* Manchester (Bramhall, Cheshire), 31045, Pte., k. in a., F. & F., 23-7-16.

PURKIS William John, *b* Manchester, *e* Manchester, 12569, Pte., k. in a., F. & F., 14-10-16.

RACE Alfred James, *b* Moss Side, Manchester, *e* Manchester (Altrincham, Cheshire), 11914, Pte., k. in a., F. & F., 2-4-17.

RADCLIFFE Emmanuel, *b* Middleton, Lancs., *e* Manchester (Middleton), 12542, Pte., k. in a., F. & F., 1-7-16.

RAMSBOTTOM Frank, *b* Pendleton, Manchester, *e* Manchester (Failsworth, Lancs.), 11644, Pte., k. in a., F. & F., 9-7-16.

RAMSBOTTOM Walter, *b* Pendleton, Manchester, *e* Manchester (Failsworth, Lancs.), 11643, Pte., k. in a., F. & F., 23-7-16.

REDDINGTON Richard Anthony, *b* Manchester, *e* Manchester, 203808, Pte., d. of w., F. & F., 3-1-18.

REED Thomas, *e* Manchester, 12743, Cpl., d. of w., F. & F., 3-4-17.

REEVES David, *b* Miles Platting, Manchester, *e* Manchester, 11660, Pte., k. in a., F. & F., 23-7-16.

REID James Arnold, *b* Ardwick, Manchester, *e* Manchester, 11646, Pte., k. in a., F. & F., 23-7-16.

RENSHAW Harry, *b* Manchester, *e* Manchester, 18436, Pte., k. in a., F. & F., 23-7-16.

RHODES Charles, *b* Disley, Stockport, Cheshire, *e* Manchester (Disley), 11916, L/Cpl., d. of w., F. & F., 22-4-17.

RILEY	James Henry, *b* Edinburgh, *e* Manchester (Dingwall, Ross Shire), 25010, Pte., k. in a., F. & F., 9-9-16.
RILEY	Thomas, *b* Marple Bridge, Stockport, Cheshire, *e* Manchester (Marple Bridge), 11657, Pte., k in a., F. & F.. 23-7-16.
ROBERTS	Aneurin, *b* Port Madoc, Carnavon, *e* Manchester, 34486, Pte., d. of w., F. & F., 7-8-17.
ROBERTS	John, *b* Manchester, *e* Manchester, 11650, Pte., k. in a., F. & F., 23-7-16.
ROBERTS	Paul George, *b* Leeds, *e* Manchester, 47382, Pte., k. in a., F. & F., 21-3-17.
ROBERTS	Thomas George, *e* Tottenham, Middlesex (Edmonton, Middlesex), 51204, Pte., k. in a., F. & F., 31-3-17.
ROBINSON	Albert, *b* Northwich, Cheshire, *e* Manchester (Northwich), 12525, Pte., d. of w., F. & F., 23-1-16.
ROBINSON	John Kendal, *b* Preston, Lancs., *e* Manchester (Preston), 12571, Pte., k. in a., F. & F., 23-7-16.
ROGERS	Ernest Stanley, *b* Salford, Lancs., *e* Manchester, 12815, Pte., d. of w., F. & F., 1-6-17.
ROGERS	William Henry, *b* Pendleton, Lancs., *e* Manchester (Moston, Manchester), 12436, Pte., k. in a., F. & F., 23-7-16.
ROSSITER	Albert George, *b* Newport, Mons., *e* Newport, 302322, Pte., k. in a., F. & F., 31-7-17.
ROSTRON	Harold, *e* Manchester (Urmston, Lancs.), 47263, Pte., k. in a., F. & F., 23-2-17.
ROTHWELL	William, *b* Longsight, Manchester, *e* Manchester, 11920, Pte., k. in a., F. & F., 23-7-16.
ROWLEY	Herbert, *b* Leeds, *e* Manchester (Woodley, Stockport), 26688, Pte., k. in a., F. & F., 20-10-16.
ROYSE	Arthur, *b* Higher Broughton, Manchester, *e* Manchester, 12197, Pte., k. in a., F. & F., 23-7-16.
ROYSTON	Albert, *b* Salford, Lancs., *e* Manchester, 12446, Pte., d. of w., Home, 1-8-16.
RUBENSTEIN	Morris, *b* Manchester, *e* Ashton-u-Lyne, Lancs. (Cheetham, Manchester), 33041, Pte., k. in a., F. & F., 23-7-16.
RUSSELL	George, *e* Manchester, 18477, Pte., k. in a., F. & F., 1-7-16.
RUSSELL	Robert Bradbury, *b* Bramhall, Stockport, Cheshire, *e* Manchester (Bramhall), 11659, Pte., k. in a., F. & F., 23-7-16.
RYAN	John, *b* Clonmel, Tipperary, *e* Manchester (Rotherham), 12818, Pte., d., Home, 31-5-15.
SALTHOUSE	Ernest Kirkham, *b* Manchester, *e* Manchester, 29027, Pte., k. in a., F. & F., 9-4-17.
SCOTT	Ernest Harry, *e* Leicester, 40930, Pte., k. in a., F. & F., 26-4-17, formerly 3203 Leicester R.
SCULTHORPE	William Henry, *b* Leicester, *e* Leicester, 41054, Pte., k. in a., F. & F., 18-10-16, formerly 4396 Leicester R.
SENIOR	William, *b* Newton Heath, Manchester, *e* Manchester, 11661, Pte., k. in a., F. & F., 23-7-16.
SHARROCK	William, *b* Wigan, Lancs., *e* Wigan, 35788, Pte., k. in a., F. & F., 9-4-17.
SHAW	Thomas, *b* Tottington, Lancs., *e* Manchester (Bury, Lancs.), 11666, Pte., k. in a., F. & F., 23-7-16.
SHAWCROSS	Walter, *b* Stretford, Manchester, *e* Manchester, 31209, Pte., k. in a., F. & F., 23-7-16.
SHEASBY	John Henry, *b* Chorlton-on-Medlock, Manchester, *e* Manchester, 11667, L/Sgt., k. in a., F. & F., 23-7-16.
SHELTON	James Patrick, *e* Manchester, 12591, Pte., k. in a., F. & F., 2-4-17.

SHIMWELL Samuel, *b* Levenshulme, Manchester, *e* Manchester, 12800, Pte., k. in a., F. & F., 1-7-16.

SHIRES Leonard, *b* Leeds, *e* Manchester (Holbeck, Yorks.), 31060, L/Cpl., k. in a., F. & F., 23-7-16.

SIDDALL Albert Vincent, *b* Chorlton-on-Medlock, Manchester, *e* Manchester, 12203, Pte., k. in a., F. & F., 1-7-16.

SIMMS Herbert, *e* Goole, Yorks., 40946, Cpl., k. in a., F. & F., 2-4-17, formerly 3506 Yorkshire L.I.

SLATER Ronald Hardy, *b* Headingly, Leeds, *e* Manchester (Bradford, Yorks.), 12205, Pte., k. in a., F. & F., 23-5-16.

SMITH Albert, *e* Leicester (Thurmston, Leicester), 41014, Pte., k. in a., F. & F., 29-7-17, formerly 3285 Leicester R.

SMITH Alfred, *b* Manchester, *e* Manchester (Bradford, Manchester), 26692, Pte., k. in a., F. & F., 23-7-16.

SMITH Andrew, *b* Weaste, Salford, Lancs., *e* Manchester (Bradford, Manchester) 11928, A/Cpl., k. in a., F. & F., 21-10-16, M.M.

SMITH Harry, *b* Leicester *e* Leicester, 40943, Pte., k. in a., F. & F., 31-7-17, formerly 3676 Leicester R.

SMITH James Willoughby, *b* Salford, Lancs., *e* Manchester, 11671, Pte., k. in a., F & F., 23-7-16.

SMITH John, *b* Manchester, *e* Manchester, 12798, Pte., k. in a., F. & F., 31-7-17.

SMITH Stanley, *b* Altrincham, Cheshire, *e* Altrincham (Hale, Cheshire), 25336, Pte., k. in a., F. & F., 21-4-17.

SOUTHERN Samuel, *b* Harpurhey, Manchester, *e* Manchester, 10950, Pte., k. in a., F. & F., 31-7-17.

SOUTHWORTH Arthur, *b* Levenshulme, Manchester, *e* Manchester, 11939, Pte., d. of w., F. & F., 8-8-16.

SPENCER Arthur, *b* Hude, Isle of Wight, *e* Manchester (Stretford, Manchester), 11674, Sgt., k. in a., F. & F., 23-7-16.

SPENCER Joseph, *e* Bolton, Lancs., 47408, Pte., k. in a., F. & F., 2-8-17.

SPINK Ernest, *b* Broughton, Manchester, *e* Manchester, 12462, Sgt., k. in a., F. & F., 23-7-16.

STANAWAY Edwin Job, *b* Manchester, *e* Manchester, 47385, Pte., k. in a., F. & F., 25-9-17.

STANLEY Robert William, *b* Manchester, *e* Manchester, 48915, Pte., k. in a., F. & F., 31-7-17.

STANSFIELD Robert Henry, *b* Nelson, Lancs., *e* Bury, Lancs. (Nelson), 44643, Pte., k. in a., F. & F., 15-12-17, formerly 26485 E. Lancashire R.

STEWART Henry, *e* Manchester, 26172, Pte., d., F. & F., 20-10-16.

STILLWELL Frederick, *b* Craffham, Sussex, *e* Chichester, Sussex (Arundel, Sussex), 51213, Pte., k. in a., F. & F., 31-7-17.

STOCKER Harry, *b* Uplyme, Devon, *e* Lyme Regis, Dorset, 41898, Pte., k. in a., F. & F., 31-7-17, formerly 4267 Surrey R.

STOTT Henry, *b* Didsbury ,Manchester, *e* Manchester (Didsbury), 11676, Pte., k. in a., F. & F., 26-12-17.

STRACHAN Percy William Boyd, *b* Lang Ditton, Surrey, *e* Kingston-on-Thames (Lang Ditton), 51244, Pte., k. in a., F. & F., 31-7-17.

STRETCH Thomas William, *b* Longsight, Manchester, *e* Manchester, 12215, Pte., k. in a., F. & F., 23-7-16.

STROMBERG Harry Cecil, *b* Sheffield, Yorks., *e* Manchester, Lancs., 11935, Pte., d., Home, 11-8-15.

STUART Charles David, *b* Wigan, Lancs., *e* Manchester (Wallingford, Berks.), 28865, L/Cpl., k. in a., F. & F., 23-7-16.

STURGESS	Henry, *b* Aberdeen, *e* Chorley, Lancs., 24202, Pte., k. in a., F. & F., 29-7-17.
SUTTON	Harold, *b* Manchester, *e* Manchester (Withington, Manchester), 33840, Pte., k. in a., F. & F., 23-7-16.
SUTTON	Harry, *b* Haslingden, Lancs., *e* Manchester, 46719, Pte., k. in a., F. & F., 23-4-17.
SWETNAM	Arthur, *b* Longton, Staffs., *e* Manchester (Stoke-on-Trent), 12695, Pte., k. in a., F. & F., 23-7-16.
TATE	Charles, *b* Belfast, *e* Manchester, 12465, Pte., d. of w., F. & F., 30-3-17.
TAYLOR	Alfred Ernest, *b* Rusholme, Manchester, *e* Manchester, 11686, Pte., k. in a., F. & F., 23-7-16.
TAYLOR	Austin, *b* Monton, Manchester, *e* Manchester, 26565, L/Sgt., k. in a., F. & F., 31-7-17.
TAYLOR	John, *b* Rochdale, Lancs., *e* Manchester (Seedley, Manchester), 11683, Pte., d. of w., Home, 8-8-16.
TAYLOR	John, *b* Radcliffe, Manchester, *e* Manchester, 11685, Pte., k. in a., F. & F., 1-7-16.
TAYLOR	John, *b* Liverpool, *e* Manchester, 49109, Pte., k. in a., F. & F., 31-7-17.
TAYLOR	Wellesley, *b* Oldham, Lancs., *e* Ashton-u-Lyne, Lancs. (Waterhead, Oldham), 48519, Pte., k. in a., F. & F., 30-11-17.
TAYLOR	William Edward, *b* Hulme, Manchester, *e* Manchester, 12473, Pte., d. of w., F. & F., 28-1-16.
THOMAS	David, *b* Bethesda, Carnavon, *e* Manchester, 12467, Pte., d. of w., F. & F., 8-7-16.
THOMAS	George Woodbridge, *b* Moss Side, Manchester, *e* Manchester, 11986, Pte., d. of w., F. & F., 2-7-16.
THOMPSON	Edward, *b* Harrogate, Yorks., *e* Manchester (Withington, Manchester), 19989, Pte., k. in a., F. & F., 2-4-17.
THOMPSON	Harold, *b* Newton Heath, Manchester, *e* Manchester, 11987, Pte., k. in a., F. & F., 23-7-16.
THOMPSON	William George, *b* Flixton, Lancs., *e* Manchester (Urmston, Lancs.), 34957. Pte., d. of w., F. & F., 18-4-17.
THOMSON	James Adie, *b* Fraserburgh, Aberdeen, *e* Manchester, 11944, Pte., k. in a., F. & F., 2-4-17.
THORNLEY	William Henry, *b* St. Helens, Lancs., *e* Manchester, 26618, Pte., k. in a., F. & F., 23-7-16.
THORPE	William, *e* Oldham, Lancs., 47077, Pte., k. in a., F. & F., 31-7-17.
THIRLWELL	William Edward, *b* Hulme, Manchester, *e* Manchester, 12473, Pte., d. of w., F. & F., 28-1-16.
THROWER	Harry, *b* Longluttlan, Lincs., *e* Manchester (Walthamstow, Essex), 33849, Pte., k. in a., F. & F., 23 7 16.
THURSTON	Edward Percy, *b* Stratford, Essex, *e* Stratford, 41902, Pte., d. of w., F. & F., 10-8-17, formerly 4222 E. Surrey R.
TIDBURY	Frederick William David, *b* Greenham, Berks., *e* Newbury, Berks., 41901, Pte., k. in a., F. & F., 9-4-17, formerly
TIERNEY	William Ewart, *b* Newton Heath, Lancs., *e* Manchester, 12608, Pte., d., Home, 23-6-15.
	32866 E. Surrey R.
TITLEY	Percy, *b* Manchester *e* Manchester, 27621, Pte., k. in a., F. & F., 23-7-16.
TOMLINSON	Arthur Collins, *b* Spotland, Rochdale, Lancs., *e* Manchester, 12469, Pte., k. in a., F. & F., 23-7-16.

TOMLINSON Richard, *b* Standish, Wigan, Lancs., *e* Wigan (Standish), 16894, L/Cpl., k. in a., F. & F., 31-7-17.

TONGE James Henry, *b* Clayton, Lancs., *e* Manchester (Clayton), 49372, Pte., d. of w., F. & F., 10-10-17.

TOOLE Walter, *b* Manchester, *e* Manchester (Cornbrook, Manchester), 12224, Pte., d. of w., 1-7-16.

TRESS Thomas Birchenall, *b* Manchester, *e* Manchester (Harpurhey, Manchester), 26691, Pte., k. in a., F. & F., 1-7-16.

TROLLOPE Christopher Victor, *b* Highgate, Middlesex, *e* N. Finchley, Middlesex), 41789, L/Cpl., k. in a., F. & F., 31-7-17, formerly 20980 E. Surrey R.

TURNBULL Arthur, *b* Manchester, Lancs., *e* Manchester, 25016, Pte., k. in a., F. & F., 23-7-16.

TURNER Fred, *b* Bury, Lancs., *e* Manchester (Bury), 11689, Sgt., k. in a., F. & F., 23-7-16.

TURNER James Edward, *b* Chorlton-on-Medlock, Manchester, *e* Manchester, 12464, Pte., k. in a., F. & F., 9-4-17.

TYLER Frank, *b* Coalville, Leicester, *e* Loughbord, Leicester (Coalville), 41071, Pte., k. in a., F. & F., 31-7-17, formerly 4139 Leicester R.

VALENTINE Ernest, *b* Stretford, Manchester, *e* Manchester, 5288, Pte., k. in a., F. & F., 31-7-17.

VAUGHAN Edward, *b* Bury, Lancs., *e* Manchester (Bury), 26621, Pte., k. in a., F. & F., 1-7-16.

WADE Harry, *b* Leicester, *e* Leicester, 40989, Pte., k. in a., F. & F., 31-7-17, formerly 2079 Leicester R.

WALDRON Michael, *b* Brenamore, Roscommon, *e* Ashton-u-Lyne, Lancs. (Longhlynn, Roscommon), 49135, Pte., k. in a., F. & F., 22-9-17.

WALKER Harold Hadfield, *b* Chapel-en-le-Frith, Derby., *e* Manchester (Chapel-en-le-Frith), 12482, Cpl., d. of w., F. & F., 11-8-16.

WALL Edmund William, *b* Kennington, Surrey, *e* Battersea, Surrey (Wandsworth, Surrey), 51216, Pte., k. in a., F. & F., 31-7-17.

WALLIS Thomas Leonard, *b* Sydenham, Kent, *e* London, 41905, Pte., d. of w., F. & F., 4-7-17, formerly 4401 E. Surrey R.

WARD Frank, *b* Weaste, Salford, Lancs., *e* Manchester (Eccles, Lancs.), 12485, L/Sgt., k. in a., F. & F., 2-4-17.

WARD John Edgar, *b* Manchester, *e* Manchester, 33860, Pte., k. in a., F. & F., 5-1-18.

WARD Thomas, *b* Bury, Lancs., *e* Manchester, 12234, Pte., k. in a., F. & F., 1-7-16.

WARNER Fred, *b* Lyddington, Rutland, *e* Oakham, Rutland (Uppingham, Rutland), 41069, Pte., k. in a., F. & F., 23-4-17, formerly 4375 Leicester R.

WARREN Robert, *b* Glasgow, *e* Leicester, 40937, Pte., k. in a., F. & F., 31-7-17, formerly 45011 Leicester R.

WATCHMAN William, *e* Colchester, Essex, 51218, Pte., d., F. & F., 27-8-17.

WATERS James, *b* Pendleton, Salford, Lancs., *e* Manchester, 11692, Pte., k. in a., F. & F., 23-7-16.

WATTS Cyril, *b* Hulme, Manchester, *e* Manchester, 12481, Pte., k. in a., F. & F., 23-7-16.

WEBB Alfred, *b* Smallwood, Cheshire, *e* Ashton-u-Lyne, Lancs. (Levenshulme, Manchester), 34184, Pte., k. in a., F. & F., 23-7-16.

WELBY John, *b* Ancoats, Manchester, *e* Manchester, 12238, Pte., k. in a., F. & F., 1-7-16.

WELSH Samuel, *b* Leicester, *e* Leicester, 41061, Sgt., k. in a., F. & F., 26-12-17, formerly 2145 Leicester R.

WEST Robert, *b* Edgeworth, Bolton, Lancs., *e* Manchester, 11953, Pte., k. in a., F. & F., 1-7-16.

WHITE Matthew, *e* Manchester, 12599, Pte., k. in a., F. & F., 19-1-16.

WHITEHEAD James, *b* Failsworth, Lancs., *e* Manchester (Failsworth), 11956, Pte., k. in a., F. & F., 2-4-17.

WHITELEY Joseph Henry, *e* Ardwick, Manchester (Gorton, Manchester), 47268, Pte., k. in a., F. & F., 9-4-17.

WHITELEY William, *b* Droylsden, Lancs., *e* Ashton-u-Lyne (Droylsden), 47070, Pte., k. in a., F. & F., 22-6-17.

WHITFIELD Samuel Handley, *b* Lower Broughton, Manchester, *e* Manchester, 12242, Pte., k. in a., F. & F., 1-7-16.

WILDE John, *b* Manchester, *e* Manchester (Irlam, near Manchester), 31219, Pte., d. of w., F. & F., 29-7-16.

WILKINSON Albert, *b* Collyhurst, Manchester, *e* Manchester, 11708, Pte., k. in a., F. & F., 23-7-16.

WILKINSON John, *b* Newcastle, Staffs., *e* Tunstall, Staffs. (Kidsgrove, Staffs.), 12683, Pte., d. of w., F. & F., 26-5-16.

WILKINSON Robert Henry, *b* Stretford, Lancs., *e* Manchester, 11962, L/Cpl., d. of w., F. & F., 1-7-16.

WILKINSON Thomas, *b* Gorton, Manchester, *e* Manchester, 12934, Pte., d. of w., F. & F., 6-2-16.

WILLCOCKS Cyril Rowe, *b* Cardiff, Glam., *e* Manchester, 12243, Pte., k. in a., F. & F., 23-7-16.

WILLIAMS Albert, *b* Salford, Lancs., *e* Manchester (Seedley, Manchester), 11704, Pte., k. in a., F. & F., 23-7-16.

WILLIAMS Arthur, *b* Salford, Lancs., *e* Manchester (Salford, Lancs.), 11960, Cpl., k. in a., F. & F., 23-7-16.

WILLIAMS Frank Sidney, *b* Camberwell, Surrey, *e* Wandsworth, Surrey, 51245, Pte., k. in a., F. & F., 6-9-17.

WILLIAMS George, *b* Bromsgrove, Worcester, *e* Manchester (Bradford, Manchester), 12493, Pte., k. in a., F. & F., 1-7-16.

WILLIAMS Peter, *b* Manchester, *e* Manchester (Salford, Lancs.), 12785, Pte., k. in a., F. & F., 23-7-16.

WILLIAMSON Harry, *e* Mitcham, Surrey, 41800, Pte., k. in a., F. & F., 2-4-17, formerly 22665 E. Surrey R.

WILLMOTT Alfred, *b* Manchester, *e* Manchester (Salford, Lancs.), 31031, Pte., k. in a., F. & F., 23-7-16.

WILSON Edgar, *b* Stockport, Cheshire, *e* Manchester (Stockport), 12487, Pte., d. of w., Home, 4-11-16.

WILSON Edward, *b* Manchester, *e* Manchester, 30140, Pte., k. in a., F. & F., 23-4-17.

WILSON Norman, *b* Manchester, *e* Manchester, 12826, Pte., k. in a., F. & F., 31-7-17, **M.M.**

WILSON Tom, *b* Bury, Lancs., *e* Manchester (Bury), 12834, Pte., k. in a., F. & F., 13-2-16.

WINDLE Arthur, *b* Salford, Lancs., *e* Manchester, 31070, Pte., k. in a., F. & F., 1-7-16.

WINN Alfred, *b* Hull, Yorks., *e* Manchester, 33583, Pte., k. in a., F. & F., 18-10-16.

WOLLEN	Albert Alfred, *b* Bristol, Glouc., *e* Manchester (Newtown, Bristol), 12476, L/Cpl., k. in a., F. & F., 1-7-16.
WOOD	Frank, *b* Manchester, *e* Manchester, 46721, Pte., k. in a., F. & F., 2-4-17.
WOOD	Harold, *b* Oldham, Lancs., *e* Oldham (Chadderton, Lancs.), 47702, Pte., k. in a., F. & F., 31-7-17.
WOOD	Harry George, *b* Drambury, New York, America, *e* Manchester (Stockport, Cheshire), 12699, L/Cpl., k. in a., F. & F., 31-7-17.
WOOD	John, *b* Hulme, Manchester, *e* Manchester, 11716, Pte., k. in a., F. & F., 23-7-16.
WOOD	John, *b* Salford, Lancs., *e* Manchester (Seedley, Manchester), 11970, Pte., k. in a., F. & F., 23-7-16.
WOOD	Thomas, *b* Oldham, Lancs., *e* Oldham, 47065, Pte., d., F. & F., 25-5-17.
WOODCOCK	Ernest, *b* March, Camb., *e* March, 51226, Pte., k. in a., F. & F., 31-7-17.
WOODFIN	Harry, *b* Swinton, Lancs., *e* Manchester (Swinton), 11715, Pte., d., F. & F., 27-1-16.
WOODHEAD	William, *b* Bury, Lancs., *e* Manchester, 11719, Pte., d. of w., F. & F., 21-8-16.
WOODRUFF	Leonard, *b* Ashton-u-Lyne, Lancs., *e* Manchester, 11969, Pte., k. in a., F. & F., 16-8-16.
WOOLLEY	Jose, *b* Butterton, Newcastle, Staffs., *e* Manchester (Sandbach, Cheshire), 12248, Pte., k. in a., F. & F., 12-2-16.
WOOLRIDGE	George, *b* Walsall, Staffs., *e* Manchester, 12650, Pte., k. in a., F. & F., 1-7-16.
WRIGHT	Frederick, *b* Crewe, *e* Manchester, 17807, Pte., k. in a., F. & F., 1-7-16.
WRIGHT	Robert, *e* Manchester (Beswick, Manchester), 28573, A/Sgt., d. of w., F. & F., 8-10-17.
WYNN	William John, *b* Rhosddn, Wrexham, Flint., *e* Manchester, 11975, Sgt., k. in a., F. & F., 31-7-17, **M.M.**
WYNNE	Jack Bernard, *b* Leeds, *e* Manchester, 47208, Pte., d. of w., F. & F., 3-8-17.
YARWOOD	Joseph, *b* Windsor, Canada, *e* Cardiff (Manchester), 32119, Pte., k. in a., F. & F., 20-10-16.
YOUNG	Henry, *b* Manchester, *e* Manchester, 48521, Pte., k. in a., F. & F., 22-6-17.
YUILL	Jack George, *b* Willesden, Middlesex, *e* Manchester (Sale, Cheshire), 11710, L/Sgt., k. in a., F. & F., 9-7-16.

CONGRATULATORY
MESSAGES

The Commander-in-Chief wishes the following wire from His Majesty the King circulated to all ranks

To FOURTH ARMY

Please convey to the Army under your command my sincere congratulations on the results achieved in the recent fighting. I am proud of my troops: none could have fought more bravely.

GEORGE R. I.

Message from Lieut.-General W. N. Congreve, **V.C.,** *C.B., M.V.O., commanding XIIIth Corps*—dated 1st July 1916

To 30TH DIVISION

Please convey to all ranks my intense appreciation of their splendid fighting, which has attained all asked of them and resulted in heavy losses to the enemy, nearly 1,000 prisoners having already passed through the cage.

LIEUT.-GEN. CONGREVE

❖

Message from the Rt. Hon. Earl of Derby, K.G., G.C.V.O., C.B.—dated 2nd July 1916

To XIIITH CORPS

Convey to 30th Division my best congratulations on their splendid work. Lancashire will indeed be proud of them.

DERBY

❖

Message from General Sir H. S. Rawlinson, Bart., K.C.B., C.V.O., Commanding Fourth Army—dated 2nd July 1916

To XIIITH CORPS

Please convey to all ranks 30th Division my congratulations on their capture and defence of Montauban. They have done excellent work and will be attacking again before long.

RAWLINSON

Message from the General Officer Commander-in-Chief of the British Armies in France—dated 11th July 1916

To FOURTH ARMY

Commander-in-Chief desires his warm congratulations conveyed to XIIIth Corps for their good work, and especially to 30th Division for gallant defence of Trones Wood yesterday and last night by 90th Brigade against such heavy counter-attacks. XIIIth Corps have not only captured all its objectives, including many strong and important positions, but has held all points gained firmly against all hostile efforts to retake them. This is a record to be proud of. Such performances lead to certain and complete victory.

❖

Extract from Report by Fourth Army Liaison Officer with the French :

General Nourrisson, G.O.C., 39th Division, XXth Corps., who took Hardecourt, expressed to General Fayolle his admiration of the British troops, his neighbours, whose bravery and discipline under heavy and continuous fire was beyond praise : " Leur attitude au feu était remarquable."

❖

Advanced G.H.Q. wire to XIIIth Corps—dated 15th July 1916

General Balfourier commanding XXth French Corps has expressed through a British Liaison Officer his admiration for the magnificent fighting qualities displayed during recent operations by our XIIIth Corps on his left and his desire to find himself fighting alongside this corps during subsequent operations A.A.A. Will you please convey this information to the XIIIth Corps A.A.A. Message ends.

269. (G)
1/8/16

As it will not be possible for me to address the 30th Division on parade as I had wished, I desire to convey to every officer and man in the Division my congratulations on the prominent and successful part that they have taken in the Battle of the Somme. The assault of the front system of trenches and the capture of the village of Montauban was a feat of arms deserving the highest praise and which has not been excelled by any Division of the New Army.

Their capture of Bernafay and Trones Woods and the heavy fighting which took place in the latter, shows a tenacity, a valour and a fighting spirit which are wholly admirable. Though they were not successful in retaining possession of Guillemont after they had so gallantly captured the greater part of the village, I am satisfied that they did all that was possible under the circumstances.

The co-operation of the Artillery with the Infantry has been most satisfactory, and the way in which the two armies have worked in unison both previous to and during the Battle of the Somme shows that a very high standard of training has been reached.

That the Division is being transferred to the First Army is a matter of great regret, and I trust that at no distant date I may again be honoured by having them under my command.

(Signed) RAWLINSON
General Commanding Fourth Army

H.Q. Fourth Army
1st August 1916

Extract from British Official—Sunday July 2nd 1916, 1 p.m.

The result of the operations round Montauban has been excellent. Our troops retain the ground gained in this sector, and repelled several counter-attacks in brilliant style. Our troops behaved brilliantly during the night. The battle went on throughout the night between the Somme and Gommecourt. The struggle was particularly keen round Montauban and La Boiselle and on both banks of the Ancre. At Montauban the enemy attacked in four columns and was repulsed with heavy loss.

Printed in Great Britain
by Amazon